Spheres of Governance

Comparative Studies of Cities in Multilevel Governance Systems

Spheres of Governance

Comparative Studies of Cities in
Multilevel Governance Systems

Edited by Harvey Lazar
and Christian Leuprecht

Institute of Intergovernmental Relations
School of Policy Studies, Queen's University
by McGill-Queen's University Press
Montreal & Kingston • London • Ithaca

Library and Archives Canada Cataloguing in Publication

Spheres of governance : comparative studies of cities in multilevel governance systems / edited by Harvey Lazar and Christian Leuprecht.

Includes summaries in French.
Includes bibliographical references.
ISBN 978-1-55339-129-6 (bound)
ISBN 978-1-55339-019-0 (pbk.)

1. Central-local government relations. 2. Comparative government.
I. Lazar, Harvey II. Leuprecht, Christian, 1973- III. Queen's University
(Kingston, Ont.). Institute of Intergovernmental Relations

JS113.S64 2007   320.8   C2007-901965-X

The Institute of Intergovernmental Relations

The Institute is the only organization in Canada whose mandate is solely to promote research and communication on the challenges facing the federal system.

Current research interests include fiscal federalism, health policy, the reform of federal political institutions and the machinery of federal-provincial relations, Canadian federalism and the global economy, and comparative federalism.

The Institute pursues these objectives through research conducted by its own staff and other scholars, through its publication program, and through seminars and conferences.

The Institute links academics and practitioners of federalism in federal and provincial governments and the private sector.

The Institute of Intergovernmental Relations receives ongoing financial support from the J.A. Corry Memorial Endowment Fund, the Royal Bank of Canada Endowment Fund, the Government of Canada, and the governments of Manitoba and Ontario. We are grateful for this support which enables the Institute to sustain its extensive program of research, publication, and related activities.

L'Institut des relations intergouvernementales

L'Institut est le seul organisme canadien à se consacrer exclusivement à la recherche et aux échanges sur les questions du fédéralisme.

Les priorités de recherche de l'Institut portent présentement sur le fédéralisme fiscal, la santé, la modification éventuelle des institutions politiques fédérales, les mécanismes de relations fédérales-provinciales, le fédéralisme canadien au regard de l'économie mondiale et le fédéralisme comparatif.

L'Institut réalise ses objectifs par le biais de recherches effectuées par son personnel et par des chercheurs de l'Université Queen's et d'ailleurs, de même que par des congrès et des colloques.

L'Institut sert comme lien entre les universitaires, les fonctionnaires fédéraux et provinciaux et le secteur privé.

L'Institut des relations intergouvernementales reçoit l'appui financier du J.A. Corry Memorial Endowment Fund, de la Fondation de la Banque Royale du Canada, du gouvernement du Canada et des gouvernements du Manitoba et de l'Ontario. Nous les remercions de cet appui qui permet à l'Institut de poursuivre son vaste programme de recherche et de publication ainsi que ses activités connexes.

CONTENTS

FOREWORD

In 2006 the Institute of Intergovernmental Relations at Queen's University published *Municipal-Federal-Provincial Relations in Canada*, a volume that explored aspects of multilevel governance in Canada with particular focus on intergovernmental relations involving the municipal sector. *Spheres of Governance* tackles similar issues from an international comparative perspective, presenting a systematic comparison of cities in multilevel governance systems in eight countries. As the demography of the world continues to tilt towards urban areas, as new global forces seem to push cities to the forefront, and as advocates of city power in Canada press for more resources and autonomy, there is much to be learned from the way federations other than Canada deal with urban issues and relate to municipal governments. The purpose of this volume is to ascertain whether, to what extent, and in what ways different countries have been restructuring their intergovernmental relationships to bring cities into the fold, and to assess the overall impact of such developments on urban governance.

The chapters in this volume underwent several iterations, and we are grateful to the authors for their diligence and dedication in working so cooperatively with us. The country chapters were first presented at a conference and subsequent authors' workshop on "Cities in Multilevel Government Systems: Lessons from Abroad." The Institute of Intergovernmental Relations (IIGR), under the leadership of then-director Sean Conway, helped organize these two linked events in Toronto on 14–15 October 2005. They enjoyed financial support from the Forum of Federations, the Canada Research Chair in Multilevel Governance at the University of Western Ontario (UWO), and the Vice-President Research at UWO. At the conference, senior scholars Caroline Andrew, Andrew Sancton, François Vaillancourt, and the distinguished former mayor of the City of Toronto, David Crombie, helped to place the international authors' observations in Canadian perspective. Toronto Mayor David Miller kindly took time to open the conference.

This research project has been supported financially by the Social Sciences and Humanities Research Council of Canada, through the Major Collaborative Research Initiative (MCRI) on *Multilevel Governance and Public Policy in Canadian Municipalities*. This MCRI is led by Bob Young, who provided intellectual and moral support throughout the project. The staff of the Institute of Intergovernmental Relations at Queen's University, Mary Kennedy and Patti Candido, along with the MCRI project manager at the University of Western Ontario, Kelly McCarthy, organized the logistical and financial aspects of this entire project. Carlotta Lemieux copyedited the chapters with her usual efficient flair. Carey Hill kindly prepared the abstracts. Several of the IIGR's student research assistants helped in the editing process; they include April Chang, Kim Johnson, Reama Khayat, Eric Leclerc, Ivy Opperman, Hillary Ryde, and Jeanette Sheehy. Stephen Ristich at the University of Western Ontario also helped. Valerie Jarus looked after publishing and layout with great care. Louise Gadbois imaginatively designed the cover.

Harvey Lazar and Christian Leuprecht
February 2007

PREFACE

It is a pleasure to introduce another Institute contribution to our understanding of comparative federalism. *Spheres of Governance* focuses on the way that cities and municipalities more generally are placed within systems of intergovernmental relations. At a time when urban issues are pressing and multilevel governance systems are evolving rapidly, the contributions collected here come at an opportune moment. We hope that they will help the Canadian debate about the role of cities in the federation.

The co-editors have worked very hard to bring this project to fruition. Harvey Lazar has produced many volumes for the Institute of Intergovernmental Relations, particularly during the very productive time when he served as director. He deserves much credit for recruiting the distinguished authors and for holding them to a strict template: this is a systematically comparative volume. Christian Leuprecht is a research associate at the Institute. His dynamism helped drive this project to completion. I appreciate the efforts of the co-editors and thank them on behalf of the Institute and the readers.

Thomas J. Courchene
Director
Institute of Intergovernmental Relations
February 2007

BIOSKETCHES

ROBERT AGRANOFF is professor emeritus in the School of Public and Environmental Affairs, Indiana University, U.S.A. He is also a senior professor in the Government and Public Administration Program, Instituto Universitario Ortega y Gasset, Madrid, Spain.

ANDRÉ BÄCHTIGER is senior assistant at the Institute of Political Science at the University of Bern, Switzerland.

JAN CHRISTOPH BODENBENDER is project manager at Steinbeis University in Berlin, Germany.

DOUGLAS M. BROWN is assistant professor of political science at St Francis Xavier University in Antigonish, Canada, and fellow and former director of the Institute of Intergovernmental Relations at Queen's University in Kingston.

EMMANUEL BRUNET-JAILLY is associate professor of public policy and co-director of the Local Government Institute in the School of Public Administration at the University of Victoria, Canada.

ANINA HITZ is research assistant at the Institute of Political Science at the University of Bern, Switzerland.

RUDOLF HRBEK is professor emeritus of political science at the University of Tübingen, Germany, where he is also director of the European Centre for Research on Federalism.

HARVEY LAZAR is senior research associate, Centre for Global Studies, and adjunct professor, School of Public Administration, University of Victoria. He is also a fellow of the Institute of Intergovernmental Relations and adjunct professor, School of Policy Studies, Queen's University.

CHRISTIAN LEUPRECHT is assistant professor of political science at the Royal Military College of Canada and research associate, Institute of Intergovernmental Relations, Queen's University School of Policy Studies.

ALLISON ROWLAND is researcher and professor of public administration at the Centro de Investigación y Docencia Económicas A.C. in Mexico City.

NICO STEYTLER is professor of law at the University of the Western Cape in Cape Town, South Africa, where he is director of the Community Law Centre. He is a member of the Municipal Demarcation Board and vice president of the International Association of Centres for Federal Studies.

RONALD K. VOGEL is professor of political science at the University of Louisville, U.S.A., and director of the Ph.D. program in Urban & Public Affairs.

RÉSUMÉS

INTRODUCTION

DE LA GOUVERNANCE À MULTI-PALIERS À LA GOUVERNANCE À MULTI-ORDRES ?

– Christian Leuprecht et Harvey Lazar

Cette enquête a comme point de départ les changements en politiques publiques de la ville. Dans les grandes métropoles en particulier, on prend pour acquis – bien qu'il s'agisse d'une hypothèse qui exige une vérification empirique – qu'une bonne partie des problématiques auxquelles les villes font face sont en train d'être gérées par des nouvelles formes de gouvernance à multi-paliers ainsi que d'autres acteurs. Ces partenariats varient selon l'échelle de l'enjeu. On estime que ces relations sont moins hiérarchiques, moins formelles, et peut-être plus égalitaires que les manifestations traditionnelles de la gouvernance verticale.

L'enquête a trois objectifs. Elle vise d'abord à saisir la nature et l'étendue des nouveaux systèmes de gouvernance à multi-paliers qui se sont développés dans différents pays pour aborder les grands défis qui confrontent leurs villes, y compris ceux de la modernisation de l'infrastructure, des programmes efficaces pour faciliter l'installation des immigrants, la préparation aux urgences et la prévention des désastres, l'aménagement et la planification urbaine, et la promotion du tourisme. Suite aux changements technologiques et économiques à l'échelle mondiale, on prétend souvent que les pouvoirs de prise de décision de l'État se sont déplacés vers les niveaux supranational et international, vers les autorités régionales et locales, et des acteurs gouvernementaux aux acteurs non gouvernementaux. Est-ce que ces relations des gouvernements locaux avec d'autres ordres de gouvernements et avec les acteurs non gouvernementaux se sont étendues ou bien sont elles en train de devenir plus importantes ? Si c'est le cas, quelle est la nature de ces relations ? Deuxièmement, si ces sortes de systèmes de gouvernance à multi-paliers se sont développés, le chapitre vise à juger jusqu'à quel point il s'agit d'une forme de gouvernance qui est capable de relever les défis qui confrontent les villes d'une manière efficace. Enfin, le chapitre considère si les tendances qui surgissent s'accordent aux valeurs et au processus démocratique.

L'ESPAGNE

« LES ADMINISTRATIONS LOCALES ET LES ENTENTES À MULTI-PALIERS EN ESPAGNE »

– *Robert Agranoff*

Sur le plan des relations intergouvernementales, en Espagne, la renégociation des statuts d'autonomie retient toute l'attention et les réformes au niveau municipal tel que le *Pacto Local* sont laissées de côté. En plus des quatre niveaux de gouvernement dont le niveau national, des régions (17 communautés autonomes), des provinces (50), et des municipalités (plus de 8 000), il existe d'autres ententes spéciales et asymétriques. Les recettes des administrations municipales proviennent entre autres de leur propre impôt, du partage des recettes fiscales, et de subventions conditionnelles. La plupart des mécanismes d'interaction municipale-fédérale sont indirects et il y a beaucoup plus d'interaction régionale-municipale que d'interaction fédérale-municipale. Chacune des régions possède un département rattaché au Cabinet qui s'occupe de l'administration locale et la plupart possèdent une forme ou une autre d'organisme consultatif. Au niveau national, il existe la Commission nationale des administrations locales, un organisme consultatif permanent. Les associations d'intérêt tel que la Fédération espagnole des municipalités et des provinces, qui font partie de la tradition corporatiste, sont plus influentes. Le caractère à multi-paliers du système espagnol s'applique aussi à ses partis politiques qui manifestent souvent des liens qui s'étendent du niveau municipal au niveau national. L'étude de cas sur le programme d'infrastructure illustre la nature « fortement intergouvernementale » des finances publiques de l'Espagne. Le financement se fait de façon directe et de façon conditionnelle et plusieurs niveaux y participent, incluant le secteur privé. Selon une autre étude de cas dans le domaine de l'immigration, le gouvernement intervient à différents niveaux et assument des responsabilités dans les processus de prévention, d'admission, de contrôle et d'intégration. Le niveau municipal est en grande partie responsable de l'intégration. Depuis les réformes de 2005, les municipalités jouent un rôle plus important dans les processus d'admission et de contrôle.

LA SUISSE

« EXTENSION DE LA MATRICE : LES RELATIONS FÉDÉRALES-MUNICIPALES EN SUISSE »

– *André Bächtiger et Anina Hitz*

Les relations entre le fédéral et les cantons en Suisse ont été qualifiées de « modèle de matrice » du fédéralisme. Les dernières tendances indiquent que le modèle a pris de l'extension afin d'y inclure les municipalités. De nouvelles institutions

ont été créées (c.-à-d. la *Tripartite Agglomerationskonferenz*), des incentifs finan-
ciers ont été accordés afin de s'assurer la coopération des municipalités, et
l'interdépendance des différents niveaux a été reconnue. Le modèle suisse suggère
que pour que la gouvernance à niveaux multiples soit efficace, il faut qu'il y ait
des institutions qui regroupent les différents niveaux, que ceux-ci coopèrent et
que chaque niveau possède des caractéristiques favorables. L'Article 3 de la Constitution suisse suggère que les municipalités sont « sous la juridiction exclusive
des cantons », mais selon les réformes de 1999, le fédéral se doit de coopérer
avec les municipalités. Les municipalités, au nombre de 2 940, sont responsables
de la mise en œuvre des politiques adoptées aux niveaux du fédéral et des cantons. Le système fiscal est « à tous points de vue non centralisé ». Les municipalités
ont le droit de hausser leur propre impôt sur le revenu. Il existe un système de
transfert. Le fédéral transfère des fonds aux cantons et les cantons transfèrent des
fonds aux municipalités. Bien que les relations fédérales-municipales soient
décrites comme étant « limitées », les structures du système fédéral suisse sont
souples et elles tiennent compte des municipalités. Il y a des référendums à tous
les niveaux, les municipalités participent aux comités spécialisés, et il existe une
procédure de consultation pré-parlementaire. Une étude de cas qui porte sur les
mesures d'urgence démontre que l'interaction se fait de manière hiérarchique.
Le niveau fédéral agit en tant que coordonnateur par le biais d'un comité spécial
au sein duquel les cantons jouent également un rôle, et les municipalités et les
organisations régionales en matière de protection civile mettent à exécution
ce que les autres niveaux ont décidé. Dans le sens contraire, selon une autre
étude de cas portant sur la gouvernance métropolitaine en matière de transport et d'utilisation du territoire, tous les niveaux jouent un rôle dans le
processus de financement fédéral et de soutien des projets en matière de
politique urbaine.

L'AUSTRALIE

« LES RELATIONS FÉDÉRALES-MUNICIPALES EN AUSTRALIE »

– Douglas M. Brown

Le système fédéral australien peut être décrit comme une « pyramide inversée ».
Le *Commonwealth* est au sommet, les administrations des six États sont au milieu,
et les municipalités (près de 730) sont au bas. Il existe trois sortes de relations
intergouvernementales en Australie (État-municipalité, fédéral-État et fédéral-
municipalité), mais elles se chevauchent de plus en plus. Selon la Constitution,
les administrations locales sont des créations des administrations des États. Les
mandats sans fonds et le transfert des charges font partie d'une relation financière
très complexe entre les administrations des États et les administrations locales.
Sur le plan fiscal, les administrations locales sont plus autonomes que les
administrations des États. Leurs principales sources de revenus sont l'impôt foncier

et les frais d'utilisation. Les administrations locales reçoivent aussi une partie de l'impôt fédéral par le biais des administrations des États. L'Association de l'administration locale de l'Australie représente les municipalités de chaque État et du Territoire du Nord et siège au Conseil des gouvernements australiens (CGA) depuis 1995. En 2006, le CGA a conclu une entente de principes au sujet des relations intergouvernementales qui touchent aux questions d'administration locale. Une étude de cas portant sur le financement au niveau de l'infrastructure et qui souligne les routes mentionne que le financement provient de deux sources principales. Les *Financial Assistance Grants* acheminent des fonds aux administrations municipales par le biais des États. Dans le cas du *Roads to Recovery Program*, l'interaction entre le fédéral et les municipalités se fait de manière directe. Les fonds sont alloués en fonction des besoins historiques, de la longueur des routes et de la population de l'État. Une deuxième étude de cas examine une réforme en matière de gestion publique qui démontre que la politique nationale sur la concurrence implantée suite aux négociations entre le fédéral et les États a permis aux États de « négocier ou dicter » des réformes en matière de concurrence au niveau municipal.

LA FRANCE

« LES RELATIONS MUNICIPALES-CENTRALES EN FRANCE :
ENTRE LA DÉCENTRALISATION ET LA GOUVERNANCE
À MULTI-PALIERS »

– Emmanuel Brunet-Jailly

La France est reconnue comme étant l'exemple parfait de l'état centralisé. Les dernières tendances semblent toutefois indiquer une plus grande décentralisation et le développement d'une forme unique de gouvernance à multiples niveaux. Les quatre niveaux de gouvernement, c'est-à-dire les municipalités, les départements, les régions et le gouvernement central participent à l'élaboration de politiques de toutes sortes. Le niveau régional devient le niveau où se trouve une convergence d'intérêts amplifiée quoique non-médiatrice. Cette transformation a amélioré le système des administrations locales sans affaiblir le gouvernement central. La France est un État unitaire et les administrations municipales ne possèdent pas de statut constitutionnel. Bien que le contrôle ait lieu depuis toujours à partir du sommet de la pyramide, la nature de l'interaction centrale-municipale a changé au cours des dernières années. Les administrations locales peuvent exercer certains pouvoirs à des fins d'expérimentation qui peuvent être généralisés au territoire national une fois testés et approuvés par les administrations locales et par l'assemblée nationale. Les ressources financières des administrations locales proviennent des frais de service, des taxes municipales, des subventions et de mécanismes de partage des recettes fiscales. Tous les niveaux, l'Union européenne et le secteur privé, participent à la négociation des contrats. De plus, l'accumulation d'instances politiques a permis aux représentants locaux d'acquérir plus d'influence. Une étude de cas portant sur les politiques de l'établissement des immigrants suggère que les politiques d'allocation des logements sont contrôlées par des municipalités et les représentants de l'état central sont incapables de réaliser les objectifs de leurs politiques. Dans le sens contraire, une deuxième étude de cas démontre que même si la technocratie du gouvernement central a maintenu en place le personnel et l'expertise pour étudier et superviser le développement du système des routes en France, ce secteur de politique devient aussi de plus en plus décentralisé.

L'ALLEMAGNE

«LES RELATIONS FÉDÉRALES-MUNICIPALES EN ALLEMAGNE »

– Rudolf Hrbek et Jan Christoph Bodenbender

En Allemagne, les municipalités, au nombre d'environ 13 500, sont sous « l'unique juridiction » des seize *Länder*. En réalité, les autorités locales sont en grande partie responsables de la mise en œuvre de politiques et de la prestation de services. Les Cités-États de Berlin, de Bremen et d'Hamburg en Allemagne remplissent des fonctions comme municipalités, comme comtés et aussi comme *Länder*. Les recettes des municipalités proviennent entre autres d'une partie de l'impôt foncier, de subventions conditionnelles et inconditionnelles des niveaux supérieurs, de frais de service et de prêts. Au niveau fédéral, les municipalités sont représentées surtout de façon indirecte par l'entremise du *Länder*. Les municipalités sont représentées directement par trois associations centrales qui coordonnent leurs efforts au sein de l'Union fédérale des associations centrales des gouvernements municipaux. La plupart des tâches municipales sont déterminées par le *Länder* ou par la Fédération. En conséquence, le gouvernement fédéral peut confier des tâches aux municipalités, mais il n'a pas l'obligation de leur fournir les ressources nécessaires. Les auteurs mentionnent cependant que « le modèle optimal » et la proposition du Comité mixte de modernisation du système fédéral aideront peut-être à remédier au problème. Selon deux études de cas, le principal rôle des municipalités est de mettre en œuvre des politiques. La première étude de cas qui porte sur les mesures d'urgence mentionne que les fondements juridique et relatif à l'organisation sont liés au *Länder*. Les autorités de contrôle en cas de désastre des municipalités jouent un rôle de niveau inférieur et ce sont les municipalités qui assument les coûts des secours apportés dans les environs. La deuxième étude de cas qui porte sur la politique en matière d'immigration démontre que les trois niveaux sont interdépendants. Par exemple, le processus d'intégration est mis en application au niveau des municipalités, financé par le fédéral à son niveau de base et par le *Länder* à son niveau avancé.

LE MEXIQUE

« L'INTERACTION ENTRE LE GOUVERNEMENT FÉDÉRAL ET
LES ADMINISTRATIONS LOCALES AU MEXIQUE :
TENDANCES, QUESTIONS, ET PROBLÈMES »

– Allison Rowland

La Fédération mexicaine inclut 31 États et plus de 2 400 administrations locales. Les dernières tendances indiquent un plus grand pluralisme. Les conflits intergouvernementaux ont augmenté, on demande la recentralisation du gouvernement et il existe beaucoup de disparités d'une région à l'autre. La lutte des États pour obtenir plus de contrôle a mené à l'usurpation des fonctions municipales, et ce même dans des domaines où la responsabilité est partagée. Selon la Constitution, les gouvernements municipaux sont des organisations qui appartiennent aux États. Même si selon les réformes de 1999, les municipalités possèdent un statut à part entière, les États continuent de croire qu'ils ont un rôle « légitime » à jouer dans toutes les affaires locales. Les recettes des municipalités proviennent entre autres de l'impôt foncier, de subventions conditionnelles des niveaux supérieurs et de partage des recettes. Les programmes et le financement destinés aux municipalités passent par l'entremise des États. Les intérêts des municipalités sont représentés par la Conférence nationale des municipalités du Mexique et par d'autres associations d'intérêt. Le fédéral a un contact direct avec les municipalités dans les régions près des frontières, dans les régions où il y a des conflits armés et dans les régions où le fédéral possède beaucoup de biens. Il arrive encore souvent que des programmes du fédéral soient mis sur pied sans avoir consulté ou ayant très peu consulté les autorités locales. Selon une étude de cas portant sur les biens fédéraux, la nature des interactions varie selon le type de biens, le degré d'activité et la capacité de réponse. La deuxième étude de cas met l'accent sur la constitution d'une image de marque grâce au tourisme. FONATUR est l'agence fédérale qui identifie et investit dans « des sites prometteurs ». Les images offertes par FONATUR ne correspondent pas toujours à l'identité et aux priorités des municipalités.

L'AFRIQUE DU SUD

« LES RELATIONS NATIONALES, PROVINCIALES, ET LOCALES :
UN MÉNAGE À TROIS INCONFORTABLE »

– Nico Steytler

La Constitution de l'Afrique du Sud de 1996 inclut la sphère des administrations municipales en plus des niveaux fédéral et provincial. Il existe une relation nationale-municipale explicite ainsi qu'une relation provinciale-municipale. La hiérachie entre les trois sphères est évidente. Le gouvernement national domine. Le niveau national et le niveau provincial se partagent la tâche de surveiller et de soutenir les municipalités. Le champ de l'interaction nationale-municipale est large et divers. Des forums intergouvernementaux officiels ont lieu, il y a « l'obligation de consulter », et il existe des programmes sectoriels nationaux. L'Association des administrations locales de l'Afrique du Sud est reconnue par le Ministère des administrations locales et des gouvernements provinciaux. La date des élections est la même pour toutes les municipalités et elle est déterminée par le ministre national. En raison des « relations à deux voies » (provinciales-municipales et nationales-municipales), il y a peu de médiation au niveau provincial. Les sources de revenus des municipalités proviennent des frais d'utilisation, de l'impôt foncier, des subventions intergouvernementales, des tarifs, des amendes, et des subsides. Une étude de cas portant sur les mesures d'urgence démontre qu'il existe différentes sortes de relations entre autres des relations hiérarchiques, parallèles et nationales-municipales. Le centre de gestion en cas d'urgence du niveau municipal est lié au centre provincial de gestion en cas de désastre et le centre national joue un rôle de coordination et d'intégration. La deuxième étude de cas porte sur l'infrastructure. À ce sujet, il y a eu un changement radical de politique. Les municipalités reçoivent désormais directement les fonds du gouvernement national. Dans le passé, les fonds leur parvenaient par l'entremise des provinces.

LES ÉTATS-UNIS

« LA GOUVERNANCE À MULTI-PALIERS AUX ÉTATS-UNIS »

– *Ronald K. Vogel*

Pour des raisons politiques et culturelles, les municipalités ont acquis la réputation d'être autonomes sur le plan municipal même si légalement, elles sont sous la responsabilité des gouvernements des États. Aux États-Unis, le gouvernement fédéral a pendant longtemps octroyé des subventions aux municipalités, mais depuis les dernières années, le soutien fédéral envers les villes a diminué. Le gouvernement national a désormais plutôt tendance à octroyer des subventions globales par l'entremise des États plutôt que par des liens directs avec les villes. Les recettes des administrations locales proviennent entre autres de l'impôt foncier, des taxes de vente, des frais d'utilisation, et sous forme d'aide des autres niveaux de gouvernement. Les lobbyistes et les membres des associations constituent des moyens de représentation municipale au niveau national. Sur le plan de l'infrastructure, l'intergouvernementalisme américain est étroitement lié au système de subventions. Dans le passé, les subventions provenant du fédéral permettaient de payer la plus grande partie des coûts des projets d'infrastructure mis en œuvre par les municipalités. Depuis les années 1980, l'aide du fédéral aux villes a diminué de façon significative et les associations municipales affirment que la crise sur le plan de l'infrastructure persiste. Dans le domaine des mesures d'urgence, les administrations locales sont les premiers répondants et les États planifient et demandent l'aide du gouvernement fédéral. Dans le passé, le *Federal Emergency Management Agency (FEMA)* était un organisme indépendant et avait des liens directs avec le président afin de faciliter son rôle de coordonnateur. Depuis le 11 septembre, le FEMA relève de la Sécurité nationale, ce qui signifie que le rôle du gouvernement fédéral en ce qui concerne les mesures d'urgence est passé de primaire à secondaire. Le système de gouvernance à multi-paliers présentement en place a été jugé plutôt négativement suite à l'ouragan Katrina et au désastre causé par les inondations.

FROM MULTILEVEL TO "MULTI-ORDER" GOVERNANCE?

Christian Leuprecht and Harvey Lazar

The majority of the world's population now live in urban areas. Cities are where the best jobs are to be found and where migrant populations overwhelmingly settle. They are centres of science, technology, and innovation, of education, culture, health care, and many other services. They are increasingly and disproportionately vital to the well-being of the regions and countries in which they are located. Yet cities are also characterized by high rents and homelessness, drug-related problems, criminal gangs, pollution, difficulties in migrant settlement, and by aging and often inadequate public infrastructure.

Some urban challenges reflect the unique geographic and demographic characteristics of individual cities. Others, however, are similar from one city to another, and these often have a national and even at times an international dimension. The latter urban challenges are of special interest here. Local governments generally lack the money and jurisdiction – and at times the expertise – to manage effectively the most acute and expensive urban issues on their own. Traditionally, these have therefore been handled through various forms of partnership between local governments and governments at the regional and national level, partnerships that have for the most part reflected top-down constitutional and fiscal realities among levels of government.

This investigation is premised on the possibility that the ways of managing urban policy matters have been changing. Especially in larger cities, there is an assumption, not yet tested fully empirically, that many of the pressures that cities face are increasingly being managed through new forms of governance that entail multiple levels of government and other political actors – partnerships that vary according to the scale of the issue. These relationships are thought to be less hierarchical, less formal, and perhaps more egalitarian than traditional vertical forms of governance. These new kinds of governance arrangements are commonly characterized as "multilevel governance" or "networked governance" when non-governmental actors are heavily engaged.

1 PURPOSE AND SUMMARY OF FINDINGS

This volume has three purposes. The first is to ascertain the *nature* and *extent* of the multilevel/networked governance systems that different polities have developed for handling the major challenges faced by their cities. The challenges we have in mind include such issues as the modernization of physical infrastructure, effective programs to facilitate migrant settlement, emergency preparedness and disaster relief, land management planning, and the promotion of tourism. In the face of changing technologies and a globalizing economy, it is often alleged that the decision-making powers of the state have shifted upward to the supranational and international level, downward to regional and local authorities, and outward from government to nongovernmental bodies, as the optimal scale for policymaking has changed (Brenner 2004). Have local governments' relationships with other orders of government and indeed nongovernmental actors grown or are they growing in relative importance? If so, what is the nature of these relationships? Second, to the extent that such systems of multilevel governance have evolved, we wish to assess just how effective this form of governance is in dealing with the urban challenges. Finally, we consider whether the trends that are emerging are consistent with democratic values and processes.

What did we learn? Our findings are based on the eight country studies that make up the rest of this volume. They include five federations, two quasi-federal systems (countries that do not describe themselves as federations but have many federal-like constitutional provisions), and one unitary country. In a nutshell, these country studies suggest that multilevel/networked governance of varying kinds is becoming widespread if not pervasive, with complex intergovernmental relationships involving international, national, regional, and municipal governments increasingly the norm. We also found, however, that this complex web of relationships among different levels of government is by no means a partnership of equals and that the role of non-governmental actors may be more modest than some of the academic literature presumes (e.g., Marks and Hooghe 2004). Across sixteen policy case studies (two in each of the eight country studies), the authors remark time and again on the hierarchical nature of the power relationships: city governments are policytakers, not policymakers, with respect to national programs that significantly affect their jurisdictions. Their role in multilevel governance is generally to deliver services or administer programs whose character has been determined by national or even international processes over which they have little control. Thus, we end up postulating a gap between the normative argument for multilevel and networked governance and the observed reality.

As well, the case studies suggest that top-down governance is not very effective in relation to urban policies. Interestingly, Switzerland and France – the two polities where the country study authors report most favourably on the influence of local government in the making of national urban programs – apparently also have the best organized governance systems for managing these policy challenges. Both have complex intergovernmental systems which at times seem to approximate theoretical notions of multilevel/networked governance – at least, more so than the remaining case studies suggest.

Finally, the impact on democracy has been mixed. Notwithstanding the modest extent of local government's role at the multilevel decision table, in countries with a strong authoritarian or centralized tradition, robust local government is identified with the spread of democracy. Conversely, in some advanced industrialized democracies with a long tradition of democratic local government, multilevel governance may actually be squeezing and threatening to stifle local government relative to what it once was.

We elaborate substantially on these findings in the penultimate section of this chapter. The country chapters tell the full story in the remainder of the volume.

2 COMPLEXITY AND INTERDEPENDENCE IN THE URBAN POLICY ENVIRONMENT

The investigation is premised on two separate but related propositions. The first holds simply that more levels of government are working more often with one another. The second proposition deals with the amorphous phenomenon of "governance." Although this term has been around for well over a century, its usage has proliferated since the mid-1980s. As Ulrich Beck (1992) and Anthony Giddens (1990) have observed, policymaking has in recent decades attained an unprecedented degree of complexity. This complexity is thought to require not only intergovernmental collaboration but also that non-governmental actors with relevant assets (such as knowledge, delivery systems, and legitimacy) be engaged in the policy process. This in turn leads to collective-action and coordination problems in an increasingly interdependent world. The compound effect of these phenomena is what some label multilevel governance. Assuming for the moment that growing multilevel governance is indeed a reality, we still can ask: Is this trend mainly the outgrowth of functional necessity – that is, the most effective way of managing complexity? Or is it inspired by a normative preference?

The term "multilevel governance" was pioneered in the context of the European Union, where it was initially meant to capture the "scaling-up" of the national state to the level of the European Union, that is, the voluntary abdication by member states of certain responsibilities to the emerging supranational structures of the European Union. In his contribution to this volume, Brown (drawing on Marks and Hooghe 2004) defines multilevel governance as "the condition of power and authority that is shared in institutional relationships in which the scope of public policy and the mechanisms of policymaking extend by necessity beyond the jurisdiction of a single government." The resulting system of government has been characterized as "[c]ontinuous negotiation among nested governments at several territorial tiers – supranational, national, regional, and local – as a result of the broad process of institutional creation and decisional reallocation that has pulled some previously centralized functions of the state up to the supranational level and some down to the local/regional level" (Marks 1993). It also has the potential of being "scaled out" to private and semi-private agencies (Marks 1996; Keil 1998; Le Galès and Harding 1998; Hooghe and Marks 2003).

While the European literature speaks of "multilevel governance," the American literature on public administration refers to "networked governance." This notion is clustered around two key concepts: patterns of interaction in exchange and relationships, and flows of resources between independent units (Jones, Hesterly, and Borgatti 1997). The contributions to this volume provide an empirical basis for testing the nature and extent of multilevel and networked governance as it relates to policymaking and implementation in cities and the local sector more broadly.

When confronted with the evidence, we realized that, empirically, multilevel governance is a more controversial term than we had anticipated. We have therefore chosen to use language that is less value-laden. To this end, we distinguish between levels, orders, and spheres. Scholars interested in federalism often refer to subnational "orders" of government when they want to describe a co-sovereign status for constituent units that is equal to that of the federal or national order. By contrast, the notion of "level" denotes a hierarchical relationship. In other words, if we use either "multi-order" or "multilevel" governance, we end up tautologically presuming what we may – or may want to – find: either an egalitarian or a hierarchical relationship. The word "spheres" is more neutral. This explains our use of the word in the title of this book. A study of "spheres of governance" is meant to take a systematic look at the way governments and other players relate to one another and to discern proclivities – be they increasingly egalitarian or persistently hierarchical.

3 METHOD

This study employs a comparative critical case-study approach. Among the seven federal and quasi-federal entities, three are largely unilingual (Australia, Germany, and the United States) and three are multilingual states (Spain, Switzerland, and South Africa), with Mexico falling somewhere in between. Two of the eight are developing or transitional economies (Mexico and South Africa). The others are advanced industrialized democracies. Three of the European countries are part of the European Union (France, Germany, and Spain); one is not (Switzerland). The sample includes different forms of governmental systems, from varieties of Westminster-type parliamentary federations (Australia, Germany) to varying forms of presidential systems (France, Mexico, and the United States). It also includes classical dual legislative federations (such as Australia and the United States) and administrative federations (Germany and, to a degree, South Africa). The sample is thus representative with sufficient variation to allow for some generalization.

To facilitate comparative analysis that will allow us to control systematically for multiple independent variables, the country authors followed a research template designed to ensure that the same key questions were addressed for each country study. The template included the following factors: relevant constitutional provisions affecting municipalities; the range of municipalities' responsibilities and functions; their fiscal position; how municipalities organize themselves to deal with the federal/national level; the scope and nature of municipal-federal/national interaction; whether and how municipal-federal/national relations are mediated by regional governments (constituent units variously referred to as states, provinces, cantons, or *Länder*); whether municipalities are bypassing federal and regional governments and engaging in international relations; and the political dimension of the relationship. The authors of the country studies also analysed two policy issues from a list of possibilities that we presented to them – studies intended to illustrate the dynamics of the intergovernmental relationships and their effectiveness. Finally, the authors were asked to discuss recent relevant trends and to judge whether the system of multilevel governance (our template used the term "multilevel"), to the extent that it existed, was up to the task of meeting the policy challenges facing municipalities, especially larger cities.

In the remainder of this section, we elaborate on some of the hypotheses and questions that arise from this template. One question relates to the forces that may precipitate multisphere governance. As alluded to above, its development is generally assumed to be largely a function of the growing complexity of policy challenges coinciding with ever-greater interdependence both within and across national borders, and possibly also between governmental and non-governmental actors. On the one hand, to the extent that this assumption holds true, we may expect to find similar if not identical trends across our country studies. On the other hand, if the trend reflects a normative preference – as opposed to a functional necessity – we may anticipate differences in its extent and its manifestation.

There are, of course, reasons that may make multisphere governance normatively attractive to political leaders and scholars. First, it can imply a dispersion of power that is attractive to those who worry about the state becoming a Leviathan or simply too large to be administratively efficient in what it does. Second, some economists consider that multisphere governance is more economically efficient than alternative forms of governance because it allows for competition among governments, provided that each government spends only or largely the money that it raises through its own taxes and levies (Weingast 1995; McKinnon 1994). (We hasten to add that there is a contrary school that considers it more efficient for the federal/national sphere to collect more revenues than it needs, while local governments spend more than they collect. This is because the federal/national sphere is presumed to be more efficient in raising taxes and the local sphere more efficient in managing expenditure programs. Intergovernmental transfers are the result.) Third, the principle of subsidiarity normatively posits delegation of decision-making responsibility to the sphere of government that is closest to the citizen and is best positioned to carry out a particular task; thus, to local government, other things being equal.

Another question we wondered about it is whether systems of *administrative federalism* might be more likely to evolve into multisphere governance than systems of *classical* or *dual* federalism. The latter is premised on a clear division of legislative power between the national government and the governments of the constituent units. The United States and Australia – in fact, Anglo federations more generally – embody this approach. Each sphere of government is, in principle, responsible for making and implementing policy in its area of constitutional competence.

Germany, by contrast, exemplifies the administrative approach to federalism. Under this arrangement, most legislative powers are concentrated at the national level, with the role of regional constituent units being mainly to administer the law. The constituent units participate in the national legislative process through their involvement in the second chamber. France also falls under this rubric: as a unitary country, it is, technically, a "pure" vertical system. Some other countries in our sample, such as Switzerland and Spain, combine elements of both systems.

The difference between the dual and administrative models is also reflected in the status of municipalities. In administrative federations, citizens seek services from the federal government at the city level, regardless of which sphere of government is actually charged with making policy decisions for that service. This tends not to be the case in dual systems.

We thus wondered whether this distinction between dual and administrative federalism would generate different degrees and forms of multisphere governance. It is plausible to hypothesize, for instance, that administrative federations might evolve into hierarchical forms of multilevel systems of governance more readily than dual federations, because the constitutions of the administrative federations already provide explicitly for hierarchical interdependent relationships. While functional necessity may also require governments in dual systems to become increasingly interdependent, the resulting relationships among the different spheres may entail less hierarchy than in administrative systems, since the dual systems constitutionally emphasize autonomy. Also, to the extent that such distinctions exist, we wondered whether urban policy tends to fare better under one or the other of these arrangements.

Similarly, differences between the European and Anglo *political cultures* may affect trends of governance. European culture tends to be more collectivist, while the Anglo culture tends to be more liberal-atomist and thus more focused on individuals than on communities. Political thinking in the Anglo culture tends to focus on checks and balances, as well as on markets; it is more skeptical than the European culture about delegating powers upward. This suggests that we may be more likely to find the more horizontal intergovernmental relationships commonly identified with networked governance in countries that share the Anglo political tradition.

In effect, our research template gives rise to questions about the political economy of the power relationships among different spheres of government. Ron Watts has written: "In virtually all federal and intergovernmental systems, financial relations have invariably constituted an important, indeed crucial, aspect of their *political* operation ... This political significance places financial relations between central and constituent-unit governments at the heart of the process of intergovernmental relations" (2003: 1–6). As intergovernmental fiscal relations was a key item in our research template, this enables us to test the Watts perspective from the broader multisphere point of view that includes local government.

4 FINDINGS

4.1 NATURE AND EXTENT OF MULTISPHERE GOVERNANCE AS RESPONSE TO MUNICIPAL/URBAN CHALLENGES

Our first purpose is to assess whether our sample polities have actually developed systems of multilevel or networked governance for policymaking and implementation in relation to the major challenges faced by municipalities, especially larger cities. Based on the evidence provided in the eight country studies, the answer here is a "qualified yes." The considerations that support the "yes" part of our answer will be discussed first.

To begin with, in six of the eight countries – France, Germany, Mexico, South Africa, Spain, and Switzerland – municipalities are maturing constitutionally as a distinctive sphere of government. This recognition was not as widespread half a century or even quarter of a century ago. However, in the constitutions of the two federations most closely associated with the Anglo-American tradition – the United States and Australia – there does not appear to be a similar development.

Although the scope and nature of the constitutional changes vary considerably among the six polities, what they all have in common is recognition of the growing interdependence among spheres of government. For example, chapter 3 (s. 40) of the South African Constitution of 1996 recognizes local government as one of three spheres of government that are "distinctive, interdependent, and interrelated." It provides that municipalities must participate in national and provincial development programs and that "[d]raft national or provincial legislation that affects the status, institutions, powers or functions of local government must be published for public comment before it is introduced in Parliament or a provincial legislature, in a manner that allows organized local government, municipalities and other interested persons an opportunity to make representations with regard to the draft legislation" (154(2)). The modernized Swiss Constitution of 1999 introduces municipalities as a potential sphere for cooperation in the federal state, declaring that the Federation shall "take into account the possible consequences for the Municipalities" of its activities. In Spain, the Constitution recognizes a multilayered interdependent framework of governments, despite the identification of autonomy as a key principle. In France, the very first article of the Constitution defines the state as decentralized, thus bolstering the autonomy of local governments; the Constitution also recognizes that any sphere of government may initiate partnerships with other spheres. Article 106 paragraphs (5) and (5a) of the German Basic Law explicitly provide that a share of the revenues from income tax and the turnover tax belongs to the communes and Article 106 paragraphs (6) and (7) designate other revenue sources to the communes. These provisions demonstrate the Basic Law's recognition of the interdependence among spheres of government, including local government. In sum, the constitutions of the three federal/quasi-federal European systems covered in this volume recognize the increasingly multisphere character of governance, while the South African Constitution does so at least in part because it borrowed heavily from the German Constitution. Indeed, even the French Constitution, in what was once a top-down unitary state, now stresses the need for cooperation among all spheres of government, including local governments.

Second, institutional arrangements have emerged that afford municipal governments or their representative organizations a role on legislative, consultative, or advisory bodies with national and regional governments. The Australian Local Government Association has a seat at the Council of Australian Governments, a body that brings together the Commonwealth prime minister and the heads of state and territorial governments. Local governments in South Africa are entitled to send ten members to the second parliamentary chamber, the National Council of Provinces, where they may participate *ex officio* in deliberations. In Switzerland, a tripartite agglomeration conference was established in 2001, consisting of the federal government, the Conference of Cantons, and the peak organizations for local government (the Swiss Union of Cities and the Swiss Union of Municipalities). In France, the Senate is made up of locally elected officials chosen by elected municipal council members. It is now normal for the central government to negotiate with regions and municipalities in drawing up contracts that span five to seven years. Spain also has an extensive system of intergovernmental interaction, including the national Commission on Local Governments, which is intended to serve as a catalyst for identifying municipal problems. In Germany, collaboration between the central associations of local government and the federal government is mandated in the standing orders of the federal ministries, as well as in the procedural rules of Parliament. These provisions state that the associations' representatives must be consulted at an early stage of the legislative process by the federal government and committees of the Parliament when there are legislative plans that affect local government interests. In Mexico, the federal government includes municipalities in three programs that are defined in its Constitution: the National System of Planning, the National System of Public Security, and the National System of Social Development.

In the United States, in contrast, there are no similar formal institutions designed explicitly to give voice to local governments and their representatives in national political decision making. Even on a less formal basis, at the political level, the relationship between the federal government and the cities is weak. There is, for example, no overarching multisphere intergovernmental body focused on national urban strategic planning. This leads Vogel to write that the "the federal partnership with cities has completely evaporated." He continues: "Increasingly, national policymaking is made without reference to the problems of cities and with little direct input from city officials." At the administrative level, however, there are ongoing multisphere governance arrangements all across the United States. For example, there are metropolitan planning organizations that include all spheres of government, local private interests, and citizen interests. These intergovernmental administrative arrangements are in significant measure "bottom up" and flat, and they focus on problem solving at the regional and local levels. This difference between the United States and the other polities is consistent with the distinctions drawn above between Anglo-American and European political cultures. It is also partly consistent with our hypothesis that systems of dual federalism may be less inclined to evolve towards relatively hierarchical multilevel governance than administrative federalisms and instead trend towards less hierarchical multi-order governance.

Third, in all the European cases and also in South Africa and Mexico, political parties have an integrative function that ensures that municipal interests are understood at the national level. This function is most apparent when national and municipal governments are constituted by the same parties.

Fourth, the accumulation of mandates, whereby politicians hold elected office at the local sphere while simultaneously serving at one or more higher spheres of government, helps to connect local governance to the national and regional spheres. As well, in the European countries in our sample it is common for national politicians to start at the municipal sphere, often as mayors of large urban agglomerations, and work their way up. The result is that many key national politicians are sensitized to municipal issues and are socialized into the workings of municipal politics. Brunet-Jailly stresses the importance of this factor in his chapter on France.

Finally, again harking back to the distinction between administrative and legislative federalism, in the polities covered here, local governments are increasingly delivering national (and often regional) programs, except in Australia and to a lesser degree the United States (where we must remember that there are still many programs mandated by the federal government, with and without funding).

While these reasons help explain our general observation about the development of multisphere governance and the rising importance of local government in it, they also explain the qualified nature of our affirmative observation. While being the administrative arm of other orders of government certainly affords local governments a substantial role in a multisphere governance system, municipalities generally do not have significant sway over national priorities or a major role in designing the broad contours of the national programs which they deliver. What influence they have is often restricted to issues of "deliverability." Local authorities, therefore, end up being relegated to "junior" partners in the emerging multisphere governance systems, with France and Switzerland as partial exceptions. This finding reflects constitutional and political realities, political party structures, and intergovernmental fiscal arrangements. Each of these explanations is discussed further below.

With respect to constitutional and political realities, Rowland characterizes the role of Mexican municipalities in the three national systems noted above as more or less "nominal." Agranoff makes clear that municipalities in Spain are constitutionally "subordinate" to the central government and the autonomous community in which they are located. (Indeed, the autonomous community determines the scope of local government's engagement in governance.) Brown observes that the Council of Australian Governments "essentially meets at the call of the federal prime minister." He continues: "Although it has been meeting regularly in the past several years, this federal dominance may limit the significance of local government having a seat on that body."[1] He also characterizes the Australian federation as an inverted pyramid with a "truly dominant" central Commonwealth government. Since the state capital is typically coincident with the largest city, Australian states are effectively capital city-states with the remaining territory as hinterland. Australian states serve as city-states "in the sense that they make all the truly strategic urban development decisions." Local government is left with "a smaller basket of goods and service provision" than is the case in most other federations. In South Africa, "the dominance of the national government is much in evidence," writes Steytler. He thus cautions that local governments risk being reduced to "mere appendages" of South

Africa's national government. Hrbek and Bodenbender use comparable language in declaring that local authorities in Germany are "under the threat of becoming little more than mere agents implementing tasks imposed and delegated by the federal and *Land* government levels."

The second above-noted reason for our qualification has to do with the way in which power is distributed within political parties. In vertically integrated parties it is typically much stronger at the national sphere than at the local. In effect, this means that vertically integrated political parties are not only a mechanism for transmitting local needs and priorities to the national sphere of the party; they are also a vehicle through which the national sphere can control the local elements of the party and thus municipal governments. This is not surprising. There is always more power at the national sphere than locally. Since locally elected officials often want to move up in the party hierarchy, it is politically difficult for them to challenge the leadership of the national party. This is the case, for example, in South Africa, where the power of the African National Congress at the national sphere can overwhelm local wings of the ANC. Indeed, mayoral candidates for the six metropolitan councils are determined by party headquarters. Similar propensities exist among political parties in some or the European case studies.

A third factor that helps explain the qualification to our observation about the development of multisphere governance systems has to do with the allocation of revenues in such systems. Typically, they are determined between national and constituent units through constitutional allocations, with the constituent units in turn determining which revenue bases should be made available to local governments. As a rule, this leaves local government short on own-source revenue and dependent on transfers from other spheres of government. Consequently, municipal government is typically cast in the role of financial supplicant in intergovernmental relations. In recent years, this has even been true in Germany, despite constitutional provisions that ensure municipalities a substantial flow of funds from designated revenue bases into municipal coffers.

The above reasons provide some of the general evidence and reasoning that helps account for the gap between "ideal models" of multilevel and multi-order governance and our sense of the empirical reality. There are other, more specific, explanatory factors that have also influenced our analysis. Asymmetry within polities is an example. The largest urban conurbations often have substantial professional competence. The opposite holds true for smaller cities and other municipalities. This detracts from the ability of the smaller cities to participate in national policy developments that affect them. In this regard, Agranoff observes a digital divide among Spanish local governments. Steytler notes that South African law recognizes municipalities with high, medium, and low capacity. Rowland stresses that in Mexico "urban municipalities tend to be more dynamic in terms of administration and governance than most rural ones." In Switzerland, Bächtiger and Hitz note that wealthy suburbs effectively resist amalgamations with core cities that are financially strained, resulting in important differences in communal capabilities.

Similarly, there is asymmetry among the countries in our sample. Multisphere governance is more advanced and prevalent in the European countries – whether or not they are members of the European Union – than in the rest of our sample. In part this may reflect the larger role of the state in Europe: the bigger the role of government, the greater is the functional need to plan its activities (see, for example, Dyson 1980). There is also a relatively more corporatist political culture in Europe compared with, say, the United States, Australia, and Mexico (see, for example, Berger, Hirschman, and Maier 1983).

All of these reasons help qualify the nature of our assessment about the trend towards multisphere governance. The development of multilevel/networked government systems is not a linear march of reason through history in the Hegelian sense. Functional necessity indubitably plays some role due to the growing complexity of the policy issues that the state must handle. In turn, this complexity may require more actors at the decision table. But the qualifications in our observations also suggest that the trend is by no means exclusively the result of an inexorable functional necessity, for the policy problems facing the United States or Australia are not all that different from those facing the other developed countries in our sample. Yet these two dual federations appear to have distinctive tracks. In Australia, the state governments continue to design and implement urban strategies, leaving local governments to get on with their relatively small set of responsibilities. In the United States, there are conflicting forces – for example, top-down mandates and fiscal incentives from Washington, on the one hand, and bottom-up administrative multipartner metropolitan planning, on the other. In the end, the trend towards multisphere governance may be as much a function of political culture and political will as of functional necessity.

4.2 EFFECTIVENESS OF MULTILEVEL GOVERNANCE IN RELATION TO THE MUNICIPAL/URBAN CHALLENGES

The second broad area of inquiry relates to the effectiveness of the multisphere governance systems in meeting challenges of urban policy and municipal policy more generally. We have decomposed this second question into three more precise queries:

- How effective are these systems of multisphere governance in fashioning national policies that meet the challenges of municipal policy, especially urban policy?
- Are municipal governments doing an effective job in delivering national and regional programs where the governance system assigns that task to them?
- Are municipal governments doing an effective job of designing and delivering policies and programs within their sphere of competence, whether constitutionally based, rooted in statute, or otherwise?

Beginning with the first of these questions, our sixteen policy case studies suggest several related conclusions. Not surprisingly, one is simply that it is difficult to make broad generalizations about the effectiveness of the different multisphere governance systems in meeting the municipal and urban challenges. With this caveat, the policy studies suggest that the different governance systems are generally mediocre in achieving desired results, although some inevitably work better than others. Differences within each of the polities are also considerable as policies in rural municipalities often turn out to be less effective than those in their urban counterparts. The performance of multisphere governance across and within each of the eight states that make up our sample thus varies.

We noted earlier that most of the governance systems we studied are largely top-down, with municipal governments as the junior partner. Interestingly, and perhaps significantly, the two political systems in our sample where the authors are most positive about the effectiveness of multisphere governance, Switzerland and France, are also the ones where local influence on relevant national policymaking and implementation is most substantial. Specifically, local governments in these two countries appear to have a greater voice in making national policies that affect them than the other six do. Since it is often assumed that unitary states are more reform-capable than federal ones, by virtue of their centralized structure, the fact that we group France together with an unabashedly federal country such as Switzerland is salient, in that it suggests that a system's capacity for reform is not merely a function of its institutional antecedents.

While starting from vastly different points on the centralization-decentralization continuum (Switzerland being among the world's most decentralized federations and France having once been the archetypal centralized state), both now have complex intergovernmental systems that seem at times to approximate our theoretical discussion of multilevel/networked governance – at least, more so than our other country studies. As the relevant chapters make clear, the French and Swiss systems of multisphere governance are not always effective (as shown by the alienation and unrest in the poorer immigrant-populated suburbs of French cities and the fact that local officials in Switzerland feel excluded from the planning for national emergencies). Yet the chapters convey the sense that the evolving multisphere governance systems in their polities work relatively well and are possibly becoming more so over time. In the case of Switzerland, Bächtiger and Hitz write of an "integrative, relatively loosely coupled system of multilevel governance which tends to protect and forward municipal interests, while simultaneously avoiding policy deadlocks and subsequent suboptimal policy results among the three levels." They relate this favourable assessment to the limitations on central government power in Switzerland, the relative clarity in roles and responsibilities among the spheres of government, and the absence of a German-like joint-decision trap.[2] In the case of France, Brunet-Jailly declares that "France has fashioned its own form of multilevel governance" and in "all social and economic policy fields all levels of government are tightly entangled and complementary," with governance of matters of local significance functioning well. This success is associated with the fact that national leaders understand local concerns (because of linked role accumulation and the integrative function of political parties) and that local government now has standing – and "equal" standing in a practical sense – in intergovernmental negotiations.

At the other end of the spectrum are Mexico and South Africa. Both are emerging from political legacies of states where the party system could hitherto have been classified as hegemonic (Sartori 1976). Thus, in the case of Mexico, Rowland writes of a "stark and persistent reality of government failures – at all levels – in key issues such as poverty reduction, crime control, and environmental protection." Despite efforts to build the local sphere, it is the weakest part of Mexico's governance system, especially outside the largest urban areas. Regarding South Africa, Steytler describes it as an "important example of a recently engineered system of multilevel governance where local government plays a significant role in the governance of the country." But he also remarks that national municipal policy overregulates local government, so that the statutory framework created for municipalities is extremely complex and burdensome.

As for the United States, where the electoral geography of presidential and congressional elections once privileged large cities, especially in the Northeast and Midwest, in recent decades the balance of power has shifted to smaller urban areas, suburbs, and rural areas, especially in the South and West. Thus, Vogel argues that "fend-for-yourself" federalism and "coercive" federalism are now much more prevalent than the "cooperative" federalism of an earlier period. The implication of this situation, he declares, is that "no level of government is seriously addressing these problems in the cities, and for this reason, the current multilevel governance system must be judged poorly."

The multisphere systems of governance in Australia, Germany, and Spain seem to fall somewhere in the middle, not as effective as France or Switzerland but outperforming Mexico, South Africa, and the United States. In the case of Australia, in part because the national governing party is based on a broadly similar coalition of interests like the current Republican presidency in the United States, the Commonwealth government has chosen not to involve itself deeply in the big-city agenda. However, there is not the same policy vacuum in relation to the cities' agenda that Vogel finds in the United States, because, as noted above, state governments in Australia coordinate urban programs, directly running many public services that municipal governments provide elsewhere.

While Brown does not answer directly the question about how effectively Australia's top-heavy system of multisphere governance handles the challenges of urban and municipal affairs, he leaves the impression that the system works tolerably well. In part, this may be because of a relatively disentangled arrangement, where it is fairly clear which sphere of government has which responsibility and what financial resources are needed to accompany those tasks.

In the case of Germany, Hrbek and Bodenbender note that municipal governments, owing to their dual role as local self-government entities and as delivery tiers for other spheres of government, have traditionally accomplished a wide range of public tasks. But in recent times of financial stress, with ever-increasing interdependence among governments, the delegation of administrative tasks to the local tier without adequate fiscal resources has weakened the capacity of municipalities to carry out their tasks effectively. While the whole system is not entirely dysfunctional, the leeway granted to local politics in the framework of Germany's federal order remains very limited. In the end, the first step of the recent federalism reform changes nothing about this reality.

As for Spain, its multitiered system has been able to catch up with its creation of a late arriving welfare state along European social democratic lines and to provide a measure of regional stability through its autonomous communities. Local governments, under the supervision of national and regional governments, have by and large delivered the necessary public services but have not been at the core of Spain's political energy in making reform happen.

The second effectiveness-related question we posed was whether municipal governments were delivering national and regional programs competently where the governance system assigns them that task. In general, most of the chapters suggest that local government performs this role satisfactorily, though less so in Mexico and South Africa.

In all four European countries, local authorities are intended, among other things, to be a delivery agent for national and regional governments. This appears to be the intention in South Africa as well. This is much less the case in Australia, while in the United States the situation is somewhere between the European and Australian models. For Mexico, it may be premature to judge, but the converse appears to prevail, with state governments to varying degrees usurping spheres of administrative activity that the Constitution assigns to municipalities.

In three of the four European cases – France, Germany, and Switzerland – there is no hint of significant shortfalls in the delivery capacity of local authorities. As for Spain, the analysis suggests that the concern about delivery capacity is confined mainly to smaller cities. On the whole, in the European cases, it is fair to say that local governments are up to, or becoming up to, the task of delivering EU, national, and regional programs as part of the reality of multisphere governance on that continent. What is more controversial is whether appropriate financial resources are attached to these responsibilities. This dispute regarding the adequacy of local finances is subject to ongoing debate in all three countries, with the German case perhaps the most contentious.

Regarding the United States, there, too, the issue of delivery capacity at the local level does not emerge as a significant concern. However, as Vogel's case study of Hurricane Katrina demonstrates, this conclusion does not necessarily hold in emergency situations, where confusion about roles and responsibilities aggravated an already difficult situation. Of equal concern is the frequency with which Congress mandates action by the local and state authorities without adequate funds. It is not by accident that, historically, the concept of "unfunded mandates" has been taken more seriously in the American academic literature than in the comparable literature of other countries.

The divide between the delivery capacity of large cities and their rural counterparts that is found in Spain is amplified in Mexico and South Africa. This obviously has less to do with any deficiencies in the concept of multisphere governance than the fact that these two economies are less affluent than our other six cases.

In short, the main issue that emerges in the developed countries has to do with inadequate funding of mandated programs from the national and other spheres, rather than delivery capacity as such. This difficulty is found in dual federalisms, administrative federalisms, and unitary France. Moreover, the country studies provide no evidence of more profligate spending or irresponsible fiscal behaviour by municipal governments in countries that rely relatively more on intergovern-mental transfers, though in isolated instances, such as Berlin, this may be the case.

The third question that we consider in our analysis of the effectiveness of multisphere governance in meeting urban and municipal challenges is whether municipal governments are doing an effective job of designing and delivering policies and programs within their sphere of competence, whether constitution-ally based, rooted in statute, or otherwise. Although this question was not put explicitly to the country authors in our research template, this emerged as an issue of growing concern from their analyses. In brief, the concern is that democrati-cally elected local governments are becoming so constrained by the mandates being imposed from above that they lack the fiscal and administrative resources – and the political energy – to respond effectively to local challenges that are within their exclusive competence.

Constitutional protections notwithstanding, we already noted the concern that local governments in both Germany and South Africa risk becoming mere ap-pendages of higher levels of government. A similar worry, though much weaker, emerges in the Swiss chapter. (The autonomy of Swiss cantons and their com-munes remains high compared with local governments in the other countries we covered.) In Mexico, local government remains in its infancy, so the risk there is not so much of losing innovative and administrative competence as in arresting any ability to develop it in the first place. Rowland observes that given some of the recent failures in Mexican governance, "it is becoming more common to hear calls for a return to centralized rule and a 'firm hand' on the part of national authorities." A 2005 Spanish White Paper on Reform of Local Government ar-gued for four general principles that should govern municipal power: autonomy, subsidiarity, flexibility, and proportionality (that is, the ability to receive funds or raise revenues proportionate to spending responsibilities). This suggests that these principles have been lacking locally, in contrast to the situation in the recently organized regional governments. In all these cases, to the extent that there may be a concern, it rests in worries about inadequately funded mandates and the lack of fiscal autonomy. Whether these trends continue – and, indeed, reduce the ability of local government to act effectively within its own sphere – is an issue worth monitoring carefully.

The American case has both similarities and differences relative to the coun-tries discussed above. Vogel surmises:

There has been "*de facto* devolution" occurring in the United States over the last four decades (Kincaid 1999). Devolution was not a deliberate policy to bolster local autonomy. Rather, the federal government abandoned cities and their problems (Caraley 1992), changing the nature of urban politics (Eisinger 1998). Cities must now be more fiscally and administratively self-reliant. Local public management takes on increasing importance, leading urban managers to focus less on issues of social justice and racial equality and more on economic development and central city revitalization. Mayors in such cities as New York, Los Angeles, and Chicago have embraced the new public management policies to reduce costs, keep taxes low, and create a good business climate, and are now being hailed as saviours of the cities (Savitch and Vogel 2005).

Washington's indifference to the big-city agenda does not mean that America's cities have been forgotten entirely. The federal government indeed continues to use them as delivery agents for the programs it mandates. In this sense, there is a similarity to the cases discussed above, especially since the mandates are often insufficiently funded and thus may stress cities financially. But since the U.S. federal government does not pretend to have an overall strategy for cities, preferring instead to connect to urban dwellers through programs for individuals such as social security and Medicare, overall urban leadership has been left to mayors. In this sense, tough love from Washington may in fact have strengthened the ability of city governments to succeed in at least some of their challenges. In effect, the decision of the federal government to withdraw from joint programs that had been part of the federal-local landscape in the 1960s has actually enhanced the autonomy of local governments and has led them to fill at least part of the void that might otherwise have been created by this disentanglement.

In contrast to the cases above, Brown points to the innovative quality of municipal government in Australia. Although its scope is considerably narrower than that enjoyed by local government in our other cases (and for this reason may be unique), municipal revenue sources seem stable and secure. This may help explain local government's good performance within its areas of competence. In the case of France, municipal governments, according to Brunet-Jailly, are "able to take up economic-development initiatives and set up tourism bureaus; they are responsible for local airports, seaports, and the building and maintenance of local roads ... they can manage public social housing ... all local schools ... as well as monuments of historical significance." These activities are not undertaken unilaterally but in cooperation with other spheres of government. French municipalities are as "reliant on other levels of government as those other government levels are on them," Brunet-Jailly writes and this networked system is working relatively effectively. In this regard, it is noteworthy that the French situation is the opposite of the Australian. The latter is based on the autonomy of the municipal sector whereas the former is based on interdependence among spheres of government. The important loose end in the case of France is the adequacy of municipal funding, a debate that has not yet been resolved to the satisfaction of municipal governments.

4.3 EFFECTS OF MULTILEVEL GOVERNANCE ON DEMOCRACY

The third broad question this chapter considers is whether and how the processes associated with multisphere governance influence democratic values and processes. Although the research template did not cover this issue explicitly, the country studies nonetheless provide some insights into it. Our main observation in this regard is twofold. On the one hand, the strengthening of local government in countries that previously had a strong authoritarian tradition (Mexico, Spain, and South Africa) or a centralized system (France) is identified with the spread of democracy. The enhanced local role is associated with a dispersion of power that had formerly been concentrated heavily in the national capital or in a single political party that was itself highly centralized. In France and Spain, this dispersion is reflected in the end of administrative tutelage from the national capital.

On the other hand, in some European countries with a long tradition of local government autonomy (Switzerland, Germany), and where local government is effectively the constituent governmental unit that predates the formation of the nation state, multisphere governance may be reducing the effective freedom of action of local government. Even in the United States, the traditional Home Rule right of local self-government was affected by the centralizing tendencies of the twentieth century. In short, because the starting points for the countries in our sample differ widely, the impact of multisphere governance on democratic values and processes appears to differ as well. On the whole, however, at the macropolitical level, the spread of multisphere governance probably entails more gains than losses, because of the checks and balances it affords and because of its more deliberative and consensual approach to overcoming collective-action problems.

At the micropolitical level, the concerns that arise most often are that systems of multisphere governance frequently lack transparency, mute accountability, and have insufficient legislative oversight. The provision for referendums in Switzerland and the still expansive if shrinking scope of cantonal and local autonomy suggest that these concerns may be least worrisome in that country. Its weak party system, the independence of members of parliament, and the fact that there is role accumulation (municipal officials may also be MPs) further facilitates a relatively open process for consensual integration. In other words, concerns for transparency, accountability, and legislative oversight do not appear to be as great an issue in Switzerland as in the rest of our sample.

In the United States, a voluminous amount of information is made available through the publication of the proceedings of committees and subcommittees of Congress. At the same time, congressional oversight of the executive branch is weaker when the party that occupies the White House also has control of Congress. Some urban literature in the United States views the growth of public-private partnerships in the urban sphere as the ceding of state authority to non-transparent private interests for unclear public benefits.[3] In the case of France, Brunet-Jailly cites Sassen's concern about "complexity and accountability" but claims that the mechanisms of governance that could make transparency a problem in France have not yet become a major issue in French political debate. Regarding Germany, the joint-decision trap has adverse implications for accountability partly because it engenders elite-driven solutions rather than grassroots public consultation. Agranoff notes in passing some concerns about transparency with respect to local government, but this issue does not emerge as significant in his study of Spain.

Our final observation with regard to the impacts on democracy concern the nature of the governance systems that our country authors encountered. As already noted, the broad thrust of their analyses suggests a relatively top-down system of multilevel governance rather than a flatter networked system. As also noted earlier, the case for networked governance is partly normative, suggesting more players, less hierarchy, and a diffusion of power that some democratic theorists might applaud. Whatever the normative arguments, however, the evidence in this volume does not suggest the growth of an extensive system of networked governance for tackling the major urban challenges.

5 CONCLUDING REMARKS

We found multisphere governance systems developing in response to contemporary municipal and urban challenges in all of our country case studies. In light of the diversity of our sample, this suggests that the trend is at least partly a functional response to the growth of interdependence worldwide. At the same time, we found that the extent of the trend and the nature of the arrangements differ from one country to another, which suggests that normative preferences also play a substantial role in evolving governance systems.

A strong result of our research and analysis is that, notwithstanding important differences among the governance systems in our sample, they remain predominantly top-down and thus multilevel (in the sense that this term was defined above). Although in each system there are institutional mechanisms for local government to voice its views on national policies that affect its sphere (except in the United States, where political institutions play a smaller role), more often than not these voices carry little weight in the multilevel policy decision process. This is unfortunate, in that the analysis here suggests that the two countries with governance systems that are the least hierarchical in their treatment of municipal/urban government, namely those of France and Switzerland, may also be the ones that best manage these policy challenges. This suggests the possibility that policymaking and implementation in other countries could benefit from a less hierarchical approach. Such an approach would also enhance democratic values and processes. The evidence also suggests that the European countries in our sample have more mature multisphere governance systems than the other polities we studied. This is consistent with the idea that the European political culture is less suspicious of the state per se than the Anglo-American culture.

We also speculated at the outset that administrative federations might be more likely to develop additional top-down governance arrangements than systems of dual federalism. The evidence here, however, is too mixed to verify this hypothesis. The cases that substantiate the hypothesis at least to some extent include both Germany and South Africa, given the hierarchical nature of their systems of administrative federalism. The cases where the evidence seems to point the other way include France, where the trend is to decentralize its unitary state, while the Australian dual federalism system remains top-heavy.

Further, the country studies did not suggest that non-governmental actors at the local level are playing a large role in the multisphere policy process. In one sense, this is understandable, since our research template did not focus explicitly on this question. Yet the country authors raised many other issues that were not directly included in our template. If non-governmental actors were indeed significant in the process of policy development and implementation as suggested in parts of the academic literature (e.g., Rhodes 1996, 1999) we should have expected to see more reference to their role in the country studies. We do not doubt that non-governmental actors are players in urban governance. But we would like to better understand the nature and weight of their role. Perhaps it is confined to helping resolve specific regional and local issues within established policy frameworks rather than in creating the frameworks, themselves. In any case, the silence of our authors on the role of non-governmental actors suggests that this is an area that merits further empirical study, with an emphasis on clarifying where non-governmental actors are influential and where they are not.

While local government may play only a small role in the policymaking process, it is nonetheless a crucial element of the multisphere system, because it is frequently counted on to be the delivery agent for national and regional programs. In this regard, the evidence here suggests that local authorities do a reasonable job administratively, with the largest urban areas generally possessing the widest range of professional skills. Without these local administrative capacities, the multisphere system would need to invent them. The analysis also indicates that local governments in Mexico and South Africa are still at an early stage of acquiring the requisite competence.

Fiscal arrangements that affect local governments' ability not only to deliver the programs mandated by national and regional governments but also to design and deliver programs within their competence are an important consideration in all of the systems. Typically, local governments are subject to fiscal arrangements that are contingent on constitutional frameworks that privilege national or regional governments. With some exceptions, they have few constitutionally entrenched own-source revenues. The imposition of unfunded and underfunded mandates on municipal governments is common in almost all of our cases, and in several they have been growing. Given the diversity among our country studies, this strongly suggests that this trend is mainly driven not by the specifics of the institutional arrangements but by a common desire at the senior spheres of government to claim maximum political credit with their voters for the least taxation they can get away with. In most of the countries covered, intergovernmental fiscal arrangements remain controversial. Municipal governments generally feel shortchanged by other spheres of government and are left without the fiscal resources they require to address urban infrastructure, emergency preparedness, and immigration settlement, or to deliver programs mandated elsewhere.

There are two distinct issues that are noteworthy here. The first is that everywhere there is a large fiscal gap between local governments and other spheres, which means that local governments spend more than they raise and they must rely on other spheres to fund the difference. For those who subscribe to the idea that this "soft budget constraint" may lead to excessive local spending, however, it should be noted that we could find no evidence to this end. Local spending, as a share of total government expenditures, has remained quite steady for the past two decades (OECD 2005), a noteworthy observation for those who claim that powers are being scaled down as well as up. This is not surprising. For one thing, other spheres of government (usually regional) typically require that local governments balance their budgets. Local governments, as argued above, remain "junior." Their room to manoeuvre financially is determined by other spheres of government that have the constitutional authority to establish the regulatory framework for local finance.

This brings us to the second issue. If municipalities cannot run deficits because of the financial rules imposed from above, it is hard to evaluate concerns about local fiscal needs. If there is indeed too little revenue available to the local sphere, this cannot be manifested in budgetary deficits, so it must show up in other ways, such as unsatisfactory physical infrastructure and inadequate local services. We are, unfortunately, not in a position to evaluate the adequacy of municipal infrastructure and services relative to the many other claims on taxpayers. We are thus unable to determine whether the programmatic and fiscal shortfalls that exist locally are of higher priority than the fiscal claims of other spheres of government. What we do sense, however, is that the process for determining the fiscal resources to be available locally is itself too top-heavy and that there is a need, within existing or amended constitutional frameworks, to make more space available for local fiscal needs to be understood and addressed in a fairer and more transparent fashion. This would not only improve the quality of local government: it would also help make local government more transparent and would facilitate accountability among governments in multisphere systems. In our own vocabulary, such changes would help make governance systems that are now heavily *multilevel* more *multi-order*.

NOTES

1 E-mail from Doug Brown to Harvey Lazar, 5 February 2007.
2 For more on the problem of the "joint-decision trap," see Scharpf 1988.
3 Conversation with Ron Vogel, winter 2007.

REFERENCES

Beck, U. 1992. *Risk Society: Towards a New Modernity*. Newbury Park, Calf.: Sage Publications

Berger, S., A.O. Hirschman, and C. Maier. 1983. *Organizing Interests in Western Europe: Pluralism, Corporatism, and the Transformation of Politics*. Cambridge: Cambridge University Press

Brenner, N. 2004. *New State Spaces: Urban Governance and the Rescaling of Statehood*. Oxford: Oxford University Press

Dyson, K.H.F. 1980. *The State Tradition in Western Europe*. New York: Oxford University Press

Giddens, A. 1990. *Consequences of Modernity*. Stanford: Stanford University Press

Hooghe, L., and G. Marks. 2003. "Unravelling the Central State, but How? Types of Multilevel Governance." *American Political Science Review* 97 (2): 233–43

Jones, C., W.S. Hesterly, and S.P. Borgatti. 1997. "A General Theory of Network Governance: Exchange Conditions and Social Mechanisms." *Academy of Management Review*
22 (4): 911–45

Keil, R. 1998. "Globalization Makes States: Perspectives of Local Governance in the Age
of the World City." *Review of International Political Economy* 5 (4): 616–46

Le Galès, P., and A. Harding. 1998. "Cities and States in Europe." *West European Politics*
21 (3): 120–45

MacIver, R.M. 1926. *The Modern State*. Oxford: Clarendon Press

McKinnon, R.I. 1994. "Market-Preserving Fiscal Federalism." Working paper. Department of Economics, Stanford University

Marks, G. 1993. "Structural Policy and Multilevel Governance in the EU." In *The State of
the European Community*, vol. 2, ed. A. Cafruny and G. Rosenthal, 391–410. Boulder:
Lynne Rienner

– 1996. "An Actor-Centred Approach to Multi-Level Governance." *Regional and Federal
Studies* 6 (2): 20–38

Marks, G., and L. Hooghe. 2004. "Contrasting Visions of Multi-level Governance." Chap. 2
of *Multi-level Governance*, ed. I. Bache and M. Flinders. Oxford: Oxford University
Press

Michels, R. 1911 [1915]. *Political Parties: A Sociological Study of the Oligarchical Tendencies of Modern Democracy*. New York: Hearst's International Library

Organization for Economic Co-operation and Development (OECD). 2005. *General
Government Account: National Accounts of OECD Countries*. Vol. 4, 1993–2004. Paris:
OECD

Rhodes, R.A.W. 1996. "The New Governance: Governing without Government." *Political Studies* 44:652–67

– 1999. *Control and Power in Central-Local Relations*, 2nd ed. Aldershot and Brookfield:
Ashgate

Sartori, G. 1976. *Parties and Party Systems: A Framework for Analysis*. Cambridge: Cambridge University Press

Scharpf, F.W. 1988. "The Joint-Decision Trap: Lessons from German Federalism and
European Integration." *Public Administration* 66 (3): 239–78

Tindemans, L. 1975. *L'Union européenne: rapport de M. Leo Tindemans au counseil
européen*. Brussels: European Commission

Watts, R.L. 2003. "Introduction: Comparative Research and Fiscal Federalism." *Regional
and Federal Studies* 13 (4): 1–6

Weingast, B.R. 1995. "The Economic Role of Political Institutions: Market-Preserving
Federalism and Economic Development." *Journal of Law, Economics, and Organization* 11 (1): 1–3

LOCAL GOVERNMENTS IN SPAIN'S MULTILEVEL ARRANGEMENTS

Robert Agranoff

1 INTRODUCTION

Spain's cities provide the major platforms in the architecture of its social, economic, and political framework. No longer isolated and dictatorial, the country is part of the European experiment and an actor on the world stage; it is governed by an inductive form of federal democracy. Most of its people now live and work in its larger cities, many of which are well known to the world: Barcelona, Bilbao, Cordoba, Madrid, Santiago, Seville, and Valencia. These and other cities offer the building blocks of the political system and enforce second- and first-level government norms, with neighbourhood offices and city halls delivering the basic services and amenities required by citizens. But the cities are more than this, for each tries to express itself in cultural, artistic, and architectural ways that were impossible just three decades ago under General Franco.

The post-Franco transition has not, however, made it possible to solve all the problems of major cities. Spain's municipal corporations are fiscally and normatively dependent on a mind-numbing set of connections with higher-level governments and with other public and nonpublic arrangements. Because of the deficit in resources and powers, cities are constantly operating with "socios," or partners, both horizontally in the community and vertically up the governmental chain. Although the Spanish state has tried to overcome a high social welfare deficit from the Franco years, the cities face myriad problems, because that is where most people with social problems live. The number of urban elderly who are somehow in need of care is just one example. Another acute social problem is the social integration of immigrants, most of whom descend on Spain's cities. Crime and substance abuse are, of course, also Spanish city problems. These social challenges are coupled with the challenge of providing affordable housing and of moving people from their homes to their work. This requires the modern infrastructure of transport, roads, bridges, tunnels, and the like. And in order to promote employment, the city must use its powers and resources to attract economic activity, putting a further demand on its infrastructure. Finally, Spain's urban construction boom of the past fifteen years has placed great pressure on the ability of city governments to provide the basics – roads, lighting, water, sewer, sanitation – and in the process has opened up the gates of land-use abuse and corruption.

These concerns all call into question the ability of Spain's cities to meet their twenty-firtst-century challenges. As this paper will demonstrate, despite the fact that most Spaniards occupy the country's larger cities, their local governments lack critical capacity in the post-Franco democratic system. Most of the reform energy has gone into decentralization, transferring powers from the central government to the second-tier autonomous communities. This important federal construction of the "state made up of autonomies," or regional governments, has more or less come at the expense of empowering cities, a practice that has continued for more than a quarter of a century. Local governments are subordinate to the central and regional levels, particularly with regard to powers such as urban planning. Indeed, municipalities have few if any exclusive powers within their sphere of operation. They have experienced less than 15 percent of shared public revenue during the entire post-Franco period. Governmentally, they not only possess limited powers but also are saddled with a form of government that involves the indirect election of mayors and independent department heads from the ruling coalition. Within city government, bottom-up democracy – for example, through neighbourhood councils – is very uneven throughout the country. Moreover, the electoral system of proportional representation virtually eliminates district representation and favours local special interests. All of this means that, from a governmental standpoint, municipalities are in a relatively weak position to offer first-rate amenities, to promote their economies, to meet environmental challenges, and to cope with indigenous social problems.

2 THE CONSTITUTIONAL DIMENSION

The Constitution of Spain became official three years after the 1975 death of Franco, on 29 December 1978. It represented the culmination of extended debate and regime reform that built on the traditions of autonomy represented in the Cadiz Constitution of 1812, the short-lived federal First Republic in the nineteenth century, and the regional autonomy movement (installed for Catalonia, adopted for the Basque provinces and Galicia, but interrupted by the Civil War) of the Second Republic of the 1930s (Crow 1985). The Constitution ushered in democracy and launched the possibility of building modern federal arrangements (Elazar 1996) and, most important for the purposes of this paper, a highly intergovernmentalized system of local, regional, state, and European-level relations.

The development of Spain's contemporary federal arrangements is, of course, integral to the entire process of the transition from dictatorship to democracy (Agranoff 1996). Aja (2003, 97) concludes that constitutional guarantees and norms, the autonomous community (AC) statutes of autonomy, interpretations of the Constitutional Court, and many forces in governing make the Spanish autonomous state "equivalent in structure and power to actual federal states," despite the fact that the "Constitution does not use that terminology."[1] Moreover, Moreno (2001, 5) suggests that what is different about Spain's federalization is that it "has developed in an inductive manner, step by step."

The Constitution, in Article 2, "guarantees the right to autonomy of the nationalities and regions" that make up the "indissoluble unity of the Spanish nation." Article 137 organizes the state "into municipalities, provinces, and the Autonomous

Communities which may be constituted. All of these entities enjoy autonomy for the management of their respective interests." Although provinces and municipalities historically preceded ACs, the primary intergovernmental emphasis has been on the connection between the state and the regional governments (Agranoff and Ramos 1997; Subirats and Gallego 2002). Governmental arrangements are in fact more complex, as figure 1 indicates. Actually thousands of governments exist if one includes the various special units of government and formal intergovernmental arrangements.

Figure 1
Spain's Governmental Units

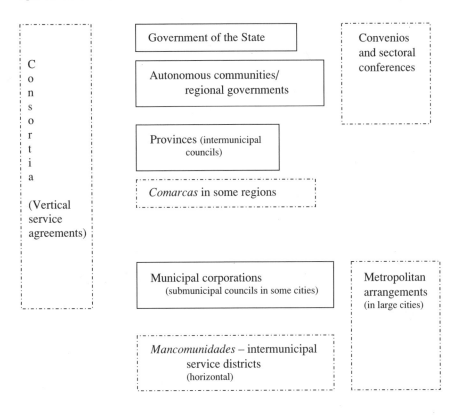

Government of the State

Autonomous communities/
regional governments

Convenios
and sectoral
conferences

Provinces (intermunicipal
councils)

Comarcas in some regions

Consortia

(Vertical
service
agreements)

Municipal corporations
(submunicipal councils in some cities)

Metropolitan
arrangements
(in large cities)

Mancomunidades – intermunicipal
service districts
(horizontal)

Legend:

Constitutional arrangements

Established by state or regional normative action

Despite rapid growth in size and functional responsibilities, local governments have not attained a role as a leading player in Spanish intergovernmental relations. Carillo (1997, 40) concludes that "the decentralization strategy employed has left local government in an area of uncertainty in terms of the definition of its role in the *Estado de las Autonomías* (the state of autonomies)." The problem, as will be demonstrated, is highly political because local government interests have never been able to muster the political power of that of the regions within the national scheme, and consequently local governments are "dually subordinated" to ACs and to the general government (Baena 2000, 13). As López-Aranguren (2001, 5) concludes, "They occupy a strong position in legal and constitutional terms but in the reality of day to day government they experience a serious lack of power in areas important to them as well as inadequate economic resources to face the responsibilities assigned to them or those they would like to assume."

The Constitution establishes a multilayered and interdependent framework of governments. Article 2 identifies unity and autonomy as the first principles, and frames a three-tiered system, including ACs and local governments. The ACs are the relatively new bodies that were "chartered" by the national parliament through statues of autonomy, which are roughly the equivalent of a state or provincial constitution for each territory (in Spanish convention and here, "AC" and "territory" are used interchangeably). The Constitution is similar to many modern European constitutions in that human rights and civil liberties, principles of social justice, and rights of association are spelled out early in the document and are important judicially enforceable rights that apply to all levels of government. For example, Article 27(8) states that "the public authorities shall inspect and standardize the educational system so as to guarantee compliance with the laws," a provision that tests principles of autonomy. It has led to acrimony between Madrid and some regions – over language, history, and other cultural instruction – with considerable tension regarding the state's role in decentralized programs.

The powers laid down in the Constitution are somewhat misleading in an overlapping system that is designed to maximize intergovernmental cooperation. Article 149 enumerates some thirty-two different "exclusive state competencies," including normal foreign and international relations, defence, international trade and organizations, state finance and debt, management of the economy, social pensions, interregional transport and economic matters, and many other matters that affect more than one region. Somewhat different from that of a number of federal systems are the administration of justice (all regional and municipal courts are, in effect, national), labour legislation, public security (except for municipal police), academic and professional degree standards, and authorization of consultative referendums. Moreover, Article 150 allows the parliament to transfer portions of state competency to the ACs, including transfer of financial means, yet maintains the state power to "harmonize the normative provisions of the Autonomous Communities even in the case of matters attributed to their competence when the general interest so demands." Not surprisingly, this clause, which is left up to parliamentary discretion, has been the source of considerable intergovernmental conflict.

In regard to AC competencies, Article 148 lists some twenty-two, ranging from the power of AC self-government to economic development and social programming, environmental protection, sport, tourism, health, and social services (Aja 2003; Argullol et al. 2004). Most important with regard to local governments is the fact that ACs are responsible for "organization of their institutions of self-government," "alterations of municipal boundaries," "in general the functions which belong to the State Administration concerning local corporations and whose transfer is authorized by the legislation on Local Governments," "regulation of the territory, urbanism and housing," and "the coordination and other functions with respect to local police forces." Five years after establishing their initial competencies, the ACs were able to expand their powers. Between 1985 and 2002, a gradual transfer of competencies from the state to the ACs occurred, most importantly the transfer of education, health, and social services to all seventeen regions.

Each AC government possesses a constitutionally required unicameral elected parliament, a council of ministers, a president who is the territorial first minister, and an administrative corps. Regional elections are held separately from statewide elections, and they follow the same patterns of partisan alignments as those of state elections (Pallarés, Montero, and Llera 1997). AC administrative agencies were partially built through the transfer of state civil servants whose programs were regionalized (Subirats and Gallego 2002).

Local government is not nearly as constitutionally elaborated. Articles 140–2, covering three short paragraphs, basically outline the structure of local governments. The Constitution "guarantees the autonomy of the municipalities." Enjoying full legal identity, their governments are composed of mayors and councillors who are elected in free and direct secret suffrage. The Constitution refers to the law determining the manner of elections and council proceedings. Article 141 names provinces as legal entities "determined by the collection of municipalities and territorial division for the fulfillment of the activities of the state." The government of the state and the ACs oversee the *diputaciones,* or provincial governments. In the two island ACs, the Balarics and Canaries, each island "shall also have their own administration in the form of *Cabildos* or councils." Finally, Article 142 enumerates the right of financial autonomy of local governments: "The local treasuries must have the means necessary for carrying out the functions which the law attributes to the respective corporations and they shall be supported basically by their own taxes and by sharing those of the State and the Autonomous Communities."

Parliamentary elaboration of local government reform in the immediate post-Franco era lagged behind that of electoral change. Not until two rounds of local elections were held in 1985 did the parliament focus its attention on the structure and power of local government and, in 1988, on local government's finances. The statutes of autonomy constitute the next "constitutional" level affecting local governments. Not all statutes of autonomy contain detailed local government provisions, but most restate their relevant constitutional competencies over local government and mention mechanisms of financing. For example, the statute of autonomy for Andalucía (*Ley Organica 6/1981*) recognizes the municipality as the basic local entity, with jural powers through its council within its territory (Article 2), and identifies provincial competencies as those delegated downward from the state and ACs and upward from municipalities (Article 4). Article 62 outlines local financing, including local governments' right to participate in AC and state revenues, the AC governments' right to fiscal oversight and supervision, the need to allocate funds according to legal criteria, and the need to follow statewide law in establishing a system of fiscal collaboration among entities.

The AC statutes of autonomy thus illustrate the dual constitutional level, with many basic laws being established by the government in Madrid and with the ACs sharing in constitutional and normative powers over local governments. As will be demonstrated, the situation is considerably more complicated in practice.

There is more besides the three basic tiers and four governments. Under state and AC government legislation, other units of government have been established, primarily for the purpose of municipal coordination. First, some ACs have created *comarcas*, or counties, for multimunicipal servicing and planning. Catalonia has the most active system of *comarcas* (forty-one); they emphasize the territorial planning coordination of rural services, and also cultural promotion.

Second are *mancomunidades*: single-purpose or multi-purpose public horizontal partnerships to deliver services, which are engaged in by two or more municipalities. They exist all over the country and are primarily designed to deliver the following services: collection of refuse, treatment and supply of water, cultural activities, fire services, social services, promotion of tourism, and economic development.

Third are consortia: vertical partnerships of public organizations from different levels (e.g., municipality or *mancomunidad*, provincial government, AC government). The most prevalent consortia, which are almost always single-function and most commonly are between provinces and municipalities, fall in the following areas: economic development, supply of water, cultural promotion, collection of refuse, management of theatres, management of hospitals, public works, urbanization, and promotion of tourism.

Fourth are several special or asymmetric arrangements. For example, the two large cities Madrid and Barcelona have metropolitan-level planning, water, and transit powers. The two North African city-territories (or possessions) have autonomy linked legally to two Andalucian provinces, even though they are independent city-states. Moreover, many cities possess submunicipal councils and have somewhat decentralized their service arms. The two island ACs emphasize their *cabildos,* or island councils (three for the Balarics and seven for the Canaries), effectively replacing the *diputaciones* at the provincial level. Finally, in the seven uniprovincial ACs, the provincial and AC governments are merged, effectively reducing the number of provinces to forty-three.

This all leads to a relatively dynamic census of Spanish governments. Table 1a provides a recent accounting of the complex array of governments, not including some 3,200 submunicipal governments. Even without these submunicipal councils, more than 10,000 governments exist in a country of about 42 million people. In addition to the government of the state, 17 ACs, and 50 provinces (with 43 *diputaciones*), almost one thousand (988) special districts or mancomunidades existed in 2004, plus just over 900 consortia or vertical structures. Most important, are the 8,107 municipalities, a subject that will be an important theme throughout this paper.

Table 1a
Census of Spanish Governmental Units, 2004: Units

Units	No.
Autonomous communities	17
Provinces	50
Comarcas	81
Mancomunidades	988
Consortia	909
Municipalities	8,107

Source: www.minhac.es (2005)

Table 1b
Census of Spanish Governmental Units, 2004: Autonomous Communities

Autonomous community	Provinces no.	%	Comarcas no.	%	Mancomunidades no.	%	Consortia no.	%	Municipalities no.	%
Andalucía	8	16.0	–	–	87	8.8	254	27.9	770	9.5
Aragón	3	6.0	32	39.5	68	6.9	22	2.4	730	9.0
Asturias	1	2.0	–	–	17	1.7	14	1.5	78	1.0
Baleares	1	2.0	–	–	7	0.7	77	8.5	67	0.8
Canarias	2	4.0	–	–	20	2.0	18	2.0	87	1.1
Cantabria	1	2.0	–	–	18	1.8	4	0.4	102	1.3
Castilla y León	9	18.0	1	1.2	216	21.9	48	5.3	2,248	27.7
Castille–La Mancha	5	10.0	–	0.0	122	12.3	30	3.3	919	11.3
Catalonia	4	8.0	41	50.6	76	7.7	244	26.8	946	11.7
Extramadura	2	4.0	–	–	83	8.4	24	2.6	383	4.7
Galicia	4	8.0	–	–	43	4.4	21	2.3	315	3.9
Madrid	1	2.0	–	–	41	4.1	38	4.2	179	2.2
Murcia	1	2.0	–	–	10	1.0	20	2.2	45	0.6
Navarra	1	2.0	–	–	63	6.4	11	1.2	272	3.4
País Vasco	3	6.0	7	8.6	36	3.6	28	3.1	250	3.1
Rioja (La)	1	2.0	–	–	25	2.5	2	0.2	174	2.1
Valencia	3	6.0	–	–	56	5.7	54	5.9	542	6.7
TOTAL	50	100.0	81	100.0	988	100.0	909	100.0	8,107	100.0

Source: Spain, Ministerio de Económica y hacienda 2005. serviciosweb.minhac.es/apps/ispl/aspx/comh300.html

ROBERT AGRANOFF

Table 1c
Census of Spanish Governmental Units, 2004: Range of Population Size

Range	Municipalities		Total population	
	no.	%	no.	%
0–2,000	5,919	73.0	2,975,840	7.1
2,001–5,000	1,007	12.4	3,138,752	7.5
5,001–20,000	854	10.5	8,236,982	19.7
20,001–50,000	205	2.5	6,070,295	14.5
50,001>	123	1.5	21,416,025	51.2
TOTAL	8,108	100.00	41,837,894	100.00

Source: National Statistics Institute, *Statistical Yearbook of Spain* 2004, 85–6. www.ine.es/prodyser/pubweb/anuario04/anu04_2demografia.pdf

Table 1b enumerates the sub-AC governments by territory, where the range appears considerable. Generally, the more provincial governments there are in an AC, the more governmental arrangements exist (with the exception of the *comarcas*, which are concentrated in Aragon and Catalonia). Municipal distribution depends largely on terrain and territorial extension (not displayed), with Castilla y León having over 2,000 mostly small towns (more than one-quarter of the total).

Table 1c breaks down the municipalities by population, demonstrating the urban nature of the Spanish population. In 2004, just over one-half of the total population lived in the 123 largest cities, and another one-third lived in cities with a population of over 5,000. Of the 8,000-plus municipalities, more than 6,900 contain just under 15 percent of the population. In other words, nearly seven out of eight municipalities have a population of less than 5,000, and almost six out of eight have less than 2,000. This makes Spain a country of urban dwellers, mostly in large cities, but with many very small municipalities.

3 RANGE OF MUNICIPAL/LOCAL RESPONSIBILITIES AND FUNCTIONS

The municipal governing code is laid out in the *Ley reguladorada las bases del regimen local* (LRBRL) of 1985 as amended. Under the LRBLR, municipalities are governed by councils (*plenos*), municipal commissions (*comisiones*) or executive committees, and mayors (*alcaldes*) elected by their councils. The law strengthened mayoral power to appoint a commission solely composed of the majority party in council, as opposed to the previous practice of proportional representation. Municipalities with a population of less than a hundred are allowed to operate in open assemblies, in which the mayor acts by following the majority decisions of all voters. In all larger cities the mayor is normally the head of the majority party in council and combines several functions: chair of the council, chief city representative, chief of municipal administration, and head of municipal police. Like the commission form of city government in the United States, departments are normally headed by elected councillors (Carillo 1991), a mayor-commission type of government. The municipal council does not have the authority to draft laws, but it can draft and enact regulations (*ordenanzas*) that are in conformity with legislation of the Cortes and/or the AC parliament. City officials are elected in constituencies called *términos municipales* by means of at-large or municipality-wide party lists in rank order, headed by each party's nominee for mayor. Electoral laws predate the LRBRL, having been enacted in 1977 and 1978, but local elections are now governed by a 1995 law, which statutorily assigns the number of councillors per municipality, with a minimum of five for small municipalities (Newton 1997).

The LRBRL specifies municipal functions, increasing the responsibilities as a city becomes larger. All municipalities must provide public lighting, a cemetery, refuse collection, street cleaning, potable water for homes, a sewage system, the paving of public streets, access (from the country) to the population centre, and food and beverage control. Municipalities with a population of 5,000 or more are additionally responsible for public parks, public libraries, markets, and solid waste treatment. Cities with a population greater than 20,000 must also include civil defence, social services, fire prevention and control, and public sports facilities. Municipalities with a population of more than 50,000 must also include urban transport and environmental protection. Of course, cities under these population limits can offer these specified services before they grow large enough for the services to be obligatory. For example, urban transport, social services, and fire protection are often offered when they are not mandatory. More important, the LRBRL states that municipalities may develop alternative servicing arrangements by soliciting their AC government; for small municipalities, this has led to a massive separation between the provision and production of services, particularly through provinces/consortia, but also by *comarcas* and *mancomunidades* (Banón and Carillo 1992). In 2003 major cities were also required to include municipal district committees, to decentralize management by districts, and to establish mechanisms of citizen participation in municipal management, but they maintained the mayor and council as the body of "maximum political representation" (*Ley 57/2003*, art. 122).

In practice, local government has become considerably more complex through expanding the organs of municipal administration. First are departments (*delegaciones,* or areas), usually headed by a council member. The types of department vary from city to city. It is not unusual for larger cities to have separate units for public works, public safety and security, traffic and transport, culture and tourism, economy and finance, commercial and industrial development, environment, and health and general government (human resources, purchasing, mayor's office, etc.). These departments are mostly staffed by non-political employees. Second, larger *ayuntamientos* often establish municipal autonomous bodies that operate like public enterprises in such areas as culture and sport, festivals, museums, water provision, and public housing. They generate their own revenue and are considerably more free of budgetary restrictions. Third, larger municipalities operate with a number of non-elected advisory committees (*comisiones informativas*), composed of councillors from the majority and minority parties. To a considerable extent, these committees mirror city administrative departments; they enable councillors of different parties to participate in matters of policy and administration, and they serve as channels of communication between the city commission and minority political parties. Fourth are the previously mentioned district committees (*juntas municipales de distrito*). They are organized by a nominated councillor, who may or may not be on the commission but normally is from the ruling party. These committees are usually composed of respected citizens who reside in the district; they work with the councillor to represent the interests of local residents (*vecinos*) and channel their concerns and service delivery complaints to the council and departments (Newton 1997, 151–2).

Bearing these structures in mind, Ballart and Ramió (2000, 28) point to four distinct arenas of municipal government structure: (1) the deliberative political structure: the *pleno* and deliberative commissions; (2) the political executive structure: the city commission and political administrative actors, mayor, deputy mayor, mayoral staff, and councillors; (3) the strategic administrative structure: the national trained corps staff (e.g., town clerks or comptrollers selected by municipalities) and the municipal inspectors, managers, and service directors/coordinators; and (4) the city operating administrative structure: chiefs of service, section heads, business managers, and operating staff. This model of organization means that unlike the position in many other countries, many city administrators and operating staff are not under the direct line supervisory control of the chief executive officer (Villoria Mendieta 2004, 38).

Provincial governments (*disputaciones provinciales*) are empowered in much less detail in the LRBRL. They have a dual character as intermediate local authorities representing municipalities as well as serving as divisions for the administration of state and AC functions. While they do not have the same type of "autonomy" as that of municipalities, their existence is guaranteed by Constitutional Court decisions. The LRBRL charges provinces with upholding intermunicipal functions, assuring "integral and suitable delivery of services in the entire provincial territory," and participating "with AC and the state governments in the coordination of local administration" (Article 31). Provincial institutions include (1) an ordinance-making council, elected indirectly by municipal councillors who, also become provincial delegates (except in the Balaerics and the Basque provinces); (2) a provincial commission or executive committee; (3) a president elected by the council, usually from the majority party; and (4) administrative departments headed by a delegate.

Within their broad mandate, provincial functions vary considerably. According to Farfán Perez (2002, 70–1), in practice they fulfill one or more of the following roles: (1) the exercise of downward-delegated state and AC competencies under Article 37 of the LRBRL, such as sports, culture, and social services; (2) the fulfilment of upward-delegated functions for economies of scale, primarily by municipalities, such as social services and social protection; (3) own-source or council-derived functions, such as rural roads, technical services, fire safety, and civil protection; (4) assistance to municipalities that cannot meet the required minimum services under Article 36 of the LRBRL, for example, water, sewerage, or others on the list of nine required services; and (5) functions that emerge to promote the general well-being of supramunicipal or "sectoral character" planning, human resource development, economic development, adult and continuing education, culture and tourism. Provincial governments are required to prepare an annual investment plan, *Plan provincial de cooperación a las obras y servicios de competencia municipal*, covering the needs of the smaller municipalities within the province, funded jointly by the provincial council, the AC, and sometimes the European Union (EU) government.

The *comarca*, authorized under Article 42 of the LRBRL, is formed by municipal assent and is subject to AC regulations. It is a form of service and/or planning district. Catalonia "comarcialized" its entire territory in 1987 (*Boletin oficial, 8 abril, 1621*), after the Constitutional Court refused to let the AC government abolish its four provinces. Catalonia did this in order to engage a process of "modernizing local administration and increasing potential management capacity, yet preserving municipal autonomy through the 'voluntary' transfer of functions." In other words, the *comarcas* would provide management where municipal functions were non-existent, thereby allowing for the functional organization of services, and would concentrate resources on a reasonable scale (Losada Marrodán1989, 77). The Aragon region is another with active *comarcas*, particularly in such basic services as fire protection, water and sewerage, emergency services, and planning/development for EU funding.

The horizontal intermunicipal partnership, the *mancomunidad,* apparently began in medieval times. The oldest recorded is from 1409 in the Basque Country, comprising thirteen municipalities that joined to manage forest resources. According to a contemporary study by Font, Gutiérrez, and Parrado-Díez (1999), 87.3 percent of the municipalities joining *mancomunidades* are towns with a population of less than 5,000. The average number of municipalities in these special districts is eight. Almost half (43.4 percent) are single-purpose units, the average belonging to the five-per-unit grouping. They are governed by boards made up of appointed municipal councillors or other politicians. Funding is largely derived from municipal coffers, with some AC contributions. Management is often delegated to a corps of professionals. *Mancomunidades* are chartered by intermunicipal agreement, whereas *comarcas* require AC parliamentary legal approval.

Vertical partnerships, or consortia, have been identified as centred around municipal (and sometimes *mancomunidad*) agreement with the provincial, AC, or central government, or some combination of them. On occasion, non-profit organizations or other non-governmental organizations also join consortia. They tend to be single-purpose, although some are multipurpose. One established between the Province of Almeria and four municipalities in Andalucía is designed to promote the related activities of public works, urban development, and tourism. Consortia more commonly involve larger cities and tend to be growing, partly in response to shortfalls in municipal budgets and partly to meet certain requirements of the European Union regarding the pooling of services and funding. Because consortia provide the maximum amount of legal and operational flexibility, a number of AC governments discourage them in favour of *mancomunidades*, for they are less able to be legally controlled, and their managerial orientation erodes the role of democratically elected municipal councillors in favour of appointed administrators and professional managers (Font, Gutiérrez, and Parrado-Díez 1999).

4. THE FINANCIAL POSITION OF MUNICIPAL AND OTHER LOCAL GOVERNMENTS

Local finances have shifted from an almost exclusively centralized tax and tax-sharing system to a mixed system more typical of federal countries (Carillo 1997, 61). Today, local governments raise their revenues through a combination of own-source taxes, tax-sharing arrangements, and subventions from higher-level governments. The overall posture for all subnational governments, ACs, and local governments alike is fiscal dependence on the taxing and spending powers of the state. For municipalities, any system of local financing did not develop until the late 1950s.

A financial framework law (39/1988), *Ley reguladora de las haciendas locales* (LRHL), addressed local government finance for the first time since regime change. The LRHL identified permissible sources of local taxes, affirmed local powers to set rates, and prohibited taxes on public services, but it permitted fees, and it set local government subventions from central and regional government as conditional. Municipalities were granted the powers to tax real estate, economic activities, motor vehicles, construction and labour, and the increasing value of urban land, and they were allowed to exempt government entities and certain non-profit organizations. Provisions were also outlined for setting rates by tax base, population, exemptions, quotas, and the like. Provincial governments were originally allowed to establish tax rates and special service fees, and were allowed a surcharge on the municipal taxes on economic activities, the only provincial own-source tax. Since 1990, this surcharge rate has been left up to provincial discretion. In the pre-LRHL years, provinces enjoyed a share of a Spanish version of the transaction tax, but when Spain joined the European Union in 1986 and the value added tax (VAT) was enacted, the transaction tax was abolished and the provincial share was replaced by an unconditional central grant. Provinces also receive important infrastructure capital grants, which are mostly distributed to municipalities as project (conditional) grants. These financing patterns were changed for some large cities between 2002 and 2004, as will be described, but this pattern remains for most local governments.

Local governments traditionally rely on the same type of mixed-source financing as their counterparts in other federal systems. Table 2 is a reproduction and translation of Ginénog's (2002) calculations for the 1998 tax situation for municipalities by population size, provincial capitals, *diputaciones* and island councils, and *mancomunidades*. Before the reforms of big-city revenue of 2002–4, direct taxes and fees were key sources of revenue for all cities, as are transfers from AC and central government. On the other hand, the largest cities – those with over

100,000 population – plus provincial capitals received a notably large share of transfers. Smaller cities, on the other hand, received a greater proportion of capital transfers – no doubt a reflection of their poorer capital-borrowing position. Provincial governments display a similarly mixed pattern but receive less in certain fees and inheritance taxes. As mentioned earlier, *mancomunidades* rely mostly on payments from other governments (mostly municipal) and on some capital transfers. The final column in table 2 represents sources of revenue for all municipalities in 1998. Here again, own taxes, fees, and transfers appear to be the most important categories.

Several recent financial changes have altered this picture somewhat. Since 2001, the new AC financing surcharge has included increased income tax sharing (from 15 percent in 1993 and 30 percent in 1996) to 33 percent, plus new tax sharing of 35 percent of the value-added tax, 42 percent of the beverage tax, and 100 percent transfer of electrical energy, transport, and petroleum taxes. The new system ties AC financing more to the ACs' economies and revenue systems, and places them in a better position to help finance local governments (Ruiz-Huerta, Herrero, and Vizán 2002).

With regard to local governments, in 2003 municipal tax sharing was increased to cover the elimination of the tax on small businesses. Also, beginning in 2004, municipalities and provinces received a defined share (13 percent) of transfers. Cities with populations of over 100,000, provincial capitals, and certain other cities with populations of over 75,000 began receiving a share (1 percent) of income taxes collected and will participate in tax collection. Smaller cities will continue with the previously indicated system of state transfers. In addition, in 2003 a law on the modernization of local government gave cities more direct budgetary powers, including greater regulating power over local taxes. These changes, coupled with the fact that cities do not bear major financing responsibility for health, education, and social services, should give them greater flexibility in expenditure and more leeway to offset any possible future slowing in the growth of revenues.

Local corporations continue to rely heavily on transfers, including a share of the income tax revenue now transferred to the ACs. Table 3 lists the AC transfers to local entities for each region. The first column provides the percentage of AC funds (central transfers, plus own-source revenues) that are transferred to local governments. The range is considerable, from 74.8 percent in the Canaries (where the island councils carry most responsibility) to only 12.3 percent in Valencia. Among the highest transfers are those of the special regime ACs of Navarra and the Basque Country. Apart from the Canaries, no region transfers more than about half of its revenues downward. The second column in table 3 provides the percentage of local revenue derived from transfers in relation to total revenues. The range is again considerable, but except for the special regime of Navarra, no region targets transfers as notable portions of AC funds. Overall, their local impact on revenues is generally less than one-fifth of total local revenue.

The 1988 LRHL also established budget and spending guidelines for local governments. These include calendar-year budgetary cycles, as well as requirements for investment and financing plans, performance reports on investment

Table 2
Revenue Sources, by Population Size of Municipalities and for Other Subnational Governments, 1998

			Local revenue sources (percentages)[1]					
	Direct tax[2]	Indirect tax[3]	Charge/fee[4]	Transfer[5]	Income[6]	Property[7]	Capital[8]	Total
Less than 5,000 inhabitants	22.69	3.51	15.26	29.70	4.12	1.54	23.18	100.00
5,001 to 10,000	26.73	4.52	19.71	30.49	2.32	2.28	13.95	100.00
10,001 to 20,000	30.00	4.57	21.33	28.88	1.81	3.02	10.39	100.00
20,001 to 30,000	31.47	4.72	19.00	29.79	2.20	3.57	9.24	100.00
30,001 to 50,000	34.81	5.32	20.67	27.10	2.68	3.13	6.29	100.00
50,001 to 100,000	34.26	5.01	18.67	28.63	1.53	4.03	7.88	100.00
More than 100,000	33.84	3.64	13.98	37.31	1.10	3.03	7.09	100.00
Provincial capitals	31.57	4.02	15.58	36.48	2.18	3.62	6.55	100.00
Provincies and island councils	29.82	32.61	4.36	26.39	0.79	0.38	5.65	100.00
Service districts (mancomunidades)	2.43	0.00	10.48	67.92	0.77	1.13	17.28	100.00
TOTAL	29.41	13.01	12.91	31.74	1.79	2.20	8.93	100.00
TOTAL (cities only)	30.38	4.22	17.09	32.74	2.32	3.12	10.13	100.00

[1]Compiled from Public Administration Accounts, 1998
[2]Property, business, and vehicle taxes
[3]Capital gains tax
[4]Charges and fees
[5]Current transfers
[6]Income from own assets
[7]Sale, cession, or transfer of property rights
[8]Capital project transfers
Source: Ginénog 2002, 417 (translation)

Table 3
Relative Importance of AC Transfers, 2002

Autonomous community	Percent of AC transfers to local entities	Percent of total revenues
Andalucía	25.1	8.3
Aragón	25.0	9.7
Asturias	41.8	18.2
Baleares	43.7	9.1
Canarias	74.8	15.7
Castilla y León	28.0	10.1
Castilla–La Mancha	36.5	14.6
Cataluña	25.1	6.1
Extremadura	37.9	18.7
Galicia	16.5	9.5
La Rioja	38.5	13.6
Madrid	25.8	4.5
Murcia	40.1	12.4
Navarra	52.2	44.0
País Vasco	41.6	3.3
Valencia	12.3	4.6

Source: Ramos and Cicuéndez 2005

programs/financing, debt forecasts, and the status of consolidating budgets with local autonomous and municipal business enterprises. The latter is a move towards EU standards. The EU's new EAS95 accounting system requires consolidation of debt of public companies, in as much as Spanish ACs and municipalities tend to fund parts of their investment programs through public companies, attempting to avoid debt limitations. A 2002 law on local government debt tightens the ability of governments to engage in off-balance short-term financing and modifying local bond market conditions designed to encourage more reliance on municipal bonding. The responsibility for budget preparation is placed in the hands of the mayor or the president of the provincial council. Controls on expenditures are enumerated, and budget management must include authorization, execution, liquidation, and reporting. Accounting principles are established and monitored according to guidelines set by the Ministry of Economy and Finance.

The general expenditure categories for Spanish subnational government demonstrate the heavy influence that the welfare state places on AC and local governments. Table 4, compiled by the Spanish Ministry of Economy and Finance, breaks down 2002 expenditures by standard Spanish expenditure categories. Social services, economic development, and regulation of productive sectors (e.g., manufacturing, commerce, agriculture) take up the bulk of AC spending. Transfers

Table 4
Budget/Spending Classifications of AC and Local Entities, 2002 (in percentages)

Autonomous community	General services		Public security		Social protection and growth		Social services		Economic development		Economic regulation		Regulation of industry		Transfers to public entities		Public debt	
	CCAA[1]	EELL[2]	CCAA	EELL	CCAA	EELL	CCAA	EELL	CCAA	EELL	CCAA	EELL	CCAA	EELL	CCAA	EELL	CCAA	EELL
Andalucía	1.90	14.89	0.08	5.95	5.83	13.19	55.80	39.00	5.03	10.32	0.86	5.24	12.21	1.58	11.53	0.79	6.73	9.02
Aragón	4.76	22.87	0.24	1.58	8.90	7.95	34.84	39.61	10.09	11.85	5.27	2.35	26.06	2.09	0.00	2.76	5.83	8.95
Asturias	30.68	9.00	0.47	5.82	14.34	15.64	44.98	45.92	16.19	9.44	2.44	2.94	12.12	2.74	0.00	0.47	3.39	8.02
Baleares	5.34	10.80	0.46	8.03	10.42	13.52	51.15	44.20	11.96	13.80	2.15	2.28	10.36	1.56	4.74	0.44	3.42	5.38
Canarias	2.84	10.28	0.42	4.07	8.81	11.86	70.76	39.50	7.19	15.32	2.61	2.83	3.42	4.59	3.04	6.35	0.92	5.21
Cantabria	3.44	12.36	1.60	6.06	7.13	9.66	53.70	45.46	13.41	13.03	2.84	4.32	10.69	0.23	3.47	0.23	3.71	7.17
Castilla y León	1.14	13.77	0.09	4.63	13.28	11.38	41.35	42.79	11.85	13.66	1.50	2.87	26.87	2.21	1.17	1.05	2.76	7.65
Castilla-Mancha	2.90	13.72	0.12	4.87	11.03	14.91	32.74	43.21	10.95	11.46	0.84	3.03	28.39	1.66	11.28	1.16	1.75	5.98
Cataluña	5.10	17.79	2.83	5.82	5.73	7.41	62.91	49.52	5.18	10.21	0.94	3.16	1.52	0.90	9.87	3.35	5.91	7.84
Extremadura	1.98	18.79	0.12	5.34	14.42	10.64	38.45	40.49	9.87	11.88	1.85	3.61	29.30	1.60	0.00	1.12	4.03	6.52
Galicia	2.21	11.73	0.28	4.83	6.44	11.25	60.77	39.46	7.25	17.24	1.74	3.12	7.27	1.31	8.97	2.85	5.07	8.23
La Rioja	5.06	13.37	1.33	5.23	16.03	9.67	47.04	43.07	15.70	9.39	2.87	12.85	8.01	1.90	0.00	0.11	3.96	4.41
Madrid	4.28	10.03	1.11	10.05	13.89	9.33	56.89	54.88	13.52	6.81	1.47	2.73	1.96	0.49	0.00	0.04	6.88	5.64
Murcia	3.08	11.58	0.72	8.07	10.18	9.04	57.32	50.10	8.37	7.45	1.93	3.49	14.61	2.09	0.11	0.17	3.69	7.99
Navarra	4.50	10.17	1.86	5.98	9.17	14.64	42.65	58.09	9.95	3.23	2.30	2.62	5.18	1.75	22.23	0.26	2.15	3.27
País Vasco[3]	4.01	5.53	7.26	1.53	4.01	6.36	63.97	9.92	5.81	7.55	0.93	1.38	5.58	0.94	0.53	64.90	7.90	1.89
Valencia	2.72	12.23	0.57	7.44	7.94	10.28	69.77	45.37	8.30	9.61	1.82	3.82	4.30	1.47	0.00	1.65	4.56	8.15

[1]Abbreviation for "autonomous communities"
[2]Abbreviation for "local entities"
[3]In the Basque Country the provinces designate 80 percent of their funds for transfer to other public entities.

Source: Spain, Ministerio de Económica y hacienda 2002

amount to a small portion of the budget, though some central government funds are passed through in ways that would not show up in this set of calculations. Local entities spend the largest share of their funds on social protection and social services, with smaller but significant amounts going to economic development and regulation. The expenditure levels on public security are also notable. What does not show up in this category is the large amount of provincial expenditures to municipalities. In fact, all but the line items for general services and civil protection – the social and economic categories – are really spent either by or on behalf of municipalities, particularly the smaller ones. Earlier data that separate out cities (Farfán Perez 2002, 76) indicate that municipalities spend more on civil protection (police and fire) but also a substantial share of their revenue on social services. Table 4 suggests that cities and provinces have somewhat higher proportions of public debt than that of the ACs, owing to a combination of lower fiscal transfer ratios and large capital expenditures. Overall, the welfare state costs of health, education, and social programs that were transferred between 1982 and 2002 comprise more than half of all subnational expenditures.

Two additional sources of Spanish project grants have a notable impact on local finance: the Interterritorial Compensation Fund (FCI) and the Regional Incentives Program. The FCI was established in Article 157(1)(c) of the Constitution and is designed to correct regional fiscal imbalances, especially for public works and economic development infrastructure projects. Established in 1984, it initially was oriented to poorer regions, but subsequently it was used as a vehicle to transfer funds to all ACs. In the 1990s, the FCI was realigned to be complementary to EU investment funds, particularly the European Regional Development Fund (ERDF), and thus was "rededicated" to poorer regions. By the year 2000, FCI had gradually been overshadowed by ERDF (known in Spain as FEDER) and other EU funds. Nevertheless, the Ministry of Economy and Finance (2003, 81) reports that a total of 692 projects were funded in 2002, totalling just over 8.5 billion euros. Of this, 3.5 billion euros were further subvented to local governments for projects in the areas of tourism, economic development and job creation, and public works. With the addition of ten new countries to the EU, Spain's proportion of development funding will decrease and the FCI may gain greater prominence. The other EU source is project funding – projects under the Regional Incentives Program (PIR), designed to match AC and local funds, aimed at job creation. The Ministry of Economy and Finance awards over 400 such projects every year (Newton 1997).

Spanish public finance is thus highly intergovernmentalized in character. The trends in the financing of local governments reveal that revenues are being shifted downward from the central government and controls on taxes and budgets are gradually being lifted. The Spanish mode relies heavily on the ceding of taxes and on conditional and unconditional transfers. Local self-financing is, however, operative to a greater degree than that of AC governments, which are the most dependent. While fiscal supervision of local governments is largely AC in orientation, it follows a template established in Madrid in the same way that municipal services are enumerated (Agranoff 2004). Fiscally, it is clearly a system of vertical imbalance, which Solé-Vilanova (1990, 351) has characterized as "consumption federalism."

5 MUNICIPAL ORGANIZATION FOR FEDERAL
ACTION

As competencies moved to the level of ACs from 1985 to 2002, there was less and less contact between local governments and Madrid. Nevertheless, a variety of political and governmental mechanisms exist for municipalities to take action at the national level. Many of these mechanisms are indirect, but they are real, and clearly some municipalities take greater advantage of this type of representation and action than others do. In general, the larger the city, the more action is likely to be taken on more than one of these fronts. Most small municipalities, especially those in isolated areas, have virtually no direct contact with the national government.

At the governmental level are many sectoral conferences, *convenios,* and the aforementioned vertical cooperative agreements. Börzel's (2000) study of the "Europeanization" of Spanish regional policy indicates that, for both domestic and European policy arenas, ACs to some extent participate in the implementation of sectoral conferences. In many non-European conferences, municipalities and other local government interests have a *de facto* role in these joint intergovernmental administration exercises. Under the law (*Ley 30/1992*), conferences are designed to facilitate the exchange of views and positions, the joint examination of problems in each sector, and the exploration of joint means of meeting such problems. Among the sectoral conferences that have a direct bearing on local government are those on social affairs, industry and energy, infrastructure and territorial planning, civil protection, water, public housing, and traffic.

Vertical cooperative mechanisms are also points of municipal-national and municipal-AC contact. For example, many infrastructure projects are funded by these consortia, which amount to agreements outside the normal legislative process. Few regulations or normative standards (including debt limitations) govern these arrangements, and local officials normally have greater discretion in funding opportunities. According to one discussant, "consortia allow municipal and provincial officials to direct funding to those projects they feel are of the greatest priority without the hurdle of regional permission." On the one hand, only three AC parliaments have appointed standing commissions (parliamentary committees) on local government. On the other hand, all seventeen regions have a cabinet department that devotes all or most of its efforts to local administration, and all but two ACs have some form of local or municipal consultative body (Ramos and Cicuéndez 2005).

A number of national standing advisory bodies also play important intergovernmental roles from time to time. The one devoted to local affairs is the national Commission on Local Governments. Comprising of public officials and local-government interests from all levels, it is the most symbolic advisory body and forum for local government interests. While the commission has been the catalyst for identifying municipal problems, it is not a particularly important intergovernmental body. More important bodies are the Fiscal and Financial Policy Council, the Council of State, numerous interministerial committees, and other special bodies. Local governments have only indirect influence in these bodies.

Local governments' influence at the national level is affected most directly by the major interest associations that comprise the Spanish Federation of Municipalities and Provinces (FEMP). Formed by big-city mayors in 1981, FEMP draws governmental members from most regions (there are also Basque and Catalan municipal associations) and from most political parties. About 6,000 of the 8,000-plus municipalities, amounting to 94 percent of the population, belong to FEMP, as do 49 of the 50 provinces. FEMP's stated purposes include the propagation and defence of local autonomy, representation of local interests before other public administrative bodies, development of the European spirit of the role of local governments, international cooperation, assistance to local governments of all types, forging partnerships to advance local government, and interpretation of local competencies. Most important, FEMP sees its role as "intervention, if such role is necessary, in the normative legal sphere that affects local entities" (*Estatutos de la FEMP*, Article 7). FEMP has been a major force in trying to promote increased municipal autonomy, exclusive local competencies, and a greater share of state financing. It has been the catalyst for the *pacto local* movement, pressuring the government in Madrid to authorize increased local powers without AC supervision. FEMP was the driving force behind the change in financing for large cities and provincial capitals. This new legislation followed an accord signed in November 2002 between FEMP, the Ministry of Economy and Finance, and the Ministry of Public Administration.

Direct contact is a time-honoured Spanish mode of interaction for local governments that choose to exercise this option. First, in a country where ties to political parties matter, it goes without saying that mayors and other local elected officials who have connections or affiliations with the party in power in Madrid will from time to time exploit these contacts. Most of the country experiences a two-party system, the right-of-centre Popular Party (PP) and the left-of-centre Spanish Socialist Workers' Party (PSOE), which have alternated in power for some years. Both parties are federal in structure, and local and regional elections are highly national in influence (Carillo and Díaz 2003). When the big-city mayors are of the same party, they use these ties. One reason why this party channel is important is that the PP and other non-state parties (Pallarés, Monteros, and Llera 1997) of the right have absorbed the local clientelistic networks and agents characteristic of previous regimes. At the same time, left-wing parties, including PSOE, have exercised measures of regional-local discipline, and local elected officials play an important role in the PSOE structure. There is a saying in the PSOE, "El que se mueva no sale en la foto" (Whoever moves will be out of the picture).

Second, even when party ties do not coincide, there will be important matters that require the mayors of the larger cities to have some contact with national officials. Because of the importance of ties to parties, they may bring along one or more of their influential minority-party councillors who belong to the national party in power. Local notables who are known in Madrid may also be brought along.

Third, although they are decreasing because of the transfer of power to ACs, there are direct administrative contacts with the national government. For example, many infrastructure projects involve EU, national, and AC financing and, sometimes, approval. This generates regular direct administrative contacts, which begin at the proposal stage and continue through the design, approval, engineering, construction, and inspection stages. In this process, local administrators learn who the players are and how they may be handled. Although less apparent and visible than, say, interest-group representation, direct contacts are critical and are time-honoured in Spain, where the term *enchufe* has more than an electrical-outlet meaning; it also refers to the action or effect of personal connections.

Provincial governments provide an additional but declining channel of interaction with the national government. Until 1996 there was a civil governor (*gobernador civil*) in each province, representing the national government – a holdover from the prefectural system of the Franco regime. The civil governor was responsible for public order and public safety and was in charge of national police and security forces operating at the provincial level, especially in emergencies such as floods, storms, and droughts. The civil governor was also responsible for coordinating services of the national government between state and local authorities. With the advent of the ACs, a governor's delegate (*delegado del gobierno*) was also assigned at this level to perform similar functions. Upon the advent of the PP government of José Maria Aznar in 1996, the civil governors disappeared in favour of a provincial subdelegate, who was directly responsible to the delegate in the regional capital. While clearly downgraded in importance, this is another form of local-federal interaction, particularly regarding matters of policing and emergencies.

One clear pattern is that as functions are increasingly devolved to the ACs, local-regional interactions have increased. In regard to infrastructure policy, one local manager said, "Municipalities are in a position of dependency on [the regional government of] Madrid. There is very little contact with the central government." Similarly, a local councillor of public works said, "When we want to initiate a project we do not go to Madrid. We go to the government of Valencia [AC] for two things: permission and money." Many of the patterns outlined above – conferences, regional bodies of FEMP, and direct contacts – would hold at the level of the AC.

6 THE SCOPE OF FEDERAL-MUNICIPAL INTERACTIONS

In a system where competencies are concurrently divided between exclusive state and exclusive AC, with all of the nuances this brings, the scope really varies with the issue. The best way to illustrate this principle is by providing concrete examples that affect municipalities.

The state has retained one exclusive competency (in addition to foreign affairs, defence, and immigration) that touches most municipalities: public safety, including aspects of traffic control. There are two national police forces, largely rural and urban, that patrol and provide many non-routine policing functions, conduct most of the criminal investigations and arrests, and work alongside municipal police in an emergency. Meanwhile, municipal police are primarily responsible for traffic control and for matters of minor order, such as beach and festival patrol. The various police forces often need to work together on issues of major concern, such as large gatherings and fires, demonstrations, bomb threats and bombings, and in criminal investigation. Traffic control and planning remains centralized in the Ministry of the Interior, and so do certain types of local public-works "sign-offs" that are of police concern. Also, the rules and procedures of municipal traffic control are heavily regulated from Madrid. In this sense, the national government's exclusive competency on public order reaches deep into the municipal realm.

This phenomenon can be contrasted with the most important concurrent competency under examination, that of the operation and regulation of local governments. As demonstrated, the national government has established the basic patterns and forms of local governments, has established baseline competencies for municipalities and finance formulas, and authorizes the ACs to establish further degrees of autonomy, through such means as the proposed *pactos locales* (described below). The Constitutional Court has upheld this basic central-government establishment and framework power (Baena 2000). It is up to the AC governments to establish the pattern of governments beyond those of basic laws, to transfer powers to them, and to regulate their actions regarding autonomous municipal functions under the LRBLR and the financing regulations. But they have not done so. One official put it this way, "Ellos legislan, municipios cumplen" (the [AC] authorities legislate and the municipalities comply). Even if this is not always the case, the ACs hold the key municipal legal and fiscal cards in terms of most programs.

Normally, in arenas of exclusive AC competency, there is only indirect federal interaction, if any. One example is social services, which were passed virtually exclusively to the ACs in the 1980s. Since then, social services have been legislated and delivered by ACs and municipalities, along with some contracting with non-governmental organizations, mostly with the Red Cross and Catholic Charities. In most ACs, municipalities directly contract with the regional governments for such services as integrating immigrant populations, to supplement social help that would go along with education, health, and housing. The regional governments develop plans and designate the services to be funded. The only central government involvement is some funding and the *Plan concertado de servicios sociales*, a program in which the ACs (with municipal representation) negotiate and voluntarily agree to provide minimum basic services in all regions (Chacón 1995). The national government gathers reports but does not regulate or supervise general social services. Thus, municipal intervention is almost exclusively by ACs.

Other types of competencies are those that are compartmentalized for each of the two spheres of government. The most important in this arena are railroads and rail traffic, highways and roads, transport, hydraulic improvements and works, ports and airports, and museums and libraries. Some of these program arenas are AC in operation and some belong to the state. For example, rail transport includes a national network, and most ACs operate regional transit systems. Both of these systems connect the larger municipalities, particularly provincial capitals and cities of over 100,000 in population. In the same way, cities deal with the central government directly regarding state highways, but with the ACs for regional roads, and with the provincial governments for minor, intertown roads. Museums and libraries are within cities, as are airports and ports. This means that affected municipalities must interact directly with the relevant governments, a situation of dual intergovernmental interaction.

Finally, there are special types of competencies, where either the roles of the national and AC governments are unclear or there is considerable confusion and application on an almost case-by-case basis (Aja 2003, 131). This includes such areas as culture, public enterprises, television, public order, and certain types of taxes. Culture, for example, involves virtually every level of government. On the one hand, national and regional governments clearly take the lead in planning and programming, but it is the municipalities that actually put on most cultural programs out of their own and subvented funds. Ordinarily they deal with the ACs regarding funding for most of these programs, but there may be occasions when a national program is temporarily or potentially located within a city – for instance, a travelling art exhibit or the possible location of a national museum. Then the interaction will be national. By contrast, public order in an emergency such as the 11 March 2004 Madrid rail-station bombing became a municipal-national issue immediately. Each issue in this category is somewhat different, and involvement may entail any two or all levels of government.

The pattern of interaction thus varies. Programs of the central government involve central expenditures, while AC programs involve AC expenditures. That is why it is almost impossible to unbundle expenditures for programs such as policing, where two national forces are allocated by province and city but remain on the national payroll. Even where competencies are exclusively AC, the national government is often indirectly involved, as in the case of social services. This is emblematic of the complicated pattern of governmental relationships that exist in Spain.

7 THE NATURE OF MUNICIPAL-FEDERAL INTERACTION

In a constitutional legal sense, municipalities enjoy much the same measure of autonomy as that of other governments. In practice, the foregoing discussion indicates that this is not the case, since national framework legislation provides a legal and fiscal framework for municipal operation along with AC competencies over local government, urban planning, and urbanization. Moreover, since tax revenues flow downward, the fiscal ties create substantial dependency that serves to limit legal autonomy (Agranoff 2004). Nevertheless, municipal governments do have the means of autonomous interaction with the federal government.

First, there is the corporatist tradition of Spanish politics. As Wiarda (1993, 48–9) explains, Spain is one of several Southern European countries that not only has the tradition of recognizing the rights and obligations of certain social institutions – family, community, church, armed forces, organized labour, universities – but also has a way of structuring state-society relations in a hierarchical, disciplined, monopolistic, and state-centred manner: "Corporatism, in this sense, typically seeks to integrate labor, business and government in a functioning, well-ordered, harmonious, and technocratic regime." While some of this has been broken down in the three decades since the end of the Franco regime, there remains a tradition of placing issues such as municipal concerns on the national policy agenda by negotiating agreements (*pactos*). This occurs in many policy areas (see Lancaster 1989). Clearly, the AC *estado de las autonomías* was largely built on a series of agreements that involved not only ethnoterritorial concurrence but also a series of negotiations during times of minority government, when the party in power was weak (Agranoff 1996; Moreno 2001). The same holds true with major labour-management negotiations, where bargaining normally occurs between top industry leaders, officers of the largest unions, and the national government (Salmon 1995).

With regard to municipalities, the corporate tradition has meant that the interests of cities are normally carried to the national government, including the effort to pass the LRBRL in 1985, the finance law of 1988, the *pacto local* in 1999, the big-city reforms in 2003, and, most recently, the 2005 *White Paper on Local Government* (discussed below). Each of these has involved negotiations between FEMP – almost always led by big-city mayors (who are officers and usually of the same party as those in national power) – and high officials within the national government. For example, the 2003 reforms followed a negotiated agreement between these two parties that provides substitute financing for the elimination of the tax on business activities, new tax sharing arrangements, and new means of local taxation (see www.femp.es/documentos/financación.pdf). In this very important sense, the corporatist tradition leads cities to try to negotiate with the centre, often through FEMP.

Second, various central government initiatives have reached through the governmental system to include local governments, particularly municipalities. In the early 1990s the national government launched a massive modernization campaign that included upgrading the managerial and analytical skills of government employees throughout the system. The effort was geared to introducing information technology into the system and readying Spanish public administration for increased EU participation. Local governments were among the primary targets of this program, which included programs in finance and budgeting, contract administration, organizational design, budgetary execution, information systems, and urban management (Spain, MAP 1991).

Third, as suggested earlier, large cities have the capacity and regularly the need to reach the national government through direct contact with Madrid. The reverse is also true, where large projects or events mean that Madrid must reach into the municipality. For example, the amount of municipal-federal interaction and flow of resources to ready Barcelona for the 1994 Olympic Games was immeasurable (the city government and the central government were of the same party). Likewise, the City of Madrid is regularly touched by various national ministries, as the central government promotes cultural affairs and special celebrations.

Fourth, as autonomy through devolution evolves, the non-hierarchical relationship means that some forms of direct interaction are more the exception than the rule. Spain has rid itself of the prefectural system, where representatives of the central government (the civil governors) gave prior permission or approval to local actions or budgets. Article 137 guarantees that, along with other governments, municipalities "shall enjoy self-government for the management of their respective interests." In effect, this has meant removal of the civil government's power of tutelage. In ordinary circumstances, most local governments are left to their own devices to implement the functions that are assigned to them. Inspectors do not regularly monitor these activities, nor is noncompliance ordinarily reported. Instead, provincial or other forms of intergovernmental cooperation is recommended and ordinarily pursued.

Fifth, frequently citizen or group reports of noncompliance, fraud, or abuse – or some combination of all three – is reported to the central government. If it involves an AC competency, it is passed down or it becomes a court matter. Court litigation over alleged municipal infractions is common, particularly with regard to land use or zoning issues. These are AC competencies and local responsibilities. Since, under Article 127, the judiciary system is considered to be a single, unified system of courts (even though a high court sits in all seventeen regions), public law is considered to be the same in the whole country. Thus, if municipalities become involved in court litigation, they are really dealing with the intervention of the national court system and helping to forge a national system of laws involving municipalities.

On the one hand, while autonomous and self-governing, the national-local government agenda building is clearly asymmetrical, with the ability of intervention weighted in favour of the national government; it frames basic legislation, directly or indirectly provides a large share of revenue, is the strongest negotiating actor in the corporatist bargaining scheme, and its courts ultimately resolve local government disputes. On the other hand, the removal of the prefectural system has greatly enhanced the everyday operating autonomy of local governments; there is considerably more control over implementation. In this sense, self-governance has been allowed to work, for better or worse, at municipal and other local government levels.

8 REGIONAL GOVERNMENT MEDIATION

The involved system of dual, exclusive, concurrent, compartmentalized, and special cases makes it difficult to generalize about mediation. In regard to issues such as the autonomy and home rule powers of local governments, the AC governments have in effect become obstacles, inasmuch as no region has meaningfully adopted the principles of the *pacto local* into its municipal code. Local officials complain that AC governments have not really supported further decentralization of power on their behalf. One official in a suburb of Madrid said that the "Madrid [AC] *Ley de Pacto* remains undeveloped. It only enters debate around election time when opportunist parties refer to decentralization. The goal of further decentralization should be to promote 'co-responsibility' in delivery of services between local entities, on the one hand, and regional and central authorities, on the other." Another local official, from Andalucia, said that instead of ACs intervening with the state on behalf of local government, their neglect and unwillingness to share power had led to an alarming stagnation: "In 1975, 14–15 percent of public funds were managed and spent by local entities. In 2005, long after the 'grand' revolution of decentralization, that figure *decreased* to 13 percent. Apparently, decentralization has great limits."

Local governments have largely been left out of the picture of AC-Madrid interventions on many questions of a basic intergovernmental nature. The pattern of negotiations, whether multilateral or bilateral, has led to waves of systemic asymmetry, followed by moves towards symmetry at the AC level (Agranoff 1999). For local governments, Carillo (1997, 53) concludes that the pattern follows at that level, "making the fate of a local government depend on its own AC either on account of its degree of self-government or on account of the policy it chooses to follow with regard to the local authority, or both." For local governments, it has meant that to get the attention of the central government, they normally must get the attention of their AC government. In addition to direct contacts, and with some representation on national councils (e.g., the social services sectoral conference has local government representation), the process depends on the circulation of elites from local governments into AC policy and administrative positions, forming clusters of AC officials who have experienced local government and understand it, and who can become a "major influence on [local] policy questions and infuse more service capacities into intergovernmental cooperation" (Carillo 1991, 168).

9 MUNICIPALITIES AND INTERNATIONAL AFFAIRS

Municipalities' roles in international issues fall into two general categories, ordinary and extraordinary. Ordinary affairs such as trade missions, commercial and cultural exchanges, "sister city" alliances, transport linkages, promotion of tourism, and other aspects of intermestic politics generally flow freely and directly between Spanish and foreign cities. Ordinary issues would include EU affairs, for example, for financial assistance. They are, of course, conducted under the umbrella of the national powers of foreign policy, currency, and commerce, and of relevant AC powers, for example, in infrastructure, urban planning, and social services. Extraordinary issues (for example, municipal appeals to the European Court of Justice, high-level meetings of foreign dignitaries, and cultural and sporting events) may require more direct involvement with the central government in Madrid. For instance, in March 2005 the City of Granada hosted an International

Summit on Security at the Alhambra Palace. The meeting was established by direct contact between city officials, the Spanish Ministries of Defence and Interior, and with foreign ministries. Between 2002 and 2005, a number of Valencian cities found themselves in the European Court of Human Rights, when Spanish courts refuse to hear landowners' appeals regarding their zoning under a controversial AC land use law (discussed below).

The most important international dimension is Spain's involvement in the EU. One the one hand, membership has negatively affected subnational (particularly AC) competencies in agriculture, fisheries, industrial policy, environment, regional planning, transport, energy policy, and culture by reducing the original autonomy of governments, either directly or through the fact that the central government has exclusive rights to final decisions on these issues within EU bodies (Colino 2001). Article 93 of the Constitution allows for transfer of sovereignty of competencies by organic law. Moreover, the central government is charged with compliance enforcement of all powers ceded. This strengthens the role of Madrid vis-à-vis subnational governments. Spanish membership, on the other hand, has enhanced AC interests in some other ways, giving them a role with regard to those domestic competencies over which they have primary control.

The Constitutional Court has approved AC international activity, so long as it does not compromise the unity of Spanish foreign policy. Where the issues between AC and Madrid become complex is when the national level sets policy and the AC implements it, as with the environment. "What emerges is a form of 'territorial complexity defined by the interaction of four levels of government (EU, national, regional, or local): which of these levels is dominant at any given moment depends on the policy stage (such as formulation, regulation or implementation) and policy sector in question" (Closa and Heywood 2004, 86). The newer arenas of EU policy development, such as gender equality, telecommunications, immigration, and environment, exhibit the greatest levels of multigovernmental involvement.

The ACs have extensive involvement with the EU, including in the following areas: representation of ACs on EU interdepartmental bodies, bodies for promotion and research, and those with regional offices in Brussels; indirect involvement in various conferences, special commissions, and the Conference on EU Affairs; direct involvement regarding funding; and participation in the EU Committee of the Regions. Actually, the latter combines representatives from both local and regional levels, a factor that Spanish ACs do not like, because they believe it dilutes regional interests and provides another opportunity for the national government to mobilize local demands against regional ones. The twenty-one-member Spanish delegation as defined by the Senate involves elected representatives. Each AC nominates one member, and the remaining four are chosen by FEMP to represent local government. FEMP has appealed this, requesting equal representation, even asking the European Commission to appeal to the European Court of Justice for equal representation (Closa and Heywood 2004, 90–1).

EU-stimulated regional development plans are anchored largely in cities, as they have been the key to receiving structural funds. The Spanish government has used these EU funds as a means of redistribution. Municipal contacts for these funds do not normally involve direct contact with AC capitals. Nevertheless, local authorities are reported to feel that they are being marginalized by the ACs. They invoke the lever of the subsidiarity principle against the regional administration, particularly when their administrations are of a different party from that of the AC.

Another international body of direct interest is the Council of Europe, which was founded in 1949 in the aftermath of the Second World War and is directed towards promoting democracy among European countries. Most important is the 1985 European Charter on Local Self-Government, which places great emphasis on municipal (and other local) autonomy in decisions affecting the community, local own-source financing, and the right to settle jurisdiction-level disputes in each country's judicial system. Among others, Canales (1999, 252–3) suggests that the Charter reinforces the elimination of tutelage. It narrows the Spanish central government's ability to supervise local administration, makes clear that local governments should have greater control over the competencies assigned to them, speaks for greater "horizontal" (own-source) rather that "vertical" (subventions) fiscal powers, and calls for a system of sorting out competencies by level of government. Under such a system, the local governments, particularly municipalities, have the potential to play a greater role in international affairs, rather than being restricted to going through their ACs or the central government. Canales concludes that if enacted by the ACs, the *pacto local* would reinforce this role of subsidiarity, both before the EU and in other foreign affairs, and would make Spanish local governments fully functioning international agents under the European Charter.

10 POLITICAL DIMENSION / POLITICAL CULTURE

Four issues stand out as characteristic of the Spanish political culture related to municipal-federal relations. First is the aforementioned corporatist tradition in Spanish politics, which often manifests itself at the local level. Second is the fact that in most of the country the political party system is national in character, pervading local elections. Indeed, local elections in Spain are highly nationalized. Third, Spain is a country of multiple loyalties – not only the devotion to region and country, but within each region there is a considerable amount of local identity and loyalty. This *patria chica* of community patriotism leads to the long tradition of local independence – for municipality and individual – and resistance to being managed from above. Fourth, as in many Southern European countries, corruption of a minor nature is fairly widespread in local governments, especially with regard to land use and development, and to a lesser extent with other forms of regulation.

Party and electoral politics at the local level resemble those at the national level in many parts of the country. The Spanish party system is tied to a proportional representation electoral system that is designed to favour major parties and stable governing groups. At the AC and local levels, the system encourages multiple parties and coalition governments (Gunther, Sani, and Shabad 1988). In some ACs, regional or "non-state" parties – such as the Convergence and Union in

Catalonia and the Basque Nationalist Party in the Basque Country – compete at all levels, including for local councils (Pallarés, Montero, and Llera 1997). But in most of the country the national party pattern is strong at the local level. For example, in the 1999 municipal elections, where over 21 million total (multiple) votes were cast, the PP received a total municipal vote of 7.3 million, capturing 24,625 local council seats. This amounted to 37.8 percent of the council seats. Meanwhile, the PSOE received 7.2 million total votes, capturing just under 22,000 seats, which amounted to 33.6 percent of all seats. The only other national party, the left-of-centre IU (Left United), captured only 3.5 percent of the seats. The remaining 25.1 percent were divided among twelve non-state and isolated municipal blocs (Olmeda and Parrado 2000).

City elections demonstrate this strong mutual influence between the levels of government. Carillo (1997, 59) says that national general elections "have thus far become a sort of primary or run-up for local elections, meaning that in most cities, local election results usually resemble those in the last general elections, with only marginal differences." Subsequent research by Carillo and Díaz (2003) for localities in the AC of Madrid indicates that this trend has continued. Local elections can also be scenarios for changing national politics. Indeed, municiple electoral behaviour is often studied as a harbinger of future national trends. It is also important to note that the so-called non-state parties rooted in the ACs usually do better in AC and local elections than they do in national and European elections, where the two major parties gain more seats.

Party government has important implications in terms of local council politics. In most cities, party discipline is reasonably tight, particularly within the majority or leading party in the case of a coalition. Party government, in the sense of the Spanish local government, means both legislative and administrative functions. As in larger parliamentary bodies that form the government, city and provincial councillors become department heads. The difference is that almost every ruling party/ruling coalition member is both a legislator and an administrator. The dominant local political culture thus stresses representation rather than administration. "Representative management" is the best characterization, where members of the *pleno* are involved in the day-to-day management of services (as in U.S. commissions). This gives rise to what Carillo calls "political inflation," where government structures tend to have a strong political weight attached to them:

> The impact of this phenomenon varies depending on the size of the organization. Small municipalities, where the number of elected members exceeds the number of public employees, serves as a prime illustration. Government being greater than that of administration allows the town council members to compensate for the lack of staff through a sort of free volunteer work. Yet, in large cities with differentiation in government, this leads to a considerable number of town councillors becoming involved in the daily administrative management of the organization's departments as their main profession. This type of behaviour leads to a fragmentation in the administrative organization, making the problem of confusion between the political and administrative spheres even more acute. Unlike other higher levels of government,

such as central government, this is not as attributable to bureaucracy's involvement in politics as it is to the invasion of politics in administration. (Carillo 1997, 60)

As a result, in the local political culture the management function often takes on a secondary or even marginal role.

While corruption can occur in any political system, it appears to be particularly prevalent in Spain, including in local government. Fernando Jiménez (1999, 80–1) refers to influence peddling as one of the major concerns of Spanish politics, on a par with terrorist violence and unemployment. This type of corruption has become a major matter of public debate and a major concern of public policy. In the democratic transition, "[i]t has constituted a lost opportunity to build sound and practical rules and traditions of political responsibility" (ibid., 85). National scandals receive the greatest attention, the most recent being the collapse of a subway tunnel under construction in the Carmel section of Barcelona, which caused multiple injuries and led to the evacuation of hundreds of residents from their homes. The contractor was found to be using substandard materials to cut costs. The regional government lost control of the project through a series of subcontracts and "shadow companies." Less visible and perhaps more prevalent are the many arrangements made by local governments with people who have a financial stake in the decisions of councils.

A notable illustration is the Valencia AC's LRAU (Law Regulating Urban Activity), a land use law, which has opened many corruption doors. Enacted in 1994, it was intended to protect small rural landholders from needless expropriation in areas that were in threat of urbanization and to protect them from having to bear large shares of infrastructure development costs. It has not worked out that way. The LRAU allows municipalities to create a *Plan de actividades integrada* (PAI) giving the urbanizing agent (developer) full autonomy in all matters related to projecting and implementing his own urban plans, and including any prices of land and or building he may see as convenient. The agent is supposed to present a "financial economic proposition" by which the developer will be paid for the work to be carried out to develop the urbanization. Moreover, the city government can benefit in that up to 10 percent of the land under the PAI can be reserved (that is, acquired) for "public use." The property owner's rights are limited to being informed, making "suggestions or alterations" to city government, and, if providing a contribution, the right to demand execution of alterations and town hall supervision (Correcher 2003, 2–3). There appears to be little or no protection of property rights in the LRAU. It has opened the door to developers – in collusion with real estate promoters and landowning commissioners in city halls – in "taking" portions of rural land to compensate for the infrastructure costs of new developments. On the Valencia coast, it is known as the land-grab law.

An additional political cultural trait is the autonomy/independence streak of the citizens of Spain. Moreno (2001, 5) explains that in all of Spain, more than two-thirds of its citizens express a form of dual identity or compound nationality to region and state, and to their institutions. This, suggests Crow (1985, 12), is largely because the geographic unity of Spain is an illusion. For years, regions were mutually inaccessible. Within these regions, Spain has a deep communal tradition, where village activity was based on the common management of lands, cooperative water rights, common access to sheep trails, and fishing cooperatives. Some communities even had their own monetary system. This led to orientation to the community over the years and a strong sense of one's own government or a local-right tradition that, in practice, has somewhat operated alongside later national and now regional regulation.

This tradition of local rule in the face of regulation "from above" is manifested in many ways. One easy illustration is that, during the Franco era, many villagers who farmed in the country had two storage places for their grain: one in the field where the grain was kept most of the year, and one in their town dwelling, which was filled at tax time in order to avoid large national inventory taxes. Municipal officials, even those sent by Madrid, were aware of this practice but tolerated it as part of the local culture. A current municipal practice is to ignore tax reassessment building-to-building and use aerial photography to reassess municipal properties to set rates for ground taxation. Where onsite assessment does not occur, many Spaniards expand their properties by building in their garages or in undeveloped lower or basement levels so as not to be detected by the tax people. Municipal officials are well aware of this practice but commonly look the other way.

Municipalities regularly and openly report that they do not deliver the required services under the LRBLR, but no one penalizes them. It is considered to be their independent prerogative to offer the services on which they decide, not to follow some list from Madrid or the regional capital. Indeed, they are "rewarded" by provincial assistance in delivering these services. As of late 2005, 20 percent of all municipal governments were reported in the newspapers as being, in total, more than 500 million euros behind in nonpayment of social security taxes for their employees. Some small towns had not paid for as long as five years (see www.spain.fipe.org). The Valencia government has repeatedly warned others against land takings under the LRAU, but the AC has yet to take action . No city has been fined, penalized, ordered to desist, or taken to court. The culture of independence means that cities are to be left alone to do either good or evil, but to "do" for the community. Few higher-level officials seem to care or wish to interfere locally. Only the courts occasionally step into these arenas, and their intervention tends to be related to human or civil rights more often than property issues. This intergovernmental culture leaves considerable operating leeway at the local level and goes back to the tradition of allowing local governments the right to operate on their own. It is part of *patria chica*. Just as every Spaniard is in many ways an autonomous subset of one, so are their communities self-organizing and governing units that limit external interference.

11 INFRASTRUCTURE CASE STUDY

There is perhaps no policy arena that is more intergovernmentalized than municipal infrastructure provision. Municipalities are required to have basic services in public lighting, water and sewers, street paving, refuse collection, and, for larger cities, parks, libraries, solid waster treatment, markets, fire services, urban transport, and environmental protection. Moreover, their role in social services, culture, and sport and recreation leads to infrastructure needs. There is also the possibility that they may become involved in activities that are shared between the national government, the ACs, and other local governments. For example, it is not unusual for municipalities to provide the land for public schools and to construct the buildings, even though education is a shared national and AC competency. Infrastructure funding, as will be demonstrated, follows a similarly mixed pattern, involving EU, national government, AC, and provincial funding streams.

The national program of infrastructure provision for municipalities is largely one of direct financing or by a series of discretionary conditional (project) grants that are channelled through provincial governments. Administered by the director general of local cooperation in the Ministry of Public Administration (MAP), these municipal projects are broad in scope or high in project eligibility, and they normally involve national, AC, provincial, and municipality financial participation – and sometimes EU and private financing as well.

Eligibility, according to the rules in the *Bulletin of the State* (BOE 30/1/04, 3721), involves a series of intergovernmental sign-offs, documentation of the relationship of the project to the Plan of Cooperation (see below), linkage to complementary plans and projects, a series of certifications (e.g., labour protection, environmental, administrative), a project timetable, and contractors' specifications. This is obviously an attempt to get municipalities to integrate specific projects with broader long-range planning, an effort that many municipalities resist, as we shall see. In addition to these targeted grants, a portion of the unconditional funds that go directly to the provincial governments are in turn subvented to municipalities.

According to discussions with officials from this MAP directorate in Madrid, municipalities with a population of over 50,000 are required to come up with some self-financing match, but they also enhance the local match with EU funds, particularly the Cohesion and the Regional Development Fund (FEDER). Large cities also have a better record of obtaining AC and national funds. Cities with a population of under 50,000 do not normally compete for national funds; they are financed through the *diputación* allocation, the EU, and small amounts of AC money. In the arena of highway and road construction, the *diputación* was reported as being responsible for 40–44 percent of all intermunicipal roads, the rest falling on the central government and ACs.

Two future infrastructure financing problems are foreseen by national government officials. The first is the loss of EU funds because of EU expansion. These funds have been important for Spain's less wealthy regions. Second are recent debt limits placed on financing local infrastructure. Both will reduce funding flexibility and will place more financing pressure on the central and AC governments.

At the local level, the province is an important unit of government for all but the very largest municipalities. Each must develop *Planes provinciales de cooperación de la obra y servicio municipal*. These city public works plans charge provinces with the responsibility of harnessing their investment efforts towards municipalities in such areas as water and wastewater, sanitation and public health, and road projects. In addition, provinces work with smaller municipalities in promoting sporting and cultural activities, secondary roads, and transportation coordination, all of which also lead to infrastructure needs. A royal decree (BOE 27/6/03, 27352-58) makes intergovernmental cooperation obligatory for infrastructure projects, while recognizing the mixed role of funding of different local entities and the EU and the central government.

Since provincial plans and local projects require AC approval, most local officials agree that regional governments do "have the last word." Provincial and local officials have become increasingly "skeptical of the powers of autonomous communities to approve their plans," commented a municipal councillor. "They [Valencia in this case] routinely act unilaterally in regard to our projects, making changes at will without discussion and consultation." An official in the Madrid AC related that "road projects (of an intermunicipal nature) and public transport are imposed by the autonomous community in response to traffic jams and the problem that in Madrid City rush hour lasts all day." With regard to a train extension project, several cities around Madrid mobilized to urge the AC government to address projects more openly and equally. One provincial official said that when plans for extending train services in a municipality arise, the management of the project becomes haphazard. The AC instructs a municipality to plan a project but does not guarantee that it will be funded. As a result, municipalities devote time to a project that may or may not ever happen. Another official said that when there was a decision to be made about building a regional hospital to centralize dispersed medical care in a series of growing Madrid suburbs, there were even municipal offers of donated land, but the Madrid AC government made a unilateral decision to locate it elsewhere.

Cities are required to submit to ACs, for approval, a *Plan general de urbanismo*, which outlines urban planning strategies and establishes specific criteria for the use of space and anticipated needs. To comply with the plan local governments must direct programs and resources for urbanization programs which are often beyond their powers and which project the use of regional resources to a greater degree than the law allows. For example, many local government officials know that the financing of new school buildings is well beyond their powers, but they are greatly encouraged (some would say coerced) into building them with local money. Social programs, such as retirement and youth centres, while locally needed and demanded, are often held up by AC governments.

Many small municipalities are reluctant to update their *Plan general*, because it reduces their flexibility to get approval if a lucrative project comes along. For example, at a general meeting in the City of Teulada (AC Valencia, Province Alicante) which the author attended, the mayor and the director of public works announced that a lucrative high-income housing project had come along at the city's beach area, Moraria. Also announced were new projects – a Moraria school building (to replace temporary classrooms), expanded parking facilities, and a renovated building for a seniors' cultural centre. None of these projects were on the *Plan general*, which had not been updated and filed since 1989. The city planned to file several amendments to the 1989 plan for AC approval. Teulada/

Moraria has grown in population from about 7,800 persons in 1989 to nearly 25,000. This regular practice of overlooking the *Plan* allows for flexibility and for greater facility in dealing with large private development corporations.

Larger cities have more difficulty in circumventing local plans because, unlike Teulada/Moraria, their projects are numerous and nearly always rely on a larger proportion of external funding, particularly from the central government. Meanwhile, the AC governments are not always particularly interested in enforcing updated general plans because that reduces their flexibility to say yes or no to a project. One municipal official said that often the message from his AC is, "Build it and then we will tell you if we can provide matching funding." When they spend a lot of money on a project, he explained, that "keeps us all very anxious," with both sides circumventing the plans and being pushed to engage in projects beyond municipal powers. To one official, it reflects little concern for public ethics: "No se dice, se hace" (This is not said, but it is done).

Cities turn to provincial governments for help on a case-by-case basis, as a rule. Initial contacts are nearly always informal. Any public works project will be *de facto* a collaborative effort. Municipalities (or other local entities) seek assistance through two separate channels: conditional grants (*subvenciones*) and less restrictive agreements (*convenios administrativos*). Conditional grants have to follow AC promulgated rules and guidelines, including inclusion in the *Plan general* (or amendment). A number of conditions follow, including intergovernmental collaboration, similar to those illustrated above with regard to national grants. Financing guidelines stipulate that provinces provide 60 percent of the funding while municipalities provide the remaining 40 percent. *Convenios*, as stated earlier, are agreements that take place outside the AC legislative process. They apply to public projects that require a significant portion (e.g., 98 percent) of public funding. There are few decrees or forms governing these agreements, and local officials can exercise considerable discretion in authorizing and executing these projects, including the channelling of funds to needed projects. These *convenio*-based projects are often the "crown jewels" of provincial and municipal governments, explained one provincial official. In his province, it is not unusual to have fifty or sixty such projects launched each year. This is not always good, he said, because many municipalities "lack a mature fiscal and budgeting capacity," and since so many are small, this is not likely to change. "Perhaps provincial governments should develop this expertise and act as municipal consultants, aiding in the decentralization process."

Finally, some infrastructure projects are not regulated and funded through intergovernmental cooperation. These tend to be projects of a private nature, such as residential and commercial development – utilities, roads, open spaces, and other amenities – which are funded either privately or through a combination of municipal financing and private funding. The latter is, of course, from property developers. It is not unusual for developers to suggest a tradeoff, by which land they have purchased or to which they have access (even when it is not in the town plan) is rezoned to residential, in return for their promising infrastructure improvements. One small coastal town exchanged permission to develop land that would double their housing stock in exchange for the developer supplying piping to the water treatment plant for the entire city. The more a city is reluctant to go into debt to finance such infrastructure projects, the more amenable it is to this form of tradeoff private financing.

To many of the local officials who were consulted for this study, the issue of power distribution is as important as the issue of money. They want more direct control over infrastructure decisions and would even be willing to spend more money if they had control. One provincial official relates that in many ways the AC governments have become "a new enemy." In addition to being against the centralization of power at the national level, local governments are more skeptical of the powers of the ACs. With regard to infrastructure, it is often the lack of concrete rules and of consistency in action. A deputy mayor said that with subsidized of affordable housing, rents often ended up higher than many could afford, thus deflating the original purpose. Without rules regarding the management of residential properties for those of moderate income, many people go without affordable housing: "This lack of explicit rules is another form of control used by the autonomous community." In other cases, the AC uses the lack of rules to push municipalities into infrastructure projects beyond the LBRLR. The same official concluded that "although the process is anti-democratic, we have little choice but to participate."

12 IMMIGRATION CASE STUDY

As one of the important "frontiers of Europe," Spain has an acute immigration problem. From a policy standpoint, the problem is mostly national and EU, but from an impact standpoint it dramatically very much affects those municipalities where foreign nationals settle. The Canary Islands AC is only 100 kilometres from Africa, and the strait between North Africa and the Iberian Peninsula is about 15 kilometres at its narrowest. Despite unemployment at around 10 percent, along with a substantial underground economy, the Spanish economy requires people willing to fill those jobs that appear to be no longer of interest to Spaniards – for example, in construction, agriculture, homecare, child care, and elder care. One government study, reported in the newspaper *Levante* (8 February 2005, 15), found that of the 17.24 million Spanish jobs, 850,000 (or 4.5 percent) are occupied by immigrants, with 34 percent of the new positions created in 2004 being taken by immigrants. Workers from North and Central Africa, Eastern Europe, and Latin America fill these jobs. In addition, older and wealthier people, mostly from Northern Europe, become "ETs" – eternal tourists looking for a milder climate, lower prices, and leisure activities. Of the estimated 2.7 million foreigners now in Spain (pop. 42.3 million), one million are believed to be there illegally. This is about three times as many as in 2001, according to the *International Herald Tribune* (23 February 2005, 8). Immigration – legal and illegal – has thus become a volatile policy issue in which municipalities have insignificant roles in policymaking but have a core role in dealing with the actual problems that these policies create.

The intergovernmental dimension of European and Spanish immigration policy can be broken into the four phases of prevention, admission, control, and integration. The first three – prevention of illegal entry, appropriate entry policies, and control over the number of immigrants – are considered to be EU and national government issues. The fourth, integration into recipient nations, regions, and cities is considered in Spain to be the business of ACs and municipalities (Zapata-Barrero 2004, ch. 1). National and EU policy reflects an ambivalence between business demands for skilled and non-skilled immigrant labour and a concern for integration, involving the control, surveillance, deportation of, and law enforcement against undocumented migrants. The latter has become particularly salient in light of the 2001 terrorist attacks in the United States and the Madrid bombings in 2004. Confounding the European approach are attempts to design a Common Asylum and Migration Policy (CAMP), in which governments have tried to play the security/integration game in their own interests. However, the EU is unlikely to replace the complex variety of labour recruitment schemes among its members. Europe's desire to promote itself as a competitive locale is not likely to change this (Menz 2005, 6–7). Spanish national policy has involved police searches and concerted sweeps; encouragement of legal nationalization and entry into the regular economy to help fill social security rolls that face a declining birthrate among Spaniards; and encouragement of coordination and planning for subnational governments (Carillo and Delgado 1998). In 2005 Spain made a dramatic change in its immigration policy, an issue that will be covered at the end of this section.

In Spain, as in other European countries, immigration is a volatile political issue. Public safety and control of immigration regularly spark interest among candidates for local, regional, and national office. In the March 2001 elections there was debate concerning which party could best control immigration. In early 2005 a woman from the Dominican Republic was killed by xenophobes and racists. Attention continues to be focused on immigration throughout the country.

Control often becomes a local government political issue. For example, in April 2005 the Popular Party of the City of Alicante (Valencia AC, 316,000 people) launched a campaign to stop a second ferry route from Algeria to Alicante. According to *El País* (1 April 2005, 3), "From its positions of power in the city council and the Valencian regional government, the PP has fomented a climate of confrontation with the Algerian residents of Alicante through its fierce opposition to the Transmediterránea line." The president of the AC, Francisco Camps, said in the AC parliament that the PP did not want more Algerian ferry passengers in Alicante because there was "no economic reason for it." In response, an opposition leader accused the PP of "xenophobia and of adopting positions more in tune with those of the extreme right." The PP spokesperson on Alicante's city council blamed North Africans for higher unemployment, for the overburdening of public health care and schools, and for other social problems. The new ferry line was said to be a threat to coexistence. The president of the Alicante *diputación* blamed the deterioration of the city's historic centre on the increasing number of Algerian shops.

In addition to national action regarding the control of borders, deportation, and the encouragement of legal entry as a path to citizenship, the national government has undertaken some action on integration planning. As integration first came on the radar screen in the early 1990s, the Ministry of Social Services began to take notice of AC actions. In particular, the importance of encouraging the existing network of NGOs – including the Red Cross, Catholic charities, labour unions, and immigrant associations – became salient. In many ways the same NGOs and public agencies involved in the Agreed Plan for Social Services (*Plan concertado*) were involved (Moreno 2000, 148–9). The result was the 1994 national plan, drawn up by the ACs, called the *Plan para la integración social de los inmigrantes* (PISI). The aim of PISI is to combat discrimination, promote mutual tolerance, guarantee social and legal rights, combat barriers to integration, and eliminate barriers and xenophobic thinking. A series of strategic actions were laid out in PISI, including a legal framework, ideal labour and professional conditions, and projected responsibilities of territorial, educational, and cultural authorities (Ramos et al. 1998, 9). PISI was followed by more plans (e.g., GRECO of 2000–4) to become compatible with EU policies, and with the creation of various government agencies, interdepartmental boards, and commissions to study and promote integrated services; between 1994 and 2001 there were six different councils, observatories, and agencies. Most important in terms of integration was the creation in 1997 of the Institute of Immigration and Social Services (IMSERSO) within the Ministry of Labour and Social Affairs (Zapata-Barrero 2004).

ACs began to turn their attention towards integration in the late 1990s. Most formed interdepartmental commissions that also incorporated the input of NGOs. For example, Andalucía formed five different bodies in 2000–1: an interdepartmental policy group, a contracted research observatory, a coordinating body, a mixed forum for popular input, and a legal assistance network. This led to an integrated plan that included (1) social integration, employment, and personal adjustment; (2) ensuring access to public services; (3) coordinated (case management) services; (4) changes in social services to accommodate new populations; (5) promotion of positive attitudes towards immigrant populations; and (6) continual improvement of the living conditions of immigrants. The particular services included: education, health, employment, social services, developmental services, social sensitivity, housing, cultural services, and legal assistance (particularly for illegal sector workers); Madrid, Catalonia, and other regions have similar plans in effect (Zapata-Barrero 2004).

In practice, less is offered by the ACs than meets the eye. For example, the Madrid Regional Immigration Office has provided information and data regarding immigration but has offered no direct services (Tamayo and Carillo 2002, interviews). In Andalucía, the Observatory has found services to be offered but in poor coordination, with the exception of a well-developed network of employers. Problems of coordination were particularly acute in public education, sanitation and health, and housing agencies.

It is at the municipal level, where immigrant populations settle, that the problems of integration occur. As mentioned earlier, municipalities with more than 20,000 people are responsible for social services, under AC supervision. But the responsibility is not the real issue, since almost all immigrants settle in large cities. Where there are reasonable concentrations of them, they inevitably affect numerous city services. The municipalities of Catalonia, Andalucía, and Valencia, particularly their coastal areas, are the heaviest hit. While immigrant populations are heterogenous, they tend to congregate residentially by country of origin. This has been a barrier to interimmigrant integration, not to speak of integration in the general Spanish population (with perhaps the exception of the small number of middle-class Latin Americans, who assimilate rapidly).

Each municipality has a different capacity to meet the influx of migrants. The local service networks include the office of social services attached to the municipality, AC-run school programs, city housing agencies, AC-operated health services within the city, AC employment services, locally based immigrant associations (e.g., local solidarity groups for Latin American women and for North Africans and Chinese), the Red Cross, catholic Charities, and municipal cultural associations. Unless a city has a local agency, such as a commission for refugee assistance, services tend to be uncoordinated. If any coordination is done without a commission, the municipal social services office is likely to perform it. In the late 1990s, municipalities began to ask for additional grants and funding to meet the increasing demand for services. Some housing and relocation assistance has trickled down through Provivienda, a housing program operated in collaboration with NGOs. For example, Andalucía has increased its service monies, largely because its cities are periodically inundated by workers who are rotated off crop harvesting as agriculture becomes more diversified. Labour unions have denounced the poor conditions of immigrant agricultural labour (e.g., housing, working conditions, hours, wages, child labour) and have promoted regulation and assistance for services. Yet, the AC of Valencia has offered no new city money, expecting municipalities to finance integration programs out of their existing budgets.

Beyond providing services for integration, higher-level governments offer little in the way of assistance. The national government and ACs provide information to municipalities in the form of lists of known "illegals." The sweeps for illegals, who are then presumably slated for deportation, are the responsibility of the national police. Municipalities have not really had a role in the enforcement side of illegal immigration, though the new policies will alter this somewhat. One problem for municipalities is that illegal immigrants do not show up on municipal registers. The same is true of the wealthy "eternal tourists," who enter the country under visitor status but stay longer than the hundred-day limit. Usually they establish a residence, but they are not enrolled citizens, nor are they on the municipal census, or *padrón*.

This leads to service demands by immigrants and others residing in the territory, though they are not counted in the allocation of grants and in service allocations. For example, Jávea (Alicante, Valencia) has a *padrón* of 32,000 people, but the estimated actual population approaches 45,000, with an estimated loss of 190 euros per person per year (just under 2.5 million euros) in revenue sharing.

Municipalities have raised the question of whether they can register (*empadronar*) persons even if they are not citizens. For those who have lived in

Spain for more than 180 days and have a *residencia* registered with the *diputación*, the answer is yes. This normally includes the wealthier immigrants. But some of these well-off migrants are reluctant to register for fear of losing health benefits back home, or in the interest of maintaining a home in their country of citizenship, or out of concern over not being able to return home. For non-documented immigrants, no policy has been established. The problem of *empadronamiento* is one of the greatest concerns of municipalities that are hit especially hard by immigration.

In summary, the problems for municipalities with immigrants are myriad. Most important, municipalities have limited powers and resources with which to tackle the social and other service expectations placed on them. While local networks of employers are relatively well developed, local education, housing, and social service networks are uncoordinated in most places. Access to many services and programs require documentation and passports, which certain immigrants do not have. Undocumented immigrants tend not to be part of the system of assistance. This set of issues has been a persistent criticism of the Spanish Commission on Refugee Aid (CLEAR), an NGO. In addition, there is animosity and intolerance to immigrant groups, along with intergroup animosity (between Moroccans and Romanians, for example), and within communities. Sensitivity to diversity and intercultural consciousness is needed, particularly in nonsegregated housing areas. Another issue is the well-off eternal tourists. Not only do they make demands on municipal services, but in some towns they establish their own enclaves, often choosing not to learn Spanish, and establishing "Little Germany" or "Little Britain" communities. Their service expectations tend to mirror their home municipal experiences, while Spain has different traditions. In this situation, it is not so much the issue of jobs, but the degree to which new residents really integrate into their new places of residence.

In February 2005 the national government enacted a reform that is designed to stop the estimated 800,000 *clandestinos* (illegal immigrants) working in the underground economy. It is aimed at getting them to pay their taxes and contribute to social security, which will facilitate their blending into the economy. Spain will now grant residence permits to immigrants who can provide proof of their registration with a municipality before 8 August 2004, along with proof that they have no criminal record and have a work contract of six months (for agricultural workers three months, and for domestic workers thirty hours per week). Immigrant employees had until 7 May 2005 to provide contracts to local authorities. Once these conditions are fulfilled and are given conditional approval, immigrants are registered with social security and start paying into the system. The government also will promote legal immigration by providing three-month visas, designed to give immigrants time to find work in Spain before applying for residence.

The program has a number of supporters, particularly those who feel that the labour market will level out somewhat and more workers will be contributing to social security. Detractors, such as CLEAR, say the policy does not protect non-workers – children, the elderly, those who can't work. Another criticism is that it will increase intergroup tension. Most important, some critics, including the opposition PP, argue that it will mean that more foreigners will be released and the underground economy will not be changed. Ana Pastor, PP social affairs spokes-person said, "Those who ask for contracts will simply be fired" (*Levante*, 8 February 2005, 15).

A report in *El País* (24 February 2005, 15) stated that in the first sixteen work-ing days a total of 48,247 immigrants registered under the new program, 63 percent of whom were from the Madrid, Catalonia, and Valencia regions. On the same day, the government announced that it planned to make half a million employ-ment inquiries between the 7 May deadline and the end of 2005. By the end of 2005, the government in Madrid reported that nearly 200,000 immigrants had registered (www.spain.fipe.org). The new registration program has been interna-tionally praised as potentially more effective than various other control means. One aspect is clear, however. The registration process has injected municipalities directly into the admission and control process in ways that previously were the responsibility of other levels of government. It is another example of what one provincial official characterized as how municipalities are treated. "Se tienen que tragar lo que les caiga" (They have to swallow whatever comes their way).

13 RECENT TRENDS

Most of the recent intergovernmental energy has been spent on renegotiating the statutes of autonomy. Most volatile is the approved Catalan *Estatut*, which begins by calling Catalonia a nation and all that this entails. Catalonia tried to shift its AC funding to a special regime (as in the Basque and Navarra cases), where all non-social security laws would be collected and a fee would be negotiated with Madrid, but failed. Catalonia will have its own accounting tribunal that would settle all money disputes, including those with Madrid. There is more to the *Estatut*, but these provisions alone were enough to raise the level of conflict. Appeals are now before the Constitutional Court. Most important, Catalan-Madrid *Estatut* issues have consumed the headlines and the primary attention of the government for over one year.

Immediately before the *Estatut* furor, intergovernmental attention was marked by the headline-grabbing action of the Basque Country's regional president, Juan José Ibarretexe, and his Basque Nationalist Party (PNV), when they moved to-wards a self-determination referendum on "a free state associated with Spain." The PNV-led AC government garnered internal backing only with political sup-port from the terrorist group ETA. The PNV platform also called for negotiation of the 1979 Statute of Autonomy. In response, the PSOE government in Madrid set aside all issues but the statute negotiations, claiming – as reported by *El País* (24 February 2005, 16) – that a referendum was unconstitutional, and asking for reasonable positions in conjunction with the state, " always guaranteeing respect for the constitution and counting on reasonable consensus among the parties." The gloomiest predictions, however, included invoking Article 155 of the Consti-tution, with Madrid dissolving the regional government. The Basque nationalists tried to turn the April 2005 regional elections into a referendum on the Ibarretexe plan. But the PNV lost four seats and the PSOE gained five, dampening the Basque plan and causing the PNV to cast about for one or more coalition partners with which to form a minority government.

While not directly relevant to this paper, the Ibarretexe plan and the Catalan *Estatut* have consumed a great deal of political energy, have heightened tensions between regionalists and centrists, and have drawn attention and effort from virtually all other aspects of the government's program of intergovernmental reform. Clearly, AC statute-of-autonomy reform has at least temporarily pushed local government change off the agenda.

Local government's second decentralization reform, the *pacto local,* is, therefore stalled. As a result of the 1999 *pacto local* FEMP-government pact, the proposed laws identified earlier were redefined and municipal authority was increased. The pact clarified local roles in public security in public places, in transport and parking, environmental protection, tourism, health, and housing. However, the ACs were not involved in this first decentralization pact, and of the 92 specific proposals identified by municipal interests, only 32 were covered by the new legislation. Most important, no AC has advanced these proposals.

The 2003 laws enhanced and clarified the fiscal and managerial powers of larger cities, but the next round of decentralization in the form of AC-legislated *pacto local* awaits the action of the AC parliaments. This would yield some of their powers in critical urban concerns, such as urban planning, economic development, employment, consumer protection, sports, and education. As one Spanish scholar of local government put it, "From a technical perspective, the legal procedure to bring about this 'Second Decentralization' will be the passing of new laws by the legislative bodies of the communities, once the pacts [between regional branches of FEMP or their equivalents and AC political parties] have been agreed to. These laws will have to abide by the central government's Local Autonomy Law of 1985, and will have to establish the procedures for municipalities' authority" (Ruiz 2002, 10).

Meanwhile, the national government did outline further reforms in its January 2005 *White Paper on Reform of Local Government*, which was primarily authored by an academic who has had long experience in local government, Manuel Zafra Victor (Spain, MAP 2005). Dr Zafra is the director general of local cooperation in the Ministry of Public Administration. The White Paper calls for four general principles to govern municipalities' powers: (1) autonomy, or the ability to meet their population's needs with concomitant powers; (2) subsidiarity, or the ability to address those needs that directly affect their populations; (3) flexibility, or recognition of the diversity among municipalities to offer services; and (4) proportionality, or the ability to receive or levy revenues in relation to their responsibilities.

Under the Zafra proposal, minimal powers would be guaranteed, including internal organization, citizen relations, public revenue and spending, management of municipal property, control over urban development, public security, and management of urban services. The proposal also calls for defining the exclusive boundaries of municipal powers and repealing the required service clauses of the LRBRL, requiring local governments to provide those services which they decide demand "universal access." Further, the paper asserts that local administrations should manage about 25 percent of the public sector, and it names some nineteen specific services that would give them direct control over basic infrastructure, urban development, police and fire, health and sanitation, culture and sport, and related urban services. Finally, the White Paper calls for a "general powers" clause that allows local entities to adopt appropriate services that other governmental bodies do not explicitly manage. In other words the Zafra paper calls for the enablement of what in the United States is called municipal "home rule," which combines the practice of the *Imperium in imperio* mode of granting exclusive authority in certain areas of local government and devolution of powers, with that of granting local governments powers to legislate in these areas as long as they do not contradict higher-level laws, as enacted by parliamentary bodies and for courts (Zimmerman 1995, 27, 29).

Practitioners of local government who were interviewed for this paper are generally positive about these proposals. One provincial official said that they try to establish local government as *las tercera pata de estado* (the third leg of the nation-state). The idea of splitting powers between the levels was particularly resonant. A number of officials responded positively to the call for direct, popularly elected mayors who would be head of local administration. This would involve a dramatic shift from the commission form of government. Others identified the call for shifting police powers downward as a positive step, along with giving municipalities general powers. One summarized the proposals as an attempt to extend the current administrative autonomy to political and fiscal autonomy, particularly to avoid what many local officials characterized as the excessive political "muscling" or bullying by AC governments, especially when using the funding influence. A deputy mayor of a large city said local home rule would move cities away from the current situation. His city, he said, "has obligations but few rights or authority. The autonomous community commands but does not negotiate. Coordination is desirable, especially to take advantage of economies of scale, but I should be equal."

The problem is that there is less political power among municipal interests; it primarily resides in the ACs. As this is a time when AC statutes of autonomy are being negotiated, it is hard for municipal interests to gain a voice. The Zafra reforms were introduced into the Congress in early 2006, and then subsequently put aside. State reform has definitely tabled them.

14 MULTILEVEL GOVERNANCE AND URBAN POLICY

Most observers of public policy and administration would say that municipalities have not only been bypassed or overlooked in the post-Franco decentralization movement but also that they are not ready, in terms of planning and operational capacity, to take on more responsibility. Yet it is hard to stereotype municipal or provincial governments as being responsible for this, because there are so many of them and they vary in terms of population and urban challenges. Spain has a number of high-capacity cities, where professionalism and effective service delivery abounds, but it also has numerous municipalities that fall very short in terms of meeting the needs of their citizens, even the basic needs required under national laws. To a certain extent, these gaps are filled by non-municipal governments. At the local level are *mancomunidades*, consortia, and *diputaciones*. At higher levels are vertical *convenios*, AC governments, and the national government filling in. This multigovernmental involvement, along with numerous forms of legislative shared competencies and responsibilities, makes the system highly intergovernmentalized, at least from an analytical perspective. From a normative perspective, many have argued that the system is overintergovernmentalized and should be reformed (Blanco and Sánchez 2002; Castells 2002), whereas others see intergovernmental cooperation as essential to avoid the confusion of roles and to facilitate a system of shared cooperation (Agranoff 2004; Canales 1999; Ruiz Almendral 2002).

In terms of a national urban policy, post-Franco governments have not emphasized the kind of initiatives that North American countries have in terms of eliminating poverty, urban blight, racial desegregation, and metropolitan development (Judd and Swanstrom 1998, ch. 8). In the European sense, many of Spain's largest cities possess long histories as centres of power, culture, and civilization. Although slow to modernize, many of these large cities – Barcelona, Madrid, Valencia, Bilbao, Seville – became engines of economic growth in the twentieth century. To be sure, the national government has launched programs to enhance affordable housing, improve water supply, facilitate intercity and intermetropolitan transportation, improve access to higher education, improve local cultural stock, and provide services and programs for youth and the elderly.

Since 1985 Spaniards have identified their urban policy as "local government reform," carried out via the *pacto local* movement, which has attempted to grant additional local autonomy in terms of powers and fiscal capacity. This has been a decade-long attempt to clarify and redefine the ambit of local powers from a decentralized, autonomous, and subsidiarity perspective (Cicuéndez 2003, 110–11). This "home rule" movement, as recently encapsulated in the Zafra White Paper, leaves a number of other important items on the table of local government development: unfinished modernization or capacity enhancement; the digital divide faced by most small governments; corruption and proximity to powerful economic interests; transparency and representation of a broad range of citizens; the commission form of government; and the need to develop "federal" or limited government attitudes to support any home rule advancements (see also Villoria 2004, 38).

Substantial reduction in corruption in local government is another issue that needs to be addressed. For example, loopholes in the Valencian land law, LRAU, have opened many doors to abuse. As a result, thousands of property owners have been forced to yield or sell their land below market value and to pay for new infrastructure which developers normally pay for, passing the costs onto the new homeowner. This could not have occurred without the collusion of corrupt local councillors who are in league with developers and real estate brokers. The Spanish national government has tried to control corruption through such measures as the 1995 Public Contracts Act, which led to new accounting, budgetary, and financial systems. Rules and qualification requirements have also been tightened regarding the appointment of administrative officials at all levels (Villoria 2000). European Union rules regarding bidding for contracts by member governments have also helped in this regard. The Zafra White Paper recommends combatting local officials' conflicts of interest by making it illegal to hold public office while one has investments in private businesses that benefit from public funds. Clearly, not all local governments are rife with corruption, but it is sufficiently widespread to require further design attention.

Transparency of local government is a related issue that is often lacking in Spain. In a few cities on the Valencian coast, actions under LRAU have been thwarted by vigilant citizen watchdogs who have mobilized against city hall's anticipated action (see www.abusos-no.org/LRAU2004). But many decisions are made without a great deal of citizen involvement. One local poll indicated that 80 percent of citizens consider that politicians are the group most taken into account in making decisions or designing projects, followed by interest groups; only 50 percent considered that citizens' views are taken into account (Villoria 2000, 22). Legal attempts have been made to enhance citizen involvement in neighbourhood or submunicipal organizations, but in the 1990s these organizations were reported as being mainly administrative and for the exchange of information.

In addition, the party list system of local elections does not allow for direct district representation (Carillo 1997, 61). Attempts to strengthen the role of district and neighbourhood councils (*juntas de distrito, consejos vecinales*) or functional consultative bodies (*consejos sectorales*) for larger cities were enumerated in the 2003 legal reforms, but they must be implemented locally, of course. Blanco and Ricardo (2003) list several emergent means of local citizen participation, including involvement in local development strategic plans, inputs on local budgets, involvement in Agenda 21, planning for land use and local public spaces, community social/cultural planning, planning for local education projects, plans for integration of immigrant populations, and plans made between city-based networks of actors to develop assistance for the Third World. This long list obviously does not include the actions of all cities, and no doubt few cities engage in all of them. But each of these actions – if carried out and if it influences municipal government – does indeed enhance transparency.

The actual form of municipal government is something that some reformers think needs to be addressed. The mayor–commission format, which is virtually universal in Spain (except in communities with less than a hundred people) is no longer considered to be efficient. It has become an invitation to corruption in most countries when it is adopted. In the United States, its adoption was almost accidental: the Texas legislature suspended the Galveston city government after a flood and imposed a temporary government of five businessmen. The commission form mixes legislative and administrative roles. In the United States it quickly fell out of favour and now is the least popular form (less than 5 percent of cities). According to Herson and Boland (1998, 104), it quickly lost favour because over the long haul it led to many problems: inept and unqualified councillors who became heads of department; problems of administrative coordination; inability to develop coherent city policies; political infighting among commissioners; and the greater possibility of commissioners having absolute power over their domains (jealously guarded territoriality). The commission form, Herson and Boland concluded, has never been able to match the initial success of the Texas City model from which it sprang (ibid., 105). The Zafra White Paper calls for the direct election of the mayor, who would be the clear head of municipal administration. This reform would allow for the "strong mayor" form of government and would overcome the many shortfalls of commission government.

15 CONCLUSION

A large part of Spain's contemporary image is related to that of its cities. Terrence Riley, a curator of New York's Museum of Modern Art, chose an exhibit of contemporary Spanish urban architecture as his last project before he stepped down. Since the building of Gehry's bold titanium Guggenheim museum in post-industrial Bilbao, said Riley, "local mayors have been emboldened, risk has been incentivized." Riley remarked that this was an attempt to overcome the antimodern state, a sense of pent-up energy unleashed: "When the clamps come off and you give up on a unified country, you get this incredible platform for contemporary culture, driven less by these overarching nationalized narratives and more by these individual and regional expressions ... The country is using architecture to stabilize neighborhoods and maintain a sense of urban life" (Pogrebin 2005, 26). One example he uses is that of Barcelona, where health, education, and social service programs have been decentralized through the city's forty-one traditional barrios in "eye-catching" centres.

As the discussion of Spain's municipal reform agenda indicates, its cities need the tools for nonarchitectural individualism and expression as well as architectural works. In a sense, there exists a legal and fiscal "democratic deficit" for cities. They do not have the capacity to govern their citizens in the sense of determining their service needs or satisfying their quality-of-life concerns, or of adopting innovative own-source public policy. Like most cities in multitiered governments, Spanish cities are highly intergovernmentalized in complex horizontal and vertical networks. Like most city governments in multitiered systems, they are the prime transmission agents of first- and second-tier policies and programs. But most local governments in other multilevel systems do possess some capacity to act independently, to represent the unique and localized wishes of their citizens. Spanish cities generally lack this ability, because of structural, normative, and fiscal limitations. As a result, the city governments are more likely to turn to officials from other governments or to special economic interests instead of to their citizens. Only when an egregious abuse arises, as with the Valencian land-use law, are citizens able to muster representational action. These limits in turn lead to poor representation and economic collusion at city hall. Cities, therefore, appear to need more citizen-sensitive independent powers and the structural and economic capacity to act independently on behalf of local needs.

Only then will the capability for urban expression in policy and program match that of architecture.

REFERENCES

Agranoff, R. 1996. "Federal Evolution in Spain." *International Political Science Review* 17 (4): 385–402
– 1999. "Intergovernmental Relations and the Management of Asymmetry in Federal Spain." In *Accommodating Diversity: Asymmetry in Federal States*, ed. R. Agranoff, 94–117. Baden-Baden: Nomos
– 2001. "Managing within the Matrix: Do Collaborative Intergovernmental Relations Exist?" *Publius* 31 (2): 31–56
– 2004. "Autonomy, Devolution, and Intergovernmental Relations." *Regional and Federal Studies* 14 (1): 26–65
Agranoff, R., and A. Ramos. 1997. "Toward Federal Democracy in Spain: An Examination of Intergovernmental Relations." *Publius* 27 (4): 1–38
Aja, E. 2003. *El estado autonómico: federalismo y hechos diferenciales.* 2nd edn. Madrid: Alianza
Argullol, E., et al. 2004. *Federalismo y autonomía.* Barcelona: Ariel
Baena, M. 2000. "Problemas de gobierno local en España." *Cuadernos de gobierno y administración* 1:11–22. Madrid: Universidad Juan Carlos
Ballart, X., and C. Ramió. 2000. *Ciencia de la administración.* Valencia: Tirant lo Blanch
Bañon, R., and E. Carillo. 1992. *Tipología de municipios de la comunidad Valenciana.* Valencia: FVMP
Blanco, I., and G. Ricardo. 2003. "Gobiernos locales y redes participativas: retos e innovaciones." Centro latino americano de administración para el desarrollo *Boletín* 26:73–100
Blanco, P., and Á. Sánchez Sánchez. 2002. "La financiación impositiva municipal: propuestas para su reforma." *Papeles de económica española* 92:101–19
Börzel, T.A. 2000. "From Competitive Regionalism to Cooperative Federalism: The Europeanization of the Spanish State of Autonomies." *Publius* 30 (2): 17–42
Canales Aliende, J.M. 1999. "Gobierno local y democracia." In *Gobierno y pacto local*, ed. M. Arenilla and J.M. Canales. Madrid: MAP
Carillo, E. 1991. *Gestión de recursos humanos, presupuestión y hacienda local en España.* Madrid: Instituto de estudios fiscales
– 1997. "Local Government and Strategies for Decentralization in the 'State of the Autonomies.'" *Publius* 27 (4): 39–65
– 1998. "El etorno, los instrumentos y la evolución de la política de inmigración en España (1985–1996)." Madrid: Instituto universitario Ortega y Gasset
Carillo, E., and L. Delgado. 1998. *El etorno, los instrumentos y la evolución de la política de inmigración en España (1985–1996).* Madrid: Instituto universitario Ortega y Gasset
Carillo, E., and J.A. Diaz. 2003. "La nacionalización de la política local en España (1979–99)." *Cuadernos de gobierno y administración* 3–4:83–107. Madrid: Universidad Rey Juan Carlos

Castells, A. 2002. "Algunos comentarios sobre la reforma de las haciendas locales." *Papeles de economía española* 92:8–26

Chacón, F., ed. 1995. *Jornadas nacionales de servícios sociales comunitarios.* Madrid: Ministerio de asuntos sociales

Cicuéndez, R. 2003. "El pacto local? medidas para el desarrollo del gobierno local." *Cuadernos de gobierno y administración* 3–4:109–31. Madrid: Universidad Rey Juan Carlos

Closa, C., and P.M. Heywood. 2004. *Spain and the European Union.* New York: Palgrave Macmillan

Colino, C. 2001. "La integración europea y el estado autonómico: europeización, intergubernamentales." In *La europeización del sistema político español,* ed. C. Closa, 225–62. Madrid: Istmo

Correcher, S. 2003. "Comments on the Law Regulating Urban Activity in the Valencian Community." Jávea International Civic Society *Bulletin*, January

Crow, J. 1985. *Spain: The Root and the Flower.* Berkeley: University of California Press

Elazar, D.J. 1996. "From Statism to Federalism: A Paradigm Shift." *International Political Science Review* 17 (4): 417–30

Farfán Perez, J.M. 2002. "El papel de las diputaciones y mancomunidades en la administración local española." *Papeles de economía española* 92:68–84

Federación española de municipios y provincias (FEMP). 2005. *Estatutos de la federación española de municipios y provincias.* Madrid: FEMP. Available online at www.femp.es

Font, J., R. Gutiérrez Suárez, and S. Parrado-Díez. 1999. "Intergovernmental Partnerships at the Local Level in Spain: *Mancomunidades* and *Consortia* in a Comparative Perspective." Paris. Online at OECD [PUMA/RD(99)4/Final]

Ginénog Montero, A. 2002. *Federalismo fiscal: teoría y práctica.* Valencia: Tirant lo Blanch

Gunther, R., G. Sani, and G. Shabad. 1988. *Spain after Franco: The Making of a Competitive Party System.* Berkeley: University of California Press

Herson, L.J.R., and J.M. Boland. 1998. *The Urban Web: Politics, Policy, and Theory.* Chicago: Nelson-Hall

Jiménez, F. 1999. "Political Scandals and Political Responsibility in Democratic Spain." In *Politics and Policy in Democratic Spain*, ed. P. Heywood, 80–99. London: Frank Cass

Judd, D.R., and T. Swanstrom. *City Politics: Private Power and Public Policy.* 2nd edn. New York: Longman

Lancaster, T.D. 1989. *Policy Stability and Democratic Change: Energy in Spain's Transition.* University Park: Pennsylvania State University Press

López-Aranguren, E. 2000. "The Present and Future of Local Governments in Spanish Intergovernmental Relations." Paper presented at the 2001 Conference of the Research Committee on Federalism and Federation, International Political Science Association, 4–7 October, at Jávea (Alicante), Spain

Losada Marrodán, C. 1989. "El gerrente comarcal." *Autonomios* 2:95–107

Menz, G. 2005. "Europe's Migration Conundrum: The Contested Borders of a Common Asylum and Migration Policy." Center for West European Studies, University of Pittsburgh. *Newsletter*, January

Moreno, L. 2000. *Cuidadanos precarious: la última red' de protección social.* Barcelona: Ariel

– 2001. *The Federalization of Spain*. London: Frank Cass

Newton, M.T. 1997. *Institutions of Modern Spain*. Cambridge: Cambridge University Press

Olmeda, J.A., and S. Parrado. 2000. *Ciencia de la administración*. Vol. 2. Madrid: UNED

Pallarés, F., José Ramón Montero, and Fracisco Llera. 1997. "Non State-wide Parties in Spain: An Attitudinal Study of Nationalism and Regionalism." *Publius* 27 (4): 135–70

Pogrebin, R. 2005. "Curator Spotlights Spain's Unique Architecture." *International Herald Tribune*. 15, December, 26

Ramos, J.A., and R. Cicuéndez. 2005. "La dimensión institucional de las relaciones autonómico-locales en un contexto de gobierno multinivel." Paper presented at the Congreso de Ciencias politicas española, 15–19 September, at Madrid

Ramos, J.A., I. Bazaga, L. Delgado, and E. Del Pino. 1998. "La política para integración social de los inmigrantes: una perspectiva intergubernamental." Madrid: Instituto universitario Ortega y Gasset

Ruiz Almendral, V. 2002. "More Power for Spain's Municipalities?" *Federations* 2 (5): 9–10

Ruiz-Huerta, J., A. Herrero, and C. Vizán. 2002. "La reforma del sistema de financión autonómica." Madrid: Instituto universitario Ortega y Gasset

Salmon, K. 1995. *The Modern Spanish Economy.* 2nd edn. London: Pinter

Solé-Vilanova, J. 1990. "Regional and Local Government Finance in Spain: Is Fiscal Responsibility the Missing Element?" In *Decentralization, Local Government, and Markets*, ed. R.J. Bennet, 331–54. Oxford: Clarendon

Spain. Ministerio de las Administraciones públicas (MAP). 1991. *La modernización de la administración del Estado*. Madrid: Ministerio de las Administraciones públicas

– 2003. *Informe económico-financiero de las administraciones territoriales 2002*. Madrid: Ministerio de las Administraciones públicas

– 2005. "Primer borrador de libro blanco para la reforma del gobierno local en España." Madrid: Ministerio de las Administraciones públicas. Prepared by Dr M. Zafra

– Ministerio de Económica y hacienda. 2002. *Liquidaciones presupuestarias de las CCAA y de las EELL, ejercicio 2002*. Madrid: Dirección general de Fondas comunitarios y financiación territorial

Subirats, J., and R. Gallego. 2002. *Viente años de autonomias en España: leyes, políticas públicas, instituciones y opinion pública*. Madrid: Centro de investigaciones sociológicas

Tamayo, M.S., and E. Carillo. 2002. "La gestión intergubernamental y la integración de los inmigrantes." Paper presented at the 7th Congreso Internacionál del CLAD, 8–11 October, at Lisbon

Villoria Mendieta, M. 2000. "The Modernization of the Spanish Public Administration: The Role of Bureaucracy." Paper presented at the International Political Science Association World Congress, 1–6 August, at Quebec

– 2004. "Democracia y territorio en España: rasgos, retos del gobierno multilevel español." *Circumstancia* 4:1–38. Madrid: Instituto universitario Ortega y Gasset

Wiarda, H.J. 1993. *Politics in Iberia*. New York: HarperCollins

Zapata-Barrero, R. 2004. *Inmigración, innovación politica y cultura de acomodación en españa*. Barcelona: Fundació CIDOB

Zimmerman, J.F. 1995. *State-Local Relations: A Partnership Approach*. Westport, Conn.: Praeger

THE MATRIX EXTENDED: FEDERAL-MUNICIPAL RELATIONS IN SWITZERLAND

André Bächtiger and Anina Hitz

1 INTRODUCTION

In the literature, Switzerland has been described as a matrix model of federalism (Bächtiger and Steiner 2004; conceptually, see Elazar, 1962, 1987; Agranoff 2002), involving collaborative and accommodative relationships among the diverse levels of government. It is also viewed as a bottom-up political system, with strong governance capacity and autonomy of municipalities (see Joye 1995; Fleiner 2002, 111; Wälti 2004). While this may certainly be true – especially from a comparative perspective[1] – a closer inspection reveals a somewhat hazier picture.

First, while the matrix is well developed for the relationship between cantons and the federal state (see Linder 2005; Bolleyer 2006), this has been less true for the relationship between municipalities and the higher levels of government. Swiss municipalities and cities are strongly embedded within "their" cantons, and interaction and institutional density between the municipal/city level and the federal level has been quite sparse for a long time. Certainly, municipalities and cities have several venues to influence federal politics, but the overall pattern has also featured hierarchy, with municipalities and cities sometimes acting as mere executive organs of cantonal and federal policies. In recent times, this pattern has even gained strength. While law-making powers have shifted to the cantonal and federal level, implementation has shifted to the municipal level. Consequently, the autonomous policymaking capabilities of municipalities and cities have decreased. In times of increased policy interdependence and complexity, however, there is growing awareness that such a top-down approach may not be adequate to attain a high quality of governance.

Second, a further challenge to the traditional Swiss federal system is the "urban question." While the importance of urban areas has steadily increased in the postwar period, the traditional territorial structuring of the Swiss state seems increasingly inadequate for dealing with urban problems. In practice, there is a growing incongruence between functional urban spaces and territorially bound decision-making structures (Kübler et al. 2003). A third challenge is the extreme fragmentation of the Swiss municipal space. About 60 percent of municipalities have less than a thousand inhabitants. This has spurred a debate on whether the governance capabilities of very small municipalities can meet the policy challenges of the twenty-first century (Ladner et al. 2000).

Since the 1990s, the matrix of Swiss federalism has been extended, with enhanced institutional cooperation and closer interaction between the municipal level of government and the higher levels. The new Constitution of 1999 provides a special section for the protection of municipalities and cities. This combines with institutional innovations – such as a tripartite coordination forum – that give larger cities and municipalities additional venues to influence the policymaking of the higher levels. In addition, there is a new financial equalization scheme for the centrality costs of large cities and agglomerations, as well as financial incentives from the federal level to stimulate cooperation in the urban space. These innovations have been conducive to more policy-oriented cooperation, more policy networks, and the recognition that the three territorial levels cannot function in isolation from one another. Finally, we have noticed changes at the municipal level: not only has intermunicipal collaboration increased, but there is a noticeable trend towards municipal fusions. However, the effective functioning of the Swiss federal matrix substantially hinges on the behaviour of the participating actors at the different levels of government. In this regard, there was increasing political polarization among the major political parties during the 1990s, decreasing cooperative attitudes. This tends to hinder the potential of the extended matrix of Swiss federalism from being fully exploited.

In this paper, we first describe Swiss federal-municipal relations from a constitutional point of view. We then give an overview of municipal responsibilities and functions. This is followed by a description of the fiscal position of municipalities. Next, we focus on the organization, scope, and nature of federal-municipal interactions with a particular eye on the interaction patterns between the federal and municipal levels of government. This is followed by two case studies, one on emergency planning and one on metropolitan governance of land-use and transportation policy. We then look at recent trends in Swiss federal-municipal relations and finally make an overall evaluation of the adequacy of the current system of multilevel governance in the production of (good) urban and municipal policy.

2 THE CONSTITUTIONAL POSITION OF MUNICIPALITIES VIS-À-VIS THE CANTONAL AND FEDERAL GOVERNMENTS

The relationships between the federal state and municipalities in the Swiss political system are regulated in Article 3 of the Constitution. Article 3 indirectly stipulates that the regulation of municipal competencies is in the exclusive jurisdiction of the cantons (Meylan, Gottraux, and Dahinden 1972, 29). Strictly speaking, the federal state cannot interact directly with the municipalities but has to do so via the cantons. However, the Constitution of 1999 explicitly mentions municipalities for the first time as a potential sphere of cooperation for the federal level (Article 50). Even though this may not imply a qualitative change in the legal situation of municipalities, it has encouraged institutional cooperation and closer interaction between the federal and municipal levels. This topic will be addressed in the fourth section. Furthermore, while municipalities are not mentioned as autonomous and independent forces in the decision-making processes of the federal state, this does not mean that participation in federal decision-making processes would not be allowed from a constitutional point of view (Thürer 1986, 203).

The constitutional position of municipalities is anchored in the cantonal law. Thus, it is the cantons that decide on the existence of municipalities and the range of their competencies. Since the competencies of the municipalities are regulated in cantonal laws, general statements about municipal autonomy are difficult to make (Schenkel and Serdült 2002, 473–4). From a comparative point of view, it is assumed that Swiss communes have a considerable amount of autonomy within cantons and could maintain their position well over time (in 1848, when the new federal state was founded, there were 3,203 political communes, only about 10 percent more than today). Moreover, the Swiss system is based on a subsidiarity principle, which stipulates that the higher unit only intervenes where the lower unit cannot fulfill its tasks anymore.

So how much municipal autonomy is there in reality? From a purely legal perspective, Giacometti (1952) assigns French-speaking cantons a relatively low level of municipal autonomy, while German-speaking cantons have greater municipal autonomy. This is corroborated by a survey of all Swiss municipal authorities conducted in 1994, in which the latter evaluated the autonomy of their municipalities in their respective cantons. The results, reported in table 1, represent average scores, ranging from 1 (very low municipal autonomy) to 10 (very high municipal autonomy),

As table 1 shows, Giacometti's estimation is largely confirmed. In most German-speaking cantons, municipal authorities ranked municipal autonomy higher than their French- and Italian-speaking counterparts did. However, the survey of Swiss municipal authorities also indicated their growing dependence on the higher government levels. Some 70 percent of the municipal authorities stated that municipal autonomy had decreased in recent years.

A NOTE ON CITIES AND URBAN AGGLOMERATIONS

There has been a long tradition of nonrecognition of cities in the Swiss federal state. Until its 1999 revision, the Constitution contained no reference to cities, thus making them political nonplayers in legal terms. Yet the importance of urban areas has steadily increased since the Second World War. Today, over two-thirds of Switzerland's population live in urban areas. In spite of urban growth, "metropolization" (see Sager 2002), and increasing territorial interconnectedness, the institutional structure of urban (local) government in Switzerland has virtually not changed since the beginning of the twentieth century. Kübler, Schenkel, and Laresche (2003, 267) note that "there is a manifest lack of congruence between functional urban spaces and territorially bound decision-making structures." This has created a number of problems, especially for large cities.

First, while most suburban municipalities were able to consolidate their economic base, the large cities ran into financial difficulties because of the loss of wealthy taxpayers and the subsequent concentration of socially disadvantaged segments of the population. This in turn led to the uncompensated centrality expenses of large cities and substantial benefits for "free-riding" suburban municipalities. At the same time, this configuration proved to be an obstacle to territorial reform in most urban areas. Not only have wealthy suburban municipalities opposed steps towards fusion with financially distressed large cities (Geser 1999, 426), but the degree of horizontal cooperation between cities and the suburban municipalities has remained very modest and conflict-ridden (Horber-Papazian and Soguel 1996, 160).

Table 1
Degree of Municipal Autonomy (evaluated by the municipal authorities)

Canton	Degree of municipal autonomy
Schaffhausen[1]	6.1
Obwalden[1]	6.0
Zug[1]	6.0
Thurgovia[1]	5.9
Appenzell, Outer-Rhodes[1]	5.8
Grisons[2]	5.8
Glarus[1]	5.6
Nidwalden[1]	5.5
Valais[2]	5.5
Uri[1]	5.4
Zürich[1]	5.4
Argovia[1]	4.9
St Gallen[1]	4.9
Solothurn[1]	4.9
Vaud[3]	4.7
Bern[2]	4.6
Schwyz[1]	4.6
Basel Country[1]	4.3
Ticino[4]	4.3
Fribourg[2]	4.2
Lucerne[1]	4.1
Neuchâtel[3]	3.7
Basel Town[1]	3.2
Geneva[3]	3.2

[1]German-speaking
[2]Bilingual or trilingual (French- and German-speaking, with the exception of Grisons, which is trilingual: German, Romansch, and Italian)
[3]French-speaking
[4]Italian-speaking
Source: Ladner 1994

Second, social segregation within urban areas leads to important differences in political preferences. In large cities, the electorate and the political elites are more sensitive towards social policy issues. Hence, large cities are usually governed by left-wing (or left-green) majorities, while surrounding municipalities are more likely to be governed by right-wing majorities. This means that the political majorities of large cities differ from those of their respective cantons and this leads to conflict over which of them is in charge of urban policy. However, as we shall demonstrate in section 5, urban and agglomeration problems are increasingly being addressed.

3 THE RANGE OF MUNICIPALITIES' RESPONSIBILITIES AND FUNCTIONS

Before discussing municipalities' responsibilities and functions, we should note some specificities of the municipal organization in Switzerland. First, there are the 2,940 political municipalities, or communes. These belong to type 1 multilevel governance and represent traditional general-purpose jurisdictions with territorial membership and a systemwide, durable architecture. The fragmentation of the territorial space in Switzerland is very high, with about 60 percent of political communes having less than a thousand inhabitants. Besides the political communes, there are 5,000 overlapping, functional special communes, which are aptly called *Zweckverbände* or *Gemeindeverbände*. These are goal-oriented or functional associations and can be assigned to type 2 multilevel governance (Marks and Hooghe 2003). Type 2 multilevel governance aims at solving particular policy problems; membership is voluntary, and multiple memberships are possible. Frey and Eichenberger (1999) identify seven types of functional jurisdictions that complement or even compete with general-purpose local governments.

The most important form of municipal organization is the political commune. The following tasks are in the prime competency of political communes (though all the task listed are not necessarily performed by all political communes in all cantons): municipal finances (taxes), schooling (primary and secondary education), social security and public health, law and order (police), public works, local public transport (in larger cities), and culture (Meylan, Gottraux, and Dahinden 1972, 27). As such, political municipalities are general-purpose jurisdictions that have political organs such as an executive, a legislature, and an administration (Ladner 1991). However, the smaller the municipalities, the more circumscribed are the political organs and the less professionalized is the administration.

Even though political communes have their own responsibilities and functions, Switzerland is an example of cooperative federalism (Geser et al. 1996). Exclusive or competing competencies barely exist. In other words, there are practically no areas where municipalities have sole responsibility. This follows the general trend of Swiss federalism. Although in 1848 the drafters of the Swiss constitution had a model of dual federalism in mind, which would assign exclusive competencies either to the central state or to the cantons (Bucher 1977, 996), the principle of dual federalism was never fully realized in practice. One reason is that the

Table 2
Types of Commune in Switzerland, 1996

Commune type	Number
Political communes	2,940
Citizen communes[1]	1,519
School communes	516
Church communes	
Catholic	1,455
Protestant	1,100
Corporations	309
Fractions[2]	78
Further types of commune	73
TOTAL	7,990

[1]Citizen communes grant communal citizenship; corporations are associations for pooled resources (such as pastures and woods).
[2]Fractions are subcommunal jurisdictions that have traditional competencies in construction politics.
Source: Frey and Eichenberger 1999, 49

Swiss federal government does not possess its own implementation apparatus and is dependent on the cantons and municipalities for executing its policies. With the increasing intervention and the rise of the welfare state, Swiss federalism began to resemble the model of cooperative federalism with the centre providing the basic legislation and the cantons and municipalities in charge of implementation. Hence, a clear-cut separation among the three layers of government has become less possible (Schenkel and Serdült 2002, 470). Although the principle of subsidiarity still has validity, tasks and competencies in many policy fields cross-cut the three levels. Especially when it comes to new policy fields such as environmental protection, the federal state, cantons, and municipalities are simultaneously in charge (Nüssli 1985, 283). This is also true in the context of transport, social policy, and educational policy, where legal prescriptions are found at all three levels. This has also led to strong financial integration, as we shall see in the next section.

The sharing of competencies does not necessarily mean collaborative relations between the different levels of government. Traditional cooperative federalism in Switzerland features hierarchical relations between municipalities/cities and the higher levels, with the former sometimes acting as mere executive organs of cantonal and federal policies. In recent times, this pattern has been accentuated; there has been a shift of law-making and financial powers to the federal level and wider implementation powers to the cantons. Thus, municipalities' financial and legal room for manoeuvre has been reduced, while the range of functions they must fulfill has grown (Klöti et al. 1993). An increasing number of municipalities report

Table 3
The Sharing of Competencies between the Federal State, Cantons, and
Municipalities

Competencies	Examples
Mainly federal state	Coinage; national defence; customs; postal system; organization of federal authorities; aviation; railway system; conclusion of international treaties; television and radio institutions; nuclear energy; criminal law; alcohol administration; ETH (Swiss Federal Institutes of Technology); asylum; vocational education; research
Mainly cantons	Police system; churches; health service and hospitals; energy; regional building and planning; secondary education; cantonal administration organization; penal system; regional business development
Mainly municipalities	Public transportation system (in cities); gas, electricity, and water supply; waste management; tax base; social welfare; culture; local planning; municipal administration
Federal state and cantons	Urban and regional planning; agriculture; environment protection; civil protection; work law and regulations; civil and criminal law; road construction; pension and disability security system; trade and industry; health insurance
Cantons, cities, and municipalities	Cantonal roads; health system; schooling and education; environment protection; urban and regional planning; sports

Source: Schenkel and Serdült 2002, 473

that they have reached their capacity for solving policy problems on their own (Ladner et al. 2000, 3; Ladner and Steiner 2003, 243ff). This particularly concerns the larger cities, which are confronted with increasingly complex policy problems (for example, in the social domain).

As mentioned above, political communes are supplemented by 5,000 communal associations (*Zweckverbände* or *Gemeindeverbände*). Since 1980, no less than 216 communal associations have been formed; 93 percent of the Swiss political communes belong to at least one such association and often to several. The communal associations are organized as jurisdictions according to the public law, and in some cantons they have the power to impose income and wealth taxes. In principle, all tasks can be subject to such cooperation, but in some cantons there are restrictions on cooperative ventures. These communal associations perform specialized tasks, such as providing local schooling, electricity, gas, water, and street lighting. They also provide specialized public services on a larger scale, for example, hospitals, nursing homes, and garbage collection. In rural areas, the major goal of communal associations is to gain more professional administration and more effectiveness, while in urban areas the major goal is to solve problems that concern several municipalities (such as social services and traffic) or to get financial compensation (Geser 2002, 460–1).

However, as Frey and Eichenberger (1999) note, the communal associations in Switzerland do not represent FOCJs (functional, overlapping, and competitive jurisdictions) in their pure form. FOCJs are a radical version of type 2 multilevel governance. Besides the functional requirement, they are competitive (they compete for communes and citizens and are subject to democratic political competition, e.g., popular referendums), and the jurisdictions should have the power to raise taxes with which to finance their expenditures. While communal associations in Switzerland do share some characteristics with FOCJs, such as the functional requirement, most of them have limited competition, cannot be instituted freely by the citizens because of the restrictions imposed by cantonal law, and cannot impose taxes.

4 THE FISCAL POSITION OF MUNICIPALITIES

The Swiss fiscal system is thoroughly decentralized. Cantons and municipalities are provided with considerable fiscal competencies. The municipalities can levy a surcharge on cantonal direct taxes and raise their own property taxes. The federal government relies mainly on indirect (proportional) taxes, specific consumption taxes, a general sales tax, and small but highly progressive income taxes. Since the municipalities are responsible for a wide range of duties, they also have the right, within the bounds of cantonal legislation, to raise their own income tax. This right is quite far-reaching, including individual and corporate income and wealth taxes that yield large revenues. The right to raise taxes – and also the right of people in municipalities to set the rate of taxation – is an important element in ensuring the autonomy of the municipalities and giving municipal autonomy some real teeth (Adamovich and Hosp 2003).

Table 4
Overview of Tax Types at the Level of the Federal State, the Cantons, and the Municipalities

Level	Taxes
Federal state	Progressive income tax, consumption tax, and corporate income tax
Cantons	Personal and corporate income tax, inheritance tax, and property tax
Municipalities	Personal and corporate income tax, surcharge, and property tax

Source: Adamovich and Hosp 2003, 9

Municipalities also have other sources of revenue, both from the federal government and the cantonal government. The financial integration between federal and cantonal governments as well as between cantonal governments and municipalities involves a complex array of vertical transfer payments (Schenkel and Serdült 2002, 474–5). Transfer payments include contributions (conditional payments that are bound to more or less strict rules of compliance with executive prescriptions); reimbursements (conditional payments compensating for the municipal execution of duties for which the federal or cantonal government is responsible); investment contributions (conditional payments linked to specific projects); and revenue shares (unconditional payments for financial equalization). It is important to note that the transfer system is generally two-tiered: the federal state transfers money to the cantons, and the cantons transfer money to the municipalities. As table 5 shows, the percentage of direct payments from the federal state to the municipalities is very small (less than 1 percent).

Table 5 gives the percentage of municipalities' own-source revenue and that of transfer payments from the federal state, the cantons, and other municipalities. As can be seen, the share of own-source revenue is very high (more than 80 percent). However, these are average scores, and there is considerable variation across municipalities. Moreover, we should not overlook the fact that around 80 percent of a typical municipal budget consists of "bound" expenditures. These involve tasks that municipalities must fulfill because of cantonal or federal laws (Bischof 1994, 7).

Table 5
Revenues of Swiss Municipalities, 1997–2003: Own-Source Revenue and Transfer Payments

	1997	1998	1999	2000	2001	2002	2003
Own-source revenue (%)	83.5	83.5	85.2	83.1	82.9	83.0	82.6
Transfer payments by the federal state (%)	0.07	0.05	0.04	0.04	0.03	0.03	0.03
Transfer payments by cantons (%)	12.6	12.6	10.9	13.0	13.1	13.1	13.5
Transfer payments by other municipalities (%)	3.8	3.9	3.9	3.9	4.0	3.9	3.9
Total revenues of municipalities (in SF millions)	37,894	38,770	40,545	42,068	43,033	43,652	44,123

Source: Eidgenössische Finanzverwaltung 2005, 80

Table 6 gives the total revenue and expenditures of all levels of the Swiss polity (federal state, cantons, and municipalities). The figures for municipal and cantonal revenues and expenditures include transfer payments. Generally speaking, Swiss municipalities raise about one-third of all public expenditures. As the table shows, there is also no centralization trend. Quite the opposite. Over the past fifty years, the federal state's share of total revenue decreased from 47 percent to less than 40 percent; the budgets of the Swiss cantons grew larger than average during the expansion of the welfare state, while the municipalities' portion of all public expenditures remained constant at around 30 percent (Geser 2002, 434).

Table 6
Total Revenues and Expenditures of the Federal State, the Cantons, and the Municipalities, 1950–2002

	1950	1960	1970	1980	1990	2000	2002
Federal state:							
Revenues (%)	47.0	45.3	40.5	35.4	37.1	39.5	38.2
Expenditures (%)	42.3	40.4	38.6	37.1	36.5	39.0	38.7
Cantons:							
Revenues (%)	35.3	37.6	46.8	46.8	47.2	47.8	49.3
Expenditures (%)	38.2	43.2	47.0	46.4	47.5	48.7	49.6
Municipalities:							
Revenues (%)	29.2	30.1	32.3	36.4	35.4	32.0	32.4
Expenditures (%)	31.9	31.5	33.7	34.9	34.9	32.8	31.7
Total revenues, all levels (in SF millions)	4,226	7,356	19,840	46,464	83,161	131,491	134,560
Total expenditures, all levels (in SF millions)	3,897	6,478	20,285	47,240	86,614	123,612	134,253

Source: Linder 2005, 151

In sum, while Swiss municipalities enjoy considerable financial competencies and autonomy, we should not overlook the importance of "bound" expenditures in municipal budgets (Geser 2002, 435). In addition, one-third of all municipalities ran a deficit in the mid-1990s, especially the larger cities (Ladner et al. 2000). These two factors considerably reduce the space for municipalities to pursue their own (and new) policy projects.

5 ORGANIZATION, SCOPE, AND NATURE OF FEDERAL-MUNICIPAL INTERACTION

As Armingeon (2000) holds, Swiss federalism is a relatively loosely coupled system. A loosely coupled system is one where the demands of the lower levels of government are heard and evaluated by the higher levels, but the decisions of the latter are not fully bound by the interests of the former (Benz 1998, 563–5). This is particularly true of Swiss municipalities (including cities), which have no formal or fiscal veto power to block decisions of the higher levels. It is also partly true of the cantons, at least when it comes to the production of policies. While the array of the cantons' formal veto points is impressive at first glance, many of these veto points are not – or only partly – effective.[2] Hence, the federal state is not fully bound by the will of the cantons. Furthermore, since the municipalities are subordinate to cantonal law, the relationship between federal and municipal governments is, in general, not conducted at the bilateral level. For a long time, relations have been mediated by the cantons (which directly interact with the federal level). Among a total of seventy forms of vertical collaboration, there is no example of direct collaboration between cities and the federal level; twenty-six forms of collaboration include all three state levels, and thirty concern cities and cantons (Kübler, Schenkel, Leresche 2003, 271–2). These figures indicate that the scope of formal federal-municipal interaction is limited; and for a long time, major policy programs for municipalities and planning activities by the federal level have largely been absent. As we shall see, this has not prevented municipalities from voicing their interests at the federal level and influencing federal policies. For this purpose, municipalities and cities organized themselves in associations: the Swiss Association of Municipalities (Schweizerischer Gemeindeverband, founded in 1897) and the Swiss Association of Cities (Schweizerischer Städteverband, founded in 1953). During the 1990s, the position of municipalities and cities towards the higher levels gained strength and the scope of federal-municipal interactions expanded considerably. Before describing how this was accomplished, we shall highlight some key features of the Swiss political system.

First, the Swiss political system can be considered a relatively inclusive and accommodative one – though there has been rising polarization among the four major parties since the 1990s (see Hug and Sciarini 1995). One major reason for the integrative character is direct democracy. The referendum (especially the optional one) produces the continual danger of a veto for policy proposals in a popular vote (Neidhart 1970, 292). Empirical evidence suggests that political parties have only partial control over their voters in referendum votes, since voters frequently view policy issues differently from political and interest group representatives. Furthermore, referendum votes are frequently negative: the rejection rate in optional referendums between 1947 and 1995 was 43 percent and was 23 percent in the case of the mandatory referendum (Trechsel and Sciarini 2000, 106). This limited control of the electorate produces uncertainty among elites about the outcome and creates institutional pressure for risk-averse policymakers to adopt cooperative strategies and build large supporting coalitions for policy proposals (Neidhart 1970; Linder 2005; Trechsel and Sciarini 1998, 110). The referendum threat has led to the establishment of an institutionalized grand coalition (called "magic formula" since 1959). Since referendums are also held at the cantonal and municipal level, the aforementioned mechanisms also come into play at the lower levels.

As Armingeon (2000, 124) notes "direct democracy at all major levels of the political system (local, cantonal, federal) penalizes political elites which consistently pursue conflictual policies." This congruent logic of negotiation and accommodation in the federal arena is supported by the composition of local and cantonal governments, which tend to follow a pattern of coalitions similar to those at the federal level (on average, cantonal governments involve 3.34 parties; Vatter 2002; see also Geser et al. 1994; Geser 1999). The exceptions – as mentioned earlier – are the larger cities, which are frequently governed by left-wing and green parties, while in smaller municipalities, in cantons, and at the federal level, right-wing parties dominate. In addition, cooperative interaction orientations are stabilized by the fact that the Swiss political elite is a very small circle, and actors in different arenas know each other and need to work together for a long time. This can create habits of working together, friendships, group loyalties, and knowledge about others; it can also create convergence, mutual confidence, and positive trust spirals.

Another reason for the integrative political system is the "weakness" of the federal level. The federal government has no implementation apparatus at its disposal and hence cannot directly control the implementation of its policies by the cantons and municipalities. The major means of federal control are the subsidies offered to the cantons and the municipalities. The lack of a federal implementation apparatus and the absence of coercive means induce the federal authorities to negotiate with the lower levels. Given the necessity of maintaining cooperation over the long term, the federation prefers cooperative to conflictual strategies (Kissling-Naef and Knöpfel 1992; also Neidhart 1975, 22). The fact that many federal policies have to be implemented by municipalities gives the latter an important voice at the design stage of federal policies. This partly compensates them for their lack of formal veto power.

At the federal level, a key arena for integrating the diverse demands is the pre-parliamentary consultation procedure, where bills are submitted to a number of political and societal actors, among them the cantons and, less frequently, the municipalities. The pre-parliamentary consultation procedure consists of two stages: first, an expert commission evaluates or elaborates a first draft of the bill; second, the political and societal actors evaluate the draft of the bill. Although in the latter stage the consultation procedure does not involve direct negotiating among the actors (the federal administration only collects the different opinions and then prepares a bill), the consultation procedure can still be considered a functional equivalent of classical "consociational" arenas: it is the locus where corporate actors express their interests and where consensual solutions are crafted. Unlike cantons, municipalities have not automatically been consulted for a long time.

However, a new law on consultation (introduced in 2005) previews a better participation of municipalities' and cities' associations in this process.

Another important feature of the Swiss political system is the fact that Switzerland is the only "consensus democracy" that has "non-parliamentary" features. Although MPs elect the government (the Federal Council), the legislature cannot stage a vote of no confidence; if a government proposal is defeated by parliament, it is not necessary for the Federal Council to resign (Steiner 1974, 43). Accordingly, MPs are quite independent in drawing up legislation and party discipline is relatively weak compared to other European parliamentary systems; (see Kriesi 2001). This means that there is a good chance for municipalities and their associations to influence individual MPs during parliamentary deliberations. In addition, there is a specific parliamentary group, the Kommunalpolitik, dealing with municipal affairs.

The realization of municipal interests is helped by four additional factors (see Thürer 1995). First, municipal politicians are often recruited by regional and federal parties; second, there are frequent role combinations between municipal authorities and national MPs (role combinations are not prohibited in Switzerland). Third, there are municipal-friendly attitudes in Parliament. Fourth, the party system is weakly centralized: local and cantonal parties play an important role in national politics (Ladner 1991; Kriesi 1995, 144; Armingeon 2000).

While it is certainly true that the Swiss federal state is basically responsive to municipal and urban interests, there has still been a deficit in the degree of interaction and institutional cooperation. In the last few decades, there was growing awareness that in the context of increased policy interdependence and complexity, a top-down approach might not be adequate to attain a high quality of governance. There was also growing awareness that the problems of large cities and agglomerations had to be tackled in a more comprehensive fashion.

In its spatial order report (*Raumordnungsbericht 1996*), the federal state recognized that urban agglomerations in Switzerland – and especially the large cities – are exposed to significant centrality expenditures which are largely uncompensated. It was stipulated that the implementation of these new objectives required the establishment of platforms of collaboration and communication involving all three state levels. The Constitution of 1999 explicitly mentions that federal policies must take into account the special situation of cities and agglomerations (as well as the situation of municipalities in mountainous regions). This, together with a report on city problems (*Kernstadtbericht 1999*) and a report on a new urban policy (*Agglomerationsbericht 2001*) provides the basis for improving federal urban policy in several policy fields and promoting better cooperation between cities, urban areas, cantons, and federal authorities (see Kübler et al. 2003, 274). An important step was the creation of the Tripartite Agglomerationskonferenz (TAK) in 2001, a discussion and coordination platform consisting of the federal state, the Conference of Cantons (KdK), the Swiss Union of Cities (Schweizerischer Städteverband) and the Swiss Association of Municipalities (Schweizerischer Gemeindeverband). The TAK aims to strengthen vertical forms of cooperation and to develop a common agglomeration policy (Schenkel and

Serdült 2002, 478). In addition, there are conferences of cantonal social, transport, construction, and planning directors, which city representatives are now invited to join. The federal state also provides financial and knowledge-based support of innovative model projects in urban network building (public authorities, city planners, private landowners, investors). Finally, the new financial equalization scheme (introduced in 2004) previews compensation for the centrality expenditures of large cities and agglomerations.

There is not much concrete research on the municipal level's real influence on federal politics and the respective evolution of municipal influence in the 1990s. In order to get more information in this critical yet underresearched area, we conducted two interviews with the chairmen of the two key associations of municipalities: Urs Geissmann from the Schweizerischer Städteverband (SSV) and Sigisbert Lutz from the Schweizerischer Gemeindeverband (SGV).[3] The interviews focused on the chance of influencing federal politics, the nature of interaction with the federal state (and the cantons) in the diverse phases of federal decision making, and the effect of recent institutional innovations on the relationship between municipalities/cities and the higher levels of government.

With respect to the representation of urban and municipal interests at the federal level, both the SSV and the SGV make use of the same instruments: participation in committees of experts and the pre-parliamentary consultation procedure as well as participation in parliamentary deliberations. The SGV, however, is better represented in the National Assembly than the SSV, since there are many current and former representatives of smaller municipalities in the National Assembly. The two associations voice their concerns both directly to MPs and in hearings of parliamentary committees. As mentioned earlier, there is also the group Kommunalpolitik which holds meetings twice a year. According to Geissmann, this group is a "showroom for representation purposes" rather than an arena for the effective enforcement of municipal interests. Real influence is exercised via MPs who represent municipal and urban interests. The enforcement of SSV interests occurs mainly through informal talks (according to Geissmann, around 80 percent is through informal talks). These talks have gained great importance during the last twenty years and are now even more important than the official consultation procedures.

As mentioned above, there have also been institutional innovations to strengthen the position of municipalities vis-à-vis the federal level (Article 50 of the Constitution of 1999 and also the TAK). According to Geissmann and Lutz, the TAK allows cities and municipalities to have better contact with the federal level, since it forces the cantons and the communal associations to work together. In the past, the cooperation of the SSV with the cantons was very poor and had competitive features. In the course of the establishment of the TAK, this cooperation has greatly improved. However, as Geissmann holds, cantons are still not always pleased when the municipalities enter into direct negotiations with the federal government, thereby bypassing the cantons.

When asked whether municipal and urban interests are taken seriously at the federal level, both Geissmann and Lutz stated that their associations have the capacity to successfully influence federal politics. However, the SSV and the SGV are only single actors in a system that contains numerous interest groups. According to Geissmann, the SSV has gained influence in federal politics, but the rising polarization of Swiss politics makes it more difficult to articulate municipal interests. Both the SSV and the SGV are only successful when they can build alliances with other actor groups (for instance, acting together or with the Conference of Cantons). The associations' interaction with the federal government depends to a great extent on the respective federal departments as well as on the issue at stake. However, since the federal level depends on the municipalities to implement its policies, the federal authorities tend to be cooperative.

In sum, we would describe the nature of municipal-federal relations as one with relatively cooperative interaction orientations embedded in a relatively integrative and accommodative system of multilevel government. As the interviews show, municipalities can influence federal politics at various stages, and in general their interests and demands are seriously evaluated and taken into account. While for a long time there was a lack of appropriate intergovernmental forums between the federal and municipal levels, the TAK and the projected law on consultation provide for more direct interaction between the highest and lowest level. Moreover, the current federal-municipal interaction is an interesting mixture of pluralism and concertation. The pluralist aspect is manifest in the preparliamentary and the parliamentary phase, where the municipal associations are players among others. The concertation aspect is manifest in the TAK, as well as in the new consultation law, which turns the municipal associations into fixed players in the political network, albeit without compulsory veto power. Moreover, as the interviews show, the increasing polarization among major parties at the federal level raises hurdles for the articulation of municipal and urban interests. This is particularly true for urban interests: cooperation among large cities, the cantons, and the federal state is complicated by the fact that the actors are of different political parties. Party competition and incongruent actor logics can decrease cooperative interaction and render policy negotiations (as in the TAK) more difficult.

6 MUNICIPALITIES AND INTERNATIONAL RELATIONS

To date, Swiss municipalities have not been very active internationally. Unlike France and Germany, Switzerland is not a member of the European Union – a fact that tends to restrict Swiss multilevel government to a three-level system and largely precludes Switzerland's having a full-fledged four-level system, including the European level, as in France and Germany (see, Brunet-Jailly, this volume). Whether this will change with the bilateral treaties between Switzerland and the European Union (effective since 2002) is an open question. There are, however, regular contacts of Swiss municipalities with municipalities across the border, including a number of functional cooperation schemes in the areas of waste disposal, tourism, and the environment. In addition, in 1998 Switzerland ratified an international treaty on the cooperation of municipal and regional organization in border cantons (INTERREG). Yet more formalized international relations are mostly mediated by the cantons (such as the *Regio Basiliensis* project of the Basel cantons).

7 CASE STUDIES

7.1 EMERGENCY PLANNING (CIVIL PROTECTION)

In this case study, we analyse how emergency planning works in practice, specifically with reference to multilevel governance and the interaction between municipalities and the federal level. We decided to focus on civil protection because this is a policy field where the policies of the federal state create a strong link to the municipalities (Meylan, Gottraux, and Dahinden 1972, 30; Bassand and Perrinjaquet 1986, 210–12; Thürer 1995, 6–8). We considered this to be a critical case whereby to obtain information about the actual interaction patterns between the federal, cantonal, and municipal levels.

Civil protection – or "protection and support services" – is jointly regulated by federal and cantonal provisions.[7] The federal state establishes the legal framework for civil protection and sets up provisions relative to its areas of competence, particularly with regard to recruitment and personnel. The federal level is also the coordinating institution while cantons are in charge of implementing the federal provisions. In general, however, municipalities are the real agencies of civil protection. How civil protection is organized depends on the canton. Frequently, municipalities have joined to form regional civil protection organizations. The rationale is that not every municipality needs its own organization; rather, the civil protection is related to the actual dangers and the topographic conditions and structures of a canton, region, or municipality. For instance, the Basel agglomeration with its chemical industry needs a different civil protection structure from a mountainous region in the canton of Valais.

As regards interactions among the three levels of government,[5] the pattern in emergency planning is hierarchical: the federal government does not directly intervene with the municipal civil protection organizations. The partners of cooperation are the cantons and the form of organization between the three government levels is top-down. The civil protection organizations at the municipal/regional level receive their orders from the cantons and the cantons receive orders from the federal government. In the case of a disaster, the coordination function is taken up by the federal level, and there is a special committee composed of federal and cantonal authorities; the municipal and regional protection organizations have to execute what the higher levels have decided. This hierarchical pattern also permeates the stage of policy formulation: ideas and demands from lower levels – the municipal and regional civil protection organizations – do not seem to be very welcome at the higher levels. In addition, even informal contacts with organizations take place only at the cantonal level. To further their interests, municipal and regional civil protection organizations have to choose the pluralist option and lobby cantonal authorities and MPs.

This case displays the traditional hierarchical pattern of multilevel government in Switzerland. The higher levels are in charge of the planning, while the municipal level has to execute what the higher levels have decided, without much input, voice, or participation from below. Granted, one might argue that emergency planning requires hierarchy in order to be effective. While this undoubtedly is true when it comes to emergency action in a disaster, one might well ask whether a modicum of input from the local level at the design stage of emergency planning might help to produce better policies.

7.2 METROPOLITAN GOVERNANCE OF LAND-USE AND TRANSPORTATION POLICY

The second case study focuses on the coordination of land-use and transportation policy in Swiss urban areas. The urbanization problem is also a problem of rising mobility and growing space needs: the more people move to the suburbs, the more commuter traffic there is in the central city, and the less attractive it becomes for city residents. Therefore, the integration of the policies for urban development and transportation constitutes the crucial means for curbing the spread of urbanization.

In the course of its new urban and agglomeration policy, the federal state provides financial and knowledge-based support to innovative model projects in urban network building (involving public authorities, city planners, private landowners, and investors). To date, the federal government's financial engagements are rather modest, but substantial amounts have been reserved to finance improvement of public transport infrastructure. A high-performance public infrastructure (e.g., transportation and communication networks) is considered crucial for the competitiveness of a metropolitan area. The condition for support is that these urban policy projects involve area-wide cooperation between the large city, the surrounding communes, and the canton. Projects supported by the federal state in this context concern the creation of new urban policymaking structures (Lucerne, Fribourg, Argovia, Bern) or the upgrading and conversion of urban areas into a broader spectrum of urban functions (Neuchâtel, Zürich, Lausanne, Delémont, St Gallen; Tobler 2002). While in Zürich and Geneva/Lausanne urban governance consists merely of ad hoc cooperation, steps towards the institutionalization of urban cooperation can be observed in the areas of Basel and Bern/Fribourg. As such, the nature and extent of vertical and horizontal interactions is shifting towards a network approach involving more collaborative modes of policymaking. Yet an analysis of multilevel governance must also be sensitive to additional, municipal-specific factors. The impact of both municipal-specific factors and coordination schemes in "metropolitan" areas on the production of metropolitan policies was the focus of a study of land-use and transportation policy conducted by Fritz Sager (2002, 2005).

Sager analysed nine infrastructure projects marked by a need for policy coordination in four urban areas.[9] The research question was whether different "metropolitan" institutional settings affect the quality of political negotiation processes and the respective policy outputs. In this regard, Sager focused on four institutional variables: centralized vs. decentralized metropolitan governance structures; fragmented vs. consolidated metropolitan areas; professionalized vs. amateur self-administering bureaucracies; and bureaucracies with a clear distinction between the administrative and political spheres of negotiation and those lacking such a distinction.

The comparison of the nine decision cases yielded the following results. Policy-driven coordination and substantially rational coordination decisions were found in centralized institutional settings rather than in decentralized ones, in fragmented metropolitan areas rather than in consolidated ones, and in project structures that have a strict separation of the political sphere of negotiation from the technical sphere. While the fragmented territorial order is a precondition for coordination processes, the fact that all the actors involved (large cities and the suburban municipalities) possess veto power can contribute to policy blockade and suboptimal policy outcomes. This effect can be offset, however, in centralized organizational structures, especially when combined with bureaucracies that make a distinction between an administrative and political sphere of negotiation. These two factors are strongly conducive to "evidence-based rather than interest-oriented negotiations" (Sager 2005). In addition, by making decisions more binding for the participating actors, centralization and professional bureaucracies help the implementation process in that the negotiation output is actually put into practice.

Sager's study underlines the importance of additional municipal-specific factors in the production and implementation of urban policy that entail quality aspects, such as policy-driven coordination, with the goal of finding a common solution that satisfies all the stakeholders' interests. Thus, effective multilevel government not only depends on institutionalized and cooperative relations among the different levels – as highlighted by the new Swiss urban and agglomeration policy – but also depends on favourable "individual" level characteristics, such as the centralization of metropolitan areas and professional bureaucracies.

8 RECENT TRENDS

As we have seen, the recent trend in Swiss federalism has been an extension of multilevel governance, involving institutional innovations – such as the TAK – as well as financial incentives from the federal level to stimulate cooperation in the urban sphere. As Kübler et al. (2003, 275) observe, "These new initiatives have given birth to a series of federal and cantonal programs and measures to improve social and technical infrastructure in cities, and to increasingly involve them in the formulation of federal policies that affect them." While it may be too early to assess to what degree these new coordination devices have an impact on the production and implementation of "good" public policy, it is clear that there has been a qualitative change in Swiss federal-municipal relations. What is new is the recognition that the three territorial levels are not only highly interdependent but cannot function without one another. The federal state needs the cantons and the cities for the effective implementation of federal policies, and the cities and the cantons need the financial and organizational resources of the federal state in order to attain their goals successfully. Moreover, the new agglomeration policy makes intermunicipal cooperation within agglomerations a condition for gaining federal support. This provides a strong incentive for large cities and the surrounding communes to overcome their conflicts (Kübler et al. 2003, 276).

Cantons, too, have become more actively involved in urban governance. Again, cantonal regulations often cast the shadow of hierarchy, thereby fostering cooperation among municipalities. The strengthening of area-wide governance in metropolitan areas will see more intergovernmental forums, more purpose-oriented cooperation, and more policy networks. But the creation of true regional institutions will be fairly exceptional. To date, the creation of a new regional layer of multipurpose government between the cantons and the communes is projected in only one urban area (the rather small Fribourg agglomeration). Due to widespread reluctance and high institutional hurdles in the form of direct democracy, significant reform of territorial institutions has not taken place in Switzerland.

Nonetheless, we should not overlook the fact that there is ongoing institutional change at a more subterranean level of the Swiss federal matrix. Confronted with increasing policy interdependence, policy complexity, and the financial distress of municipalities and cities, reform discussions about a new division of functions and finances between cantons and municipalities have been launched. In fact, some cantons have restructured their system of financial compensations, for large cities as well as for other financially distressed municipalities (Schenkel and Serdült 2002, 480–1). Moreover, as Ladner et al. (2000) note, in almost two-thirds of municipalities (especially the larger municipalities) intercommunal, functional cooperation increased during the 1990s. Second, there are experiments with new forms of administration (such as the implementation of "new public management" schemes), especially in the German-speaking part of the country. Finally, while fusions of municipalities have been very rare for a long time, the respective frequency has increased considerably. Already, 25 percent of municipalities have discussed the possibility of a fusion, and many cantonal authorities consider municipal fusions a very important tool for strengthening governance capabilities at the municipal level (see Steiner 2002). Hänggli (2006) shows that financial problems – combined with cantonal financial support – significantly enhance the chances of municipal fusions.[7]

In sum, two parallel trends characterize the current Swiss federal system. Vertically, the "matrix" has been extended with increased institutional cooperation and closer interaction density between municipalities/cities and the higher levels. This has led to the development of urban development programs involving multiple stakeholders in network governance. Horizontally, the mapping of the municipal space is evolving too. Not only did intermunicipal functional collaboration in the sense of type 2 multilevel governance increase during the 1990s, but we also detect a noticeable trend towards municipal fusions.

9 ADEQUACY OF THE INSTITUTIONAL FRAMEWORK FOR THE PRODUCTION OF (GOOD) URBAN AND MUNICIPAL POLICIES

What leads to the production of good urban and municipal governance? On the basis of a global inquiry, Gerring, Thackers, and Moreno (2005) provide evidence that institutional arrangements which increase the quality of governance must involve two features. On the one hand, they must be authoritative: "they must provide an effective mechanism for reaching agreement and implementing that agreement" (ibid., 569). On the other hand, they must be inclusive: "they must reach out to all interests, ideas, and identities" (ibid., 569). Regarding the institutional preconditions for good governance, current Swiss multilevel governance has increasingly embodied one of these requirements, namely, the inclusion of relevant interests (in this case, municipal and urban interests). As for authoritative government, the other requirement for good governance, Switzerland is not a paragon at first glance. Featuring a nonparliamentary consensus system with no federal implementation apparatus at hand, the possibility of authoritative and effective government seems to be severely limited. But on closer inspection, the Swiss system is not so ineffective when it comes to reaching agreement and implementing policies. First, the levels are relatively loosely coupled, with the higher levels not being fully bound by the will of the lower levels. Second, Swiss multilevel government is premised on consensus systems across all levels (with the partial exception of larger cities), leading to relatively congruent actor logics at the different levels of government. Cooperative interaction orientations are further backed by direct democracy and the referendum threat. These factors create a governance system that can be quite innovative and is less prone to deadlock than the more tightly coupled German system which involves joint-decision traps and suboptimal policy outcomes (Armingeon 2000). In addition, the mixture of type 1 and type 2 jurisdictions in Swiss multilevel governance creates considerable flexibility. Political communes are supplemented by a great number of functional communes (*Zweckverbände* or *Gemeindeverbände*). These type 2 jurisdictions, which aim at solving actual policy problems and cross-cut traditional territorial boundaries, allow for a more efficient provision of public services (see Marks and Hooghe 2003). Combined with the still relatively strong governance capabilities of municipalities, the current institutional framework thus seems to be quite adequate for the production of good urban and municipal policy. Indeed, the performance of metropolitan public services, for instance, can be high (e.g., public transport), and the outcomes of metropolitan policymaking generally meet the expectations of the citizens (see Kübler et al. 2005).

However, loosely coupled multilevel systems (and authoritative government schemes alike) tend to come at a price. Lower levels, and particularly municipalities, cannot be certain that their interests and demands are taken into account. As our interviews revealed, there are indeed complaints that municipal and urban interests do not receive enough consideration in the policy production of the federal and cantonal levels (Schenkel and Serdült 2002, 486, 488). And as our case study of emergency planning shows, there are policy fields where both the policy production and the implementation process can be hierarchical, without partici-pation or input from the municipal level. Hence, one may wonder whether formalized veto positions and tight coupling of the three levels might be the better option for furthering municipal interests. In a comparative study on the effects of veto power on cooperative and deliberative policymaking, we found neither posi-tive nor negative effects (Bächtiger and Hangartner 2005). The findings did not support the arguments that veto power and unanimity is strongly counterproduc-tive to the production of cooperative policymaking entailing policy learning and argumentative change (Austen-Smith and Feddersen 2002); nor did the findings support the argument that veto power forms an "enabling constraint" in this re-spect (Steiner et al. 2004). What matters for cooperative and deliberative policymaking are consensual decision-making patterns. This may be a hint that productive multilevel governance does not primarily hinge on tightly or loosely coupled multilevel governance systems but seems to be highly dependent on the cooperative interaction orientations of the relevant actors.

In conclusion, we would like to stress the importance of the complementarity aspects of multilevel governance. In Switzerland, the production and implemen-tation of "good" urban and municipal policies seem to depend on a complex array of factors, involving favourable institutional and actor-related factors at all three levels: a dense interaction and institutional network among the federal state, the cantons, and the municipalities; cooperative interaction orientations of the actors involved; and a professional bureaucracy at the municipal level. Put differently, multilevel governance can be adequate for municipal and urban policy only if both contextual and individual level characteristics are complementary – that is, if the presence (or efficiency) of one increases the returns from (or efficiency of) the other (Hall and Soskice 2001, 17). The current challenge in Swiss multilevel governance is the growing political incongruence among different levels (differ-ent political majorities in large cities and cantons), combined with increasing political polarization among the participating actors. This may prevent the poten-tial of the extended matrix of Swiss federalism from being fully exploited.

NOTES

We thank Hans Hirter, Andreas Ladner, Regula Zürcher, Nicole Bolleyer, and the partici-pants of the Conference on "Cities in Multilevel Government Systems" (October 2005) for extremely helpful comments.

1 In a comparison of twenty-two OECD countries, Switzerland scores highest on a feder-alism scale as well as on a fiscal decentralization scale (Wälti 2004).
2 A first potential veto point for cantons at the federal level is the Council of States, which is composed of two representatives for each canton (one for each half-canton). The Council of States has equal competencies with the National Council – the people's chamber – and its consent to federal laws cannot be denied. However, the councillors are not appointed by the cantonal parliaments or government but are elected directly by the residents of the cantons. Hence, they do not have to defend the interest of cantonal

governments, and councillors of state frequently defend the same group and party interests as MPs in the National Council (Heger 1990). For a long time, councilors of state rarely made use of their blocking power, and the relationship between the Council of States and the National Council was not very conflictual (Trivelli 1974). This pattern has changed since the 1990s, with increasing differences in political preferences between the two chambers. But there is no clear evidence that the Council of States has started to defend cantonal interests more forcefully (Wiesli and Linder 2000). Furthermore, for changing the constitution, both a majority of the national electorate and a majority of the cantons is needed (majority of the cantons clause). This may represent the most important veto point, since risk-averse actors might anticipate it at the design stage of policies. Nevertheless, the majority of the cantons clause does not affect all bills at the federal level, nor does it represent a strict veto point. In addition, there is another federalist veto point, the cantonal referendum allowing a minimum of eight cantons to challenge parliamentary bills. However, these two veto devices have not been critical veto instruments. The majority of the cantons clause did not play an important role for a long time, and there were very few collisions of a people's majority and a federalist majority (eight collisions between 1848 and 2000). Canton referendums, in turn, seem to be extremely difficult to orchestrate. A collective of eight cantons has to support them, and prohibitive procedures within the cantons add barriers too. Not surprisingly, there has been only one case where a cantonal referendum has been used successfully. For a detailed overview of cantonal veto points and their effects, see Bächtiger and Steiner 2004.

3 The interviews were conducted on 12 and 18 April 2005.

4 Civil protection organizations are responsible for providing the protective infrastructure (e.g., shelters) and resources needed to alert the population and those made homeless in the case of disasters. Public and private buildings and premises, shelters and protected premises, and/or parts of the army infrastructure are available to this end. Another aspect is protecting the country's cultural property, particularly in the event of disasters and emergencies. Where necessary, civil protection units back the other partner organizations and may be deployed for long-term operations (days up to months) alone or jointly with partner organizations. Civil protection personnel may be called upon to reinforce management support. When necessary, civil protection units provide logistics services for the other partner organizations and are in charge of logistics coordination for management support. They are also in charge of repairs of infrastructure (Schweizerisches Bundesamt für Zivilschutz 2004).

5 Interview with Gerhard Baumgartner, director of the regional civil protection centre (Regionales Kompetenzzentrum Bevölkerungsschutz, RKZ) in Bern. The interview was conducted on 13 April 2005.

6 The agglomerations in the study were Basel, Bern, Lausanne, and Geneva. The nine case studies comprised the following policy projects: new tramlines and the building up of a rapid transit network (Basel), the extension of a suburban regional railway line to the city centre as well as the planning of a coherent rapid transit system (Lausanne), traffic hubs and sports and shopping facilities at the city periphery (Bern, Geneva), and the renewing of a light railway transport supply (Geneva). The selected cases all took place within existing public administrative structures in the four metropolitan areas.

7 However, a recent study (Lüchinger and Stutzer 2002) shows that fusions have not yet led to increasing "economies of scale," with an improved financial capacity, compared with municipalities that have not merged.

REFERENCES

Adamovich, Ivan Baron, and Gerald Hosp. 2003. "Fiscal Federalism for Emerging Economies: Lessons from Switzerland?" *Publius* 33:1–21

Agranoff, Robert. 2002. "Managing Within the Matrix: Do Collaborative Intergovernmental Relations Exist?" *Publius* 31:31–56

Armingeon, Klaus. 2000. "Swiss Federalism in Comparative Perspective." In *Federalism and Political Performance*, ed. Wachendorfer-Schmidt, 112–29. London: Routledge

Austen-Smith, David, and Timothy J. Feddersen. 2002. "Deliberation and Voting Rules." Working paper, Northwestern University, Evanston

Bache, Ian, and Matthew Flinders. 2005. "Themes and Issues in Multi-Level Governance." In *Multi-Level Governance,* ed. Bache and Flinders, 1–11. Oxford: Oxford University Press

Bächtiger, André, and Dominik Hangartner. 2005. "When Political Philosophy Meets Political Science: Theoretical and Methodological Challenges in the Study of a Philosophical Ideal." Paper presented at the Third ECPR General Conference, 8–10 September, Budapest

Bächtiger, André, and Jürg Steiner. 2004. "Switzerland: Territorial Cleavage Management as Paragon and Paradox." In *Federalism and Territorial Cleavages,* ed. Amoretti and Bermeo, 27–54. Baltimore: Johns Hopkins University Press

Bassand, Michel, and Roger Perrinjaquet. 1996. "La politique locale." In *Handbuch Politisches System Schweis.* Vol. 3: Foderalismus, 201–19. Bern: Haupt

Benz, Arthur. 1998. "Politikverflechtung ohne Politikverflechtungsfalle: Koordination und Strukturdynamik im europäischen Mehrebenensystem." *Politische Vierteljahresschrift* 39:558–89

Bischof, Kurt. 1994. "Handeln statt Jammern." Traktandum Magazin 3:7

Bolleyer, Nicole. 2006. "Federal Dynamics in Canada, the U.S., and Switzerland: How Sub-States' Internal Organization Affects Intergovernmental Relations." *Publius* 36 (4): 471-502

Bucher, Erwin. 1977. "Die Bundesverfassung von 1848." In *Handbuch der Schweizer Geschichte*, 2:987–1018. Zürich: Berichthaus

Eidgenössische Finanzverwaltung. 2003. Öffentliche Finanzen der Schweiz 2003. Neuchâtel: Bundesamt für Statistik

Elazar, Daniel J. 1962. *The American Partnership: Intergovernmental Co-operation in the Nineteenth-Century United States*. Chicago: Chicago University Press

– 1987. *Exploring Federalism*. Tuscaloosa: University of Alabama Press

Fleiner, Thomas. 2002. "Recent Development of Swiss Federalism." *Publius* 32:97–123

Frey, Bruno S., and Reiner Eichenberger. 1999. *The New Democratic Federalism for Europe: Functional, Overlapping and Competing Jurisdictions*. Cheltenham, UK, and Northampton, Mass.: Edward Elgar

Gerring, John, Strom C. Thacker, and Carola Moreno. 2005. "Centripetal Democratic Governance: A Theory and Global Inquiry." *American Political Science Review* 99:567–81

Geser, Hans. 1996. "Die Beziehungen der Gemeinde zur kantonalen Ebene. Ein Beitrag im Rahmen des Nationalfondsprojektes." *Aktuelle Wandlungstendenzen und Leistungsgrenzen der Gemeindeorganisation in der Schweiz.* Available online at www.socio.ch/gem/001g.htm (accessed 17 February, 2005)

– 1999. "Die Gemeinden in der Schweiz." In *Handbuch der Schweizer Politik,* ed. Klöti et al., 421–68. Zürich: Verlag Neue Zürcher Zeitung

– 2002. "Die Gemeinden in der Schweiz." In *Handbuch der Schweizer Politik,* ed. Klöti, Kriesi, and Papadopoulos, 421–68. Zürich: Neue Zürcher Zeitung

Geser, Hans, Peter Fargo, Robert Flunder, and Ernst Gräub. 1987. *Gemeindepolitik zwischen Milizorganisation und Berufsverwaltung.* Bern and Stuttgart: Haupt

Geser, Hans, François Höpfliger, Andreas Ladner, and Urs Meulo. 1996. "Die Schweizer Gemeinden im Kräftefeld des gesellschaftlichen und politisch-administrativen Wandels." *Aktuelle Wandlungstendenzen und Leistungsgrenzen der Gemeindeorganisation in der Schweiz.* Zürich: Abschlussbericht des Nationalfondsprojekts No. 12-32586.92

Geser, Hans, Andreas Ladner, Roland Schaller, and Than-Huyen Ballmer-Cao. 1994. *Die Schweizerischen Lokalparteien.* Zürich: Seismo

Geser, Hans et al. 1994. *Die Schweizer Lokalparteien.* Zürich: Seismo

Giacometti, Zaccaria. 1952. "Die rechtliche Stellung der Gemeinden in der Schweiz." In *Die direkte Gemeindedemokratie in der Schweiz,* ed Marcel Bridel. Zürich: Polygraphiques

Hall, Peter A., and David Soskice. 2001. "An Introduction to Varieties of Capitalism." In *Varieties of Capitalism. The Institutional Foundations of Comparative Advantage,* ed. Hall and Soskice, 1–68. Oxford: Oxford University Press

Hänggli, Regula. 2006. "Gemeindefusionen: Ein Beitrag zur Erklärung und Beschreibung institutioneller Reformen." Master's Thesis: Universität Bern

Heger, Matthias. 1990. *Deutscher Bundesrat und Schweizer Ständerat: Gedanken zu ihrer Entstehung, ihrem aktuellen Erscheinungsbild und ihrer Rechtfertigung. Beiträge zum Parlamentsrecht,* Vol. 17. Berlin: Duncker und Humblot

Héritier, Adrienne. 1999. *Policy-Making and Diversity in Europe: Escape from Deadlock.* Cambridge: Cambridge University Press

Horber-Papazian, Katia, and Nils C. Soguel. 1996. "La répartition des tâches canton-communes ou le rendez-vous manqué des réformes." *Swiss Political Science Review* 2:143–64

Hug, Simon, and Pascal Sciarini. 1995. "Switzerland – Still a Paradigmatic Case?" In *Towards a New Europe: Stops and Starts in Regional Integration,* ed. Schneider, Weitsman, and Bernauer, 55–74. Westport, Conn., and London: Praeger

Joye, Dominic. 1995. "Le government métropolitain: entre efficacité technique et démocratie." In *Métropolisations: interdépendances mondiales et implications lémaniques,* ed. Leresche, Joye, and Bassand, 39–157. Geneva: Georg éditeur

Kissling-Näf, Ingrid, and Peter Knoepfel. 1992. "Politikverflechtung dank zentralstaatlichem Immobilismus? Handlungsspielräume kantonaler Vollzugspolitiken im schweizerischen politisch- administrativen System." In *Staatstätigkeit in der Schweiz,* ed. Abromeit and Pommerehne, 43–69. Bern: Haupt

Kloti, Ulrich et al. 1993. "Die Stadt im Bundesstatt – Alleingang oder Zusammenarbeit? Umweltschutz und öffentlicher Verkehr in den Agglomerationen Lausanne und Zürich." In *Zürcher Beiträge zur Politischen Wissenschaft*. Vol. 17. Chur/Zürich: Rüegger AG

Kriesi, Hanspeter. 1995. *Le système politique suisse*. Paris: Economica

– 2001. "The Federal Parliament: The Limits of Institutional Reform." In *The Swiss Labyrinth. Institutions, Outcomes, and Redesign*, ed. Lane, Jan-Erik, 59-76. London: Frank Cass

Kübler, Daniel, Fritz Sager, and Brigitte Schwab. 2005. "Governing without Government: Metropolitan Governance in Switzerland." In *Metropolitan Governance: Capacity, Democracy and the Dynamics of Place*, ed. Hubert Heinelt and Daniel Kübler, 169–87. London: Routledge

Kübler, Daniel, Walter Schenkel, and Jean-Philippe Leresche. 2003. "Bright Lights, Big Cities? Metropolisation, Intergovernmental Relations, and the New Federal Urban Policy in Switzerland." *Swiss Political Science Review* 9:261–82

Ladner, Andreas. 1991. *Politische Gemeinden, kommunale Parteien und lokale Politik: Eine empirische Untersuchung in den Gemeinden der Schweiz*. Zürich: Seismo

– 1994. "Finanzkompetenzen der Gemeinden: ein Überblick über die Praxis." In *Finanzföderalismus*, ed. Franz Eng, Alexnader Glatthard, and Beat H. Koenig. Zürich: Emissionszentrale der Schweizer Gemeinden

Ladner, Andreas, and Reto Steiner. 2003. "Die Schweizer Gemeinden im Wandel: Konvergenz oder Divergenz?" *Swiss Political Science Review* 9: 233–59

Ladner, Andreas et al. 1998. *Gemeindereformen in den Schweizer Kantonen: Konzeptionelle Grundlagen und empirische Ergebnisse einer Kantonsbefragung*. Bern: Institut für Organisation und Personal der Universität Bern

Ladner, Andreas et al. 2000. *Gemeindereform zwischen Handlungsfähigkeit und Legitimation*. Bern: Institut für Politikwissenschaft und Institut für Organisation und Personal der Universität Bern

Linder, Wolf. 2005. *Schweizerische Demokratie: Institutionen – Prozesse – Perspektiven*. 2nd Edn. Bern: Haupt

Lüchinger, Simon, and Alois Stutzer. 2002. "Skalenerträge in der öffentlichen Kernverwaltung: Eine empirische Analyse anhand von Gemeindefusionen." *Swiss Political Science Review* 8:27–50

Marks, Gary. 1993. "Structural Policy and Multilevel Governance in the EC." In *The State of the European Community*, ed. Cafruny and Rosenthal, 391–411. Boulder, Colo: Lynne Rienner

Marks, Gary, and Liesbet Hooghe. 2003. "Unraveling the Central State, but How? Types of Multi-level Governance." *American Political Science Review* 97:233–43

Meylan, Jean. 1987. *Die Schweizer Gemeinden*. Lausanne

Meylan, Jean, Martial Gottraux, and Philippe Dahinden. 1972. *Schweizer Gemeinden und Gemeindeautonomie*. Lausanne: Imp. Populaires

Neidhart, Leonhard. 1970. *Plebiszit und pluralitäre Demokratie: eine Analyse der Funktion des schweizerischen Gesetzesreferendums*. Bern: Francke

– 1975. *Föderalismus in der Schweiz*. Zürich and Köln: Benziger

Nüssli, Kurt. 1985. *Föderalismus in der Schweiz: Konzepte, Indikatoren, Daten*. Grüsch: Rüegger

Sager, Fritz. 2002. *Vom Verwalten des urbanen Raums: Institutionelle Bedingungen von Politikkoordination am Beispiel der Raum – und Verkehrsplanung in städtischen Gebieten*. Bern: Haupt

– 2005. "Metropolitan Institutions and Policy Coordination: The Integration of Land Use and Transport Policies in Swiss Urban Areas." *Governance* 18:227–56

Scharpf, Fritz W. 1988. "The Joint-Decision Trap: Lessons from German Federalism and European Integration." *Public Administration* 66:239–78

– 1997. *Games Real Actors Play: Actor-Centered Institutionalism in Policy Research.* Boulder, Colo: Westview Press

Schenkel, Walter, and Theo Haldemann. 2003. "Schweizerische Agglommerationspolitik: Stillstand oder Bewegung?" In *Politik im Fokus: Festschrift für Ulrich Klöti,* ed. Serdült and Widmer, 143–68. Zürich: Neue Zürcher Zeitung

Schenkel, Walter, and Uwe Serdült. 2002. "Bundesstaatliche Beziehungen." In *Handbuch der Schweizer Politik,* ed. Klöti et al. 469–506. Zürich: Neue Zürcher Zeitung

Steiner, Jürg. 1974. *Amicable Agreement Versus Majority Rule: Conflict Resolution in Switzerland.* Chapel Hill: University of North Carolina Press

Steiner, Jürg, André Bächtiger, Markus Spörndli, and Marco R. Steenbergen. 2004. *Deliberative Politics in Action: Analysing Parliamentary Discourse.* Cambridge: Cambridge University Press

Steiner, Reto. 2002. *Interkommunale Zusammenarbeit und Gemeindezusammenschlüsse in der Schweiz: Erklärungsansätze, Umsetzungsmöglichkeiten und Erfolgsaussichten.* Bern: Haupt

Thürer, Daniel. 1986. *Bund und Gemeinden* (Beiträge zum ausländischen öffentlichen Recht, Vol. 90). Berlin: Springer

– 1995. "Die Stellung der Städte und der Gemeinden im Bundesstaat." *Recht* 5:217–22

Tobler, George. 2002. "Agglomerationspolitik des Bundes: Ziele, Strategien, Massnahmen." *Forum Raumentwicklung* 1:5–7

Trechsel, Alexander H., and Pascal Sciarini. 1998. "Direct Democracy in Switzerland: Do Elites Matter?" *European Journal of Political Research* 33:99–124

Trivelli, Laurent. 1974. *Le bicamérisme, institutions comparées: étude historique, statistique, et critique des rapports entre le Conseil national et le Conseil des Etats.* Thesis. Lausanne: Payot

Vatter, Adrian. 2002. *Kantonale Demokratien im Vergleich: Entstehungsgründe, Interaktionen und Wirkungen politischer Institutionen in den Schweizer Kantonen.* Opladen: Leske and Budrich

Wälti, Sonja. 1996. "Institutional Reform of Federalism: Changing the Players rather than the Rules of the Game." *Swiss Political Science Review* 2:113–41

– 2004. "How Multilevel Structures Affect Environmental Policy in Industrialized Countries." *European Journal of Political Research* 43:599–634

Wiesli, Reto, and Wolf Linder. 2000. *Repräsentation, Artikulation und Durchsetzung kantonaler Interessen in Stände- und Nationalrat.* Bern: Institut für Politikwissenschaft, Universität Bern

FEDERAL-MUNICIPAL RELATIONS IN AUSTRALIA

Douglas M. Brown

1 INTRODUCTION

1.1 FEDERALISM AND LOCAL GOVERNMENT

A number of new realities are challenging traditional perspectives on federalism in the first decade of the new millennium. The boundaries of all states are increasingly porous, and many policy matters increasingly overlap or entail joint responsibilities of governments. Global economic forces are present in everyday local economic transactions, and local government actions can be as important as national or international ones in responding effectively to global competition. This interdependence is challenging – and changing – the role of the nation-state. Policy fields are more naturally concurrent and interdependent; for example, externalities of international trade and competition and of environment extend through all the levels of government in a federation – indeed, beyond them to international governance institutions.

A renewed emphasis on the significance of cities to the globalized economy is also contributing to the changed context in federations. With the focus on urban economic and social development also comes renewed attention to city governance. This inevitably raises the relative importance of local government. In this paper, assume that local government is an important part of what may be termed the governance requirements of competitiveness. However, more important for the federation as a whole may be the effectiveness of local government within a wider system of intergovernmental relations.

Thus, a key reality of the twenty-first century may be more intense multilevel governance, in which policymaking and intergovernmental relationships will span from local to global. For the purposes of this paper, one may define "multilevel governance" simply as the condition of power and authority that is shared in institutional relationships in which the scope of public policy and the mechanisms of policymaking extend by necessity beyond the jurisdiction of a single government (see Marks and Hooghe 2004). In particular, this paper examines whether municipal-federal relations in Australia contribute to multilevel governance in that country in ways that empower local government as a partner and not merely as a dependent or supplicant party. As will be shown, modest but significant movement is being made towards multilevel governance, as a result both of recent developments and of structural features that have been present for decades.

1.2 THE AUSTRALIAN CASE

Compared with many other federal systems, Australia is significantly more centralized in legislative, financial, and programmatic terms. The Commonwealth
(federal) government has a very dominant fiscal position, and many of its transfers to the states are highly conditional. It is responsible directly for social programs
that elsewhere would be designed and delivered by the state or provincial governments – for example, medical care insurance and social assistance (welfare). The
federal government also makes direct transfers to the local governments. The state
governments in turn dominate metropolitan and regional finances and functions,
directly undertaking roles which elsewhere would be devolved to local government, such as policing, education, social and community services, land-use
planning, and public transportation. In some policy fields, local governments act
as agents of the state governments. In sum, the system resembles an inverted
pyramid (see figure 1), with the Commonwealth at the top, the state governments
in the middle, and local governments occupying a relatively small corner of government activity at the bottom.

Still, federalism as a political value remains strong in Australia, particularly in
the more recent context of political and economic liberalization, as many had
perceived the public sphere as being overly centralized and interventionist. None-

Figure 1
Australian Governments: Share of Total Government Expenditure, 2002–3

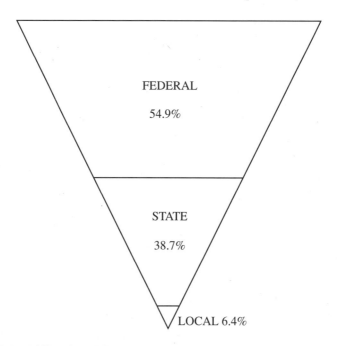

Source: National Office of Local Government 2005

theless, local governments, while relatively stable in fiscal and functional terms, continue to be subordinate. They are vulnerable to attack in terms of democratic integrity and autonomy from the federal government and especially from the state governments (Kiss 2001). Part of the context for this vulnerability is that public policy solutions in Australia continue to take on a flavour of uniformity, stressing equitable national standards. The same public sector values – including, in recent years, thoroughgoing public management reform – extend through all three orders of government. In addition, federal and state funding to local government is strongly conditional and programmatic or, where it is meant for general purposes, comes with conditions concerning equitable redistribution.

Australia as a whole is highly urbanized. What has been called the "mega metro" regions surrounding the state capital cities have retained a stable 70 percent share of the national population since 1981 (ABS census figures cited in O'Connor et al. 2001, table 3.7). Moreover, Sydney has emerged as the foremost globalized city in the South Pacific, and it is also significant in comparison with its hugely dynamic Southeast Asian neighbours. It is an exemplar for the effects of globalization on urban society: multicultural, an advanced postindustrial economy, and a tourist mecca. However, Australia as a whole exhibits a serious case of urban/rural divide in terms of population growth and, more particularly, economic development.

It is notable that despite this urban dynamism (which by no means is confined to Sydney), there are so few metropolitan governments in Australia. The only urban areas to have consolidated metropolitan governance are Brisbane (even though it does not extend to the entire urban area) and the Australian Capital Territory (ACT), where the territorial government is in effect a metropolitan government for Canberra and the surrounding rural municipalities of the ACT. In effect, as will be outlined more fully below, most important urban governance functions in Australia are undertaken by the state governments, all of which, in addition to their dominant capital regions, have extensive hinterlands, which on some issues may be seen as the tails that wag the city dogs.

In summary, Australia is an intriguing and instructive case for the set of federations examined in our research program. It is relatively centralized yet resolutely federal and democratic in spirit; and although it is highly urbanized, local government is not a dominant player in urban decision making. Nonetheless, as discussed in the following sections, there is much to be learned from the Australian experience, including the depth and directness of the federal role in supporting local government, the relative fiscal autonomy of local government entities, their record of innovation and reform in terms of public management, and their modest but important integration into intergovernmental decision making.

2 CONSTITUTIONAL SETTING

2.1. OVERVIEW OF THE AUSTRALIAN FEDERAL SYSTEM

Six self-governing British colonies joined in 1901 to form the Commonwealth of Australia. To the six states were added two territories, the Australian Capital

Territory and the Northern Territory; the total national population in 2005 was approximately 20.4 million. Over its first century the federation engaged in a nation-building process with a strong central government and a political culture that valued uniformity, equity, and national standards. As noted, the population is increasingly urban, with most states dominated by the state's capital city. Yet there is a growing tension between urban and "regional" Australia (the latter consisting of smaller cities, towns, and rural shires, including the outback).

The basic features of the federal Constitution and federal system[1] may be summarized as follows:

- Westminster-type parliamentary institutions providing a fused executive and legislature at both the federal and the state level. The state parliaments have all adopted state constitutions, and all states but Queensland have an upper house.
- No explicit constitutional bill of rights.
- A distribution of powers modelled on the U.S. Constitution with enumerated federal powers, some concurrent with the states, and the residual power to the states. The Australian High Court has interpreted federal powers widely, granting the federal parliament authority to occupy any area of previous state jurisdiction, provided that federal legislation covers the field. The federal parliament has also fully occupied most major tax fields.
- A federal parliament with two houses. The lower House of Representatives is elected by 148 constituencies on a single transferable-vote electoral system; the upper house, the Senate, is elected on state-wide constituencies with equal representation (twelve) per state. Party discipline rather than state loyalties have tended to determine Senate proceedings.
- A seven-member High Court appointed by the federal government with full authority for constitutional judicial review.
- Intergovernmental relations with a strong executive dominance and an extensive network of first ministers', ministers', and officials' meetings. While not constitutionally entrenched, reforms in the 1990s provided a significantly upgraded and rationalized intergovernmental decision-making process. As will be discussed more fully below, there is an important and growing integration of local government representation in the federal-state intergovernmental network.
- In cultural terms, Australian cities are increasingly multicultural as a result of diverse immigration. The rights of the Aboriginal population (2 percent of the national total population), particularly for traditional land use, are gradually being extended. However, one could argue that overall the federation is not as diverse in regional, social, or cultural terms as Canada or the United States.

As emphasized above, Australia is a relatively centralized federation. The constitutional founders adapted the American federal model with its concurrent distribution of legislative competences and the states holding the reserve. With the help of interpretation of the distribution of powers by the High Court, the effect of the concurrent scheme has been significant centralization over time. This has been reinforced by fiscal arrangements in which the states have narrow taxing authority, the Commonwealth has a broad spending power, and the states are dependent on federal transfers for nearly 40 percent of their revenues on average. However, in 1999 the federal and state governments agreed to a major revenue-sharing scheme where all the proceeds of a nationally collected goods and services tax (GST) are divided among the state and territorial governments.

Another notable feature is the system of intergovernmental relations. Of all federations except for the European Union and Germany, Australia may now be judged as having one of the most advanced intergovernmental decision-making systems. In the context of a shared agenda of microeconomic and fiscal reform tied into Australia's competitiveness strategy, Australian governments decided in the early 1990s that they needed to upgrade their intergovernmental mechanisms significantly in order to achieve a more comprehensive and coordinated program of reform. While the initial impulse for reform has passed, the upgraded inter-governmental capacity remains (Painter 1998; Brown 2002). What one can call the Australian model of intergovernmental co-decision consists of the following elements:

- the formal establishment of the Council of Australian Governments (COAG) to meet on an annual basis (the council includes the president of the Australian Local Government Association [ALGA] as a constituent member); [2]
- a parallel leaders' forum of state and territorial first ministers;
- a rationalized and streamlined set of ministerial councils (MCs), under the scrutiny of COAG if not always reporting directly to it (at least one of which also includes ALGA representation);
- MCs that can take binding decisions, backed up by uniform Commonwealth and state legislation;
- voting rules in these MCs that allow the councils to take decisions by majority or qualified majority vote;
- several new joint national agencies in such fields as environment, food standards, road transport, training, and competition policy; and
- coordination through non-centralized devices such as mutual recognition of standards, and negative integration through such policies as national competition.

Contrasted with the unreformed state of Canadian intergovernmental relations, these innovations enable the Australian federation to reach substantive, binding joint decisions. The chief (and significant) caveat is that the new machinery in Australia still requires political will – particularly by the federal prime minister – to make it work. This political will has sometimes been lacking in John Howard's period in office (now in his fourth term since 1996), though it has by no means been absent, as demonstrated by major agreements on the GST, water reform, mutual recognition, gun control, and antiterrorism.

These institutional features of federalism are underpinned by political values that differ somewhat from those of other federal systems, such as Belgium, India, and Canada, but which are nonetheless typical of federalism. Australian society is less diverse than Belgium, India, or Canada, and its regional identities appear to be somewhat less drawn than those in Canada. Overall, the system places an emphasis on national uniformity, fairness, and equity, while recognizing the virtues of citizen responsiveness and liberty through the dual occupancy of sovereignty (Galligan 1995). The development of national integration and nation building over the past century has led to what political scientist Campbell Sharman calls a "closed, bureaucratic and collusive" type of intergovernmental relations, able to adopt more comprehensive cooperative schemes than other federal systems (Sharman 1991). As noted, there is no constitutionally entrenched bill of rights, and there is far less use of rights discourse in the political culture than in some other federations.

2.2 CONSTITUTIONAL AND LEGAL BASIS FOR LOCAL GOVERNMENT

Local governments have never been considered as fully constitutional federal partners in Australia. Legally they are creations of the state governments. Yet local government has existed in some states since the 1840s – in some cases, even before the colonies themselves attained responsible government. The emerging cities were all incorporated by the 1860s, and general multipurpose local authority systems became established at the same time. All municipal government is now governed by the various states' Local Government Acts, as well as by other state statutes.

Local government advocates have pushed to have the roles and functions of municipalities protected by the federal and state constitutions. They received a reasonable hearing in federal constitutional review exercises in 1969–83 (the on-again, off-again Australian Constitutional Convention [ACC]) and in 1985–88 (the federal government's Constitutional Commission). The ACC was initiated by the states, seeking broader fiscal and economic powers. However, the federal Labor government under Prime Minister Gough Whitlam (1972–75) sought, if anything, a further diminishing of the role of the states – indeed, promoted regional government and a direct relationship with local government as a way of undermining state influence. Thus, the Whitlam government agreed to participate in the states' ACC only on condition that local governments also be represented. In the ensuing discussions, the federal government sought reform, among other things, to confirm a federal role in borrowing on behalf of local governments and to make direct fund transfers to them as the federal parliament saw fit (Coper 1988, 355). Thus, two specific amendments to the Constitution, related to borrowing (s.51(ivA)) and to the spending power (s. 96), were proposed in the national referendum of May 1974. However, along with three other proposals that were unrelated to local government, these amendments did not receive the required support to proceed, albeit by a relatively narrow margin of 53 percent opposed nationally (Mathews and Grewal 1997, 72). In the context of significant federal-state and party rivalry, the Whitlam referendum proposals were cast by the conservative parties and state governments as a Commonwealth power grab.

A similar fate befell the next attempt to include local government in the federal Constitution. The 1988 referendums put to the people, among other things, a proposed amendment, as recommended by the Constitutional Commission, to add a new section 119A, which called upon each state (but not the territories) to "establish" and to "continue" local government bodies but stipulated that their elections and their legal authorities were to be in accordance with state law. In other words, the amendment would have provided bare symbolic recognition and would hardly have been a charter for local autonomy. The proposal received about 33 percent support nationally, following a referendum campaign in which neither the Hawke federal government nor the states exhibited enthusiasm for the measure (Galligan 1995, 126–32).

Despite the failure of efforts to recognize local government in the federal Constitution, the general advocacy did have a more positive outcome at the state level. All the states have separate written constitutions, and all of them were amended in the 1970s and 1980s to provide for the general recognition of the status and role of local government. Rosemary Kiss describes the general tenor of these state constitutional provisions:

> Each state's Constitution Act provides that there shall be or continue to be a system of local government in the state, [e.g., section 74A *Constitution Act 1975* (Victoria); section 54(1) *Constitution Act* (Queensland)]. This does not mean, however, that the constitutions guarantee the continued existence of local governments. Every constitution expressly provides for the suspension and dismissal of individual councils and for appointees to perform the functions of local government. (Kiss 2001, 10)

In any case, if there was any doubt, the state constitutions' grant of general power to the state legislatures makes it doubly clear that any state legislation shall prevail over local government enactments.

Finally, there has been a trend in the 1990s in some states (e.g., Victoria and Tasmania) to provide greater regulatory autonomy through a more general legal expression of the scope of municipal powers (Tasmania 1996; Mathews and Grewal 1997). These provisions have been undermined, however, by detailed reporting prescriptions. For example, senior governments in Australia have included local government in broad-sweeping microeconomic reform aimed at creating a more competitive public sector (as discussed more fully below). In the State of Victoria, municipalities continue to seek more extensive constitutional protections. In general, only Queensland seems to stand out in terms of allowing somewhat more leeway to local government and greater protection against state government intervention. These more liberal provisions are located in its *Local Government Act* – but not in the Queensland constitution (Kiss 2001).

3 RANGE OF LOCAL GOVERNMENT FUNCTIONS AND RESPONSIBILITIES

Local government functions are shaped by three key characteristics: a narrow initial allocation of functions, a conservative disposition to municipal consolidation, and the strong influence of intergovernmental relationships. As noted above, the state governments assume directly many functions that are assumed by local governments in other federations. The key remaining functions are local streets

(but not highways), sewers (but not trunk systems), garbage and waste management generally, local utilities (in some states), building and food inspection, public
health, local environmental management and planning, and recreation and parks.
Local governments are also used as agents to deliver state programs, such as sports
and recreation, cultural services, and land use planning. Other functions are shared
with the state and federal governments, and require extensive negotiation, including major roads, utilities and water supply, environment, and some aspects of
housing and community services. There is some variation among the states and
territories, with local government in Queensland, rural New South Wales, and
Tasmania being responsible for water and sewer, for example (May 2003; NOLG
2005).

The narrower allocation of functions results in a smaller share for local government expenditures in terms of the public sector, or as a percentage of gross domestic
product – again when compared with other federations.[3] For 2002–03, for example, local government expenditures amounted to only 2.3 percent of GDP and
only 6.4 percent of total government expenditures. This compares with the states
making 38.7 percent of total government expenditures, and the Commonwealth
54.9 percent.[4] The inverted triangle is even more pronounced for the revenue
figures, with local government levying directly only 3.02 percent of the Australian total, the states 15.3 percent, and the Commonwealth 81.8 percent – although
the federal share includes the GST revenue, which it passes on entirely to the
states, as will be discussed below (NOLG 2005, tables 1.13 and 1.14). Of course,
there is considerable variation among municipalities and within and between states
as to per capita expenditures and revenues in the local government sector. For
example, in the more densely populated State of Victoria, local government spends
Aus$ 820 per capita, whereas in more sparsely populated Queensland (where
local government has more to do in any case) the per capita expenditures are
$1,226. The national average is $916 (figures are for 2002–03, see NOLG 2005).

The pattern of urban development has been crucial to the comparatively small
role of local government as such. Over 85 percent of the population now lives in
cities. With the exceptions of the Gold Coast area of Queensland and the federal
capital, this development has been mainly in the state capitals of Perth, Brisbane,
Adelaide, Hobart, Melbourne, and Sydney. In all these cities development has
been highly suburban, based on a general preference for single-home ownership.
The pattern of local government is for a consolidated but rather small core city,
surrounded by a patchwork of suburban councils. The core cites are now little
more than the central business districts (similar to the official City of London in
relation to metropolitan London), where business interests usually dominate the
municipality. By far the largest share of the population lives in the surrounding
suburban municipalities. In total, in all of Australia there are currently only approximately 720 local government councils, about 90 of which are Aboriginal
and Torres Strait Islander community councils. Of the 720, about 22 percent are
urban and 78 percent rural (NOLG 2005).

Municipal consolidation and amalgamation has occurred across several states,
principally those in the grip of major economic retrenchment and restructuring in
the 1990s, namely, Tasmania, South Australia, and Victoria. The latter state reduced

the numbers of local governments in the 1990s from 210 to 78 (May 2003; Australia 2003, 83). However, there has been no significant movement either to the megacity or to extensive regional intercouncil arrangements. Instead – and one might say by design – it is the state government itself that assumes the functions of (often coercive) coordination of overlapping responsibilities (Chapman and Wood 1984). As a result, and especially when compared with the United States, there is less room for strong interlocal competition.

4 THE FISCAL FRAMEWORK

The federal Constitution makes no explicit provisions for local government either to tax or to spend. Rather, these powers are wholly delegated to local governments by State law. (Note the brief discussion above of the failed attempt in 1974 to amend the federal Constitution. This would have strengthened the federal parliament's powers to make direct transfers to local bodies and to borrow funds on their behalf.) Despite the lack of constitutional provision, local government revenues have remained relatively stable for several decades, at about 1.2 percent of GDP. Own-source revenues (widely defined) account for over 87 percent of the total, compared with intergovernmental transfers at approximately 13 percent. In the figures provided in table 1, where local own-source revenues are defined by the IMF somewhat more narrowly, the 1997 proportion of grants to total local revenues is 16.3 percent. Since the mid-1980s, a reduction in the rate of growth in transfers has been partly met by increased own-source revenues, especially user fees, but this is not enough to correct what has become a modest but chronic aggregate deficit at the local government level (Mathews and Grewal, 1997). Of their own revenues, property taxes are by far the most important source at 69 percent (the figure is 100 percent in the IMF data that excludes user fees, as shown in table 2). When

Table 1
Australia: Government Revenue, including Grants, 1997

	Aus$ millions	*Percent*
Federal government: total	134,579	
Federal government: grants	–	–
State governments: total	90,969	
State governments: grants	35,656	39.10
Local governments: total	12,177	
Local governments: grants	1,986	16.30

Source: IMF 2000

Table 2
Australia: Revenue Distribution by Major Tax Type, 1991

	Income	Property	Goods/Services	Other
% Federal Revenue	71.9	0.3	22.8	5.1
% State Revenue	0	30.1	40.9	28.9
% Local Revenue	0	100	0	0

Source: Norregaard 1997, table 3

one combines the unconditional nature of most (66 percent) of the transfer funds from the Commonwealth (a sum about twice as large as the total of all state grants to local government) with the substantial record on own-source revenue, Australian local government would rank among the most autonomous in a survey of OECD countries (Caulfield 2003). Indeed, in terms of the vertical fiscal gap, local government – despite its more limited responsibilities at the small end of the inverted pyramid of Australian government (see figure 1) – is more fiscally autonomous than the states are in the overall federal system.

There has been considerable public policy debate and change with regard to the tax system in Australia in the past fifteen years (e.g., introduction of the GST, reform of other business taxes, abolition of several regressive state taxes, and the flattening and simplifying of the income tax). Municipal property rates have also been controversial, but the more problematic issue for local government is the fact that the states in general reap even more from property than the municipalities do. The states, however, raise their funds in the form of property sales transactions and financial and other capital transactions.

Of the intergovernmental transfers, the Commonwealth provides the largest set of payments. Key features include the following:

- The largest transfer is designated as "general purpose assistance" (GPA). It began in 1974–75 as a 2 percent share of federal income tax revenue, and since then has been tied into the general system of transfers to the states, with a formula for escalation for inflation and economic growth. The level of funding has been judged to have been maintained in real dollar terms since the mid-1980s, with the exception of modest cuts in 1996–97 as part of broader budget reductions (Johnson 2003, 53).
- The GPA is made to the states, on condition that they pass through the entire funds to the local governments. Both the block of funds to the states and the allocation to local governments within the states are subject to equalization formulas, the former through the Commonwealth Grants Commission, the latter through State Grant Commissions, set up along national standards.[5]

- The general purpose assistance is delivered in a program entitled Financial Assistance Grants (FAGs) in two separate funds, one totally untied, which in the financial year 2005–6 was estimated at Aus\$1,127 million; the other a loosely conditional fund for 'identified road grants," at Aus\$500 million (ALGA 2006).
- The federal government also makes a variety of conditional Specific Purpose Payments directly to local governments, totalling about Aus\$440 million in 2005–6 (for both current and capital outlays). These grants cover such social services as municipally run child care, aged and disabled persons care, and programs for Aboriginals.

As noted, state transfers to local government are about one-half the size of the overall federal transfers, and they tend to be highly program specific, for such purposes as roads, housing, libraries, aged-care facilities, and recreation and culture. Otherwise the states have a complex financial relationship with local government through such instruments as subsidized loan interest on approved infrastructure borrowing programs; ad hoc capital grants for infrastructure; and exemption from state payroll, land, and other taxes. In turn, local governments provide the state governments with shared levies for fire protection, planning, and other purposes. Neither the federal nor the state governments appear to make payments in lieu of taxes for their property within municipal boundaries.

While the overall fiscal framework has changed only incrementally in the past decade, there are several emergent fiscal issues of concern to local government that figure prominently in intergovernmental relations (for a good summary, see Johnson 2003, 41–53). A chronic problem for local government with respect especially to the state governments is the growing occurrence of what in the U.S. literature (and increasingly in Australia) is referred to as "unfunded mandates." These are especially onerous now in terms of state legislative and regulatory requirements on local government in the fields of planning, environment, and waste management. A more recent problem, termed "cost-shifting" by local governments, seems to incorporate unfunded mandates, but it also relates to the cutbacks of state or federal funding for previously funded and relatively mature programs delivered by local government in such areas as community security, fire services, health, welfare, libraries, and airports. These funding cuts leave local councils with the difficult choice of cutting services or raising new revenues (Australia 2003, 25–38). As with unfunded mandates, this is a worldwide problem. Recently it was the subject of an extensive federal parliamentary inquiry, the Hawker Report (Australia 2003). Infrastructure funding is another important current concern, but one now involving very substantial intergovernmental cooperation (discussed below). In addition, more or less perennial problems, some of which may be perceived as worsening in the current decade, include the lack of transparency in state to local funding, the inelasticity of local property tax revenues, and concern about the escalation or growth formula and the interstate distribution of the major federal transfer, the FAGs.

5 FEDERAL-LOCAL RELATIONS

5.1 BRIEF HISTORY, SCOPE, AND DYNAMICS OF FEDERAL-LOCAL INTERACTION

The Commonwealth government takes a strong interest in both urban and rural development. This interest goes back to 1920s programs for roads, but the most activist federal government since Federation has been the Labor government of Gough Whitlam, 1972–75. His government's political objectives were complex, but they seem to have included a deliberate attempt to outflank the states by appealing directly to local government and by creating a regional administrative structure of its own. This reflected a traditional position of hostility to federalism by the Australian Labor Party (Galligan 1995; Mathews and Grewal 1997). As noted, the Whitlam government introduced the payment of general-purpose funds to local governments and sought, unsuccessfully, to amend the Constitution to entrench a federal role in local government finance. Also it began to spend heavily in state-local programs such as housing, urban social services, public transport, and recreation. Transfers to local government from the federal government doubled in four years – all aimed at promoting greater equity in services. A new federal Department of Urban and Regional Development undertook a wide array of direct federal programs as well, for "growth centres, land acquisition and development, area improvement and a national sewerage program" (Mathews and Grewal 1997). The Fraser (conservative coalition) government (1975–83) retreated from such programming and ended overtly hostile moves towards the states. It continued the basic, general-purpose financial support to local government, but made the payments "through" the states on condition that the states establish State Grants Commissions to allocate the funds at arm's length from the Commonwealth and state governments.

The Hawke-Keating Labor governments of 1983–96, inheriting large economic and fiscal problems, accomplished a significant amount of microeconomic, fiscal, and intergovernmental reform. Their incursions into urban and local affairs were selective but important. They continued a strong federal presence in housing programs (delivered generally by the state governments, not the local), and the Building Better Cities program, again with a strong intergovernmental component of capital grants for social and physical infrastructure. On the broader intergovernmental front, Prime Minister Hawke initiated a series of special premiers' conferences in 1991, ultimately leading to the creation of the Council of Australian Governments (COAG) in 1992. As noted above, COAG includes the first ministers of the Commonwealth, state and territorial governments as well as the president of the Australian Local Government Association (ALGA). Particularly in 1992–95, COAG led a highly coordinated and integrated set of economic and public-sector reform processes, to which numerous federal-state ministerial councils reported.

While the current conservative coalition government (since 1996) under Prime Minister Howard maintains these intergovernmental mechanisms, it tends to take a more standoff attitude to local government. Yet on rural issues in particular, the prime minister is faced with a restive coalition partner in the National Party, which is under pressure to reverse the economic decline of "regional" Australia. This has had the effect of a distinct federal emphasis on rural and regional funding.

In more general fiscal policy terms, the Howard government proposed in 1998 to roll GPA payments (i.e., the lion's share of the FAGs to local government) into overall state funding, as part of the negotiations over the introduction of the GST. However, the federal government relented in the face of widespread local government pressure, but not before raising considerable worry among local government about the stability of this key funding relationship and the long-term nature of the federal commitment to local government (interview with Rosemary Kiss, University of Melbourne, July 2004). Finally, and most recently, in June 2004 the Howard government announced a major renewal of its Roads to Recovery infrastructure program, costed in the 2005–6 federal budget at approximately Aus$1.4 billion over four years to 2008–9.

5.2 ORGANIZATION OF FEDERAL-LOCAL RELATIONS

Due in large part to the smallness of local government entities, especially in the cities and in comparison with many other countries, Australian local government relies heavily on its organized representative bodies for relations with the federal government. Only rarely are there formal or bilateral discussions between elected mayors and councillors (or municipal managers) with federal cabinet ministers or departmental officials, although informal meetings occur frequently with local federal MPs.

The ALGA is a federation of the associations of municipalities of every state and the Northern Territory. Its board of directors comprises two representatives of each of the state and territorial local government associations. The Australian Capital Territory, which represents its local governments directly, also sends two representatives to the board of directors. The president and two vice-presidents of the ALGA are elected, by the annual national general assembly, from among the state and territorial delegates of local government associations. These associations in turn are composed of elected officials (e.g. mayors or councillors) from each of the 730 municipalities in Australia. Thus, the president and other senior executives of the ALGA are all elected officials from one or other of these local governments.

The ALGA seems to have achieved legitimacy as the sole and credible voice of local government interests throughout Australia. Of course, the president of the ALGA cannot speak authoritatively for all individual local governments in intergovernmental forums in the same way as the first ministers can speak for their governments. In any case, most of the specific COAG commitments and undertakings do not apply directly to local government, though some very important ones do. For example, the microeconomic reform agenda has been extended to the local sector, both on its own initiative and through conditions placed on funding and, in some states, by political fiat.

The ALGA receives support from (and its work in general is buttressed by) the National Office of Local Government (NOLG), part of the federal Department of

Transport and Regional Services (DOTAS). In addition, this federal agency convenes an annual meeting of the State Grant Commissions. The NOLG, as an arm of the federal bureaucracy, is somewhat less visible within the federal ministry structure than the former Department of Urban and Regional Government of the Labor governments of the 1970s. However, the NOLG has survived, albeit within a series of larger departments, through many government changes since its establishment by the Fraser Liberal-National coalition government in 1979. Its current home within DOTAS reflects the Howard government's priorities with respect to local government on regional infrastructure and services, especially roads.

Since the ALGA took its seat at COAG in 1995, it has also been represented at the Local Government and Planning Ministerial Council. This council has made some important intergovernmental strides, including the completion of a national review of local government labour markets (Baker 2003, 121). However, until recently, the trilevel intergovernmental relationship lacked much in the way of structure. A federal House of Representatives committee examined, inter alia, the nature of these relationships (Australia 2003). It recommended that COAG – i.e., the first ministers – negotiate a broad intergovernmental agreement to better identify local government roles and responsibilities, establish policy priorities, allocate funds, and improve performance. It further recommended that COAG host a summit on intergovernmental relations, with the express purpose of bringing state governments to heel on such issues as their grants to local government and measures to reduce cost-shifting. The report was met initially with some skepticism in state circles, and the Howard government chose to assuage local government concerns with the increased funding to infrastructure that is discussed below (interviews with senior officials, Municipal Association of Victoria and the Department of Infrastructure, Victoria government, July 2004; and with Rosemary Kiss, University of Melbourne, July 2004).

However, the idea of a federal-state-local intergovernmental agreement did get taken up by the Local Government and Planning Ministerial Council, which includes the ALGA, as noted. In April 2006 the council reached an "Inter-Governmental Agreement Establishing Principles to Guide Inter-Governmental Relations on Local Government Matters."[6] While meant to establish a framework of broad principles for later more specific agreements, this new agreement seems to mark a significant milestone in the extension of the Australian intergovernmental apparatus and culture to local government. It stresses the need for federal and state governments to take more care in assessing the financial impact on local government when mandating or otherwise agreeing with them to provide a federal or state legislated public service or good. The new agreement should provide for a greater degree of transparency, planning, and mutual consensus for locally delivered roles and responsibilities, and it should also provide some leverage for the local government sector in continuing consultations and negotiations at the national level.

In sum, the municipalities of Australia have well-functioning organizations with a growing capacity to be significant actors in national policy debates and deliberations. Their participation in the pinnacle of executive federalism of COAG, through the ALGA, is much more than token representation, and they seem to be making strides towards integrated decision making. Nonetheless, key limitations remain, as illustrated more clearly in the two policy cases discussed later in this paper.

6 SUMMARY CHARACTERIZATION OF MUNICIPAL-FEDERAL INTERACTION

As the above discussion makes clear, municipal-federal interaction mainly falls within a category of *nonhierarchical interdependence*. The local government sector has a significant financial relationship with the Commonwealth, but one in which it enjoys a reasonable degree of discretion over expenditures – indeed, full discretion over the largest portion of federal transfers. This relationship differs significantly, as outlined below, from the municipal-state dimension, which can be characterized as *hierarchical interdependence*, marked by heavily conditional financial transfers and a strongly supervisory and regulatory role for state governments.

In areas where local government remains independent, this independence seems to have little impact by way of direct competition with the federal government. Rather, competition tends to occur in the municipal-state dimension and, of course, in the state-federal. In any case, the overall tendency in Australia, compared with federations such as Canada and the United States, is for cooperative and coordinated federalism rather than competitive federalism.

7 STATE GOVERNMENTS AND THE MEDIATING ROLE

As noted already, state governments take a dominant role in urban affairs as well as in specific regional and rural development. A recent example is the successful bid and implementation of the 2000 Olympic Games in Sydney, which was almost entirely a state-run affair. The Government of New South Wales passed the legislation, coordinated the bid, provided and managed the budget and the infrastructure, and took over the local organizing committee (in which the local governments per se played only a minimal role) when it looked as if facilities would not be ready on time. Federal funding to the Games went to the state government, not to the city or cities. In general, the states run directly many public services that elsewhere are associated with local government, such as police, housing, and welfare; and for all the major cities, it is the state government that delivers directly the major urban infrastructure (Murphy and Wu 2001, 407). State transfers to local government tend to be disaggregated across departments and are, highly project-specific and conditional. Indeed, some state budget documents – those of New South Wales, for example – provide no consolidated information on transfers to local government at all (New South Wales 2004).[7] Nonetheless, the most important role of the states towards local government is regulatory: departments of local government tend to be overseers of municipal councils, rather than funding agencies.

While state agencies pursue various bilateral relations with individual municipalities, all states have peak associations empowered by statute to represent the interests of local government, as noted above. In Tasmania there is also a "premier's forum" in which the premier meets quarterly with the executive of the state-wide municipal association (elected mayors or councillors). In some states, such as Victoria, the peak municipal body has signed protocols with key state departments to ensure that its view is considered apart from the regular interest-group consultations.

The peak municipal bodies, both state and national, are wholly independent of the state governments as such. State governments do not attempt to coordinate local government input to the national (federal) level. They play no overseeing role; nor, it seems, do they make any significant effort to influence or steer the state-wide municipal associations in their relations with Canberra. This does not mean that municipal-state relations do not affect federal-municipal relations. Of course they do. But there is an acceptance, if not always an enthusiasm, among the state and territorial governments that the local government associations will pursue their own relationship with the federal government and have a place at selected intergovernmental tables. And there is the realization on all sides that on some issues the local government representatives will seek to exploit state-federal differences to their own advantage.

How, then, do state-local relations – described above as essentially hierarchical – fit with federal-state and federal-local relations that are increasingly nonhierarchical? For much of Australia's history up to the 1990s, intergovernmental relations were in three separate spheres – a three-ring circus with little overlap. With the creation of COAG and the ALGA's participation in the Local Government and Planning Ministerial Council, there is considerable potential now for the three rings to overlap and occasionally to join up, if not to become fully integrated. This occurs because, while the states retain a dominant and often domineering role with respect to the local governments within their jurisdiction, they have not been able to assert this dominance as a monopoly on mediating local interests on the national scene. On the contrary, the federal government has developed a direct relationship (notably, through fiscal transfers) with local governments, assisted significantly by a strong national peak organization, the ALGA.

Finally, a few comparative comments help place the state mediating role in context. Unlike Canada's provincial governments, the Australian state governments have not been very successful at keeping federal intrusion at bay, a fact that limits their mediating role. Unlike Germany, state governments are not directly represented in the federal parliament. However, like the United States, they do have significant informal power through integrated state and federal party structures, but these relations are limited by the norms of executive federalism. These norms are for a weak to non-existent role for ordinary federal, state, or local legislators in intergovernmental relations (unlike the stronger roles in the U.S. system). In particular, the elected federal senators from each state have traditionally not held strong state government briefs, although they do reflect state and regional preferences, within the confines of strong party discipline.

8 THE FOREIGN RELATIONS OF LOCAL GOVERNMENTS

It would be a stretch to characterize local government in Australia as playing any significant role in foreign relations. Municipal government functions are too constrained and metropolitan government too undeveloped for city governments to become major transnational players as they are in Europe or North America. The state governments assume the kinds of role in international exchange and promotion that match those of a New York, Frankfurt, or Toronto (Ravenhill 1990). That said, in the larger state capitals the central city governments have been drawn into some internationally focused activities, such as tourism and trade and investment promotion. For example, the City of Melbourne has a twinning arrangement with New Delhi (i.e., both were host cities of the Commonwealth Games); and the City of Sydney is active in the International Council for Local Environment Initiatives.

9 THE POLITICAL DIMENSION OF THE MUNICIPAL-FEDERAL RELATIONSHIP

In political terms, municipal government in Australia fits into what has been termed the "anglo model": self-governing entities, constrained but not normally dictated to by senior governments, with directly elected officials (mayors and councillors) and independent public servants; that is, they are not part of a larger national or state-run bureaucratic hierarchy (Sancton 2002). In three states – Queensland, New South Wales, and Victoria – voting in local elections is compulsory (as it is in all state and federal elections across Australia). Moreover, local councils and mayors in Australia, with some exceptions, do not take on partisan labels, and party politics plays no significant role in local elections as such. Elected office is on a fixed term basis, meaning that local elections are not held simultaneously with state and federal elections, because the latter do not have fixed terms and therefore their elections can be called at any time.

Owing to the absence of organized party politics, the same basis for political integration through party allegiances with the state or federal parties is dissimilar to that in some other federations (for example, Germany and the United States). Nonetheless, local politics is often a stepping stone to state and federal elected office; and as noted above, local issues are interpreted somewhat differently by the two major federal parties. When the Australian Labor Party is in power federally, it has been more activist with respect to urban development, sometimes in cooperation and sometimes in competitive relations with the states. By contrast, when the coalition (Liberal and National) parties are in power, they have been more active on regional rather than urban issues.

10 BRIEF POLICY CASES OF FEDERAL-LOCAL RELATIONS

10.1 INFRASTRUCTURE FUNDING

While the direct federal role in the provision of urban infrastructure has declined over the past three decades, targeted federal initiatives continue to be negotiated and implemented. As noted, the Labor federal government that was in office until 1996 initiated the Building Better Cities program, with specific-purpose conditional grant funding both to state governments and, through the states, to local governments, covering a variety of housing, recreation, cultural, and related programs. These programs have been maintained in general terms through specific-purpose payments through the state governments.

The current federal government's newer initiatives tend to be targeted to "regional" (i.e., non-urban) Australia, which includes the smaller cities and towns, remote resource and farming communities, and the "outback" in general. A major issue has emerged in recent years over the level and quality of services to regional Australia. This has occurred as the Australian population becomes increasingly urban and as the role of government as a whole has declined, both in the direct provision of goods and services – for example, through state-owned monopolies for air and rail transport, electricity, and telecommunications – and in the liberalized regulatory structure of private markets (Gray and Lawrence 2001). In response, a political coalition of rural municipalities, resource industries, and the National Party (the latter being the minor partner of the Howard government coalition in the federal parliament) has emerged to fight back for regional services. This coalition of regional interests has been especially concerned with the effect of public sector reform, especially privatization, on service availability and access. A prime example has been the ongoing debate over the conditions to be placed on the final privatization of the once wholly publicly owned telephone utility, Telstra. Nonetheless, the most pressing infrastructure need identified by virtually all local governments in regional Australia continues to be road construction, repair, and maintenance.

Urban infrastructure needs are also pressing, as local and state governments face constrained fiscal capacity, as infrastructure built in the mid-twentieth century requires replacement, and as there is an increasing need to deal with urban congestion and growth, particularly in Sydney, Melbourne, and the urban area of southeast Queensland (Murphy and Wu 2001, 415–17). Yet while the Howard government sees political capital to be gained by investing in rural (and resource export) transportation infrastructure, it has jumped less quickly to assist the state governments in their task of directly delivering key aspects of urban infrastructure, notably major highways and public transit, including commuter railways. The latter were under state control through direct ownership until recently.

Since the early 1990s, many of the larger investments in urban roads in particular have been through state-based public-private partnerships that entailed considerable controversy. Critics charge, among other things, that private funding and/or the operation of major highways (usually involving tollways), for example, reduces the strategic capacity of the state governments to plan and execute overall infrastructure needs (Murphy and Wu 2001). In any case, an additional political factor in the lack of direct federal support for urban infrastructure has been the unusual conjunction during the past several years of all eight state and territorial governments being led by the Australian Labor Party, which is in opposition in the federal parliament. One might surmise that, as urban infrastructure tends to be heavily associated with the political fortunes of the state governments, the conservative federal coalition government has left them to their fate.

In any case, funding to local governments for roads remains the most important form of federal infrastructure support. It has come in two ways. First, as noted above, a portion of the otherwise unconditional funding in the FAGs program is devoted to untied roads funding. This was as much as Aus$365 million in 1997–98, growing to $500 million in 2005–6. These funds, as part of the FAGs, come to local governments through the states and have been allocated not only by the interstate equalization methodology of the Commonwealth Grants Commission but also by individual State Grant Commissions for equalized allocation within states. Through this program, the State of Victoria, for example, received $103 million in funding in 2005–6 to allocate to local councils, which spend as they see fit.

The second major program is the Roads to Recovery (R2R) program, announced by the Commonwealth in 2000, which from 1 January 2001 to the end of 2004 spent an initial $1.2 billion. Highly popular politically, the program was renewed in June 2004 for another four years at a second $1.2 billion, which has since been budgeted at approximately $1.4 billion to 2008–9. The program funds local government directly, without a state role, allocating funds according a formula based on historical needs (from the FAG formula), road lengths, and state population. Compared with the FAG program, R2R entails a bigger and more direct federal role, including the requirement of uniform standard data gathering as a condition of funding. Moreover it is the Commonwealth government that ultimately decides on the size of the pool and its allocation among the local councils (interview with senior official, Municipal Association of Victoria, July 2004; see also Australia 2003, 57–74). However, the program is said to be simpler for local government than the FAG-based one; it was negotiated with the heavy involvement of state-based municipal associations (led, it seems, by the dynamic Municipal Association of Victoria) and by the national peak body, ALGA. Certainly, observers see the R2R program as delivering considerable branding and credit for the Commonwealth government (interviews with senior official, Municipal Association of Victoria, and with Rosemary Kiss, University of Melbourne, July 2004).

Federal involvement in infrastructure continues to evolve with the establishment of "Auslink" (first proposed in November 2002), a federal agency designed to consolidate programs and federal support for all land-based transport systems, responding in particular to concerns about getting resource products to world markets. The municipal lobby has been satisfied thus far that the Auslink plans will not dilute their existing funding arrangements for roads, and the states seem cautiously optimistic that intergovernmental agreement can be reached on the many coordination issues (ALGA 2003; 2004). Funding and regulatory issues surrounding Auslink and transportation infrastructure in general were on the agenda of the Council of Australian Governments, meeting in June 2005.

Since the late 1980s, Australian governments have undertaken a wide-ranging agenda of microeconomic reform to increase the size and competitiveness of the national economic union, mainly to improve international competitiveness (Brown 2002). The objective has been to increase competition in labour markets, in agricultural and other inputs to industry, and in the provision of public goods and services. The agenda has included much privatization, deregulation, and provision of national infrastructure. Since 1995 the agenda has been expanded gradually to include the local government sector. Initiatives being pursued by local governments – with varying degrees of intensity and success, depending on the state – include the contracting-out of services, financial management reforms, commercialization of functions, the enforcement of competitive bidding on the procurement of goods and services, and the adoption of standardized performance measurement (Australia, Productivity Commission 1997).

These competition reforms are part of the broader movement, in which Australia and New Zealand were enthusiastic participants, of what has been called "new public management" (Aucoin1995; Hood 1996; Pollitt 1998). The interesting feature about both Australia and New Zealand is how thoroughgoing the adoption of reforms has been, and how a uniform ideology and wide-scale standardization and desire for uniformity extends to multiple levels of government. Financial reporting is but one important example of this, where federal-state agreement was, it would seem, achieved readily in the 1990s on uniform standards for the adoption of accrual accounting by all public entities in Australia, including local government (Ryan 2003).

More broadly, these reforms have encouraged such local government practices as competitive tendering for the procurement of goods and services, performance measurement and assessment, contracting-out of services, corporatization of utilities, deregulation of labour relations, and market pricing mechanisms, among others (Australia, Productivity Commission 1997; Caulfield, 2003). The most prominent device for reforms, the National Competition Policy, was the result of extensive federal-state negotiation, allowing each state considerable flexibility to achieve the overall goal of competitive neutrality in the public provision of goods and services (especially important in utilities such as gas, water, and electricity, and in rail transport) (Brown 2002). In return for adopting an integrated policy approach to competition policy, including the establishment of a major new national regulatory watchdog and extensive Commonwealth legislation that is binding on all the states, the states received compensation and adjustment funds of Aus \$2.4 billion over eight years. Through these arrangements, states were able to negotiate or dictate competition reform onto the local government sector, employing such broad options as full cost pricing, commercialization, and corporatization (which of course included in some cases privatization and the sell-off of public corporations). While local government representatives were at the table, they had small bargaining power over the timing and extent of the application of competition policy to their sector. For example, there is no indication that they played an important role in the initial bargaining over the National Competition Policy in 1993–95.

Observers have compared the different approaches of Victoria and Queensland to the implementation of competition reforms by local government. The Kennett government (1992–99) in Victoria adopted a basically Thatcherist approach to the public sector and, like the United Kingdom government, imposed the microeconomic reform agenda (including a heavy emphasis on cost cutting) onto local government, engendering considerable conflict in the process (Hughes and O'Neill 2000; Baker 2003; Kiss 2001). In particular, the Victoria government's imposition of compulsory competitive tendering was seen as misguided and later had to be withdrawn. The Queensland approach seems to have been more cooperative and gradual, targeted to those local governments with heavier service responsibilities in key utility fields, including the Brisbane City Council, the largest municipality in the country. Queensland also decided to pass on to local governments a part of the compensation payments provided by the Commonwealth (Australia, 2003, 45–7), one of the few states to do so. While this discussion cannot attempt a full comparative assessment, there does not seem now to be an enormous difference in the efficiency and performance of the local government sectors in the two states, but at least one observer notes that values of local autonomy and democracy have been more fully preserved in Queensland (Kiss 2001; also Baker 2003).

11 CONCLUSIONS AND ASSESSMENT

To conclude, we return to the questions posed at the outset: Do federal-municipal relations contribute to multilevel governance in Australia and, if so, does this governance preserve or diminish local government autonomy? In addition, as outlined in the introduction to this volume, Leuprecht and Lazar seek summary assessments with respect to various criteria by which developments in intergovernmental relations may be judged. These include the health of federal values in the evolving constitutional order, the promotion of democratic institutions and values, and the pursuit of broader public policy values such as equity, effectiveness, and efficiency.

To begin, three sets of summary comments seem to be in order. First, local government plays an important but clearly limited role in Australian governance. The striking feature of the governance system overall is what one may call the inverted pyramid: a truly dominant central government in the Commonwealth, with strong legislative resources and an overwhelmingly strong fiscal position, directly regulating or providing public goods and services that in other federations are done by the regional or intermediate level of government. The states in turn are almost city-states. The largest urban population centres are also the state capitals, which have developed historically in a strongly dependent relationship with the state governments. All the states as well as the Northern Territory, however, govern large hinterlands comprising smaller cities and towns and rural municipalities, sometimes at the expense of urban priorities and development. Yet the states *are* city-states in the sense that they make all the truly strategic urban development decisions. What is left for local government is a smaller basket of goods and services provision than in most other federations. Nonetheless, in respect of the relatively narrow set of functions, local governments retain an important degree of autonomy, largely because of their fiscal position, which relies heavily on own-source revenues, and because of their largest transfer, an unconditional grant from the federal government. This funding relationship has been stable for the past twenty years or more.

Local governments remains relatively minor players, in part because of their small size as governments. With the partial exception of one city, Brisbane, there is neither metropolitan government in Australia nor the kind of intermunicipal or interregional cooperation that one sees in North America. The states, by design, have assumed the regional coordination function. Nor does Australia provide any significant models for constitutional autonomy for local government. The provisions for local government in state constitutions provide plenty of room for regulatory and other forms of direct intervention by the state governments.

In making these assessments, I do not wish to suggest that models of governance elsewhere are superior. Australia, despite its huge geographic territory, has a relatively small population at just over 20 million, and it is less diverse demographically, even regionally, than many other federations. There has been (as seen in other federations) a historic process of nation building in which any really important public issue is going to have a strong central stamp to it, regardless of the values of federalism and local self-government. Rather than being squeezed as the more constrained order of government, the states have naturally assumed the role that elsewhere might be assumed by metropolitan or sub-state regional governments.

My second general conclusion is that the federal role in local affairs waxes and wanes; it depends significantly on the party in power. Labor governments have taken on a more direct interventionist role, especially on urban issues and, at least before the late 1980s, were considerably hostile to the states. The conservative coalition parties have traditionally been more favourable to federalism and the states. However, their strong support of local government through direct funding can be seen as a way of limiting the influence of the states and helping to maintain local fiscal autonomy. Significantly, the Commonwealth does not seem to desire a large role in urban development, at least under the Howard government. More negatively, federal involvement has become increasingly targeted and bureaucratic as far as local governance is concerned.

These dynamics are illustrated by the two policy cases in this paper. The case of infrastructure policy demonstrates a role common to the central governments of many federations in what otherwise might be deemed a local responsibility, based on the rationales of national economic competitiveness, development, and equity. In Australia, federal funding for infrastructure is increasingly earmarked for projects that meet federal policy criteria rather than local needs as such, in particular the federal interest in regional roads. The second policy case involves broad-based public management reform, where local government has been drawn into a comprehensive intergovernmental web of reforms. Here the Howard government has been more interventionist, pursuing standards that are applied uniformly across the public sector. This it has achieved through cooperation with the states and local governments. Thus, it seems that where regulation is the chief policy instrument involved, Australian norms for uniformity and national standards constrain local autonomy. The latter is retained, or at least much more flexibly exercised, when the federal policy instrument involves primarily the expenditure of funds.

A third observation relates to the assessment of the role and future of multilevel governance. In federal systems – Australia is no exception – intergovernmental relations have often been bifurcated: a federal-state system, and a state-local system. To these two can be added the more limited but certainly active federal-local relationship. In Australia the principal traffic remains in these dyadic patterns, but there are important and interesting signs of a more truly multilevel (i.e, trilevel) system emerging. The Council of Australian Governments and its related intergovernmental mechanisms provide a strong set of instruments for co-decision and joint action. The president of the ALGA has been a member of COAG since the beginning, a role that seems to have promoted a greater policy capacity in the ALGA as the national representative body of local government, as well as in the state-wide local government associations.

In Australia, the harnessing of the COAG process to any given set of issues requires executive political will, particularly the lead of the federal prime minister. This will has not been significantly present for action on urban issues thus far, though it has been for more generic public management reform, including, as noted above, the introduction of broad-reaching competition principles in the public sector, as well as for other issues significant to local government as a whole, such as water supply and management and other environmental issues.[8] More recently, the federal and state ministers of local government have concluded a potentially significant framework agreement with the ALGA on their continuing intergovernmental relationship, very much building upon and in keeping with COAG norms.

In the meantime, the main action in multilevel governance is likely to continue to be in the separate municipal-state and federal-state arenas. For urban issues, and the sustainability and competitiveness of Australian cities, the focus seems increasingly to be on the state governments and their fiscal and policy capacities. Indeed, one recent and impressive set of academic analyses of local government finance, governance and reform ended by not mentioning the federal role at all, let alone an expansion of it, in its prescriptions for the future, but it had plenty to propose for action by the states and municipalities as such (Dollery and Marshall 2003, 238–50; Murphy and Wu 2001). Perhaps a renewed avenue for inquiry, then, would be to start with a fresh survey of just exactly how the Australian state governments manage urban issues, with or without local government. But that is for another day.

In sum, multilevel governance involving local government is a real phenomenon in Australia. It is constrained by the narrow allocation of powers and responsibilities to local government, by the strong role of the state in urban and regional governance, and by the seeming decline of federal interest in urban matters. And, as noted above, while the three rings of the intergovernmental circus increasingly overlap and join up, it is the traditional dyadic patterns of federal-state, state-local, and federal-local that remain the most heavily used.

Some Australian features stand out as particularly helpful and promising for the continued development of integrative and nonhierarchical multilevel governance. Both the relative fiscal autonomy of local government and the significantly small degree of fiscal gap between revenues and responsibilities allow local government to enter into interdependent relations on a more equitable and less subordinate basis than would otherwise be the case. Of course, the long-term federal-local relationship has greatly nurtured these conditions.

Finally, one turns to the overarching criteria addressed throughout this volume to make what must be rather concise and preliminary assessments. First is whether the overall mode of multilevel governance that is emerging in Australia retains federal values. Clearly, the trend has been towards more rationalized cooperation and less open competitive federalism. This is demonstrated in the integrated and highly structured nature of COAG and the ministerial council process, in the binding reforms of public management, and the propensity to setting standards even in infrastructure funding. Yet these trends are hardly inimical to federal values and broader political norms as traditionally played out in Australia, as I have argued elsewhere (Brown 2002).

Second, the style and substance of multilevel governance in Australia also lends itself to heightened national performance of prevailing policy goals and values. These, as noted, have in recent years been guided less by equity considerations and more by efficiency and competitiveness. Sweeping economic and fiscal reform has been achieved by intergovernmental means; and this reform has been easier to achieve following the coincident reform of intergovernmental machinery. The bias in policy outcomes has been greater economic efficiency compared with equity, but Australia is hardly alone in this respect. What is clearly enhanced, however, is the effectiveness of intergovernmental outcomes.

Third, in all this, is local democracy and autonomy preserved? This discussion has not been primarily addressed to democratic considerations, including the ongoing health of local democratic culture (see Kiss 2003). One notes, however, that general Australian discourse does not seem to place much emphasis on potential democratic deficits in their emerging multilevel governance. Yet in terms of such democratic values as local autonomy, participation, and flexibility, the arguments about how globalization affects nation-state sovereignty would seem to apply to subnational (state and local) governments as well; that is, sovereignty is exercised, not denied, by multilevel governance. From the perspective of local governments in Australia, being at the table and shaping decisions, in however minor a role, is surely preferable to being on the receiving end of centralized decision making in an interdependent world. They may be very small players at the end of the inverted pyramid, but Australian local governments are getting more adept at performing in multilevel governance.

NOTES

1 For a concise discussion of Australia's federal constitutional principles, structure, and history, see Saunders 2005; for insightful commentary, see Galligan 1995.

2 COAG membership is restricted to the Commonwealth prime minister, the six state premiers, the two territories' chief ministers, and the president of the Australian Local Government Association.

3 An overview of local government functions and finances is provided in the annual reports of the federal government's National Office of Local Government. See NOLG 2005. The website is also useful: www.dotars.gov.au/local govt. Also, for the Australian Local Government Association, www.alga.asn.au

4 The federal share of expenditures does not include transfers to state and local governments. See NOGL 2005, table 1.14.

5 Aspects of these arrangements dealing with the mandatory flow through to local governments as a condition of overall Commonwealth–state transfers were subject to a constitutional challenge by the states in the 1970s. In the 1975 case *State of Victoria and Another* v *The Commonwealth and Another* 7 ALR 277, the High Court found in favour of the Commonwealth practice as an exercise of its general spending power (Mathews and Grewal 1997). See also Watts 1999.

6 See www.alga.asn.au.

7 However, for an estimate provided by the federal government, see NOLG 2005, table 1.16.

8 See, for example, the extensive National Water Initiative agreed upon at the COAG meeting of June 2004, detailed in COAG 2004.

REFERENCES

Aucoin, Peter. 1995. *The New Public Management: Canada in Comparative Perspective.* Montreal: Institute for Research on Public Policy

Australia. 2003. *Rates and Taxes: A Fair Share for Responsible Local Government.* Report of the House of Representatives Standing Committee on Economics, Finance, and Public Administration (Hawker Report). Canberra: Parliament of the Commonwealth of Australia

– Productivity Commission. 1997. *Stocktake of Progress in Microeconomic Reform.* Canberra: AGPS

Australian Local Government Association (ALGA). 2003. *Annual Report 2002–3.* Canberra. Available online at www.alga.asn.au

– 2004. "*Auslink* Confirms $1.2 Billion Boost for Local Roads." Media release, 7 June. Available online at www.alga.asn.au

– 2006. "Federal Budget 2005–06 Analysis: A Local Government Perspective." Available online at www.alga.asn.au/policy/finance/federalBudgetAnalysis2005/factSheet02.php

Bache, Ian, and Mathew Flinders, eds. 2004. *Multi-level Governance.* Oxford: Oxford University Press

Baker, Geoff. 2003. "Management Reform in Local Government." In *Reshaping Australian Local Government: Finance, Governance, and Reform*, ed. Dollery et al., 117–38. Sydney: University of New South Wales Press

Brown, Douglas M. 2002. *Market Rules: Economic Union Reform and Intergovernmental Policy-Making in Australia and Canada*. Montreal: McGill-Queen's University Press

Caulfield, Janice. 2003. "Local Government: Reform in Comparative Perspective." In *Reshaping Australian Local Government: Finance, Governance, and Reform*, ed. Dollery et al., 13–34. Sydney: University of New South Wales Press

Chapman, R.J.K., and Michael Wood. 1984. *Australian Local Government: The Federal Dimension*. Sydney: Allen and Unwin

Coper, Michael. 1988. *Encounters with the Australian Constitution*. Sydney: CCH Australia

Council of Australian Goverments (COAG). 2004. *Communiqué*, 25 June. Available online at www.coag.gov.au/meetings/250604/index.htm

Dollery, Brian, and Neil Marshall. 2003. "Future Directions for Australian Local Government." In *Reshaping Australian Local Government: Finance, Governance, and Reform*, ed. Dollery et al., 231–50. Sydney: University of New South Wales Press

Dollery, Brian, Neil Marshall, and Andrew Worthington, eds. 2003. *Reshaping Australian Local Government: Finance, Governance, and Reform*. Sydney: University of New South Wales Press

Galligan, Brian. 1995. *A Federal Republic: Australia's Constitutional System of Government*. Melbourne: Cambridge University Press

Gray, Ian, and Geoffrey Lawrence. 2001. *A Future for Regional Australia: Escaping Global Misfortune*. Cambridge: Cambridge University Press

Hood, Christopher. 1996. "Exploring Variations in Public Management Reform." In *Civil Service Systems in Comparative Perspective*, ed. P.T. Bekke. Bloomington: Indiana University Press

Hughes, Owen, and D. O'Neill. 2000. "The Limits of New Public Management: Reflection on the Kennett 'Revolution' in Victoria." Paper delivered at International Public Management Conference entitled "Learning from Experiences with New Public Management," held 4–6 March in Sydney, Australia. Online at www.inpuma.net/research/papers/sydney

International Monetary Fund (IMF). 2000. *Government Finance Statistics Yearbook*. Washington, DC: IMF – 2002. *Government Finance Statistics Yearbook*. Washington, DC: IMF

Johnson, Andrew. 2003. "Financing Local Government in Australia." In *Reshaping Australian Local Government: Finance, Governance, and Reform*, ed. Dollery et al., 37–63. Sydney: University of New South Wales Press

Kiss, Rosemary. 2001. "Are We Kidding about Local Autonomy? Local Government in Australia." Paper prepared for the workshop on local autonomy and democracy., ECPR, held in Grenoble, April

– 2003. "Reasserting Local Democracy." In *Reshaping Australian Local Government: Finance, Governance, and Reform*, ed. Dollery et al., 101–16. Sydney: University of New South Wales Press

Marks, Gary, and Lisbet Hooghe. 2004. "Contrasting Visions of Multi-level Governance." In *Multi-level Governance*, ed. Bache and Flinders, chapter 2. Oxford: Oxford University Press

Mathews, Russell, and Bhajan Grewal. 1997. *The Public Sector in Jeopardy: Australian Fiscal Federalism from Whitlam to Keating*. Melbourne: Centre for Strategic Economic Studies, Victoria University

May, Paul. 2003. "Amalgamation and Virtual Local Government." In *Reshaping Australian Local Government: Finance, Governance and Reform*, ed. Dollery et al., 79–97. Sydney: University of New South Wales Press

Municipal Association of Victoria (MAV). 2004. "Response to the 2004–2005 Federal Budget." Unpublished paper available online at www.mav.asn.au

Murphy, Peter, and Chung-Tong Wu. 2001. "Globalization and the Sustainability of Cities in the Asia Pacific Region: The Case of Sydney." *Globalization and the Sustainability of Cities in the Asia Pacific Region*, ed. Fu-chen Lo and Peter Marcotullio, 399–427 . Tokyo: United Nations University Press

National Office of Local Government (NOLG). Department of Transport and Regional Services. 2005. *Local Government National Report, 2002–03*. Canberra: Commonwealth of Australia. Available online at www.dotars.gov.au/localgovt/publications/national_report/03_04/index_downloads.aspx

New South Wales. 2004. *Budget Paper No. 2, 2004–05*. Sydney: Government Printer

Norregaard, John. 1997. "Tax Assignment." In *Fiscal Federalism in Theory and Practice*, ed. T. Ter-Minassian, 49–72. Washington, DC: International Monetary Fund

O'Connor, Kevin, Robert J. Stimson, and Scott Baum. 2001. "The Regional Distribution of Growth." In *Reshaping Australia's Economy: Growth with Equity and Sustainability*, ed. J. Nieuwenhuysen, P. Lloyd, and M. Mead, 50–63. Cambridge: Cambridge University Press

Painter, Martin. 1998. *Collaborative Federalism: Economic Reform in Australia in the 1990s*. Melbourne: Macmillan

Pollitt, Christopher. 1998. "Managerialism Revisited." In *Taking Stock: Assessing Public Sector Reforms*, ed. Guy Peters and Donald Savoie, 45–77. Kingston: McGill-Queen's University Press

Ravenhill, John.1990. "Australia." In *Federalism and International Relations: The Role of Subnational Units*, ed. Hans J. Michelmann and Panayotis Soldatos, 76–123. Oxford: Clarendon Press

Ryan, Christine. 2003. "Local Government Financial Reporting." In *Reshaping Australian Local Government: Finance, Governance, and Reform*, ed. Dollery et al., 64–78. Sydney: University of New South Wales Press

Sancton, Andrew. 2001. "Municipalities, Cities, and Globalization: Implications for Canadian Federalism." In *Canadian Federalism: Performance, Effectiveness, and Legitimacy, ed.* H. Bakvis and G. Skogstad, 261–77. Toronto: Oxford University Press

– 2002. "The Legal and Political Setting of Municipalities." Unpublished report. Kingston: Institute of Intergovernmental Relations, Queen's University

Saunders, Cheryl. 2005. "Australia." In *Constitutional Origins, Structure, and Change in Federal Countries*. Vol. 1 of *Global Dialogue on Federalism* series, ed. John Kincaid and G. Alan Tar, 1–40. Montreal: McGill-Queen's University Press for the Forum of Federations

Sharman, Campbell. 1991. "Executive Federalism." In *Intergovernmental Relations and Public Policy*, ed. B. Galligan, Owen Hughes, and Cliff Walsh, 23-38. Sydney: Allen and Unwin

Tasmania. 1996. *Budget Overview, 1996–97, Budget Paper No. 2*. Hobart: Government Printer

Ter-Minassian, Teresa, ed. 1997. *Fiscal Federalism in Theory and Practice*. Washington, DC: International Monetary Fund

Watts, Ronald L. 1999. *The Spending Power in Federal Systems*. Kingston: Institute of Intergovernmental Relations, Queen's University

MUNICIPAL-CENTRAL RELATIONS IN FRANCE: BETWEEN DECENTRALIZATION AND MULTILEVEL GOVERNANCE

Emmanuel Brunet-Jailly

1 INTRODUCTION

The global economy, as many scholars have noted, modifies the politics of state relations in the intergovernmental and international arena (Courchene 1999; Duchacek 1988; Risse-Kappen 1995; Brown and Fry 1993; Balme 1998; Keating 1998; Young 1999). There seems to be no consensus, however, on the general transformation of states. Is the state hollowing out? Is it a functional reorganization? Is it multilevel governance? New technologies of information and communication affect states, free trade integrates the economies of Europe and North America, and free trade regimes pressure governments to ease regulations and open new markets (Keohane and Milner 1996). Furthermore, these changes seem to enhance subnational entities as economic players (Ohmae 1991). So it seems that the global economy, new technologies, and free trade transform the relations of states and other governmental tiers with market forces. Governing is becoming much more complex.

Federal and unitary states, such as Canada and France, adapt and mediate these international market and governance changes with varying difficulty (Young 1999; Sassen 1996; Salmon and Keating 1999). Focusing on the impact that globalization has on states, Saskia Sassen explains that new legal regimes "un-bundle sovereignties" and "denationalize territories" (Sassen 1996, 28) a process that also reconfigures the links between rights and territories and thus has "disturbing repercussions for distributive justice and equity" (ibid., 1996, 29–30). Brenner, focusing on the politics of scale and the rescaling of national states, claims that state spaces are being recalibrated, which leads regional-central government relations to be redefined from vertical, coordinative, and redistributive to horizontal, competitive, and developmentalist (Brenner 2005). Keating, focusing on multination states in Europe, finds that along with constitutional reforms, an asymmetry of rights develops that further differentiates local and regional constituencies in a process in which federal and centralized states progressively seem to resemble each other (Keating 1999a, 1999b; Salmon and Keating 1999).

Thus, this literature suggests that decentralizing or devolving, along with constitutional reforms, have implications for institutional structures and the allocation of functions, and for the governing capacity of lower-level governments. In some instances, central governments are less able to regulate, to organize fiscal equalization, and to reduce interregional or provincial competition; in other instances, central governments actually encourage intergovernmental competition at lower-government levels. Overall, policymaking is increasingly based on "territorially overarching policy networks" that involve public- and private-sector organizations and all levels of government (Marks 1992). In the end, it seems that such changes in federal territorial politics characterize tendencies towards greater legal, institutional, and functional complexity and an asymmetry of rights, while institutional capacity, as well as functional allocation, increasingly characterizes disparate and decentralized politics.[1]

Although these features may seem clear in most federal state systems, where they tend to provide mechanisms of power sharing among the various levels of government that are more flexible, they are not found in central state systems in the same way (Keating 1999c, 8–12). The Constitution of the French nation-state does not recognize asymmetry. In this nation-state, asymmetries seem to develop functionally but with much greater regulatory constraint because France's institutional system is less flexible than that of most federations (ibid., 22). After an introductory overview of the key features and recent evolution of the French system, this paper is divided into twelve sections that address successively the constitutional dimension of municipalities; their range of functions; their fiscal position; their relationship with the central government; the scope of municipal-federal interaction; the nature of municipal-central interaction; regional mediation; international relations; immigrant settlement and road infrastructure policies (case studies); recent trends; and the central question of multilevel governance.

The material presented in this paper suggests that, over the last decade, France has been creating its own blend of multilevel governance. This ongoing process results from a series of constitutional reforms but is in part motivated by the specifically French practice of accumulating electoral offices at central and local levels of government and creating personal political fiefdoms. Of additional importance is the progressively influential role of the European Union in regional and local policies, which privileges the regional dimension in matters of development. Today, multilevel governance supplants top-down and hierarchical territorial politics in France. It results in intermeshed policy networks, where all levels of government are near equals and where intergovernmental negotiations are based on contracting. The scope and depth of these reforms is clear. They are likely to be part of an ongoing process of interaction where left-leaning political actors will push for further decentralization and re-enforcement of the French regions as the new locus where policies and actors converge.

1.1 OVERVIEW OF CENTRAL-LOCAL RELATIONS IN FRANCE

France is known to be an archetypical centralized state. It emerged out of the nineteenth- century Napoleonic reforms, which modelled the central state bureaucracy on a hierarchical military model that controlled and divided French territories into 100 *départements*, each of which was subdivided into 4 or 5 counties and more than 36,000 *communes*, or municipalities. The legislature and the judiciary remained an exclusive feature of the central government. The administration of the central government was ingrained with a fundamental distrust of local and regional democratic institutions. Prefects, those "Napoleons with small feet," centralized and controlled all the executive and administrative activities of each level of government from the top down.

Until the 1960s and 1970s, local and regional policies in France were the result of national regional policy. Every four or five years, from 1946 through the mid-1970s, a so-called *Plan* played a key role in rebuilding and modernizing the country (Quinet 1990). Plans I to VIII were useful tools for disseminating ideas and methodologies, top-down, across the country, with municipalities at the bottom of this Russian doll type of system.

However, a weakened governing system in the 1970s necessitated a change in these relations. Plan VIII remained in project form, and the intermediary plan of 1982 missed its goals because of a gap between the legal goals which the plan had to target and its accomplishments (Levy 1994). The 1982 laws on decentralization initiated a new approach to regional and local politics. Regional coordination of policies was to be the role of a new institution, a government elected at the level of the *région*. Some have argued that the 1982 laws on decentralization effectively resulted in the democratization of France (Schmidt 1993).

Since 1982, the French system of local government has comprised *régions*, *départements*, and *communes*. Each level of local government – regional, departmental, and municipal – is elected; but decentralization notwithstanding, the central government has maintained a strong presence at each level. The *prefectures* and *sous prefectures* are headed by prefects, subprefects, and their staff. Tension persists between local governments and the field offices of the central government. It is precipitated by the tradition of submission to field administrators and the many mechanisms of control embodied in the tutelage system, despite the contemporary decentralized nature of their authority and their strong political existence.

In French public law, this dual system of government is understood as being made up of "territorial administrative units" that have specific competencies on a specific territory. Their functions, however, are generally recognized as relevant only to local affairs and are subdivided into two types of territorial administrative units: those that are decentralized from central government and those that are deconcentrated from central government.

Decentralized administrative units serve three types of elected local governments called – namely, "collectivities" Communes, which are territorially and functionally similar to municipalities in the United States and Canada; Departments, which administer territories as large as four to six English, Canadian, or American counties; and Regions, which group four to six Departments. The level of the county remains a deconcentrated unit of the central state and has not been affected by decentralization.

There are two kinds of "decentralized local administrations" (DLAs): those that are subject to tutelage by the central government and those that enjoy full authority over a specific bundle of policies. Legally, they are distinguished as "local public establishments" and "territorial public establishments."

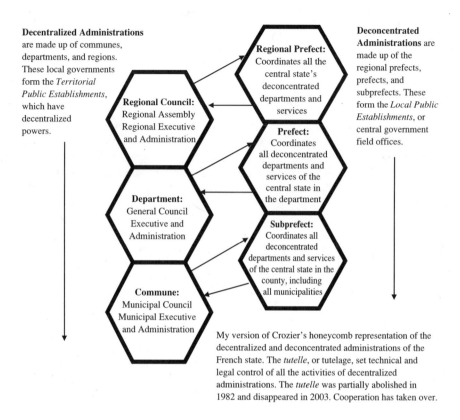

Decentralized Administrations are made up of communes, departments, and regions. These local governments form the *Territorial Public Establishments*, which have decentralized powers.

Regional Council: Regional Assembly Regional Executive and Administration

Department: General Council Executive and Administration

Commune: Municipal Council Municipal Executive and Administration

Regional Prefect: Coordinates all the central state's deconcentrated departments and services

Prefect: Coordinates all deconcentrated departments and services of the central state in the department

Subprefect: Coordinates all deconcentrated departments and services of the central state in the county, including all municipalities

Deconcentrated Administrations are made up of the regional prefects, prefects, and subprefects. These form the *Local Public Establishments*, or central government field offices.

My version of Crozier's honeycomb representation of the decentralized and deconcentrated administrations of the French state. The *tutelle*, or tutelage, set technical and legal control of all the activities of decentralized administrations. The *tutelle* was partially abolished in 1982 and disappeared in 2003. Cooperation has taken over.

Local public establishments consist of the central government's field offices, which are unifunctional deconcentrated administrative units. These include, for example, schools and hospitals. Territorial public establishments have decentralized powers; they include intermunicipal organizations such as the commune communities and "union of communes," as well as the traditional communes, Departments, and regions. They have delegated powers and resources. Their decision-making bodies – the municipal council, the general council, and regional council – are made up of locally elected officials. The municipal and the general councils are creations of the Third Republic, dating back to 5 April 1884 and 10 August 1871, respectively.[2] The region, the most recent creation, dates back to 2 March 1982; the law was subsequently amended, in 1986, to create councils elected at the level of the region. In principle, regions have full powers over specific policy arenas: economic development, professional training and the real estate of colleges, and regional roads and planning. The 1992 law no. 92-125 clearly states, however, that decentralized local governments and the deconcentrated services of the state are to ensure the administration of the territory of the Republic, which suggests that elected governmental bodies and the field offices of the central state are to collaborate.

Deconcentrated administrations have field offices of the central government with specific territorial competencies. The most important and best known of these is the prefect. The prefect is the highest deconcentrated territorial authority. In principle, all other deconcentrated field offices fall under the authority of the prefect, though there are four partial exceptions: finance, education, justice, and health. Each has its own deconcentrated system.

The basic territory of deconcentration is the department (*département*), originally established and designed by Napoleon, who argued that a man on horseback should be able to cross a department in one day; hence their round or oval shape. Above the department (since 1982) is the region, whose prefect, the regional prefect – accumulates all functions of the central government concerned with departments and regions. Departments are made up of counties whose deconcentrated authority is in the hands of a subprefect. There are very many communes in each department and in each county. Their mayors are elected locally. They head the commune's executive, and in matters of public security they are the local representatives of the central government under the authority of the prefect and subprefect. The prefect heads the local administrations of the central government. His signature is required on all documents that involve any department or agency of the central government in his constituency (law 92-125 of February 1992). This control extends to all deconcentrated government funds.

Analysts of the French system question whether the end of the unitary state has occurred (Loughlin and Mazey 1995). Levy's interpretation of French decentralization is that the weakness of French civil society limits the transformation of the *dirigiste* state. The state remains a coordinator and a "firefighter"(Levy 1994). Baverez and Olivennes (1989) contend that the state apparatus faces "public powerlessness" because it remains an ambitious state that supports a large bureaucracy that lacks productivity. From Crozier's (1989) standpoint, the French bureaucratic state is archaic because it orders and regulates but is unable to put either its citizens or entrepreneurs first. Others contend that the central government actually maintains control, having decentralized only the few policy arenas where new investments and funding were required.

Decentralization took place in three stages. The first framework laws were enacted between 1982 and 1992. Then, from 1992 until 2002, and again in 2003–4 a second and a third set of reforms were implemented. The first and third periods are deemed successful; not so the second.

The 1982 reforms did not change in depth the territorial organization of France, nor did they actually transform the principles that organized its local administrative and institutional systems. The debate over the abolition of the tutelage system illustrates the persistence of those foundations. For instance, legalists often argue that the minister in charge of the decentralization laws of 1982, Gaston Deferre, did not attempt to pass a new framework law.[3] Rather, he initiated changes with a "locomotive law," to use his own words, launching a long list of reforms, that primarily affected local institutions on specific aspects of decentralization: downloading of responsibilities, local finances, and the role and functions of local elected and public officials. Four major reforms of 1982, three of which primarily concerned local institutions, have had a lasting impact on democratization and decentralization.

First, the Deferre Acts created twenty-one regional governments. Second, instead of the prefects, the elected presidents of regions and departments became heads of their executives. Third, the principle of tutelage, which gave all of the executive powers of regions and departments as well as supervision over all municipal decisions, was subjected to legal scrutiny, whereby the prefect had to refer those decisions to administrative tribunals. The fourth and final central element of the reform was the downloading of the economic development function to all local authorities under the leadership of the region, including some taxing and financial-incentive powers.

Soon after this primarily institutional reform was in place, two laws – one passed on 7 January 1983, the other on 22 July 1983 – downloaded functions to each level of local government. The 1982 laws attempted to disentangle functions and funding. They were partly successful in that they organized all primary responsibilities or the leadership role, for each level of government. This emphasis is important because today, as discussed in section 3 of this paper, no level of government seems to have exclusive control of any given policy arena, not even the central government. Municipalities primarily govern planning and housing issues, while solidarity, social and health issues, and rural transportation are policy arenas of the departments. The regions tend to be in charge of economic development. Nevertheless, responsibilities in many policy arenas are actually shared by all levels of government. For instance, in education and transportation, each level governs different parts of the policy. Municipalities manage and maintain primary school buildings; departments are in charge of middle school buildings; and regions and the central government are responsible for high school and university buildings, respectively, and all teachers, professors, and other school and university staff are on the central government's payroll. Similarly, the central government plans and manages the national railway system, while regions manage regional railways and departments manage school buses. All levels have to work together for the successful implementation of any of these policies and contracting appears to be the "new" essential mechanism that organizes and both entangles and disentangles these complex partnerships. In fact, the 1982 laws explicitly instituted contracting as a policy mechanism to link all four levels of government – central, regional, departmental, and municipal – for the successful management of policies in the spirit of the pre-existing plan launched after the Second World War.

In the wave of reforms between 1992 and 1999, new legal initiatives addressed the statutory position of all local administrations, including intermunicipal partnerships. Because of their perceived importance, the statutes of 6 February 1992 were labelled Act II of Decentralization, also known as the Chevènement Acts. Yet they were largely unsuccessful. Their intended aim of enticing municipalities to pool functions was compromised because there were no specific funding incentives. As a result, very few municipalities pooled functions, and Act II was again reformed with the passage of the July 1999 Act on urban reorganization and municipal cooperation, which proposed new forms of intermunicipal partnerships. Today, most scholars and policy analysts agree that these reforms constitute an important yet quiet revolution that has profoundly transformed mechanisms of municipal service delivery and the local government map. Intermunicipal partnerships have allowed for greater economies of scale and greater policy differentiation that further entrenched policymaking at the local level.

Most scholars and experts view the first wave of decentralization in the 1980s and 1990s as a significant success in the policy arenas where all four levels of governments cooperate, such as education and public transportation. This consensus does not extend to the 1992 and (5 February) 1995 reforms, which are generally seen to have failed. However, the 1999 Acts on intermunicipal partnerships and territorial development and planning – the LOADT (*Loi d'orientation pour l'aménagement et le développement du térritoire*) and the LOADDT (*Loi d'orientation pour l'aménagement et le développement durable du territoire*) of 25 June 1999 – which allowed rural municipalities to organize themselves into "*Pays*" (countries) around specific partnership goals, are perceived as a successful silent revolution.

The Chevènement Acts of 1992 had attempted to reduce them from seven to five. "Districts" and "city communities" disappeared, and the new Act (1999) created "commune communities," an "agglomeration of communes," and "urban communities." These three new types of partnership, however, have had to cohabit with the pre-existing "unions of commune" which set up either unifunctional or multifunctional upper-tier special-purpose bodies.[4]

Regourd (2004) argues that five such local mechanisms of cooperation only add to the complexity of the French system, which also includes four levels of government and the European Union. He also points to the progressive emergence of intermunicipal partnerships – more than 25,000 in 2004 – which focus on one or more local functions and seem to add much complexity to the French local government system. The system is now made up of about 36,000 municipalities as well as 25,000 local governments. Knowing who does what is just about impossible (ibid., 2004, 7). These intermunicipal partnerships are criticized for limiting accountability; in short, 61,000 local governments seem overwhelming.

The constitutional reforms of 2003, detailed in the next section of this paper, confirm the growing influence of local elected officials and the power of local authorities. The European Union's legal framework[5] also contributed to the current transformation of the French local government system, particularly the Charter for Local Authorities (Ziller 2003).

The central themes of this paper address the issues of decentralization, the influence of local elected officials, and the power of local authorities. The central arguments are that over the last twenty-five years, France has undergone a historical transformation that has enhanced its local government system without necessarily weakening that of the central government, and that no one level of government is the clear beneficiary of those reforms that further entangle and structure France as a unitary yet decentralized republic within the multilevel governance system that currently organizes the European Union.

2 CONSTITUTIONAL DIMENSION

French policymakers and legal and constitutional experts believe that there is a French exception to the global movement of government decentralization. Critics will, however, point to the recent French constitutional reform that entrenches the principle of a decentralized republic. Yet this important reform cannot be taken at face value because, as much as it is correct to say that France is succumbing to the decentralizing trend, it is doing it the "French way." French scholars argue that it is very different from any form of regionalization or federalism found in other European countries (Delpree 2004).

Today, the first article of the Constitution of the French Republic states: "Its organization is decentralized." This suggests a contradiction with the indivisibility principle. France is a unitary state in which constitutional history (see, for instance, the Fourth Constitution of 1946) suggests that local governments had no constitutional standing. Nevertheless, Article 1 clearly strengthens the autonomy and constitutional standing of local governments. Commentators have suggested that the legislature enacted the reality that France is *de facto* decentralized. The assertion in Article 1 also entrenches the French Republic as a form of government that is clearly not federal, suggesting as well that there are many variants of decentralization. The interpretation of how decentralized France may become is a future legal conundrum.

While Article 1 recognizes that the Republic is decentralized, the Constitution also specifies that officials of the central governments are to be in charge of national interests (Article 72.6), thus suggesting, *a contrario*, that non-central government officials may focus on their territorial interests. The French Republic remains indivisible; the key role of prefect seems greater, since prefects now have to work with all non-central government officials to make the best possible decisions in cooperation with officials working for other levels of government.

The constitutional reform establishes that any level of government can take policy initiatives to develop partnerships with all three other levels when appropriate. communes, departments, and regions, as well as the central government can make use of this power to engage in cooperation with any other governments and may organize *ad hoc* modalities of their cooperation (Boeuf 2003; Luchaire and Luchaire 2003). In the law of March 1982, the question of the nature of the relationship between local governments and the central government was not addressed: communes, departments, and regions were to concur with the central government on matters of administration and territorial planning. This principle considerably limited the 1982 ideas of decentralization because it allowed central state officials to make the point that all partners – the central government, communes, departments, and regions – were to work together and complementarily, according to their specialization, as stipulated by law. The 2003 constitutional reform clarified this ambiguity, recognizing that cooperation is necessary to organize a coherence of action among all four government levels.

It also decrees that no one level of government may make use of tutelage over any other (Article 72.5). Administrative lawyers have interpreted this reform as a new constitutional principle that imposes cooperation on all four levels of territorial government. *De facto* co-decision becomes the new principle that organizes the interactions of the newly decentralized republic (see Article 72.1).

The third important reform (see Article 72.2) is that each territorial level of government "has the vocation to take decisions using all competencies necessary at their level of government." It suggests that non-central governments share all regulatory and executive powers with the prefects. These local governments freely administer themselves. They have an elected council and regulatory powers (72.3).

The fourth constitutional amendment consists of the new principle of "experimentation." This controversial legal change implicitly recognizes that local governments and the central government are jointly responsible for making new laws. Indeed, a controversial principle (Article 37.1, regarding regulatory power and experimentation, and Article 72.4, regarding legislative and regulatory powers and experimentation) suggests that local governments have special dispensatory powers – for the purpose of experimentation – on a specific object and for a limited time. An experimental project or proposal should be generalized to the national territory once it has been tested successfully and approved by local governments and the National Assembly. Commentators have been very clear that the constitutional wording was ambiguous and gives legislative and regulatory powers to those local governments during the experimentation period, which may last five years (Luchaire and Luchaire 2003; Boeuf 2003a; Brisson 2003b, 2003; Crouzatier-Durand 2004; France, *Journals officiel* 2003; Verpeaux 2003, 2004).

A noted constitutional analyst has pointed out that, since the 1982 reforms, local governments have been granted greater administrative and executive powers and that this recent constitutional amendment not only strengthens those early reforms but also ushers in a new type of relationship between the executive and legislative bodies of both central and local governments (Brisson 2003a). In Europe, decentralization has been common, since most countries, save France, ratified the Charter of Local Authorities in 2002. The French Senate introduced the ratification bill in December 2004.

France is primarily "one and indivisible," yet as noted above, it is also decentralized. It balances two polarized ideas: the need for autonomous local authorities and for unified administrative and political action. Hence, in France, coordination is key to political, executive, and administrative actions. How is the unitary characteristic of the French state preserved in a decentralized environment? First, the legislative authority remains primarily in the hands of the National Assembly, but regions, departments, and municipalities have specific delegated legislative authority. Their administrative decisions are susceptible to a control of legality that is the separate responsibility of administrative tribunals, the State Council, and the courts. In matters where lawmakers have explicitly transferred all legislative and executive authority to non-central governments, they keep the authority to establish minimum standards. Ergo, a decentralized France is not yet federal, but it has a plural legislative system that is a prominent feature of federal systems. Future legislative practice and jurisprudence will be decisive. Furthermore, this is not a transformation towards a regional system because the central government maintains greater control over legislative action and can set minimum standards in those regions that push the limits. What, then, is the so-called French exception?

3 THE RANGE OF MUNICIPALITIES' RESPONSIBILITIES AND FUNCTIONS

Two principles organize the division of labour between local and central governments: proximity and national coherence. In line with the European principle of subsidiarity, each government is to take decisions at its level for the entirety of its responsibilities; central government officials are to work in partnership with all local governments to design and implement nationally coherent policies.

No one level of government, however, can impose its tutelage on any other. Local and central governments are expected to collaborate. Responsibilities are shared. On socio-economic policy and education, few dimensions are the exclusive responsibility of a particular governmental level. As a result of downloading, the central government shares part of all local government responsibilities, making partnerships necessary for the proper design and implementation of all policies. Each level, however, has been assigned broad and vague leadership functions over specific areas of policy that do not translate into clear authority.

A region, for instance, takes the lead in policy areas that include economic development and tourism. Social and solidarity policies are primarily the responsibility of the general councils. Furthermore, municipalities *de facto* seem to govern planning and housing issues, and the central government is left without a specific area of primary responsibility. Municipalities, for instance, have responsibilities in all policy areas delegated to local governments. They are able to take economic-development initiatives and set up tourism bureaus; they are responsible for local airports, seaports, and the building and maintenance of local roads. In the areas of social action, they can manage public social housing (for the poorest and elderly) and student housing and set minimum housing standards. In matters of education and culture, they manage all local schools, including all art schools as well as monuments of historical significance (Cabannes and Gohin 2000). The local government system is best characterized as tightly entangled while centrally governed. French municipalities and other local governments seem to be as reliant on other levels of government as those other government levels are on them. This makes accountability and policymaking extremely complex.

About one-third of all public-sector employees work for a local government. In 2001, the 56,700 local governments had about 1.6 million public-sector agents (these numbers do not account for the City of Paris and the General Council of Paris, which would add another 35,000 employees). Of those 1.6 million agents of local government, about 50,000 work for regions, 500,000 for general councils, and just over 1 million for municipalities or intermunicipal organizations. This contrasts with the more than 3 million employees of the central government and its deconcentrated services, central departments, and ministries. These numbers exclude about 850,000 public health and 1.5 million education employees.

This entanglement and the relative size of the municipal staff are also highlighted when analysing the respective budgets of these governments. The annual budget of the central government is about 288 billion euros annually. Municipalities spend about 90 billion euros, departments 40 billion, and regions 14 billion annually. All in all, local governments are about half the financial and staff size of the central government, while municipalities' staff and budgets account for about 20 percent of the whole.

4 THE FISCAL POSITION OF MUNICIPALITIES

The French local government tax system consists of grants and tax-sharing mechanisms. The first pillar is a system of *dotations* – conditional grants that are usually attached to a new transfer of responsibilities. These grants have been criticized for not addressing the issue of the level of public service and concurrent cost. Despite indexation on inflation and on GDP growth, the central government often does not devolve adequate funding to guarantee a high standard in the quality of public service. A traditional example of such imbalance in revenues is the transfer of high schools to regional governments; over time, this transfer has cost regions four times as much as the corresponding *dotations*.

The second pillar is a mechanism of tax sharing, where the central government procures either a specific portion or all of the revenues of a tax instrument to local governments. But downloading certain types of taxes contravenes European law. For instance, the transfer of the value added tax could precipitate a multiplicity of local rates, which is contrary to European law (de Courson 2003). The transfer of the "petroleum products interior tax" (TIPP), which is paid and monitored at the regional level on gas-production sites, would not allow for effective territorially varied rates. De Courson argues that there is only one type of tax that could be transferred to local governments: the traditional income tax and the newer general social contribution. Regarding the income tax, rates are already deemed to be very high, and only about 51 percent of French families pay any income tax. De Courson suggests that the general social contribution is possibly the tax most suitable for transfer to local governments because it involves 90 percent of the population and because variations in rates would be compatible with European law.

In 2001, municipalities raised about 41.71 billion euros, departments 17.91 billion, and regions 4.54 billion. Yet out of a total of 64.16 billion euros, only 8.19 billion were tax revenues based on economic activities, whereas over 80 percent, (or 55.36 billion) came from various property taxes. Between 1997 and 2001, the fiscal autonomy of local governments decreased from 52.8 to 45.4 percent. Municipalities, departments, and regions lost 7.2,, 5.7,, and 16.1 percent, respectively, of their financial autonomy, with the central government substituting conditional grants for specific local government tax revenues (DGCL 2005).

Locally elected officials have been frustrated by the central government's inability to "keep its word" since 1982. A Senate report, chaired by Patrice Gélard (2004), underlined how in the 1980s and 1990s the failure of the central government in to transfer resources, along with its extensive downloading, had frustrated locally elected officials.[6] For instance, the Constitutional Council's reluctance to oppose the central government's "recentralization" of local resources resulted in further constraints on local financial prerogatives, including equalization transfers,[7] local taxes, and the regulatory capacity of local tax rates. Contrary to the view of local government officials, the central government administration understood the principle of "free local administration" as a principle that, *de facto*, left local governments with minimal financial autonomy.

According to Didier Migaud, the member of parliament for the Département d'Isère, the underlying ideology of the central government that justified this financial disengagement and recentralization is fuelled by views that deficits and balanced-budget issues at the level of the central government can be addressed by transferring expenditures and responsibilities to local governments. It assumes that such transfers should secure balanced budgets and limit the overall deficits to less than the 3 percent of the GDP threshold mandated by the European Union. Also, local governments are perceived as being smaller, inexpensive, and efficient policy actors that can shoulder having decreasing sources of revenue. The transfer of the TIPP[8] is a good example. Its revenues accounted for about 1.94 percent of GDP in 1994 but were down to 1.6 percent in 2001. With the signature of the Kyoto Agreement and related increases in gas prices that will assuredly reduce consumption, revenues are expected to reach new lows by 2012, thus affecting local government revenues time and again. This downloading will lead to future local tax increases, which will further constrain the implementation of territorial solidarity and equity (Migaud 2003).

The Senate president and president of the Association of French Departments, Christian Poncelet, the president of the Association of French Mayors, Jean-Pierre Delevoye, the president of the local finance committees, Jean-Pierre Fourcade, and the president of the Association of French Regions, Jean-Pierre Raffarin, had been working on a proposal for constitutional reform since 2000. Similarly, the Social and Economic Council consultation produced a White Paper in June 2001, and the Mauroy Commission published its views in October 2000. The overall debate on further decentralization acknowledged that it had to include greater local fiscal capacity and autonomy.

At the annual meeting of the Association of French Mayors in November 2003, Poncelet explained that the local government tax system was "obsolete, unfair, and archaic" (Robert 2004). In 2003 the consensus was that local governments should finally gain constitutional guarantees of financial autonomy (de Courson 2003; Migaud 2003). The constitutional reform of 28 March 2003 led to full powers being transferred to municipalities; as of 13 August 2004, constitutional principles included local liberty and responsibility, experimentation, referendum, and financial autonomy and resources (Guengant and Josselin 2003). However, the idea that all local governments and municipalities now have growing financial autonomy however is controversial, because a large part of local resources are still centralized.

The reform, specifically Article 72.2, strengthens the financial autonomy of local governments by ensuring that they have their "own" resources and those resources and that these resources are to determine all their revenues. Both of the new rules are designed to protect local collectivities from the propensity of the central government to recentralize and control all local government resources. According to Article 72.2.2, a local government's resources are made up of loans negotiated with financial institutions, fees for services set by its elected council, local taxes, tax rates, and mechanisms of evaluation.

However, this aspect of the reform does not comprise "real innovations," since local government councils were already empowered to set tax rates on built and vacant properties, real estate ownership, and specific professions (Sauvageot 2003). In the end, these considerations are probably included in the reforms because the Senate committee insisted on them. The real innovation is found in Article 72.2.3, which affirms that local fiscal revenues and other resources are *fundamental* local government resources. This suggests that specific central government grants should be reduced and limited to less than half of local revenues (the "majority" principle).

The implementation of these rules leads to particular difficulties. For instance, which local governments are to be included? A restrictive understanding would limit the application to metropolitan local governments and exclude all others (Polynesia, Mayotte, and St Pierre and Miquelon). Also, how is the principle of "majority" to be understood? Is it exactly 50 percent of all resources, or should it be a significant amount as long as no local government's action is restricted? The spirit of the law seems to indicate that local elected officials be protected from having to agree with the decisions of central state officials concerning the administration of their territory. The majority principle might end up being referred to the Constitutional Council, and it could be particularly controversial for larger local governments. Article 72.2.5 suggests a constitutionally entrenched equalization mechanism. Although it suggests that the Constitution favours equality among local governments, it does not extend to an obligation that equality be the end-result.

In conclusion, the nonspecific nature of the constitutional text seems to imply that the substantive meaning of these constitutional reforms will primarily rely on future interpretations of the Constitutional Council.[9] Regarding expenditures, the new texts forbid any downloading and any new expenditures that are not entirely funded by parallel transfers of resources or fiscal instruments. The Constitution also guarantees fiscal autonomy, but vagueness in the wording left commentators without a clear interpretation. A dual interpretation is possible: fiscal autonomy is constitutionally guaranteed, but French legislators inherit the right to organize its exercise. The current debate suggests that any attempt at formulating an explanation could be thwarted by a decision of the Constitutional Council in the near future. According to this interpretation, commentators suggest that Constitutional Council jurisprudence might resemble what was in force before the 2003 reform,[10] while legislators might be able to specify mandatory expenditures and both government and parliament might be able to cap expenditures, if only to keep all local government expenditures in line with the overall budgetary obligation set by the European Monetary Union. The traditional financial control that central state officials have over public finances does not appear under threat.

In August 2005 the Direction générale des collectivités locales published its first complete report on local finances (Laignel 2005). This report reviews the financial history of local governments since 1982–83 and outlines the current state of local finances. It discusses recent reforms, particularly the transfer of new resources, such as transferring the TIPP to the regions and the TSCA (special tax on insurance conventions) to the department. Another reform discussed is the municipalities' block-grant system, which sets an allocation of 60 to 120 euros per capita that increases according to each municipality's size and population. The municipal solidarity and social cohesion grant is similarly based on a per capita ratio of the affected population. The report updates the fiscal autonomy ratios of municipalities, departments, and regions at 60.8, 58.6, and 39.5 percent, respectively; it shows an overall improvement of the fiscal autonomy of municipalities and departments, but regions are again the exception.

It seems that interpretations of these new texts may lead either to a greater focus on the designation of resources to specific expenditures or, on the contrary, to a withdrawal of the central government's funding when its agents lose control. In other words, what happens will depend on the next Constitutional Council ruling on local government expenditures. The Central government cannot download functions without downloading parallel resources or the capacity to raise revenues. This is an important innovation; however, what these transfers of resources will comprise remains unclear. In particular, the question of the specificity of these resources remains to be answered. Will the resources be new local taxes, tax rates, or specific grants or block grants? Here again, two polarized interpretations of the Constitution could lead to opposite funding mechanisms that would either transfer power back to central government officials or assert the financial authority and freedom of local governments (de Courson 2003; Geppert 2003; Hertzog 2003, 2004). In the end, the differences of interpretation are really about redistribution and equalization on the one hand (a concern of the central state) and local autonomy on the other. Both redistribution/equalization and local autonomy are perceived as too weak. But it was local financial autonomy more than redistribution and equalization that was on the minds of all involved in the constitutional reform, suggesting that the future fiscal position of municipalities is still uncertain and will largely depend on the tug-of-war between local elected and central government officials.

5 THE RELATIONSHIP BETWEEN MUNICIPAL AND CENTRAL GOVERNMENTS

What is the influence of local elected officials on French politics and policies? The authority of mayors is essential and has become particularly important over the last twenty-five years (Le Lidec 2001; Reformistes et solidaires 2005; Documentation française 1998). Mayors have always been influential because the French political system is founded on mayoralty offices and municipal councils.

Le Lidec (2001) studied the role of French elected officials and the associations of elected officials in the design of successive French regimes. He contends that the recent rise in influence of local elected officials predates the 1969 referendum that originated from a conflict between President Charles de Gaulle and French elected officials. Regarding all recent laws on decentralization law, Le Lidec argues that for the last two decades local elected officials, particularly their national representations – the Association of French Mayors, the Association of French Big City Mayors, the Association of French Departments, and the Association of French Regions – have been extremely influential in their interaction with the central government and the personnel who drafted the reform proposals, and with the National Assembly and the Senate more generally.

Why are locally elected officials so influential at the national level? Le Lidec's historical description of the genesis of their influence underlines the fact that the political system is built on a century-long practice of officials getting elected locally and then protecting this mandate as their political "base camp" before they attempt to gain influence regionally and nationally. They rely on small local networks of political friends (their spouses and close and trusted political companions) to "accumulate"[11] electoral mandates.

The history of the accumulation of mandates, according to Le Lidec, is part of the genesis of the French Republics – particularly the Third and Fourth Republics when, faced with unstable governments, elected officials were always worried about protecting their own political careers. During the seventy years of the Third Republic (1870 – 1940), there were fifty-one prime ministers and governments, and during the twelve years of the Fourth Republic (1946–58), there were thirteen prime ministers and governments. Indeed, from 1870 to 1958, a central government's tenure averaged about twelve months; the average since the beginning of the Fifth Republic in 1958 has been forty-six months.

For the last forty years, elected members of parliament, senators, and ministers and other members of the central government have not had to worry about unstable governments. Still, the practice of accumulating a local electoral mandate with other mandates – including the department, region, Senate, National Assembly, and European Union – remains a cornerstone of the political system. Often the accumulation of mandates will reinforce the position of a mayor, particularly in the case of a large municipality. Such a mayor may also control a general council or a region's presidency or both.

George Frêche is the archetypical example of a feudal political lord. After being mayor of the city of Montpellier for nearly twenty years, he resigned as mayor but remained on the city council and was nominated by his peers to become president of the "agglomeration of communes" for the Montpellier region. He also presides over the regional council and is the member of the National Assembly for the constituency of Montpellier.

Mayor Frêche also controls what happens in the Département d'Hérault because David Vezinhet, the president of the General Council, is his political friend and vassal. Vezinhet started his political career in 1977 on the municipal council of Montpellier. At the time, he was one of Frêche's closest allies and political friends in the Socialist Party, and as Frêche's political career took off, so did Vezinhet's. In 1983 Vezinhet became deputy mayor and a member of the regional council; in 1985 he became a member of the general council; and in 1998 he became its president. Today, he is also very active as chair of three local governments – special-purpose bodies – that manage transportation, planning, and economic development policies for Montpellier and its surrounding municipalities. Such an accumulation of mandates exemplifies that although the 1985 act limited the kind of mandates elected officials could have, it did not abolish the practice. The inability to accumulate a European mandate with a national one led to an increased specialization and division of labour among elected officials and their political teams.

Today, important political figures are able to accumulate by "delegation." A typical elected official wins a mandate, establishes a team and selects lieutenants, and then resigns from office, giving the office to his designated deputy, and so on and so forth, but always protecting his first local mandate. In 1988, for instance, 133 members of parliament resigned from their mandates, often opting for a mayoral or general council mandate rather than a regional one.

The 5 April 2000 "reform of the reform" of the accumulation of mandates stipulated that a member of parliament could not accumulate this mandate with that of a general or regional council member or with that of a mayor of a municipality of more than 3,000 inhabitants. Furthermore, an elected official could not resign from a recently won mandate. However, elected officials may still rely on their spouses and heads of staff. For example, Jean-Pierre Fourcade is the mayor of Saint-Cloud. He is also a senator and vice-president of the regional council of Ile-de-France. He used to be on the city council of Boulogne-Billancourt. He alternates with his spouse and deputies to remain in control. Similarly, the minister of the interior, Mr Sarcozy, is an elected council member of Neuilly and of the general council of Neuilly, after having been mayor and president of each for over a decade.

Today, most nationally elected officials hold a local mandate, with over 85 percent of all members of parliament and senators accumulating at least two mandates. In 2003, 90.8 percent of the 577 members of parliament and 80.7 percent of the 239 senators held a local elected office as well as their parliament mandate (Le Lidec 2001; Tronquoy 2004).

These vertical networks of elected officials link local politics to national decision-making processes and frame the relations of each level of government. They are critical to the efficiency of French policymaking. Today, they further the political and functional integration and coordination of each level of government that contracts organize, as the following section details.

6 THE SCOPE OF MUNICIPAL-CENTRAL INTERACTION

For the last thirty years, the central government has negotiated and signed contracts – the *Contrat de Plan État-région*, or *Plan* – with all regions and with some municipalities (Le Galès 1995; Pasquier 2003; Pontier 2004; Jouen 2002; John and Cole 2000; Digaetano and Strom 2003; De Penanros and Serfati 2000; Bourget 2002; Behar 2002b). These *Plans* lay out all contractual and planned activities for a period of five to seven years, which in turn overlaps with periods of negotiation that can last up to three years. Originally conceived as simple planning exercises that would allow central government officials to rally local key decision makers to their plans, these contracts became negotiated agreements between equal partners. Municipalities were free to participate in the negotiations – or not – which led to these contracts.

During the 1970s, the *politique de la ville* relied on these contracts to frame the use of specific grants; at the time, these agreements focused primarily on major infrastructure projects (André 2005). By the late 1970s, cities had managed to broaden the agenda to include social housing and the rehabilitation of downtown. These years that preceded decentralization also marked a pause, because these contracts were very unsuccessful at being inclusive and local elected officials were losing interest.

After 1982–83, the focus of new contracts expanded to include neighbourhood needs, especially the urban needs of the poorest populations – the underprivi-leged, the unskilled, and new immigrants. These contracts included all of the previous initiatives as well as education and security policies deemed to address issues of urban criminality. This period was a turning point. Locally elected offi-cials and their staff were able to influence the frames of references of these contracts. Each contract was to be locally negotiated to fit locally identified needs. They became broad policy frameworks which, when necessary, extended to the municipality as a whole and, in some instances, to the urban region.

Between 1989 and 2004, municipalities signed 296 contracts with the central government, including 136 neighbourhood conventions, 130 social-housing con-ventions, and 13 much broader "city" contracts that comprised 4,000 neighbour-hoods as their direct beneficiaries (André 2005). From 1994 to 1999, municipali-ties and the central government agreed to simplify procedures and to limit the number of contracts to 214 for about 1,500 neighborhoods that housed some 18 million people. Between 2000 and 2005, 247 contracts were signed, representing 2,199 communes, an increase of nearly 1,300 new municipalities partnering with others (70 percent of these were signed with intermunicipal organizations in charge of these policies), and they targeted 27 million people – half of the population of France.

Funding for these contracts is very complex, for it involves all levels of govern-ment, the European Union, and the private sector. In 2003 the central government's contribution was estimated at 1,363 billion euros. Municipalities or intermunicipal special-purpose bodies provided 664 million euros, regions 106 million, and de-partments 155 million (DATAR 2000–5). Various public and private pension funds and insurance corporations also contributed funds. Finally, various activities in-cluded in these contracts were eligible for different "Objectives and Funds" offered by the European Commission. Objectives 1, 2, and 3 contributed 200 million euros, and the Urban 2 and Equal programs contributed 20 million euros (André 2005; 2000–5).

In the past, municipalities had been encouraged by their prefects to pool re-sources, funding, and staff into one of the intermunicipal special-purpose bodies that were available to them. This contrasts with recent ministerial documentation suggesting that this prefectoral leadership was not a requirement (France, SPV 2003). An eligible municipality may enter into a partnership on its own, and in-deed, during the 1980s and 1990s a large number of municipalities acted autonomously. This explains the relatively small number of municipalities per contract and the fact that those contracts affected only a small proportion of the population. Measured by the number of intermunicipal agreements, recent reforms have been quite successful. The impact of this policy, as it now concerns half of the French population, is being transformed by municipalities' taking the initiative to collaborate. Mayors and municipal elected officials engage their colleagues in their region, their department, and the central government to co-produce and implement policies that specifically address the needs of their communities from a grassroots perspective. From a top-down policy, the *politique de la Ville* has evolved into an interesting example of a bottom-up, multilevel governance policy.

7 THE NATURE OF MUNICIPAL-CENTRAL INTERACTION

Municipal-central interactions had a long history of strict top-down control called *la tutelle*. However, this tutelage system was phased out during the last part of the twentieth century (Boeuf 2002; Masquet, Domergue, and Kiwan 2002; Remond 2002; Thoenig 1992; Gaudemet and Gohin 2004; Moreau 1978). Originally, prefects were the executive heads of general councils and municipalities; their staffs were field officers of the central government; and their control over municipal and general council decisions was tightly framed legally. Tutelage spanned issues such as the behaviour of elected officials on council, most local government decisions, including budgetary matters, and the prefect's prior approval of which decisions were presented to council.

Early in the last century, prefects were very powerful administrators of the central government. The 1910s to 1920s were a period of increased and tighter control, which eased after the Second World War, particularly in the 1960s. Its shaky start notwithstanding, local power was strengthened in the Fifth Republic (Worms and Gremion 1968). In 1982 the tutelage system disappeared in principle but remained in application regarding some budgetary matters and some technical issues. Municipalities, general councils, and the newly created regions could not vote on an unbalanced budget and were expected to request the technical views of field officers of the central government in areas such as road width, sewage tanks, and water quality.

Today, tutelage has been replaced by a judicial review of all decisions made at the local level. However, mayors still work with officials of the central government on all matters of municipal accounting, and the influence of the technical expertise of the central government, despite being challenged daily, remains important in some policy arenas, such as those concerning roads and bridges, water mains and sewage tanks, and policing. The evidence suggests that in most instances these are policy arenas where local governments have chosen to limit their staff development because of the expertise and well-known overinvolvement and control of certain professions, such as civil engineers.

The relevance and influence of the "control of legality" as a mechanism that counteracts local governments' decisions have become a matter of debate. The general view is that elected officials are not constrained by this control of legality because it is not used against them for two reasons. First, the prefects' staffs do not have the resources (human or financial) to monitor all local government decisions. Indeed, they review few of them and refer even fewer to administrative tribunals. In theory, prefects are supposed to review about 7.5 million Acts yearly, yet only about 1,500 to 1,700 Acts are brought before administrative tribunals. When prefects suspect something illegal, their office is to prepare a letter "observation" to ask for an "explanation" and to refer the case to an administrative tribunal. In 1989 no Acts were referred to administrative tribunals in seven departments. Overall, only 0.022 percent of all Acts have ever been referred to administrative tribunals: 420 of those were deemed suspended, and only 1,293 were actually struck down. As well, local governments can ask for a certification of exception from an administrative tribunal, and both a prefect and an administrative tribunal can declare an exception to an Act that would otherwise be deemed illegal.[12]

Second, the relationship that prefects and subprefects have with elected officials is central to their own administrative careers; they do not frustrate influential elected officials or their political friends for no good reason. As noted above in section 5, a mayor or other prominent elected official can have tremendous influence and control over the nomination of a new prefect in their department. Furthermore, the evidence suggests that because of their functions and delegated powers, both prefects and general council presidents are able to keep a large number of mayors of smaller municipalities in their network of influence. There are about 450 subprefects, 100 prefects, and 22 regional prefects across metropolitan France. They all know that the success of their career is proportional to their ability to work well with prominent and successful elected officials and with their networks of friends and political allies. Their primary career objective is to serve on a ministerial team for a time, not to review all new municipal decisions systematically.

In the end, because prefects work in a highly politicized environment that creates a dependency on powerful elected officials and because decentralization has increased the number of decisions made by local government, the "control of legality" is not a serious threat. The central government could limit its arenas of investigation or hire more staff to implement better controls. Such decisions, however, are the responsibility of elected officials who sit in the National Assembly and the Senate. The traditional balance of power between central and local governments, especially municipalities, has shifted. Despite limited research on the topic, cities seem to emerge as the clear beneficiaries.

8 MUNICIPAL-CENTRAL RELATIONS AND REGIONAL GOVERNMENTS

Although municipal-central relations are not mediated by regions, most actions do take place at the regional level. Regions are "young" local government institutions that were created in 1982. In France, they did not catalyze regional political movements as in Italy or the United Kingdom. However, the state-regions contracts, or *Plans*, date back a quarter of a century and constitute a well-established tradition of broad economic development and planning "contracts" that bring together, around the negotiating table, all levels of governments with a large number of public and private organizations, and which hold them accountable to each other through contracts that span at least five years. The current contracts for the 2000–2006 period concern the twelfth plan. For instance, in the last round of negotiations regarding the Nord-Pas de Calais 2000–2006 contracts, the region was a key partner alongside each level of government – the central state, both departments, and a number of key municipalities (Dunkerque, Boulogne-sur-Mer, Lille-Roubaix-Tourcoing, Lens-Liévin, Valenciennes, Maubeuge-Val de Sambre) – and the European Union. All partners fund the contract for a total of 28 billion francs: the central government contributed 10.4 billion, the region 7 billion, the departments, 2.6 billion, and the European Union 8 billion (Conseil regional du Nord-Pas de Calais 2004).

Furthermore, the European Union's Structural and Social Funds, launched in 1974, and its Community Initiatives policies, introduced in 1989, have chosen the regional level as their key territorial unit for all policy negotiations and all processes involving partnerships, funding, applications, implementations, and evaluations. Regions, however, are not the exclusive partners of the European Commission. Its funds and policies bring a multiplicity of governments and public and private organizations to the table (Manesse 1998; Auby 2003; Behar 2002c; Behar and Estebe 1997). The regional impact of European policies is detailed further in section 9 below.

After the creation of regional governments during the 1980s and 1990s, some scholars predicted that they would gain in importance – that their role as key signatories for contracts and their general responsibility for economic development policy might cause the departments to disappear and lead to a fusion of regions that could compete with German *Länder*. The scholarly debate, however, did not influence the recent reforms.

The 2003 constitutional reforms (detailed in section 2 above) and the subsequent strengthening of all local governments has revealed that regions are now well established among local governments but with no authority over any other government. The constitutional reform of 28 March, 2003 actually entrenched the principle of cooperation among all governments (Article 72.5). Also, compared with other local governments (as shown in section 4 above), regions actually remained relatively small in terms of both staff and budget, and the further downloading of 2003–4 did not affect this balance of power among local governments. As for further downloading, the early proposals to transfer the Ministry of Education's technical and administrative staff to the regions never materialized. Their responsibilities, however, expanded in economic development, professional training, and regional transportation. They were also given the leadership for the coordination of all European Union policies. Although this will obviously strengthen the position of regional council presidents in all negotiations with regional prefects, the planned reduction of all EU Structural and Social Funds by 2007 will minimize the impact of this transfer of authority. As a result, regions have not emerged as key mediators of central-municipal relations.

The prefects were also affected by new reforms, notably Act 2000-374, of 29 April, 2004, relating to the new constitutional amendment that affected the functions and organization of the central government. Its impact on regional prefects is interesting, if only to underline that this central government reform included a further deconcentration of services that strengthen the regional coordination of all de-concentrated services. Initiated in 1992 and further reformed with the government's decision of 29 April 2004, Act 2000-374 stipulated that prefects and government field offices were to be reorganized under the strengthened coordinating role of prefects. The five traditional ministries that were not affected by prefectoral rule – justice, health, education, finance, and labour – must now work with the regional prefects, who have become the exclusive coordinating representatives of the central government and the only authority for the signature of all agreements and contracts. Prefects are now the gatekeepers for all interaction with all local governments and are the only authority to engage the central government on contracts and conventions. Regional prefects are to uphold national coherence in all programs. No government activity can take place without consulting the prefect, including the activities of nationalized private-sector corporations. Prefects chair all service committees, including the "regional action" and "chiefs of staff" committees, and may organize all deconcentrated services according to regional priorities or to pools of competency. Finally, they have the authority to nominate project leaders who coordinate specific policy actions (Tronquoy 2004). These reforms attest to the need to strengthen the coordination of all field offices of the central government, particularly at the level of the region. They mark the emergence of prominent regional prefects, but they also highlight the fact that the minority position held by officials of the central government in all regional negotiations is no longer protected by legal or financial authority or by the traditional prestige of their functions; rather, it results from negotiations among varied points of views, where the primary role of prefects is to maintain national coherence while other local government officials assert what is best for their communities (Behar and Estebe 1997, 1999; Tronquoy 2004).

When the central government deconcentrated further resources and reasserted the authority of the regional prefect the regions did not see their responsibilities or authority increase. These two concurrent trends support the contention that it is at the regional level that primarily European, central, and regional governments and public- and private-sector organizations converge to organize the governance of France. What is clear, however, is that no one government is emerging as the key mediating authority; neither the prefects and their central state field officials nor regional elected officials and their regional government staff are able to dominate the regional policy game.

These interactions may benefit the large cities that are at the heart of the regional political economic and social systems – and, by extension, the mayors of these few large regional capitals. Examples include Pierre Mauroy, when he was mayor of Lille; Martine Aubry, his political protégée and successor at Lille City Hall; George Frêche, the mayor of Montpellier; Jacques Chirac, when he was mayor of Paris; and Alain Juppe who was mayor of Bordeaux. Their extensive networks of influence and control over regional political networks (as described in section 5) show that they are emerging as *primus inter pares*.

9 ARE MUNICIPALITIES BYPASSING CENTRAL AND REGIONAL GOVERNMENTS AND ENGAGING IN INTERNATIONAL RELATIONS?

French municipalities have been active internationally since the 1980s, when EU funds were made available that encouraged them and the regions of Europe to take part in pan-European networks and to design and implement programs spanning the borders. Today, it is arguable that French local governments' new vertical relations with the European Commission and their horizontal relations with their peers across the European Union interfere greatly with the traditional, hierarchical, and submissive relations they had with the central government until the 1980s. Also, the influence of EU law on the framework of action of local governments is felt everywhere – from environmental law to public service regulations (Jouen 2002; Rossinot 2003; Behar 2002c; Behar and Estebe 1997, 1999, 2004; Morin 2003).

Until the early 1980s the European Union was not particularly concerned with subnational governments, but it has since opened new arenas of policy discussion that are primarily horizontal involving non-central authorities at the same level of government across the European Union. Over the past twenty-five years, non-central authorities in France and across the European Union have gradually been able to engage and partner with one another in making use of European funds.

The EU principle of subsidiarity, partly owing to the different ways in which it has been interpreted, has also greatly influenced local-central relations across the European Union. Introduced with the Treaty of Maastricht,[13] it was first understood as a hierarchical organizing principle: subsidiarity meant that each level of governments was to deal with those policy needs that it could best address at its level. More recently, past EU president Romano Prodi (2000) argued that subsidiarity was not about hierarchies that divided powers but was about governance networks that developed mechanisms to coproduce policies.

Finally, their varied forms and functions notwithstanding, the European Union's Committee of the Regions represents all European local governments: French or Italian regions, German *Länder*, or Spanish autonomous communities. The Committee of the Regions' representatives have to hold local electoral office but are appointed by the government of each member state. Since the committee only delivers opinions, it is considered a relatively weak EU institution. Yet it is a powerful lobby group, effectively representing regions and major cities in all negotiations and consultations and in all EU institutions.

The EU Structural and Social Funds and Community Initiatives dominate European regional policies. There are five categories of funds, each addressing different regional needs, and four pan-EU Community Initiatives: Interreg, Leader, Urban, and Equal. The overall budget for the European Union in 2003 was about 100 billion euros. The Structural and Social Funds accounted for about 33 percent and the Community Initiatives for about 6.5 percent (European Commission 2005). For the period 2001–6, the French share of structural funds amounted to about 10 billion euros, or 2 billion annually. During this time, the structural funds (objectives 1 and 2) accounted for about 42 million euros, or about 8 million annually, for the Nord-Pas de Calais region, which compares well with the 140 million euros attached to the five-year *contrat de plan* (France, DATAR 2005). It is reasonable to assume that these sizable European funds are transforming local policymaking in France. There is substantial literature on these transformations: French regions are now entirely responsible for allocating European Regional Development Funds in their constituencies. More and more, they are partnering with bordering and other regions of Europe to gain access to EU Community Initiative Funds, for instance (Brillet and Feron 2006).

However, France has yet to address the fact that it does not spend all the EU funds for which it applies. For instance, in 2002 France ranked fourteenth out of fifteen EU member states in terms of how well it had spent its EU funds. This has two implications for future funding applications. First, because French local governments are underspenders, they are likely to lose out to overspenders. Second, in their partnerships and linkages with other European partners, they are perceived as incapacitated by their slow procedures. This is a serious deterrent to all future partnerships and could affect the European Union's allocation of funds. These difficulties might increase with time because, by 2013, all EU programs and funds regarding agriculture and regional policies (about three-quarters of all EU funds) will have taken into account the needs of all ten new eastern member states, whose regions are much poorer. This will likely raise concerns about the continued influence of those EU policies on French local governments.

Overall, however, European programs and the European Commission have brought French local governments into large pan-European networks that privilege cross-border cooperation and partnerships. Participating French local governments have in turn, been greatly influenced by the continuing work of European local governments, both through lobby groups at the EU level, (such as the European Association of Local Economic Development Agencies) and through public policy forums involving all European members. Yet the lack of representation of French regions and larger municipalities in Brussels is well known among lobby organizations (Gueguen 2005). French organizations are generally not well represented among lobbyists, law firms, consulting agencies, the media, and NGOs. Compared to how proactive and focused British, German, Italian, Spanish, and all Scandinavian regions are on the needs of their constituencies, French regions are underrepresented.

Nevertheless, the compound effect of these trends signals the emergence of a pan-European public policy discourse and practice. Local and regional governance is under the influence of EU policies that shape their overarching strategies as they assimilate, share ideas and "best practices" across Europe, and lead French local governments that are lagging behind to become progressively more European. So there is a constellation of local, regional, national, and European, public and private actors that are colluding in co-production, funding, and implementation of policies that are giving rise to European transnational partnerships among local interests. The future of such networks, once funding is spread thin between twenty-seven rather than fifteen members, is difficult to predict. Yet it is possible that funding may not be key at all. Instead, it may be that these networks have become the very fabric of local governance of Europe, thus influencing local government policy views and practices.

10 POLICY CASE STUDIES

10.1 IMMIGRANT SETTLEMENT POLICIES IN FRANCE: SOCIAL DIVERSITY AND URBAN SEGREGATION

Immigrant settlement policies are generally viewed as unsuccessful, fuelling segregation in France. For the last fifty years, policies designed by the central ministries in charge of transportation, infrastructures, and planning have attempted to engineer social mixing, diversity, and assimilation.[14] In effect, they have produced segregated neighbourhoods, municipalities, and cities.

During the 1950s and 1960s, urban planning was the key policy tool used to engineer social mixing and assimilation. Varied populations were targeted to live together. At the time, the idea of diversity, social mixing, and assimilation was not a clear policy choice. Instead, it was assumed that if populations with similar social and economic backgrounds were settled side by side they would naturally assimilate. The unsuccessful assimilation attempts of this era precipitated a major social crisis in the 1970s and eventually gave rise to the 1977 reform. The idea then was to socialize the populations being targeted by mixing them up within designated social-housing parks. An additional view was that transferring ownership would maintain diversity while increasing social mixing and assimilation. A tax called "1 percent lodging" was levied on all new construction projects. Loans were set up to help potential residents. The central government systematically monitored and regulated the mixing of populations in particular neighbourhoods, and prefects managed quotas for each department. But the policy only aggravated the situation. It was characterized by a rise in crime and high geographic ethnic concentrations in specific urban social-housing parks.

During the 1980s the implementation of social housing was downloaded to municipalities. This resulted in even greater fragmentation of social housing. In the 1990s the policy recommendations were that specific areas could be detached from the housing parks to be managed by social mixing and social assimilation professionals. At the same time, there was a policy of better-balanced assimilation that offered lower rents – the *Plan de Localisation de l'Habitat* (PLH). Management of PLH was extremely expensive. Municipalities limited eligible social housing; consequently, despite a steady demand for such housing, its availability actually declined.

In 2000 there was renewed interest in urban social issues, especially urban segregation, social mixing and integration, and social-housing policies. The law *Solidarité renouvellement urbain*[15] mandated that all new residential construction projects in French municipalities would have to set aside 20 percent of their units for social housing. It also introduced the possibility of public-private partnerships. Policy mechanisms included funding for targeted populations. The availability of social housing was manipulated to encourage a better mix of the middle class and groups in need of social housing. Public safety was improved, rents were controlled, and eviction procedures were set up to protect three types of landlords: municipalities, prefectures, and the private sector.

This short history gives rise to two sets of questions. First, who are the key policy actors in immigrant settlement and social integration? Second, what is the specific role of municipalities and their relationship with the responsible ministry? In 2003 the infrastructure ministry initiated a series of policy papers in order to come to grips with the failure of social-housing policy and social segregation in France. The body of research that emerged exceeds the scope of this paper. However, research by Bacqué and Fol (1998) on social mixing and assimilation in St Denis, Montreuil, and Gènevillier is particularly relevant, because it shows that these municipalities implemented strategies not to encourage social mixing or diversity but with the sole objective of protecting their electoral basis. St Denis, Montreuil, and Gènevillier are called the "red" municipalities of the Parisian suburbs; they have been controlled by communist or socialist parties since the Second World War. They have always had very ambitious social-housing policies, based primarily on rental units. A typical social-housing park in these municipalities may reach 30 percent of the overall housing stock.

Until the late 1960s, social-housing was about building residences for a growing population in a country faced with a very serious housing shortage. Twenty years later, when social housing policies became more focused on diversity and mixing populations, these same municipalities became more concerned about maintaining their well-established middle class than about responding to the need for housing. In theory, municipalities are expected to provide social housing to new immigrant populations, but their policies of allocation are closed and almost secretive. In other words, new immigrant families who are offered social housing are subject to careful scrutiny. Municipalities control social housing to prevent a pauperization of the municipal population. There are also clear ethnic criteria for the allotment of all social housing, and progressively mixed socio-economic groups are mixed within the same housing parks. This mixed social-housing policy is accompanied by innovative architecture, which further differentiates and targets different populations.

Bacqué and Fol (1998) argue that these municipalities faced a double evolution of their strategies during the 1990s. On the one hand, they were coping with mounting pressure to develop office buildings in the nearby suburbs of Paris. On the other hand, their middle class was leaving. The remaining population was becoming ever more impoverished. All three municipalities ended up diversifying offers for housing. They partnered with the private sector to attract targeted population groups as a way of redressing relative deprivation. While regulating rents to prevent gentrification, Montreuil insisted on the highest possible quality for all new buildings. Expensive properties that might attract younger and better-educated groups were to be avoided, because they threatened to transform the electoral fabric of the municipalities.

In the end, demographic factors worked against Montreuil but not St Denis. The municipality of St Denis chose to focus on developing office buildings and to make do with the overall decline of its blue-collar population. Montreuil built more social housing, but it lost its traditional electoral groups.

Officials skirt the issue of ethnicity. Yet municipalities define diversity in terms of either ethnicity or class. St Denis is a blue-collar but ethnically homogeneous municipality; Montreuil is ethnically diverse but less stratified. Municipalities are able to manipulate specific mixing and social-housing goals effectively because they mediate the policy goals of the central government, of their departments, and the private sector (Bacqué and Fol 1998). Until the late 1980s, these municipalities did not want their electorate to buy housing, so they invested in rental housing on a large scale. Their electoral base was made up of the white working class. Their social and integration housing policies *de facto* insolated those municipalities from the overarching goals of the central government.

By controlling for income, these municipalities operationalized discriminatory policies without clear ethnic criteria. By partnering to: (1) set up social-housing plans for their agglomeration, (2) fund social-housing plans together, and (3) barter social-housing projects with each other, they reached the 20 percent mandate for social housing across the urban agglomeration. Each municipality in the urban agglomeration was thus able to specialize and protect its targeted populations.

In theory, prefectoral rule should penalize those municipalities that do not reach the 20 percent threshold. Those that reach the floor cannot be forced to increase their proportion. However, the unit to which the 20 percent ratio applies is controversial. Is it to be applied at the level of the urban agglomeration, the municipality, the neighbourhood, the street, or each new building? Decisions by administrative tribunals posit that the municipality is the appropriate level. But this is very difficult to implement because, as noted above, the threshold is actually managed by intermunicipal special-purpose bodies. In those rare cases where a prefect decides to penalize a municipality, the prefect ends up managing the social-housing park directly. But prefects have limited resources to control and enforce these regulations, and municipalities are building less and less social housing. Michel Sarkozy, for instance, never reached the 20 percent threshold when he was mayor of Neuilly, a wealthy suburb of Paris. He opted to pay fines instead (Charles 2005).

Despite central government policies against urban and social ghettos, social-housing policy has currently reached a deadlock, with the targeted populations of poorer and richer municipalities increasing without any greater mixing and diversification of their social-housing parks. The 20 percent floor for social housing has in effect become a ceiling. In conclusion, this case study shows that in matters of immigrant settlement, central state officials are unable to carry out their policy objectives, despite expertise and powerful regulatory tools at their disposal. In response to immigrant settlement, the French public system put forward a policy that is highly fragmented, complex, and asymmetrical.

10.2 ROAD INFRASTRUCTURE

In 1960 France had only about 120 kilometres of highway but a good network of national roads that were well maintained, though it lagged behind other European countries. By 2003 France had 11,383 kilometres of highways, 27,893 kilometres of national roads, 363,033 kilometres of departmental roads, and 609,635 kilometers of municipal roads. Over the past twenty-five years, however, the central government has downloaded to municipalities the responsibility for more than one million kilometres of road. Whereas departmental expenditures for maintenance decreased by 31 percent between 1985 and 1995, investment in new road infrastructure had risen by 77.6 percent (France, Ministère de l'Equipement et des Transports 2006).

Between 1950 and 1990, the way transportation was administered and funded changed significantly. In 1950 the central government had full responsibility for France's network of roads and bridges. By 1990, however, about 2 billion euros came from public-private partnerships that had been set up to build new toll highways, while about 1 billion euros came from the central state and 1.1 billion came from the departments.

The bureaucracy in charge of the administration of roads modernized only slowly. In 1992 the Court of Accounts reported that the economy of roads and highways was still not subject to the general principles of free market competition, while the central government progressively was disengaging from maintenance expenditures and from funding new roads (France, Cour des Comptes 1992). In 1998 the Court of Accounts once again noted that the central government was withdrawing from building new roads, while regions and municipalities, and especially departments, shared the newly decentralized responsibilities to fund and harmonize roads in regional and municipal networks. Departments are key funding partners among local governments. Yet, they also have to take into account the regional plans and subsidize municipalities. The Court of Accounts, however, observed that equalization across departments, regions, and municipalities was based on different procedures that failed to produce equalization. The court underlined regional, departmental, and municipal variations that resulted in the creation of a national network of roads of increasingly varied quality, where maintenance varied from eight to twenty years, depending on capacity, weather, geography, and local politics (France, Cour des Comptes 1998).

More recently, with the statute of 13 August 2004, the minister of transport further decentralized to the departments 20,000 kilometres of national roads, along with administrative and fiscal resources. Following the recommendation of the Fourcade Commission, this law transferred 185 million euros in block grants to departments and forbade all future central-local funding partnerships for the construction of new roads. Furthermore, 24,000 central government employees, whose primary task is to build or maintain departmental roads, became departmental staff (France, Ministère des Transports 2006).

On the one hand, the administration of roads was slow to modernize. On the other hand, decentralization played a big part in its rapid expansion and modernization. How is one to explain such rapid change in a policy area where most of the road system has been progressively downloaded to local governments? The literature points to two major shifts in the postwar period. First, over the years, the central government was able to download responsibilities to lower-level governments, particularly to departments, which invested in roads. Second, as the central government shifted costs and responsibilities, it never lost control over the direction of policy. The training of central state officials at the School of Bridges and Roads – one of France's *grand corps* a "caste" of engineers, who were able to retain tight control over the construction of roads and bridges and to continually influence decisions about roads by lower level governments, is key.

The engineers' particular interest in modernizing roads and bridges involves a form of legal corruption, or personal interest, that would be unacceptable in any anglophone country (Mény 1996). A financial incentive causes the engineers to lobby lower-level governments for a multitude of new contracts to modernize their roads. The more contracts are signed, the greater their annual bonus (Mény 1992). When individual or commercial traffic increases, elected officials turn to those employees of the central state who are in charge of roads. Over the last twenty-five years, elected officials have been sold on their municipality being at the "heart" of Europe and in great need of renewed investment to ensure that it is properly connected to national and international transportation networks. Yet existing roads are poorly maintained, and most local solutions seem to culminate in the construction of a new toll speedway.

Since the creation of this caste of engineers by Napoleon Bonaparte – when post-revolutionary France had no resources to pay its staff – the payment of bridge and road engineers has been paid based on the portion of the works they supervise. In Jean Petot's history of the administration of bridges and roads from 1599 to 1815, he notes the progressive establishment of these technocrats and the particularity of their wages, which include a bonus of one-twentieth of all work supervised (Mény 1992, 145). Today, this "bonus" supplements their salary and in most cases doubles their annual income. It amounts to a percentage of all the proposals and studies, supervisions, and controls which they exercise over any public works contracted by a local government. Since the "bonus" is inversely proportioned to the size of a contract, it is customary to multiply and reduce the number and size of contracts, thereby maximizing the annual bonus.

This practice was abolished on 6 January 1945 but was reinstated just as quickly in 1948[16] to motivate this *grand corps d'Etat* to modernize France's infrastructure. In addition, all new suburban cities and all social housing and 50,000 kilometres of national roads were downloaded to departments and municipalities. A reform passed on 12 May 1970 specified that all new kilometres of highway were to incur a 0.5 percent payment on construction costs as well as 0.5% on all tolls. Since 1981, this annual bonus has been aggregated at the national level to equalize rich and poor departments. Critics argue that this change allows funds to be reallocated towards less-densely populated communities when areas with a high-density population oppose new infrastructure (*A contre courant syndical et politique* 2006; Mény 1992). All Bridges and Roads engineers are eligible for this "bonus," not only those staffing the Ministry of Transport. Over the past twenty-five years, the road system of France was largely decentralized to departments, along with regions and municipalities, but the staff and expertise necessary to study and supervise roadways has remained part of the central government technocracy. This is in the process of changing. Staff is being decentralized, and financial and human resources are being downloaded to local governments in order to address local and central needs to maintain a well-balanced network of roads. In this case study, as in the first, successive decentralization reforms have increased asymmetry – in this case, asymmetry of the quality of roads across France.

11 WHAT ARE THE RECENT TRENDS?

The 1982 decentralization laws democratized the system of local government. All are autonomous and elected. Traditional top-down control by the central government was replaced by judicial review. The 2003 constitutional reforms entrenched the organization of France as decentralized, with three levels of local government and other intermunicipal partnerships, and guaranteed financial autonomy. Autonomy is a contentious issue because no one level of government has any control over socio-economic policy. Policymaking results from a multitude of interactions between local and central governments and European and other public and private organizations.

Contracts are replacing top-down regulatory policymaking. Contract negotiations involve local and central government staff. Here, the regional level is emerging as the mediator. Officials of the central government are attempting to uphold national standards; therefore, they present their views as neutral. But this is controversial with officials of local governments, because the central government has shown itself reluctant to relinquish control over local finances. Future decisions by the Constitutional Council will be very decisive in this matter. At this time, however, it seems that the autonomy of local governments has expanded in spite of tight fiscal environments.

The accumulation of mandates is a fundamental feature of local government that has strengthened local elected officials and made them more influential. From the 1970s onward, elected officials challenged the authority of prefects. They now bypass the prefects to negotiate directly with ministerial or European officials. This is particularly true of members of parliament and senators, who also are elected at the local level and have built their political careers by accumulating mandates and cultivating local political networks. In France, where there are 36,000 communes and about 55,000 municipalities (including special-purpose intermunicipal bodies) a total of 1.5 million elected officials ground French politics in many territories and communities. About 680 of these officials are elected, both at the local and the national level of government. They make up a well-staffed, well-organized, and Europeanized political elite that spans all levels of government, including the European level, in a complex system of governance.

12 IS THE SYSTEM OF MULTILEVEL GOVERNANCE ADEQUATE IN RELATION TO MUNICIPAL AND URBAN POLICY?

French scholars and elected officials concur that recent decentralization reforms have been important and successful because of a rare coincidence of interests. The former prime minister Jean-Pierre Raffarin, understood local issues well. He had emerged from the political elite that accumulates local and regional mandates. Since 1988 – before becoming prime minister – he had held a council mandate in a small municipality and was the elected president of the Région de Poitou Charentes. His published work on regional political life testified to his strong beliefs in strengthening local government. In his efforts to reform the French system of local government, he coalesced with Senate President Christian Poncelet, whose ambition was to reassert the Senate's role in taking important policy initiatives.

Both leaders were quite successful. In part, the reforms merely organize and legislate a pre-existing policy practice. This is not unusual in French politics. Yet the process also allowed for serious and wide consultations and analysis. Scholars and elected officials now argue that this process established the importance and historical significance of these reforms when compared with previous ones. Voices on the left of the political spectrum, however, would like to have seen the reforms extended further. This is indicative of possible future pressure to persist with the current decentralizing and regionalizing trends.

France has fashioned its own form of multilevel governance. Elected and staff officials in central or local governments have great difficulty in pointing out a single policy arena where they dominate. All levels of governments are tightly entangled and complementary in all areas of social and economic policy. It follows that the French Republic is now decentralized and is becoming a system of multilevel governance. Even if the 2003 constitutional reforms and the 2004 laws are considered an experimental part of an ongoing process to find the appropriate level of territorial application of a particular policy, it seems that at this time the decentralized French Republic is made up of intermeshed and territorially overarching policy networks (Marks 1992), which are a classical example of multilevel governance.

Constitutional reforms have affected the organizational governance of France. French government is now about governance among equals, where contracting establishes the influence of local governments. The regional level, where all interests of the intergovernmental network seem to converge, emerges as the new locus of the political territory. This is reminiscent of Keating's (1998, 1999b, 1999c) and Sassen's (1996) work on the influence of global markets on the politics of state relations in the intergovernmental and international arenas which make governing much more complex. Yet issues of complexity and accountability – which Sassen highlights – were never discussed in the media or by elected or public officials. Few scholars actually raised questions about the complexity and opacity of the system of local government. It is assumed that its fundamental characteristic is protected; it is democratic and accountable because it is grounded in over 36,000 elected municipalities.

Territorial and policy asymmetry, however, are emerging issues. There is little doubt that the French system is now asymmetrical in nature. This may contravene the constitutional principle of equity. Even in the area of welfare funding and administration, the department is partially responsible, regions are in charge of professional training, and municipalities take care of policies of solidarity. All three levels of government get funding from an agency of the central state, the Agence nationale pour la renovation urbaine (ANRU). Partnerships of this sort also involve the *Plan* and the European Union. Multilevel governance emerges as an answer to growing policy asymmetry. These mechanisms of governance, however, make transparency an issue because they result from a very complex network of agencies and overarching policy networks.

NOTES

This paper would not have been possible without the support of the Social Science and Humanities Research Council of Canada. I would like to thank Robert Young, Christian Leuprecht, and particularly Harvey Lazar for their patience, advice, and encouragement. In France, Elise Feron helped with most of the documentation and prepared fieldwork. Elise Feron, Vincent de Briant, and Michel Verpaux should also be thanked for having had the patience and kindness to meet with me repeatedly and to read early drafts of this paper. As it turned out, their help and advice were invaluable. All errors remain mine.

1 This is Michael Keating's argument in "Challenges to Federalism, Territory, Function, and Power in a Globalizing World" in Young (1999, 8–27). The argument is also found in Salmon and Keating (1990).
2 French laws tend to become known by the date on which they were passed.
3 Gaston Deferre did not attempt to address all issues of decentralization. Instead, he focused on key issues strategically. His few initial proposals were to launch a reform (see Schmidt 1993).
4 Translated by the author. Intermunicipal partnership organizations are similar in form and function to traditional systems found in North America called districts, regional municipalities, or regional districts. They are special-purpose bodies that federate a few municipal functions often related to major infrastructure or public transportation. In France, their names vary with the size of the core municipality and also take into account whether they are mostly urban or rural special-purpose bodies. "Districts" and "city communities" disappeared in 2004; the new Act created "commune communities," an "agglomeration of communes," and "urban communities." In French, these five local institutions are called *district, communauté de ville, communauté de communes, agglomeration de communes*, and c*ommunauté urbaine*. The "union of communes" translates as *syndicat intercommunal*. They are unifunctional organizations.

5 European and North American jurists who specialize in European Union law contend that the 10,000 pages of legislation that include major treaties and a European Charter of Human Rights form a constitutional body of law that profoundly affects the legal systems of all member states. The French parliament spends half its time reviewing and enacting EU laws.

6 See the so-called Deferre Act, 82-123, regarding the freedoms and rights of regions, departments, and communes (JORF 3 March 1982, 730), particularly Article 102, which states that "resources should be transferred along with all net increases in charges resulting from state downloading to local collectivities or the region."

7 In 1993 the central government cancelled the region and department tax on "vacant properties"; the finance law of 2000 cancelled the regional share of the "habitation tax"; and the finance law of 2001 cancelled the tax on licence plates (called the *vignette automobile*).

8 TIPP translates into "petroleum products interior tax."

9 Key texts on past and present scholarly views on local public finances include M. Bouvier, M.C.Esclassan, and J.P. Lassale, *Finances Publiques* (Paris: LGDJ, 2002) ; H.M. Darnanville "L'Autonomie financière et fiscales de collectivitès locales passé par une reforme de leur fiscalité" , *Actualité juridique de droit administratif*; D. Guillaume, *La necessaire consécration constitutionnelle d'un pouvoir fiscal des collectivités territoriales* (Paris: Economica, 2002) ; and R. Hertzog, "L'ambigue constitutionalisation des finances locales," *Actualité juridique de droit administratif*, November 2003, 548–58 (Mouzet 2003; Trosa 2002).

10 See, for instance, Hertzog 2003. See also Jean-Claude Ricci, "Les nouvelles garanties constitutionnelles en matière de resources des collectivités," in *Acte du Colloque des 31 Mars et 1 Avril 2003, Revue juridique de l'Océan Indien, Saint Denis de la Réunion*, 3-2003.

11 The French expression is *cumul des mandats*, which suggest an accumulation of electoral mandates.

12 See the State Council decision of 6 October 2000, *Ministry of interior* versus *Commune of St. Florent*.

13 The Treaty of Maastricht of 1992 established the monetary union.

14 The French conceptual expression that captures the principles that organized the policy of immigrant settlement is *diversité sociale,et mixité,* which translates into social diversity and assimilation.

15 Solidarity and Urban Renewal.

16 It was reintroduced by Bill 48-1530 on 29 September 1948, with additions regarding the construction of new cities on the outskirts of the Région de Paris.

REFERENCES

A contre courant syndical et politique. 2006. "Ingénieurs de l'équipement et aménagement du térritoire." www.acontrecourant.org/108inge.html (accessed July 2006)

André, Pierre. 2005. *Contrat de ville: rénover et simplifier*. Information report to the Senate by Pierre André, Paris: The Senate

Auby, Jean-Bernard. 2003. "Décentralisation 2003: le modèle français en mutation." *Pouvoirs Locaux* 59 (4): 37–41

Bacqué, Marie-Hélène, and Sylvie Fol. 1998. *Le devenir des banlieues rouges:* ha*bitat et sociétés.* Paris: L'Harmattan

Balme, Richard. 1998. *Les politiques du neoregionalism.* Paris: Economica

Baverez, Nicola, and Denis Olivennes. 1989. *L'impuissance publique.* Paris: Calman Levy

Behar, Daniel. 2000a. "L'agglomération: entre gouvernement et gouvernance." ha*bitat et société* 19 (September): 2–3

– 2002b. "Au-delà de la décentralisation: repenser le pouvoir local." In *Pour en finir avec la décentralisation,* ed. Charles Floquet, 2–10 Paris: Editions de l'aube

– 2002c. "De l'Europe au local: vers un partage de la souveraineté politique." *Les cahiers du management territorial* 12:1–5

– 2002d "Le département: intercesseur territorial?" *Interrogations: La revue des agences de développement et des comités d'expansion* 240: 12–21

Behar, Daniel, and Philippe Estebe. 1997. "Etat et politique territoriales: de la discrimination positive à la derogation." In *L'Etat de la France,1997–98, 10–13.* Paris: La Découverte

– 1999. "Aménagement du territoire: la solution locale." In *L'Etat de la France, 1999–2000,* Paris: La Découverte

– 2004. "Aménagement du territoire: une mise en perspective." In *L'Etat des régions françaises,* 1–4 Paris: La Découverte

Boeuf, Jean-Luc. 2002. *Décentralisation et recomposition des territories, 1982–2002: problèmes politiques et sociaux.* Paris: La documentation française

– 2003. *Décentralisation et experimentations locales:* problèmes politiques et sociaux. Paris: La documentation française

Bourget, Bernard. 2002. "La région et ses départements." *Commentaire* 98:337–39

Brenner, Neil. 2005. *New State Spaces.* Oxford: Oxford University Press

Brillet, Emmanuel, and Elise Feron. 2006. "French Regions as Relevant Policy Actors" (mimeo). Paris, France: Interdiscipline Centre for Comparative Research

Brisson, Jean-François. 2003a. "Les nouvelles clefs constitutionnelles de répartition matérielle des compétences entre l'Etat et les collectivités locales." *L'actualité juridique, droit administratif,* 24 March, 529–39

– 2003b. "La France est une République indivisible ... son organisation est décentralisée!" *Revue du droit public* 1:11–114

Brown, Douglas M., and Earl H. Fry. 1993. *States and Provinces in the International Economy.* Berkeley, Calif.: Institute of Governmental Studies Press; and Kingston, Ont.: Institute of Intergovernmental Relations, Queen's University

Cabannes, Xavier, and Olivier Gohin. 2000. "Compétences et ressources des communes." *Pouvoirs* 95:55–68

Charles, Gilbert. 2005. "Logements de la honte." *L'Express,* 15 October

Conseil régional du Nord-Pas de Calais. 2004. *Contrat de Plan Etat-Région, 2005* www.cr-npdc.fr/instit/cper/intro.htm (accessed 20 November 2004)

Courchene, Thomas. 1999. *From Heartland to North American Regions State.* Toronto: University of Toronto Press

Crouzatier-Durand, Florence. 2004. "L'expérimentation locale." *Revue française de droit administratif* 1:21–30

Crozier, Michel. 1989. *Etat moderne, etat modeste: strategies pour un autre changement.* Paris: Fayard

de Courson, Charles. 2003. "Autonomie financière des collectivités locales: la voie étroite." *Commentaire* 25 (Winter): 885–7

De Penanros, Roland, and Claude Serfati. 2000. "Regional Conversion under Conditions of Defense Industry Centralization: The French Case." *International Regional Science Review* 23 (1): 66–80

Delpree, Francis. 2004. "Organisation territoriale et exception francaise." In *Cahier francais.* Paris: La documentation française

Digaetano, Alan, and Elizabeth Strom. 2003. "Comparative Urban Governance: An Integrated Approach." *Urban Affairs Review* 38:356–95

Direction générale des collectivités locales (DGCL). 2005. "Fiscalité locale: structure, autonomie." Review of Reviewed Item, *Structure de la fiscalité locale: autonomie de la fiscalité locale.* www.dgcl.interieur.gouv.fr/donneeschiffrees/accueil_donnees_chiffrees.html

Documentation Française. 1998. "Le cumul des mandats et des functions." *Les études de la documentation française,* 1–139

Duchacek, Ivo. 1988. *Perforated Sovereignties and International Relations: Trans Sovereign Contacts of Subnational Governments.* New Haven: Greenwood Press

European Commission. 2005. European Union budget

France. Cour des Comptes. 1992. "La politique routière et autoroutière: évaluation de la gestion du réseau national. Paris: Cour des Comptes

– 1998. "L'action des départements dans le domaine de la voirie routière." Paris: Cour des Comptes

– Délégation à l'aménagement du térritoire et à l'action régionale (DATAR). 2005a. *Etat d'avancement des programmes européens. synthèse générale du dégagement d'office par programme et par fonds.* www.datar.gouv.fr/datar_site/datar_framedef.nsf/webmaster/europe_framedef_vf?

– 2005b. *Les politiques européennes.* DATAR 2000–2005. www.datar.gouv.fr/datar_site/datar_framedef.nsf/webmaster/europe_framedef_vf (accessed November 2004 and November 2005)

– *Journal officiel.* 2003. "L'organisation décentralisée de la République." Paris: Les éditions des Journaux officiels

– Ministère de l'Equipement et des Transports. 2006. *Routes en France.* Paris: Direction de l'Equipement, Gouvernment de la France

– Ministère des Transports, de l'Equipement, du Tourisme, et de la Mer. 2006. *Transfert des Routes Nationales aux Département et Modernisation de L'Etat.* Paris: C. d. Ministre

– Secrétariat à la politique de la ville (SPV). 2003. *Politique de la ville*

Gaudemet, Yves, and Olivier Gohin. 2004. *La République décentralisée.* Paris, France: Panthéon-Assas

Gélard, Patrice. 2004. *Projet de loi constitutionnelle modifiant le titre 15 de la constitution.* Paris: The Senate

Geppert, Anna. 2003. "L'aménagement du territoire dans l'Acte II: clarifier les rôles et les financements. "*Pouvoirs locaux* 59 (4): 83-87

Gueguen, Daniel. 2005. "Brussels: Delusional and Defensive." *Public Affairs News* 10 (September): 1–5

Guengant, Alain, and Jean-Michel Josselin 2003. La Constitution, fournit-elle une garantie déterminante d'autonomie financière? *Pouvoirs locaux* 59 (4): 42–3

Hertzog, Robert. 2003. "L'ambiguë constitutionnalisation des finances locales." *L'actualité juridique, droit administratif,* 24 March, 548–58

– 2004. "La loi organique relative à l'autonomie financière des collectivités territoriales: précisions et complications. "*L'actualité juridique, droit administratif,* 25 October, 2003–12

John, Peter, and Alistair Cole. 2000. "When Do Institutions, Policy Sectors, and Cities Matter? Comparing Networks of Local Policy Makers in Britain and France." *Comparative Political Studies* 33 (2): 248–68

Jouen, Marjorie. 2002. "Comment l'Europe influence-t-elle les relations Etat-collectivités?" *Pouvoirs locaux* 55 (4): 69–74

Keating, Michael. 1998. *The New Regionalism in Western Europe: Territorial Restructuring and Political Change.* Aldershot, UK: Edward Elgard

– 1999a. "Asymmetrical Government: Multinational States in an Integrating Europe." *Publius* 29 (1): 71–86

– 1999b. "Les nationalités minoritaires d'Espagne face à l'Europe. "*Etudes internationales* 30 (4): 729–43

– 1999c. "Challenges to Federalism, Territory, Function, and Power in a Globalizing World." In *Stretching the Federation,* ed. Robert Young. Montreal & Kingston: McGill-Queen's University Press

Keohane, Robert, and Helen Milner. 1996. *Internationalization and Domestic Politics.* Cambridge, UK: Cambridge University Press

Laignel, André. 2005. *Rapport observatoire des finances locales.* Paris: Direction générale des collectivités locales

Le Gales, Patrick. 1995. "Du gouvernement des villes à la gouvernance urbaine." *Revue française de science politique* 45 (1): 57–95

Le Lidec, Christian. 2001. *Les maires dans la République: L' Association des maires de France. Eléments constitutifs des régimes politiques français depuis 1907.* Paris: Sciences politiques, Université de Paris

Levy, Jonah. 1994. *Tocqueville's Revenge: Dilemmas of Institutional Reform in Post-Dirigiste France.* Cambridge, Mass: Department of Political Science, Massachusetts Institute of Technology

Loughlin, John, and Sonia Mazey. 1995. *The End of the French Unitary State? Ten Years of Regionalization in France.* Regions and Regionalism Series, 5. London: Frank Cass

Luchaire, Yves, and François Luchaire. 2003. *Décentralisation et constitution.* Paris: Economica

Manesse, Jacques. 1998. *L'aménagement du territoire.* Paris: LGDJ

Marks, Gary. 1992. "Structural Policy in the European Union." In Euro-politics: *Institutions and Policymaking in the "New" European Community,* ed. A. Sbragia. Washington, DC: Brookings Institution

Masquet, Brigitte, Isabelle Domergue, and Charif Kiwan, eds. 2002. *Décentralisation: regard sur l'actualité.* Paris: La documentation française

Mény, Yves. 1992. *La corruption de la République.* Paris: Fayard

– 1996. "Politics, Corruption, and Democracy: The 1995 Stein Rokkan Lecture." *European Journal of Political Research* 30 (2): 111–24

Migaud, Didier. 2003. "Un transfert du déficit de l'Etat sur le dos du contribuable local." *Pouvoirs locaux* 59 (4): 87–90

Moreau, Jacques. 1978. *Administration régionale, locale, et municipale.* Paris: Dalloz - Mementos Dalloz

Morin, Hervé. 2003. "Aller plus loin dans l'architecture territoriale." *Pouvoirs locaux* 59 (4): 91–3

Mouzet, Pierre. 2003. Le Conseil d'Etat et le contrôle budgétaire des collectivités territoriales. *Revue française de droit administratif,* July–August; 741–50

Ohmae, Kenishi. 1991. *The Borderless World.* New York: Harpers Business Books

Pasquier, Romain. 2003. "Les régions dans la nouvelle décentralisation." *Pouvoirs locaux* 59 (4): 69–73

Pontier, Jean-Marie. 2004. "Les nouvelles compétences de la région." *L'actualité juridique, droit administratif,* 1968–77

Prodi, Romano. Address to the European Parliament, 17 February

Quinet, Emile. 1990. *La planification française.* Paris: Presses Universitaire de France

Reformistes et solidaires. 2005 *Tout savoir sur le cumul des mandats.* www.re-so.net/article.php3?id_article=565 (accessed 25 July 2005)

Regourd, Serge. 2004. "La revision constitutionnelle de mars 2003 et l'unité de la Republique. *Cahiers français: la documentation française* 318:59–67

Remond, Bruno. 2002. "Décentraliser: vraiment? Enfin!" *Pouvoirs locaux* 55 (4): 83–90

Risse-Kappen, Thomas. 1995. *Bringing Transnational Relations Back In: Non-State Actors, Domestic Structures, and International Relations.* Cambridge: Cambridge University Press

Robert, Fabrice. 2004. "Vers une fiscalité décentralisée." *Cahiers français: la documentation française* 318:52–8

Rossinot, André. 2003. "Du village à l'Europe, des territoires qui se transforment, des institutions qui bougent, des enjeux qui évoluent, et des pistes d'action qui se dessinent. *Territoires 2020* 8:7–11

Salmon, Trevor, and Michael Keating. 1999. *The Dynamics of Decentralization: Canadian Federalism and British Devolution.* Montreal & Kingston: McGill-Queen's University Press

Sassen, Saskia. 1996. *Losing Control.* New York: Columbia University Press

Sauvageot, Frederic. 2003. "Les nouvelles garanties financières des collectivités." In *Décentralisation: histoire, bilan, évolutions,* ed. E. Maestri. Paris: L'Harmattan.

Schmidt, Vivien. 1993. *Democratizing France.* New York: Cambridge University Press

Thoenig, Jean Claude. 1992. "La décentralisation dix ans après." *Pouvoir* 60:1–12

Tronquoy, Philippe. 2004. "Décentralisation, Etat, et territoires." *Cahiers français: la documentation française* 318:1–88

Trosa, Sylvie, et al. 2002. "La LOLF est une révolution, mais pas une réforme de l'Etat. *Pouvoirs locaux* 55 (4): 28–34

Verpeaux, Michel. 2003. "La loi constitutionnelle du 28 mars 2003 relative à l'organisation décentralisée de la République: libres propos." *Revue française de droit administratif,* July–August, 661–9

– 2004. "La loi du 13 août 2004: le demi-succès de l'acte II de la décentralisation." *L'actualité juridique, droit administratif,* 25 October, 1960–68

Worms, Jean Pierre, and Pierre Gremion. 1968. *Aménagement du térritoire et développement régional.* Vol. 1. Grenoble: Institut d'Etudes politiques

Young, Robert, ed. 1999. *Stretching the Federation.* Montreal & Kingston: McGill-Queen's University Press

Ziller, Jacques. 2003. *The Europeanization of Constitutional Law.* Paris: L'Harmattan

MUNICIPAL-FEDERAL RELATIONS IN GERMANY

Rudolf Hrbek and Jan Christoph Bodenbender

1 INTRODUCTION

German local self-government is constitutionally guaranteed and protected, and has a long historical tradition. But according to its Constitution, the Federal Republic of Germany has only a two-tiered structure, consisting of the Federation and the federal states (*Länder*). According to the Constitution, the municipalities are part of the executive branch while being constituent parts of the *Länder* in organizational terms (Nierhaus 2003, 31). Functionally, however, Germany's administrative structure includes the municipalities as a third tier, though the separation between the federal, *Land*, and municipal levels is ambiguous. Over time, a system of multilevel governance, marked by complex political interdependence (*Politikverflechtung*), has evolved and become emblematic of Germany. Against the background of the ongoing process of European integration, the European Union represents a fourth level, adding yet another layer of political interdependence for the German municipalities, the *Länder*, and the Federation (*doppelte Politikverflechtung*) (Hrbek 1986).

Within the European context, the concept of multilevel governance is nowadays most often associated with analytical attempts to describe the *sui generis* character of the European Union, with its highly interdependent multilevel structure (Knodt and Große Hüttmann 2005, 227). The point of departure for this approach is the "existence of overlapping competencies among multiple levels of governments and the interaction of political actors across those levels" (Marks et al. 1996, 41). The levels of political decision-making are interconnected, not nested. There is no clear division between national and supranational decision making levels. Subnational – i.e., regional (*Land*) or local – actors can operate on both levels. They do not necessarily have measurable influence on the overall decision-making process because "mobilization and influence are not synonymous" (Knodt and Große Hüttmann 2005, 241). The separation between domestic and international politics is blurred. The multilevel governance approach recognizes the "multilevelness" of a polity where authority is spread over various levels of governance and among different actors, including potential sectoral variations in patterns of governance. Multilevel governance is not a "grand theory"; it is more an "attempt to depict complexity as the principal feature" of a political system (Rosamond 2000, 111). Therefore the approach serves as an analytical tool to ascertain the established pattern of governance in Germany's political system.

In Germany, public tasks and responsibilities have been distributed among the European Union, the Federation, the *Länder*, and the municipalities. Local authorities play a key role in the entire intergovernmental setting of policy implementation, the application of law, and service delivery. A wide range of public tasks and responsibilities are accomplished on the local level by the territorially based, multifunctional, and general-purpose local governments, which are endemic to the German tradition (Wollmann 2004a, 118). Local government is an institutional, cultural, and normative component of Germany's democratic constitutional system (Wollmann 2002, 29). In an international comparative perspective, the German municipal model ranks among the functionally and politically strongest types of local government (see Goldsmith 2003). In recent years, this traditional model has been subject to challenges from the regional, national, and international levels in response to fundamental political and economic changes.

German municipalities face two major problems. First, owing to the increasing extent of legal requirements coming from the Federation and *Länder*, municipalities' capacity for autonomous decision making has been reduced. Second, municipalities have seen their financial basis erode. The crisis of municipal finances, however, is not just a by-product of the overall crisis of public finances. Rather, it is a function of the structural bias of the German federal system at the expense of the municipalities (Keller 2006, 102). Because of their growing dependence on the *Länder*, the Federation, and the European Union, German municipalities are increasingly caught between local self-determination and heteronomy (Schmidt-Eichstaedt 1998, 323). Within this specific context of multilevel governance, German local government must stand its ground.

2 CONSTITUTIONAL DIMENSION

In the aftermath of the Second World War, independent political life in Germany began to be decentralized at the local and regional levels. With some exceptions, such as Bavaria, the *Länder* were created without direct historical predecessors on an ad hoc basis in the framework of the respective occupational zones. In 1946 parliamentary elections were held at the *Länder* level in the three Western occupational zones. Political parties were influencing the formation of *Land* governments according to the rules of parliamentary government, and the *Länder* forged constitutions. In September 1948 the Parliamentary Council, consisting of delegates sent from the parliaments of the *Länder*, began to elaborate the Constitution for the Western part of Germany (which consisted of the British, French, and U.S. occupational zones). The Constitution had to be approved by the three occupying powers and ratified by the *Länder*. From the outset, the Allied powers imposed the condition that the new state must have a federal structure (Hrbek 2001, 55). This obligation mirrored the Allies' desire to avoid the creation of a heavily centralized German state. It also reflected federal traditions in the German territories over the centuries and the strong position which the *Länder* were already enjoying at that time. In this context, municipalities were given their place in the framework of the constitutional order of the new state and were regarded as constituent parts in the democratic life in West Germany.[1]

2.1 CONSTITUTIONAL POSITION OF LOCAL AUTHORITIES

The Federal Republic of Germany is a two-tiered political system consisting of the Federation and the *Länder*. This dualistic structure also determines the legal position of German municipalities. Their status is regulated by the German Constitution – the *Grundgesetz* (GG), or "Basic Law" – by the constitutions of the respective *Länder*, and by the municipal codes of the *Länder*. Within the interplay of forces between the Federation and the sixteen *Länder*, the municipalities occupy an idiosyncratic position (Dieckmann 1998, 292).

The organization of the municipal level is one of the few matters – apart from police, education and culture – over which the *Länder* have sole jurisdiction (Gburreck and Kleinfeld 2005, 122). Thus, the power to make decisions about questions relating to the territorial framework and the institutional arrangement of local government lies exclusively with the *Länder*, whose parliaments decide by legislative fiat. They are bound only by the provisions of Art. 28 (1) 1 GG insofar as their "constitutional order ... must conform to the principles of a republican, democratic, and social state governed by the rule of law."

Pursuant to the regional traditions of local self-government, as well as the influence of the respective occupying powers after 1945, the *Länder* established distinct constitutional systems and different municipal codes.[2] In recent years, however, the differences pertaining to the institutional arrangements of the local level have been aligned, following an assimilatory process precipitated by Germany's competitive federalism (Kost and Wehling 2003, 8). German local self-government encompasses two tiers: municipalities (*Gemeinden*) and municipal associations or counties (*Landkreise*). Municipalities are territorial entities under public law (*Gebietskörperschaften*). They are local authorities, that is, independent, democratically structured, political entities. Yet municipalities do not have the same statelike qualities as the Federation and the *Länder*. The directly elected local council is not a legislative body but the administrative representation of citizens (Püttner 2004, 19). Municipalities have competencies concerning the following aspects: organization (internal structure), personnel (selection, engagement, promotion, and dismissal), finances (independent management of revenues and expenditures, including fees and charges), planning (land use and building plans), and legislation (statutes and bylaws). These rights apply only within the limits prescribed by law.

Most of the municipalities belong to counties (*kreisangehörige Gemeinden*). The counties are also territorial bodies under public law. They administer the public tasks which cannot be fulfilled by the municipalities on their own or which go beyond the sphere of action of individual municipalities. Yet counties are also the lower administrative authority of their *Land*. Thus, they are hybrids, having local and state authority at the same time. The function of an association of municipalities (*Gemeindeverband*), as envisaged by the Basic Law, has only little practical relevance (Püttner 2004, 33). In addition, there are urban municipalities (*kreisfreie Städte*), which exercise the responsibilities and powers of both municipalities and counties.[3] In some *Länder*, umbrella associations of local government bodies (*höhere Kommunalverbände*) have been created, which are responsible for tasks that cannot be carried out by individual municipalities or counties.[4] The *Länder* have also installed *Land* authorities, mostly called *Regierungspräsidien*, as an intermediate authority between the Ministry of the Interior of the *Land* and its counties and municipalities.

As a result of shifts in the way settlements are structured and – in answer to the ensuing debate on regional planning – territorial reforms were initiated in the mid-1960s to enhance the administrative capacity and efficiency of municipalities. In the course of this reform, the overall number of municipalities in the Federal Republic was cut by 65 percent, from 24,300 to 8,500. There were two strategies for territorial reform. The first included redrawing the boundaries of all existing municipalities by amalgamating them and forming territorially and demographically enlarged unitary municipalities. The second strategy allowed existing municipalities to remain as political local government units, while a set of joint authorities was created of which the municipalities are members and serve as administrative support units. The way these reforms were carried out varies considerably from *Land* to *Land* (Wollmann 2004a, 111).

After Germany's unification in 1990, the number of municipalities in the new *Länder* was not initially reduced further. Today, there are about 13,500 municipalities in Germany. They vary considerably in number and size among the thirteen *Flächenländer*.[5] In the most populous *Land*, North Rhine–Westphalia (18 million residents), there are only 396 municipalities with an average of 45,500 inhabitants. Rhineland-Palatinate, by contrast, has only 4 million residents but 2,320 municipalities, with an average population of 1,700. The five *Länder* in the eastern part of Germany have 7,564 municipalities. Compared with the differences in the territorial reform of municipalities, the *Länder* proceeded rather uniformly with the territorial reform of counties. The number of counties was reduced by more than 40 percent to 323, with an average size of 170,000 (Wollmann 2004a, 112).

All municipalities and counties possess the same legal status irrespective of their size. The local charters apply to small municipalities as well as to large cities, leaving no sign of asymmetry (Püttner 2004, 31). For citizens, there is no qualitative difference between state and municipal administration, since local administrative activities are equivalent to the exercise of state authority according to Art. 20 (2) GG. Therefore, municipalities and counties constitute the third administrative level in Germany.[6] Constitutionally, however, they are not an autonomous third level within the federal structure but are constituent parts of the *Länder* (see Decision of the Federal Constitutional Court, BVerfGE 39, 96 (109)).

2.2 LEGAL PROTECTION

Art. 28 (2) 1 of the Basic Law determines that "municipalities must be guaranteed the right to regulate all local affairs on their own responsibility, within the limits prescribed by the laws." According to Art. 28 (2) 2 GG, associations of municipalities (i.e., counties) also have the right of self-government according to the laws and within the limits of their functions designated by a law. The Federal

Constitutional Court as well as the entire judiciary and legal doctrine have interpreted these provisions guaranteeing the principle of local self-administration (*Wesensgehaltsgarantie*) (Andersen 1995, 180). A "general competence clause," Art. 28 (2) 1 GG, recognizes the special status of local government. It binds the *Länder* accordingly. Its core and essence are therefore immune to legislative encroachment by the Federation or the *Länder*. But there is also a consensus that the Basic Law neither guarantees that the single municipality will continue to exist in its territorial boundaries nor that specific municipal functions and responsibilities will remain unaltered (Gburreck and Kleinfeld 2005, 122). The same article also determines that the municipalities can exercise their functions only within the framework of existing legislation. This clause has been used as a "door opener" for legislation – particularly by the *Länder* – to curb local autonomy (Wollmann 2002, 24).

Since local self-government is conceived as an institutional guarantee rather than a basic right, municipalities have their own indefeasible but not unrestricted legal position. Municipalities and counties have the right to bring constitutional complaints to the Federal Constitutional Court on the grounds that their right to self-government under Art. 28 GG has been infringed by a law. In the case of an infringement by a *Land* law, the Federal Constitutional Court rules only if the law in question cannot be challenged in the constitutional court of the respective *Land* (Art. 93 (1) 4b GG). A municipality can also, analogous to a bearer of basic rights, appeal to the Federal Constitutional Court with regard to general flaws under constitutional law following Art. 93 (1) 4a GG, if its rights under Art. 20 (4) or under Arts. 33, 38, 101, 103, or 104 GG have been infringed by public authority.[7] Municipalities and counties are independent corporations of public law, that is, legal personalities separated from the state. However, they are not entitled to have their Basic Rights protected in accordance with Art. 19 (3) GG (see BVerfGE 21, 362; 45, 63).

On the international level, German municipalities are protected by the provisions of the European Charter of Local Self-Government, which was ratified by Germany in 1988. The operative meaning of this charter is limited, for it does not bind the European Union and its institutions (Thränhardt 1998, 366). The treaty on the EU Constitution introduces a legal guarantee of self-government on the European level (see Püttner 2004, 30).[8] The inclusion of local self-government in future European primary law not only protects the status of local self-government vis-à-vis the European Union but also serves as an additional basis for the legitimization of local authorities. In 2005 the ratification process was put on hold after the negative outcome of the referendums in France and the Netherlands.

2.3 SUPERVISION

As integral parts of the state, municipalities and counties are subject to supervision. Since local self-government is supposed to provide local politics with a certain leeway, a complicated system of supervision was established, distinguishing between legal supervision (*Rechtsaufsicht*) and expert supervision

(*Fachaufsicht*) (Püttner 2004, 57).[9] This supervision can be seen as the "correlative of the right to self-government" (BVerfGE 26, 228). Owing to the constitutional assignment of municipalities to the *Länder*, each *Land* is in charge of the supervision of its municipalities. County administrations (*Landratsämter*) are responsible for the legal supervision of smaller municipalities, while the *Regierungspräsidien* are responsible for the supervision of urban municipalities. Yet the Federation is legally obliged to ensure that the *Länder* fulfill their constitutionally mandated supervisory obligation (Art. 28 (3) GG).

2.4 CITY-STATES

The cities of Berlin, Bremen, and Hamburg not only perform the functions of both a municipality and a county but also are a *Land*. As so-called city-states, they are members of the Federal Council (*Bundesrat*) with rights equal to those of all other *Länder*. When the *Länder* were established after the Second World War, the historical tradition of Bremen and Hamburg as city-states did not run counter to the interests of the occupying powers. But Berlin was a different matter. As the former capital of Germany (and of Prussia), it was divided amongst the four occupying powers into "sectors." Although West Berlin (composed of the three Western sectors) functioned as a de facto part of West Germany, it remained occupied territory with a special status under the formal supremacy of the Allies until 1990.[10] Since Germany's unification, Berlin has possessed the same legal status as the other two city-states while at the same time performing special functions as Germany's capital; an amendment to the Constitution (expected to enter into force by the end of 2006) will serve as the basis for defining the responsibility of the Federation in this context.

Over time, there have been numerous attempts to reduce through mergers the number *Länder* (see Arts. 29, 118, and 118a GG). Art. 118a GG explicitly provides for the possibility of revising the "division of the territory comprising Berlin and Brandenburg into Länder … without regard to the provisions of Art. 29." The procedural provisions to do this, however, are complicated. Hamburg and Bremen also have always been part of considerations on delimitation (on the basis of Art. 29 GG), which illustrates the fact that city-states as such are not regarded as integral to Germany's federal structure. They are a historical artifact. In addition, there are big differences between the three cities that cannot be attributed to their status as city-states. It is, therefore, difficult to generalize about all three city-states, and their situation differs from that of other large German cities. Their special status compared with other municipalities nevertheless implies a series of special duties and tasks as well as special features of their fiscal position.

Instead of having their own local charters, the specific features of local government are laid down in their respective constitutions (Kipke 2000, 83). According to its constitution, Berlin is both a *Land* and a city; its parliamentary assembly also serves as a municipal assembly and its government as a local government. Hamburg, by contrast, is by definition only a *Land*, yet one that also performs the functions of a municipality. The case of Bremen is special in that it is composed of two independent municipalities: Bremen and Bremerhaven.

3 THE RANGE OF MUNICIPALITIES' RESPONSIBILITIES AND FUNCTIONS

The Basic Law stipulates that local self-government does not encompass a specific catalogue of functions and duties but has the right "to regulate all local affairs." Local affairs have been defined by the Federal Constitutional Court as "those needs and interests, which are rooted in the local community or to which they bear specific reference, which are common to the local citizens, because they affect the cohabitation of the people within the municipality" (BVerfGE 79, 128). Following this principle of universality, municipalities and counties are bearers of all tasks that need to be performed at the local level.[11] Municipalities have a functional preponderance as territorially based "multifunction and general-purpose" local authorities for the coverage of public activities and functions (Wollmann 2004a, 109).

3.1 OWN AND TRANSFERRED SPHERES OF RESPONSIBILITY

The dual status of German municipalities as local self-government entities and as the lowest level of administration is also reflected in the range of their responsibilities and functions. From a formal point of view, these responsibilities can be classified into two categories, based on the respective degree of autonomy and the freedom of decision: functions within the own sphere of activity, that is, genuinely local self-government tasks; and functions within a transferred sphere of activity, that is, on behalf of the state (Andersen 1995, 182). In reality, however, there is no strict dualism between the municipalities and the state; rather, it is a more differentiated situation according to the gradual influence of higher political levels (Kost and Wehling 2003, 17). Tasks without directives include voluntary (where the *Länder* are not allowed to interfere at all) and compulsory ones (which have to be fulfilled, but without specific guidelines from the *Land* concerning the exact means). Tasks bound by directives include compulsory (which must be fulfilled in the specific manner) and governmental tasks (a municipality serves as a governmental subagency). Owing to the dual position of local authorities, the relation between the principle of local self-government and administrative heteronomy remains difficult.

3.2 ADMINISTRATIVE FUNCTIONS

The wide range of tasks and duties of municipalities reflects a basic feature of intergovernmental relations in Germany. Whereas legislation is primarily the responsibility of the federal level, the subnational level is responsible for administrative tasks, including the implementation of federal laws and policies. The *Länder* are responsible for executing federal laws in their own right (Art. 83 GG). In these cases, the *Länder* shall, in accordance with Art. 84 (1) GG, decide on the establishment of administrative authorities and the administrative procedure. The establishment of such authorities also remain the concern of the *Länder* where they execute federal laws on federal commission (Art. 85 (1) GG).

The *Länder* have mostly delegated administrative functions to the local level. Following the principle of administrative legality, all actions and functions of municipalities and counties must have a distinct legal basis. Altogether, between 70 to 80 percent of all legal provisions of the Federation and the *Länder* are implemented by local authorities (Schmidt-Eichstaedt 1998, 325). The process of European integration affects the administrative functions of German municipalities as well.[12]

German local authorities are administratively responsible for a wide variety of public functions which in other countries are carried out by single-purpose local field offices of the state government (Wollmann 2004a, 108). Municipalities receive compulsory tasks with the authority to issue directives in such areas as civil registration, citizenship, and food quality control. However, the Federation is prohibited from dictating to the *Länder* whether or not a task has to be transferred to municipalities. The Federal Constitutional Court has allowed exceptions to this rule only if it can be deduced from the factual connection that a concurrent regulation of responsibilities is appropriate (BVerfGE 77, 288). The federal level is constitutionally denied the right to have administrative offices of its own at the sub-*Länder* level, except for a constitutionally enumerated minimal number of functions, such as customs and border police. This also corresponds with the limited array of special-purpose administrative units (*Sonderbehörden*) that have been installed by the state via federal laws, such as employment offices and the internal revenue service (Püttner 2004, 124). Finally, the Federation and the *Länder* may transfer warrants or tasks to a specific municipal organ, which then acts as a federal or *Land* agency rather than a local one (so-called *Organleihe*) (Püttner 2004, 124). Some areas, including the school system and police, are subject to direct administrative responsibility by the *Länder*.

3.3 PROVISION FOR PUBLIC GOODS AND SERVICES

Since German municipalities are close to the citizens, they are best suited to the needs-oriented allocation of public goods and services (Scherf and Hofmann 2003, 314). Thus, they focus mainly on the provision of public utilities and welfare. These include the following areas: museums, theatres, schools, sports and recreation grounds, hospitals, construction, habitation, sewerage, waste disposal, electricity, gas and water supply, public transportation, promotion of trade and business, measures related to immigration and integration policy, and social assistance. Unlike municipalities, counties do not have a specific area of activity but are even more occupied with administrative tasks, which are delegated to them by the *Land*. They do, however, intervene if individual municipalities cannot perform their tasks on their own.

Local authorities are the major providers of public utilities. Over 60 percent of all public investments are carried out by local authorities. In 2004 municipalities and counties spent more than 20 billion euros on construction and other infrastructure measures and on acquiring assets (see table 1).

Table 1
Municipal Spending, 2004 (in billion euros and percentages)

	Germany		West Germany		East Germany	
	Billion euros	Percent	Billion euros	Percent	Billion euros	Percent
Overall	149.95	100.0	124.80	100.0	25.15	100.0
Human resources	39.90	26.6	32.80	26.3	7.10	28.2
Material expenses	29.35	19.6	24.70	19.8	4.65	18.5
Social services	32.25	21.5	27.60	22.1	4.65	18.5
Interest	4.80	3.2	4.00	3.2	0.80	3.2
Investment	20.10	13.4	15.50	12.4	4.60	18.3
Other	23.55	15.7	20.20	16.2	3.35	13.3

Source: Statistisches Bundesamt

Since the mid-1990s, the Federation, the *Länder*, and the local governments have reduced their bureaucracy by more than 15 percent (see table 2). In 2002 the Federation had 490,000 civil servants (this includes the armed forces), while the *Länder* had 2.1 million employees (this includes personnel in schools and tertiary education). The municipalities and counties had a workforce of more than 1.4 million, which accounted for almost 35 percent of the bureaucracy. In 2004 the municipalities spent almost 40 billion euros, or 26.6 percent of their budgets, on human resources.

Table 2
Public Service Personnel (in thousands)

	Federation	Länder	Municipalities / counties	Zweckverbände
1994	577	2,482	1,806	66
1998	516	2,363	1,580	67
2002	490	2,156	1,441	71

Source: Statistisches Bundesamt

3.4 ECONOMIC ACTIVITIES

Public services comprise economic activities of the municipalities and municipal enterprises, such as the public utility companies (*Stadtwerke*), which are owned by local government. In principle, municipalities are allowed to be economically active and make a profit. But the *Länder* have drawn restrictive lines. These activities are permitted only if they fulfill a public purpose and if the private sector cannot fulfill the same task adequately. Especially in economic matters, municipalities join forces with one another in special-purpose associations (*Zweckverbände*), which are independent bodies under public law. They act on their own abilities and possess the right of self-administration. The purpose of these *Zweckverbände* is to foster and ease intermunicipal cooperation in specific areas of local responsibility. The cooperation takes place on different levels and on different scales, that is, in small or large areas.[13] Owing to heterogeneity, there is no reliable and comprehensive data on the extent of intermunicipal cooperation in Germany. Yet very few municipalities are not part such of cooperatives (Püttner 2004, 158). In 1998, 3,500 municipal enterprises employed more than 530,000 persons. The overall turnover of these enterprises amounted to more than 82 billion euros (COR 2004, 256). Municipal enterprises are responsible for 95 percent of water treatment, 85 percent of water distribution, 95 percent of waste disposal, 50 percent of urban waste collection, 75 percent of gas distribution, and 65 percent of local public transport.

3.5 SOCIAL POLICY

The German welfare system has an important local dimension. Local authorities play a major role in the provision of social transfers and services as a result of the "general competence clause" of Art. 28 (2) GG. Another reason for their involvement in social policy relates to the fact that municipalities have traditionally been a "last resort" in the German welfare system (Bönker and Wollmann 2004, 246). Social policy at the local level encompasses four fields: social assistance, personal social services, social housing, and employment programs.

Generally, local authorities are responsible for upholding the social service infrastructure. Furthermore, they finance most of the individual social services. Following the principle of subsidiarity, these services (e.g., kindergartens, nursing homes) are mainly provided by welfare associations (*Wohlfahrtsverbände*) – non-public, non-profit organizations usually affiliated with churches or trade unions. Since the mid-1980s, these welfare associations have lost their virtual monopoly as providers of personal services. The field of municipal employment policy is of relatively recent origin. Municipalities became active in this field in the 1980s when they were confronted with mounting unemployment rates and rising social assistance expenditures. Since then, they have developed measures to expand employment opportunities for the locally unemployed. These measures are complementary to the activities of the Federal Employment Agency (*Bundesagentur für Arbeit*), which acts through local employment centres (*Arbeitsämter*).

4 THE FINANCIAL POSITION OF MUNICIPALITIES

Germany's financial system, which was altered distinctly by a comprehensive reform in 1969, is characterized by a mixture of several types of fiscal sovereignty.

There are elements of a discrete, a combined, and an allocative system.[14] The underlying political goal of this mixed financial system is the adjustment of differences in tax revenue (Kipke 2000, 82). The allocation and separation of powers, in connection with the principle of political competition within a federal state presuppose that all levels are able to exercise their powers independently from one another. This includes the availability of financial resources. Autonomy in this respect requires that each level is equipped with sufficient funds to fulfill its tasks. It also presupposes the right to decide on expenditures independently.

4.1 CONSTITUTIONAL AND LEGAL FRAMEWORK

While municipal tasks are regulated by the Basic Law only in very general terms, it spells out the financial position of German municipalities in considerable detail. The Constitution mandates that tax revenues be distributed among the different levels of government. The most fundamental rule concerning the municipalities is stipulated in Art. 28 (3) GG: "The guarantee of self-government shall extend to the bases of financial autonomy; these bases shall include the right of municipalities to a source of tax revenues based upon economic ability and the right to establish the rates at which these sources shall be taxed." Chapter 10 of the Basic Law deals with the details of the financial relations between the Federation, the *Länder*, and the municipalities. Art. 106 GG regulates the way tax revenues are divided among the different levels of government. Paragraph (1) lists the tax revenue that accrues to the Federation even if it is collected by the *Länder* (e.g., customs duties). The second paragraph enumerates the taxes whose revenue accrues to the *Länder* even if governed by federal laws (e.g., property tax, motor vehicle tax, beer tax). Paragraph (3) stipulates that the "revenue from income taxes, corporate taxes, and turnover taxes shall accrue jointly to the Federation and the *Länder* (joint taxes) to the extent that the revenue from the income tax and the turnover tax is not allocated to municipalities pursuant to paragraphs (5) and (5a) of this Article."

Municipalities are entitled to a share of the revenue from the income tax. The amount of their share is transferred by the *Länder* on the basis of the income tax paid by the inhabitants of the municipality (Art. 106 (5) GG). Since 1998, municipalities have also been receiving a share of the turnover tax from the *Länder* on the basis of a formula reflecting geographical as well as economic variables (Art. 106 (5a) GG). Municipalities or counties receive the revenue from taxes on property and trades (the so-called "real tax guarantee"). Local authorities are authorized to decide on the rates at which taxes on trades and property are levied (*Hebesätze*) (Art. 106 (6) GG). These *Hebesätze* are an important element of the fiscal autonomy of local self-government, even if the leeway for changing these rates is limited.[15]

Implicitly, the provisions of this article also affect the city-states. The revenue from real taxes as well as from local taxes on consumption and expenditures shall accrue to the *Land* if there are no municipalities.[16] Municipalities must give a share of the tax on trades to the Federation and the *Länder* (*Gewerbesteuerumlage*) (Art. 106 (6) 4 GG). Since the 1990s, the Federation and the *Länder* have used this as an instrument to coerce municipalities to co-finance the burdens of German unification via the Fund for German Unity (*Fonds Deutsche Einheit*) and the Solidarity Pact (*Solidarpakt*). Contrary to the original plans, the *Gewerbesteuerumlage* was not abrogated with the reform of municipal finances (*Gemeindefinanzreform*) in 2003. Instead, the participation of the Federation and the *Länder* in the municipal trade tax was reduced from 28 to 20 percent. This reform was intended to provide local authorities with additional revenues of at least 2.5 billion euros per year. Overall, financing through taxes is marked by a high degree of heteronomy for the municipalities, because they can only decide independently on the *Hebesätze* for real taxes.

From a formal point of view, the different levels of government are financially independent and autonomous because they set their own budgets. According to Art. 106 (9) GG, however, revenues and expenditures of municipalities and counties are also deemed revenues and expenditures of the *Länder*. In principle, the dual structure of Germany's political system therefore also applies to its financial system, because the financial power of municipalities and counties is legally attributed to the respective *Land*. Municipal claims for adequate financial strength are therefore primarily targeted at the *Länder*, which supposedly function as guarantors. This term describes the obligation of the *Länder* to take responsibility for their municipalities (Dieckmann 1998, 296). Nevertheless, the Federation influences the financial situation of municipalities by its legislation. With the exception of Art. 106 (8) GG, the Basic Law does not provide for direct financial flows between the Federation and the municipalities. If the Federation demands the establishment of special facilities in individual municipalities or counties that would directly result in an increase of expenditure or in reductions of revenue, compensation may be granted.

4.2 MUNICIPAL REVENUE

Whereas the Federation and the *Länder* finance themselves mainly by taxes, municipal budgets are composed of various sources of revenue (see table 3). The main taxes of the German fiscal system are income and turnover taxes, which account for 40 and 30 percent, respectively, of overall revenue. Without a share of these taxes, the *Länder* and the municipalities would be unable to cover their financial needs. Municipalities receive a share of the income tax (15 percent of the respective *Land* revenue, plus 12 percent from the capital yields tax revenue) and a 2.2 percent share of the turnover tax from the *Länder*.

Structural assessments of municipal revenue need to distinguish between the Western (the old FRG) and the Eastern (former GDR) part of Germany. In the West, the main share of income comes from taxes. In the East, financial allocations are the most important source of income.

Taxes are the most important source of revenue for West German municipalities. They account for almost 40 percent of their budget (46.5 billion euros in 2004). In East German municipalities, less than 20 percent (4.6 billion euros in 2004) of the budget comes from tax income. This is mainly because of weak revenue from the tax on trades. Property tax accounts for 14 percent of the

Table 3
Municipal Revenue, 2004 (in billion euros and percentages)

	Germany		West Germany		East Germany	
	Billion euros	Percent	Billion euros	Percent	Billion euros	Percent
Overall	145.85	100.0	120.90	100.0	24.95	100.0
Taxes	51.10	35.0	46.50	38.4	4.60	18.6
Trades	20.45	14.0	18.53	15.3	1.92	7.6
Income	18.55	12.7	17.50	14.4	1.05	4.2
Turnover	2.61	1.8	2.22	1.8	0.39	1.6
Fees	16.14	11.0	14.15	11.7	1.99	7.9
Grants	47.02	32.3	33.01	27.3	14.01	56.0
Others	31.59	21.6	27.24	22.6	4.35	17.5

Source: Statistisches Bundesamt

Table 4
Tax Yield, 2004

	Billion euros	Percent
Overall	442.971	100.0
EU equity capital	19.640	4.4
Federation	186.950	42.3
Länder	179.887	40.6
Municipalities / counties	56.494	12.7

Source: Statistisches Bundesamt

municipal income in the West and for 26 percent in the East. Other taxes – such as those levied on entertainment and dogs – account for only 1.5 percent of local budgets. These taxes mainly serve as elements of regulatory policy (Karrenberg and Münstermann 1998, 444). For cities and towns, the tax on trades is the most valuable source of revenue; in smaller municipalities, the income tax is more important (ibid., 439). Compared to municipalities, counties do not have significant tax revenues of their own. They rely mainly on revenues from fees and financial subsidies and on municipal allocations (*Kreisumlage*), which amounts to 40 percent of the income of the counties.[17]

Both tied and unconditional financial grants from the *Länder*, the Federation, and the European Union also make a considerable contribution to municipal budgets. These financial transfers are carried out by the *Länder* within the framework of "municipal equalization" (*kommunualer Finanzausgleich*), using their annual financial equalization laws. These grants serve several purposes: to increase the financial clout of municipalities (fiscal function), to soften and alleviate differentials in revenue (redistributive function), and to help finance special needs (political regional planning function) (Karrenberg and Münstermann 1998, 452). According to Art. 104 (4) GG, the Federation may also "grant the *Länder* financial assistance for particularly important investments ... by municipalities or counties ... to avert a disturbance of the overall economic equilibrium, to equalize differing economic capacities within the federal territory, or to promote economic growth." On average, 45 percent of the grants and allocations from the *Länder* and the Federation are tied, while 55 percent are unconditional. Overall, they amount to one-third of the municipal budgets. Regional differences, however, matter. For municipalities in West Germany, these grants account for 27 percent of their budget (33 billion euros in 2004). In East Germany, with 14 billion euros in 2004, which is more than half the municipalities' revenue, the financial allocations they receive from the upper levels of government constitute their most important source of revenue.

In return for rendering certain services, municipalities charge fees, which are the third significant source of municipal revenue. These fees include, among others, administrative charges, entrance fees for public service institutions, and payments for infrastructure development on construction sites. There are, however, administrative, legal, economic, and political limits to an expansive fees policy.

4.3 MUNICIPAL LOANS

The municipal budget is divided into two parts. The administrative budget covers all revenues and expenditures for the performance of municipal tasks (e.g., personnel and material costs, social benefits). The property budget includes the investment in assets as well as taking out and repaying credits and loans. Municipalities are allowed to borrow from the capital and money market only to the extent that they are able to service their debt permanently from the income of the administrative budget. Municipal budget laws permit borrowing only for investment purposes and for investment-promotion programs (Karrenberg and Münstermann 1998, 438). In addition to traditional loans, municipalities are allowed to use cash advances (*Kassenkredite*) to secure their solvency. To raise these cash advances, municipalities need to be authorized accordingly by the respective budget law or statute. To borrow the maximum amount of cash advances, municipalities need the approval of their supervisory body – the county administration or the regional government. In recent years, the amount of cash advances to German municipalities has almost tripled, from 7 billion euros in 2000 to approximately 20 billion euros in 2004.

Still, when compared to the Federation and the *Länder*, financing by loans plays only a minor role for municipalities (see table 5). Traditional loans account for only a small proportion of the revenue of local budgets. The comparatively low ratio of new indebtedness of the municipalities can be attributed to the specific

Table 5
Public Debt Burden (in billion euros)

Public corporations		Dec 2000	Dec 2002	Dec 2004
Federation	Money / capital market	715.626	719.397	802.994
	Cash advances	0.192	6.008	9.088
Länder	Money / capital market	333.187	384.773	442.922
	Cash advances	4.886	7.350	5.700
Incl. Berlin	Money / capital market	33.453	44.647	53.876
	Cash advances	2.252	1.489	0.189
Bremen	Money / capital market	8.522	9.584	11.270
	Cash advances	–	–	0.104
Hamburg	Money / capital market	16.626	18.183	20.359
	Cash advances	0.583	0.998	1.434
Municipalities /	Money / capital market	82.991	82.662	84.257
counties	Cash advances	6.880	10.670	19.936

Source: Statistisches Bundesamt

debt ceiling, which does not exist in the same way at the levels of the Federation and the *Länder*. However, differences in the amount of loan financing in the budgets of municipalities are substantial. Economically underdeveloped cities with weak tax power and a high burden of social benefits tend to have a lower debt ceiling than cities in economically stronger regions. Nevertheless, throughout the 1990s, deficits in the budgets of larger cities were the rule rather than the exception. Whereas the rise in the debt load in the West has been gradual, East German municipalities have plunged into debt very quickly. They now have the same level of indebtedness as West German municipalities. City-states are in a special situation. Because of their status as *Länder*, they are not bound by the same strict debt ceiling as other municipalities. In 2004, the level of debt of Berlin (53.9 billion euros), Bremen (11.3 billion euros), and Hamburg (20.4 billion euros) equalled the level of debt of all German municipalities together.

4.4 FINANCIAL CRISIS

The financial situation of German municipalities deteriorated throughout the 1990s. In 2004 the municipal share of the overall tax revenue was 12.7 percent (see table 4), which is 2 percent less than twenty years earlier (Keller 2006, 102). The gap between revenue and expenditure widened, leading to the steady erosion of the financial pillars of municipal self-government. Reasons for the aggravation of local finances and municipal budgets include macroeconomic and structural problems; shifts in age, population, and social structure; financial ramifications of German unity; erroneous trends in the system of municipal financing; increasing encroachment on local revenue; municipal responsibilities and the way they were fulfilled by the Federation and the *Länder* (Karrenberg and Münstermann 1998, 437). This municipal financial crisis differs from the financial situation of the Federation and the *Länder*, insofar as the latter can decide more or less independently on their revenue and their expenses. For municipalities, revenue as well as spending are marked by a high degree of heteronomy.

The traditional concept and financing of the local welfare system is especially a cause for massive budgetary concern. The mounting burden of social services is the largest reason for the growth in municipal expenses. Between 1980 and 1996, municipal spending rose by 80 percent, while spending on social services tripled (Karrenberg and Münstermann 1998, 456). The importance of the social assistance scheme is complemented by the strong employment benefit nexus in the German pension system and in the unemployment insurance scheme. Since the mid-1970s, municipalities have been faced with a growing social assistance burden, mainly because of the high degree of (long-term) unemployment and the growing number of elderly people in need of assistance. The increasing number of unemployed individuals turn to social assistance benefits, which are co-financed by the local authorities. In addition, the Federation and the *Länder* have saddled municipalities with new tasks without securing the necessary funding (e.g., the legal right to a place in a kindergarten; joint financing of child benefits). As a result of all these factors, municipal social spending has risen substantially.

This has forced municipalities and counties to consolidate. In 2004, overall municipal budgets amounted to 150 billion euros. That was roughly equal to municipal expenses in 1992. A deficit of more than 4 billion euros remained. Many municipalities are struggling with chronic deficits. In addition, more and more government agency expenses (e.g., payrolls) are financed by continually increasing cash advances (Articus 2002, 5). Although the number of personnel has been reduced, payroll costs still amount to 26.6 percent of the overall expenses. In most cases, municipalities have started to reduce their personnel for voluntary tasks. In addition, the discretionary items of the local government budget, which are crucial for the funding of original self-government tasks (e.g., culture) are shrinking rapidly (Dieckmann 1998, 300). In 2004 the municipalities still invested more than 20 billion euros (13.4 percent of their budgets) in construction projects and in acquiring assets. Even so, the local government investment policy, as the nucleus of municipal rights and as a keystone of public services and utilities, is on the wane (Articus 2002, 5). In response to their financial constraints, local authorities have been privatizing municipal activities. Outsourcing to the private sector is not limited to municipal economic activities but can also include core activities of local authorities such as property management (Wollmann 2002, 30). Recently, municipalities have begun to use "cross-border-leasing" or "sale-and-lease-back" methods to ease their financial problems by selling parts of their real estate (e.g., school buildings) to private investors, who then lease them back to the municipality.

5 REPRESENTATION OF MUNICIPAL INTERESTS VIS-À-VIS THE FEDERAL LEVEL

The *Länder* participate in the legislation and administration of the Federation through the Federal Council (Art. 50 GG). There is no equivalent body to the Federal Council for the nationwide representation of municipal interests. Their political legitimization and their grass roots level notwithstanding, municipalities do not have an institutionalized opportunity to participate in the legislation process of the Federation (Gburreck and Kleinfeld 2005, 122). Due to the complexity of the process of policy formulation, the representation of interests is getting more complicated for the municipalities. Because of their nature and their number, municipalities are not ideally suited to participate in a bottom-up process of opinion formation and political agenda setting at the national level (Thränhardt 1998, 367). Hence, local authorities have to rely on the commitment of the *Länder*, to which they are assigned under constitutional law. Most *Länder*, however, are keen to represent their municipalities vis-à-vis the Federation without the actual participation of the local authorities (Dieckmann 1998, 302). A direct means of influence for municipal interests are the three associations of local government.

5.1 CENTRAL ASSOCIATIONS OF LOCAL GOVERNMENT

To avoid being marginalized in Germany's federal structure, municipalities need lobbying institutions and advisory bodies (COR 2004, 374). In light of the trend to transfer certain areas of legislation from the Federation to the *Länder*, municipal lobbying will become even more difficult, because lobbying activities at the federal level tend to be more powerful than on the regional level (Dieckmann 1998, 302).

Three central associations of local government (*kommunale Spitzenverbände*) seek to promote the constitutional right of local self-government. They also encourage and facilitate the exchange of experiences and represent the common interest of all local government bodies vis-à-vis the state and the public. The German Association of Cities (*Deutscher Städtetag*) represents the interests of its 216 direct members, including the three city-states; the German Association of Towns and Municipalities (*Deutscher Städte- und Gemeindebund*) speaks for more than 12,500 towns and municipalities within counties (*kreisangehörige Städte und Gemeinden*); and the German County Association (*Deutscher Landkreistag*) represents all 323 German counties. The division of labour between these three central associations reflects the differing needs and problems of smaller municipalities, larger cities, and counties. In order to coordinate and ease cooperation between the three central associations and to increase their clout in relations with the Federation, the Federal Union of Local Government Central Associations (*Bundesvereinigung der kommunalen Spitzenverbände*) was formed. In accordance with Germany's federal structure, the central associations are also organized along federal lines. Except in city-states, there are regional sections of the three central associations of local government in all thirteen *Länder*.

5.2 COOPERATION WITH THE FEDERAL LEVEL

Collaboration between the federal government and the central associations has been regulated within the joint standing orders of the federal ministries. A similar regulation can be found in the rules of procedure of the Federal Parliament. Both ensure that the central associations' representatives are involved and consulted at an early stage by the federal government and by the committees of Parliament in connection with legislative projects that affect local interests (DLT 2005). Contrary to provisions in the constitutions of eight *Länder* (including Baden-Württemberg and Bavaria), the central associations' right to be heard during the legislative process is not included in the Basic Law. Demands from the central associations to amend Art. 28 GG to guarantee such a right in the Constitution have not been met.

Occasionally, central associations have talks with federal ministers or with the chancellor. Since 1993, there have been sporadic meetings with the conference of the prime ministers of the *Länder* and with line ministries from the *Länder* (Dieckmann 1998, 302). In addition, central associations participate in several institutions of the *Länder* and the Federation in a decision-making or advisory capacity, including the Financial Planning Council, the Economic Planning Council, the Federation-*Länder* Council for Educational Planning and Research Support, and the Concerted Action in the Health Service Group (DLT 2005).

6 SCOPE AND NATURE OF MUNICIPAL-FEDERAL INTERACTION AND THE ROLE OF THE REGIONAL LEVEL

As mentioned earlier, German municipalities do not constitute an independent level of government; they are a constituent part of the *Länder*. However, with respect to the norms of the Constitution, the division between the federal, regional, and municipal levels is not as strict in political reality as one might expect (Dieckmann 1998, 299). Germany's political system is characterized by a high degree of political interdependence and joint tasks (*Politikverflechtung*). Over the years, the tasks and responsibilities have been distributed among the Federation, the *Länder*, and the municipalities. To assess the scope and nature of federal-municipal relations in Germany, it is thus necessary to take into account the interaction with the regional level as well.

German municipalities complain about the growing imbalance between local self-government and administrative heteronomy (Schmidt-Eichstaedt 1998, 323). As the delegation of tasks by the *Länder* and the Federation has becomes ever more regulated, the local authorities' room for manoeuvre has shrunk, thus depriving them of the basis for effective self-government. According to the German Association of Cities, 95 percent of municipal tasks are decided by higher orders of government (Kuban 2004, 114). Local authorities criticize the structural incongruity between the determination, execution, and financing of municipal tasks, which results in a structural bias to the detriment of municipalities (Gburreck and Kleinfeld 2005, 122). The increasing governmental influence from the Federation and the *Länder* on the execution of municipal tasks is further curbing local autonomy.

6.1 THE PRINCIPLE OF CONNECTIVITY

Constitutionally, the *Länder* execute federal laws in their own right (Art. 83 GG). They are bound by the so-called connectivity or costs-cause principle (*Konnexitätsprinzip*) if they delegate the execution of federal laws to their municipalities. This principle is enshrined in the constitutions of the *Länder*. Connectivity encompasses the link between the competencies for tasks and for spending, including the concurrence of political decision makers and the cost units of governmental services. For the relationship between the Federation and the *Länder,* this principle already applies via Art. 104a (1) GG. Both must separately finance expenditures that result from the discharge of their respective responsibilities. This implies that each of them is not allowed to impose financing of its proper tasks on the other.

Based on Art. 84 (1) GG, the Federation possesses the right of direct access to the municipalities (*Bundesdurchgriff*). In order to execute federal laws enacted with the approval of the Federal Council, the Federation can directly entrust the municipalities with specific tasks. In this case, the connectivity mechanisms of the *Länder* level are circumvented. The Federation is not legally obliged to provide the municipality with financial resources, because the Basic Law does not envisage the direct flow of financial means between the federal and the municipal level. This is widely regarded as a major flaw of current constitutional practice (Keller 2006, 104).

For municipalities, this situation poses a severe problem, because the Federation and the *Länder* violate the principle of connectivity by transferring duties to municipalities without providing them with the necessary funding. The municipalities suffer from the present burden-sharing principle, which assumes that the executing level must bear the costs that arise. This problem is aggravated by the fact that municipalities are not directly involved in the decision-making processes at the *Länder* and national levels. The Federation and the *Länder* can pass laws that impose financial burdens on local budgets without the participation of the municipalities. Recent examples of such federal laws involving direct access to the local level include social welfare (§ 3 *Sozialgesetzbuch* (SGB) XII), the Law on Child and Youth Welfare Services (§ 69 SGB VIII), and the accommodation costs for the long-term unemployed (§ 6 SGB II).

Municipalities and their central associations demand that legislative authority and the financial responsibility coincide by extending the costs-cause principle to the relationship between the Federation and municipalities (see section 10, below).[18] A clause on connectivity, recognizing the principle of legal causality (*Gesetzeskausalität*), should be included in Art. 104a (3) GG. In addition, municipalities demand that their right to be heard in the legislative process be constitutionally enshrined in the form of an amendment to Art. 28 (2) GG (Gburreck and Kleinfeld 2005, 126).

6.2 LACK OF REGIONAL MEDIATION

There are no specialized ministries or agencies in charge of municipal affairs at the federal level. At the regional level, there are no institutional structures devoted to relations with municipalities that are equivalent to the protection of the interests of the *Länder* via the Federal Council; nor are there regional ministries of intergovernmental affairs that could mediate between the local authorities and the federal government. The *Länder*, which are supposed to support their municipalities, often pursue their own interests. By delegating responsibilities to the municipalities, the federal and *Länder* governments are attempting to find ways to shift the onus to local authorities to solve their own fiscal problems and reduce their own backlog of unaccomplished tasks (Articus 2002, 6).

7 MUNICIPALITIES AND INTERNATIONAL RELATIONS

As a rule, foreign relations are conducted by the Federation (Art. 32 (1) GG); they fall under its exclusive legislative power (Art. 73 (1) GG). The *Länder* may, insofar as they have the legislative power, conclude treaties with foreign states with the consent of the Federation (Art. 32 (3) GG). Within their competency to exercise state powers and to perform state functions, the *Länder* have, since 1992, enjoyed the constitutional right to transfer sovereign powers to transfrontier institutions in neighbouring regions (Art. 24 (1a) GG). All German territorial entities, including municipalities, have to respect the principle of *Bundestreue* – the constitutional obligation to contribute to the consolidation and safeguarding of the interests of the Federation as a whole (Art. 20 GG; BVerfGE 1, 315). This principle applies to foreign affairs as well.

7.1 CROSS-BORDER COOPERATION

Germany borders nine countries, all of which are members of the European Union, except Switzerland. In times of increasing political and economic interdependence, the possibility of establishing cross-border institutions responds to the needs of many bordering areas. At present, there are more than thirty so-called *Euregios* – agreements in which subnational authorities, including municipalities, cooperate and coordinate their actions on a variety of issues of mutual interests. Most of these cooperation agreements are bilateral, but some have members from three countries. In 1996 Germany, France, Luxemburg, and Switzerland concluded the Karlsruhe Agreement, with the goal of fostering transfrontier collaboration in the adjoining regions. As a result, the participating territorial entities of four countries – including municipalities – are authorized to conclude mutual agreements independent of the federal level.

7.2 FROM TOWN TWINNING TO DEVELOPMENT ASSISTANCE

The encroachment of German municipalities as constituent parts of the *Länder* in the sphere of foreign affairs is sensitive and controversial from the point of view of constitutional norms (Wollmann 2004a, 106). Whether, and to what extent, foreign relations can be seen as part of "all local affairs" (Art. 28 (2) GG) and therefore part of the municipal domain remains controversial. Nevertheless, German municipalities have been actively engaged in international relations for decades. At first, their engagement was restricted to the establishment of bilateral town-twinning programs. For a while, these twinning activities were limited to municipalities from Western Europe and North America, but later they were extended to partners from all over the world. German municipalities thus discovered development assistance as a field of activity. Especially in the aftermath of the United Nations Summit on Environment and Development in Rio de Janeiro and its (local) Agenda 21, German municipalities have intensified their involvement in coordinated development activities.[19]

7.3 INTERACTION WITH THE EUROPEAN LEVEL

German municipalities have become the target of European policies that do not necessarily focus directly on the local level but are increasingly affecting the tasks und functions of local authorities. European treaties transfer few powers to intervene in areas of strictly municipal responsibilities to the bodies of the European Union (Articus 2002, 5). Still, the politics of the European Union exert greater influence on municipalities in many legislative and administrative areas than German national or *Land* politics. The separation between domestic and international (EU) politics has become ambiguous because this reality is reflected in a multilevel governance structure.

EU policies, such as competition law and the Internal Market project, have undermined the municipal authority to provide essential public services – a core area of the right to local self-government. In reaction, the municipalities have repeatedly complained that there is a lack of "local urban impact studies" prior to the enactment of EU measures that affect German localities (Articus 2002, 21). Despite the provisions of the EU constitutional treaty, local government autonomy has not been guaranteed at the EU level thus far. Against the backdrop of the continuing process of European integration and its impact on local affairs, German municipalities have identified the need to articulate their interests vis-à-vis the institutions of the European Union. In the EU's Committee of the Regions, German municipalities are underrepresented. Of the twent-four German members, twenty-one represent the *Länder*, while only three speak for local authorities.[20] In view of the absence of other established arrangements for comprehensive municipal participation in EU policymaking, German municipalities must rely on national and *Länder* governments. The latter, however, have made no moves towards establishing formal procedures for municipal participation in EU-related issues. As constituent parts of the *Länder*, German municipalities are forced to rely on advocates whose concern has primarily been to protect their own autonomy and rights of representation vis-à-vis the European level. Thus, local self-government is caught in another trap, jeopardizing the representation of its vested interests in political processes that serve European integration (Articus 2002, 22). Unlike the *Länd* level of government, the position of German municipalities has not really been strengthened by European integration.

As a result, single municipalities as well as the central associations of local government are directly engaged in various lobbying activities to further the interests of German local authorities within the European Union. They are trying to achieve this through their representations in Brussels, via members of the European Parliament who have special links to the local level, or by lobbying the European bureaucracy, especially the Commission (Thränhardt 1998, 370). Over the past decade, the German central associations and their regional branches have established offices (some of which are joint) in Brussels. The *Länder* have been closely observing these direct contacts between EU institutions and German municipalities (Thränhardt 1998, 369). In addition, the three central associations are direct members of the Council of European Municipalities and Regions, the largest organization of local and regional government in Europe (in the framework of the Council of Europe), and they are also members of the European section of the worldwide organization United Cities and Local Governments.

8 THE POLITICAL DIMENSION OF THE MUNICIPAL-FEDERAL RELATIONSHIP

In theoretical terms, the political status of German local government remains controversial (Ott 1994). On one hand, local councils must be treated as purely administrative organs, rather than as local parliaments, if the local government level is seen as a constituent part of the administrative structure of the *Länder* (Wollmann 2002, 28). On the other hand, the constitutional provision of Art. 28 (1) GG suggests that local councils have the same constitutional quality as *Länder* parliaments (Wollmann 1998, 61).

In practical terms, however, it is widely agreed that local government has been increasingly politicized. Political parties perform the same functions at the local level as at the *Land* or federal level. The influence of local media, civic action groups, and other associations notwithstanding, they shape local politics by dominating local agenda setting and decision making. The level of politicization, and with it the influence and relevance of national political parties, corresponds to the size of the municipality (Holtmann 1998, 209). But especially in smaller municipalities, the "city hall parties" or "independent voters' associations" (*Freie Wählergemeinschaften*) enjoy equal footing with the nationwide parties. These associations focus mainly on local issues and are thus restricted to the local level; 39 and 43 percent of the municipal mandates in Baden-Württemberg and Bavaria, respectively, are held by members of such independent (non-party) associations. Relative to the size of the municipality, these associations become more politicized and the nationwide parties gain more ground regarding offices and issues. Although the personality of the candidate is often more important than membership in a party, a growing number of these associations' politicians are close to traditional political parties (Kipke 2000, 86).

Parties are the major political players in local politics. This *de facto* situation has gradually been recognized *de jure* in local government charters as amended by the *Länder* parliaments. The introduction of local referendums and the direct election of the mayor and the chairman of the county have further accentuated the political and partisan profile of local government (Wollmann 1998, 56).

It is difficult to assess systematically whether voters in municipal elections cast their votes based on regional and national topics or on very specific local issues (Holtmann 1998, 211). Likewise, it is difficult to measure whether, and to what extent, (national) party politics programmatically influence policy outputs at the local level. Several empirical studies have tried to show that local decisions on factual issues reflect the programmatic options of national political parties only to a small degree. These studies argue that variables from the local and regional context – such as the need to solve local problems or to maintain local continuity in spending patterns – seem to be more important (ibid., 212). But the distinction between decisions on specific single issues in the local context and program-oriented decisions on the overall direction of politics is at least questionable. Owing to the advanced political interdependence between the European Union, the Federation, the *Länder*, and the municipalities, issues in the municipal area are subject to cross-level preliminary decisions (or non-decisions). In other words, political interdependence fosters the politicization of local affairs (ibid., 215).

Since the very beginning of the Federal Republic of Germany, local politics has been considered a democratic stepping stone. This applies not only to the active involvement of the population but also to the training of politicians. While most local politicians limit their involvement to the local sphere, municipal parliaments serve as the most important preparatory stage for the careers of politicians at the *Land* and federal levels. But the importance of personal involvement in local politics and the significance of nominations and elections at that level to launch a career in the regional or federal arena have been reduced. Since the 1970s, political parties have increasingly been nominating younger politicians, who do not have extensive experience in local politics, for seats in the *Länder* parliaments or the Federal Parliament (Dieckmann 1998, 302). However, certain ties with the grassroots of political parties still seem to be necessary and unavoidable. In some *Länder* (e.g., Baden-Württemberg), numerous mayors and county chairpersons are at the same time members of the *Länder* parliaments. This accumulation of offices, which does not exist between the local and federal levels, entails closer ties between the municipalities and the *Länder*.

The standing and influence of municipal incumbents depends to a large degree on the size of the municipality they represent. Only the mayors of very large cities appear on the national political scene and are thus able to play a certain role in national party politics. It is rare for municipal incumbents to take office at the national level. The situation is a bit different for the mayors and civil servants of the city-states. They are able to use their membership in the Federal Council as a platform to further their federal ambitions.[21]

9 POLICY CASE STUDIES

The two case studies that follow illustrate the position, tasks, and responsibilities of the local level in the policy fields of emergency planning and immigration. Both examples show that municipalities are integral parts of Germany's multilevel governance structure.

9.1 EMERGENCY PLANNING

The structure of the German federal system, with its division of competencies between the Federation and the *Länder,* is reflected in the distribution of tasks and responsibilities in the field of emergency planning. In times of peace, the *Länder* have the legislative, administrative, and executive authority for disaster control. Except for minor divergences, disaster control has the same legal basis (in the respective *Land* Law on Disaster Control) and organizational structure in all sixteen *Länder*. In a state of defence, the Federation possesses the exclusive legislative power with respect to the protection of the civilian population (Art. 73 GG; Law on Civil Protection). To avoid a costly duplication of manpower and technical equipment, the Federation and the *Länder* do not maintain independent systems of disaster control. Even in a state of defence, the disaster control of the *Länder* remains the basis for civil protection. In assuming this role, the *Länder* are acting on behalf of the Federation. The latter supplements the peacetime equipment and manpower of the *Länder*.

In contrast to fire control or the police fight against crime, disaster control as such is not a precisely definable task to avert danger. Disaster control is not in the hands of forces that are permanently assigned to a specific agency in order to fulfill certain duties. Instead, it is an organizing principle for a plethora of agencies and specialized organizations.

The *Länder* Laws on Disaster Control include provisions concerning the duty to help in a disaster. This duty applies to all *Länder* authorities, regional governments, counties, municipalities, fire brigades, and relief organizations. In certain circumstances, even private persons have to provide help. Yet the most important actors in the disaster control are voluntary members of public and private organizations. The local fire brigades of the municipalities, which are termed dependent institutions under public law (*unselbständige Anstalten des öffentlichen Rechts*), have about 1.2 million members. Their deployment and organizational structure are regulated by *Land* laws. Relief organizations that are active in the field of disaster control include the German Red Cross, the Worker Samariter Federation, Malteser International, New Johanniter, and the German Lifesaving Association with a total number of 500,000 volunteers. These voluntary organizations constitute an enormous potential resource, which is unique throughout the world.[22]

The *Länder* do not have specifically organized units for disaster control. By contrast, the federal Ministry of the Interior can rely on the federal Agency for Technical Relief (*Technisches Hilfswerk*) with its 75,000 voluntary members to provide disaster assistance (often abroad and worldwide; for example, in the case of earthquakes or tsunamis). Under the framework of administrative assistance, the federal armed forces and the federal border police can also be asked to provide assistance during disasters (Art. 35 GG). Recent catastrophes have shown that the armed forces are critical to large-scale disasters where a large number of highly organized and structured hands are needed at short notice.

The distribution of competencies and responsibilities in the field of disaster control follows the principle of subsidiarity. The administrative offices of Germany's 323 counties and 117 urban municipalities are the lower disaster control authorities (*untere Katastrophenschutzbehörde*). The regional governments serve as upper disaster control authorities (*obere Katastrophenschutzbehörde*), while the *Land* Ministry of the Interior has the status of the supreme disaster control authority (*oberste Katastrophenschutzbehörde*). It is within the discretion of the upper and supreme authorities to take over responsibility for disaster control. Yet as long as a state of disaster has not been declared, the municipality is responsible, coping with smaller emergencies. The *Länder* Laws on Disaster Control lay down criteria for the circumstances in which the authorities can declare a state of disaster. These regulations have a qualitative and a quantitative dimension.[23]

As soon as a state of disaster has been declared, responsibility automatically shifts from municipalities to the lower, upper, or supreme disaster control authorities, which then take over coordination and execution. All other actors and authorities are then placed under the command of the highest authority involved. Within these authorities, the disaster control teams (*Katastrophenschutzstäbe*) are responsible for strategy, logistics, and communication. They supervise and coordinate the necessary personnel and equipment.

According to the legislation of the *Länder*, the counties and urban municipalities must bear the costs that arise from disaster control in their territory. They must also bear the costs of compensating third parties, the deployment of fire brigades from other areas, and for the support from their *Land* and the Federation. Yet in cases with a special dimension and intensity, the *Länder* or the Federation provide counties and municipalities with special financial grants. The volunteers of relief organizations continue to receive pay from their employers, who can make claims to the responsible disaster control authority.

Since the late 1990s, new strategies for civil protection and disaster control have been developed in an effort to establish closer coordination and cooperation among the Federation, the *Länder*, and the municipalities. The question is whether the dual structure of disaster control and civil protection meets present-day requirements. The tragic events of 11 September 2001 made it clear that the established division of responsibilities in Germany is ill prepared to deal with terrorist attacks of such magnitude. The massive flooding of the Elbe and Danube river systems in the summer of 2002 demonstrated once again the need for trans- and supraregional cooperation and coordination mechanisms to deal with large-scale emergencies. It has also become clear that the distribution of resources across the *Länder* needs to be improved.

In response, in June 2002 the Federation and the *Länder* devised the New Strategy for the Protection of the Population. Its aim is joint crisis management by the Federation and the *Länder* in cases of extraordinary, large-scale danger. They also decided to set up an interministerial coordination group and a joint coordination centre for large-scale danger situations. As a result, the Joint Federal Situation and Information Centre, the German Emergency Information System, and the Academy for Crisis Management, Emergency Planning, and Civil Protection were established. Finally, the new Federal Office for Civil Protection and Disaster Response (*Bundesamt für Bevölkerungsschutz und Katastrophenhilfe*), under the auspices of the federal Ministry of the Interior, began operations in May 2004.[24] This office underlines the importance of civil protection for national security in organizational terms and responds to the need of a federal agency with competence to provide effective protection for the civil population when faced with a large-scale and nationally significant threat. Yet the original competencies and responsibilities of the *Länder* remain untouched by the new federal office, because the *Länder* are still responsible for the operative management of crises.

Generally, Germany seems to be well prepared and equipped for coping with large-scale disasters. Counties and urban municipalities play an important role as lower disaster control agencies. Still, there is room for improvement. Often the technical equipment of the fire brigades and the relief organizations is not up to date and not fit to deal with emergencies that involve many casualties. In addition, continued fragmentation of competencies is widely criticized. The federal Office for Civil Protection and Disaster Response, for example, is not allowed to take the coordinating lead during large-scale disasters. The Federal Minister of the Interior pushed for more centralization in the field of disaster control during the meetings of the Committee on Modernizing the Federal System (see section 10) but failed in the face of persistent opposition by the *Länder*.

9.2 IMMIGRATION

Fifty years ago there were approximately 500,000 foreigners in Germany (about 1 percent of the total population). These figures have since increased considerably; today there are 7.3 million foreigners (8.9 percent). If one also includes the 3.1 million recent repatriates of ethnic German origin – most of them from the former Soviet Union and Poland – as well as naturalized Germans (2.1 million) and illegal immigrants (between 500,000 and 1.5 million), the total number of people of immigrant origin amounts to approximately 13 million (16 percent of the total population). Demographic projections show a decline in Germany's "indigenous" population, whereas the share of people of immigrant origin (with a "migration background," as they are called in officialese) will rise. The 1990s were characterized by massive migration movements. Between 1991 and 1995, almost 6.2 million people moved to Germany, while 3.6 million left the country. During the following five years, 4.3 million people entered Germany, while 3.5 million departed. Between 1991 and 2004, more than 13.7 million immigrated to Germany, while almost 9.7 million emigrated, leaving a positive net balance of more than 4 million people.

The high numbers of migrants in the early 1990s were a direct result of the radical political and social changes in middle eastern and southeastern Europe. The large number of people who are leaving Germany suggests that the migratory movements were, on the whole, temporary in nature. There were four main types of migrants: recent repatriates (especially until the mid-1990s), asylum seekers (whose numbers also have dropped drastically since the mid-1990s), civil war refugees from the Balkans (who for the most part have returned to their home countries), and a small number of labour migrants. In 2003, fewer than 800,000 people moved to Germany, while more than 600,000 left.[25] Today, the most significant and stable form of legal immigration is family-member immigration (*Familiennachzug*), with 55,000 to 80,000 migrants per year. The numbers mentioned above suggest that Germany is as an immigration country.[26]

The spatial distribution of people with a migratory background shows a significant regional imbalance. The share of legal foreigners in former West Germany ranges between 6 and 15 percent. In the East German *Länder*, they account for less than 2 percent of the population. Immigration is predominantly an urban phenomenon all over Germany: 80 percent of people without German citizenship live in cities of more than 100,000 inhabitants. They represent 15 percent of the urban population. In large cities and urban agglomerations, this number is even higher.[27] Consequently, immigration policy is of major importance for Germany's cities and towns. The local level plays a key role in the integration of immigrants. After a lengthy and very controversial legislative process marked by intense public discussions, the Immigration Act (*Zuwanderungsgesetz*) came into force in January 2005. It consists of the Residence Act (RA), the Act on the General Freedom of Movement for EU Citizens, and amendments to other pieces of legislation. The Immigration Act provides a comprehensive legislative framework for dealing with immigration, especially control.

Unlike previous legislation, there are now only two types of residence title: the (temporary) residence permit and the (permanent) settlement permit (chapter 2 RA). The right of residence is determined by the purpose of residence, such as education, employment, humanitarian reasons, and subsequent family-member immigration. Foreigners who are in the country legally are free to decide where to take up residence in Germany. By contrast, foreigners who have entered Germany illegally, who do not submit an application for asylum, and cannot be repatriated immediately are allocated among the *Länder* (section 15a RA). This procedure follows the provision for the distribution of asylum applicants and is intended to spread the financial burden among the *Länder*.[28] The Residence Act also codifies legal claims for measures to promote the integration of legal immigrants in Germany. The new integration policy tightens requirements and puts a greater emphasis on integration.

Knowledge of the German language is considered to be an essential prerequisite for successful integration into German society. Chapter 3 of the RA includes detailed provisions for a basic package of measures to promote integration. This integration course is the central element of the new immigration policy, covering measures to acquaint foreigners with the language, legal system, and culture of Germany. The course consists of a basic and an advanced language course and an orientation course. The basic language course and the orientation course are financed by the Federation. In 2005 the Federation spent 200 million euros on these courses. The *Länder* must pay for the advanced language course. They also have to bear the costs associated with child care and social counselling. The

Immigration Act's Regulation on Integration Courses specifies that integration courses are to conform to a nation wide standard. The Federal Office for Migration and Refugees is responsible for the development of these standards. This reorganization represents an improvement over previous support for language courses.

Following the provisions of Art. 30 GG, the "exercise of state powers and the discharge of state functions is a matter for the *Länder.*" In addition, Art. 104a (1) GG stipulates that the *Länder* and the Federation "shall separately finance the expenditures resulting from the discharge of their respective responsibilities." These provisions apply to immigration as well as to integration policy; consequently, each *Land* is responsible for the general costs that arise from the integration of immigrants. In addition, the *Länder* are responsible for executing federal laws in their own right, including the right to regulate the establishment of authorities and their administrative procedure. These provisions also apply to the new immigration law (Art. 83 GG).

Counties and urban municipalities have been designated by the *Länder* as "foreigners' authorities" (*Ausländerbehörden*), which are responsible for residence- and passport-related measures. The local foreigners' authority, as a government agency of its respective *Land*, is subject only to directives by its supervising regional government which serves as the central foreigners' authority. According to section 71 (1) RA, the Länder may determine that only one or several foreigners' authorities are competent for specific tasks or areas of activity. Within Baden-Württemberg, for example, the regional government of Karlsruhe is responsible for the regional distribution of foreigners who have entered the country illegally.

Local authorities are responsible for the implementation of the Residence Act, which has organizational, personnel, and financial ramifications for the local level. Tasks must be redistributed, integration programs must be modified, and the implementation of the integration courses by the responsible organizations must be planned and coordinated. However, many municipalities, especially those with a high share of residents with a migratory background, were well prepared for these challenges since they already had experience in the development of integration programs. In addition, the Federal Office for Migration and Refugees has appointed regional coordinators to assist the local authorities in dealing with the changes that are induced by the Immigration Act.

For a long time, the policy on foreigners was mainly perceived as regulatory policy. Yet integration policy is also social policy. The local administration must, therefore, understand integration as a cross-sectional task. Many municipalities are working on a comprehensive approach to the coordination of integration policy. There is a growing need for increased inter- and intra-administrative cooperation and coordination. A central coordination office within the local administration seems to be necessary. In Stuttgart, for example, a central department for integration policy coordinates the work of other departments. But especially in smaller municipalities, the commitment of individual members of the administration is indispensable. In addition to the official authorities, welfare associations, civic action groups, churches, and clubs are actively engaged in the field of integration.

10 RECENT TRENDS

Currently, the high unemployment rate, the permanent financial crisis of the public budgets, and the interdependence of competencies are among the most pressing problems in Germany. The broad consensus is that comprehensive reforms are long overdue. Agenda 2010 and the attempts to modernize the federal system are steps in that direction. The former primarily addresses economic and social policies and thereby has an indirect impact on the situation at the local level. The latter targets the very core of Germany's federal system, including the relationship between municipalities and the federal and *Länder* levels.

10.1 AGENDA 2010

Agenda 2010 consists of several reform measures aimed at stimulating economic growth, the creation of jobs, and the modernization of the social security system. Until recently, the Federal Employment Agency and its local offices were responsible for job seekers. Municipal social welfare offices were in charge of the social assistance beneficiaries. This dual structure has proved to be inefficient and too costly. Thus, its reform was to eliminate problems associated with the traditional coexistence of institutions for unemployment benefits and social assistance.

The Fourth Bill on Modern Services in the Labour Market marks a cornerstone of the comprehensive reform package. After being approved by the Federal Parliament in late 2003, the Federal Council passed the bill in July 2004. This law, called *Hartz IV* in everyday usage, came into effect in January 2005. It has dramatically changed the coverage of the social assistance scheme. The introduction of new benefits for the elderly and for those of the unemployed who are capable of working has substantially narrowed down the traditional social assistance clientele, bringing it closer to its original mission. *Hartz IV* merges unemployment compensation and welfare benefit payments to form a new unemployment benefit system. This universal second-tier unemployment benefit (*Arbeitslosengeld II*) applies to all unemployed people capable of working who are not or no longer eligible for unemployment insurance benefits. The merger should enable the authorities to provide more effective advice and support to those concerned.

The responsibilities of the *Arbeitslosengeld II* have been split between the Federal Employment Agency and local governments. This scheme is the result of a compromise between the federal government and the opposition in the Federal Parliament, following a very controversial debate on how to administer and finance the new scheme. Originally, the opposition wanted municipalities to be responsible. Instead, the newly established Job Centers – which are part of the local offices of the Federal Employment Agency – are responsible for administering the payment of benefits and for job placement. Local governments provide supplementary benefits, such as the costs of accommodation for the long-term unemployed, child care, and social counselling.

The aforementioned compromise has led to the introduction of the "optional model" (*Optionsmodell*), which allows a predetermined number of counties and municipalities to decide whether or not to be in charge of the long-term unemployed on their sole responsibility or in cooperation with the local job center. Overall, sixty-three counties and six urban municipalities have decided to make use of the optional model. They are also in charge of the long-term unemployed, including their job placement. Yet the Federation remains responsible for the payment of the *Arbeitslosengeld II* as well as for administrative costs.

Municipalities are ambivalent about the changes associated with the *Hartz IV* reform. Local governments will get rid of a substantial part of the financial burden of unemployment, while the overall fiscal effects remain unclear because of incalculable follow-up costs (Gburreck and Kleinfeld 2005, 119). Owing to the higher accommodation costs of *Arbeitslosengeld II*, the Federation donated 3.2 billion euros to the municipalities as financial grants in 2005. At the same time, the local government's role in labour market policy is changing. The sixty-nine counties and urban municipalities that are making use of the optional model will be able to increase their role because of a new and broader set of activities. However, the influence of the majority of municipalities and counties will decline, because the traditional instruments of local labour-market policy are no longer available to them. As a result of the reform, local governments lose a major part of their traditional responsibilities, thus probably reducing their role and visibility in the German welfare system (Bönker and Wollmann 2004, 255).

10.2 REFORM OF THE FEDERAL SYSTEM

In recent years, there has been a broad debate about the need to modernize Germany's federal system comprehensively. The present system (euphemistically termed "cooperative federalism") is being criticized for its disorder in the allocation of competencies. The critics are demanding new jurisdictional provisions of the Federation and the *Länder*, a clear division between federal and *Länder* issues, a reallocation of competencies to the *Länder*, and a reduction of the Federal Council's influence on federal legislation. In exchange, the *Länder* should receive more autonomy. As a result of these discussions, a joint Committee on Modernizing the Federal System (CMFS) was established by the Federal Parliament and the Federal Council in the fall of 2003. The agenda of the CMFS included the allocation of legislative powers, the competencies of the *Länder* and their right to participate in the Federation's legislative activities, and the financial relations between the Federation and the *Länder*. The role of municipalities was also taken into account.

Yet because of irreconcilable differences between the Federation and the *Länder* on a series of major and crucial points (including education), the CMFS was unable to reach agreement on a joint proposal for amending the Basic Law. It concluded its work in December 2004 without adopting a formal proposal (Gburreck and Kleinfeld 2005, 135). Thus, the "mother of all reforms" – as it was euphorically labelled by many politicians – failed, at least for now. After the federal election of September 2005, a revised version of the joint proposal for the reform of the federal system was included in the coalition agreement between the Christian Democrats and the Social Democrats as an annex (Bundesregierung

2005). This proposal included municipal demands, a major aspect of the whole reform package. With the new government in office, chances have improved that the reforms will be approved by a two-third majority in both Houses of the Parliament.

The CMFS was composed of the Federal Parliament and the Federal Council (each of which sent sixteen representatives), the sixteen *Länder* parliaments (each of which sent six), and the federal government (which sent four members in an advisory capacity). Municipalities were represented by three members from the three central associations; although their membership was *ex officio*, they were entitled to speak and make proposals (Gburreck and Kleinfeld 2005, 123).

The main concern of the municipalities was to ensure that local self-government was respected and protected in accordance with Art. 28 (2) GG, which allows them to "regulate all local affairs on their own responsibility." The central associations argue that this principle of self-government has been put at risk by the structural flaws and shortcomings of German federalism and that it has caused the sustained financial crisis. Municipal representatives have identified the decline in local tax revenue and the imbalance between delegated tasks and financial compensation by the Federation and the *Länder* as the main reasons for their financial malaise (Gburreck and Kleinfeld 2005, 125).

It was clear from the outset that the municipalities would not succeed in getting their proposals for a radical reform of local finances onto the CMFS's agenda. But the prospects were better concerning another core demand. The municipal representatives insisted on the introduction of the connectivity principle in federal-municipal relations, unless the direct delegation of tasks by the Federation to the municipalities was not generally prohibited in Art. 84 GG. *Länder* governments across all parties supported this municipal demand. Among the CMFS's delegates from the Federal Parliament only the liberal faction supported this cause-costs principle (Gburreck and Kleinfeld 2005, 132). But as of February 2004, a two-thirds majority of the CMFS supported local authorities with regard to their demands concerning Art. 84 GG. The two chairmen of the CMFS introduced a proposal which stipulated that federal laws should no longer be allowed to delegate tasks to municipalities and to associations of municipalities (Gburreck and Kleinfeld 2005, 133). In November 2005 this proposal was included in the annex of the new coalition agreement. Within the context of the overall reduction of responsibilities of the Federal Council, Art. 84 (1) and Art. 85 (1) will be amended. Both articles now prohibit the transfer of tasks and responsibilities to municipalities and associations of municipalities by federal law. This prevention of the *Bundesdurchgriff* symbolizes an important improvement for local self-government.

11 IS THE SYSTEM OF MULTILEVEL GOVERNANCE ADEQUATE IN RELATION TO MUNICIPAL POLICY?

The previous sections, including the case studies, have argued that it is appropriate to use the concept of multilevel governance to analyse the established pattern of governance in Germany's political system. Within this system, which is marked by its high degree of complex political interdependence, municipalities have traditionally played a decisive role in the intergovernmental setting of the implementation of policy, the application of law, and the delivery of services. Owing to their dual function as local self-government entities and as the lowest administrative tier, municipalities have been able to accomplish a wide range of public tasks and responsibilities. For a long time the division of labour between the federal, the *Länder*, and the local level worked well. Furthermore, the introduction of direct-democratic elements has accentuated the political profile of local self-government and has strengthened the citizens' ability to control policies. But in times of chronic financial crisis and ever-increasing interdependence, German municipalities are forced to defend their autonomy against growing heteronomy by the *Länder*, the Federation, and the European Union. The delegation of administrative tasks by the Federation and the *Länder* without adequate financial compensation have a negative effect on the capability of the municipalities to perform properly the tasks that have been basic elements of the traditional multifunctional model of German local government. Local authorities risk becoming little more than agents implementing tasks imposed and delegated by the federal and *Land* governments. They risk degenerating into a "subordinate organizational and social agency" (Wollmann 2002, 33).

The central goal of the municipal level must, therefore, be to achieve the congruity of determination, execution, and financing of local tasks and responsibilities. Limiting the tendency of the Federation to overload municipalities is a first but important step towards alleviating the financial crisis at the local level. With an adequate financial basis, it will be easier for the local level to assert its position within the federal political system, which is marked by its multilevel-governance structure and by its high degree of political interdependence.

Finally, multilevel governance and political interdependence influence not only the perception and behaviour of actors at the local, *Land*, and federal level but also make it difficult to attribute objectively to one level of government or another the negative effects and positive achievements of political decisions. It is, therefore, in the interest of all responsible actors to strengthen transparency and to reduce the disorder of jurisdictions that blur the responsibilities in Germany's system of multilevel governance.

NOTES

1 Similar definitions can be found in the first article of most local government codes of the *Länder* (e.g., Art. 1, Local Government Law of the Free State of Bavaria).
2 There are four models of local self-government. Their main differences relate to the relationship between the elected representation of the people (assembly, council with part-time "deputies") and the full-time executive, as well as to the type and selection of the executive body (Andersen 1995, 184).
3 In addition, there are district capitals (*große Kreisstädte*) in some *Länder*. These towns fulfill several administrative functions for the county to which they are subordinated.

4 Examples include the Westphalia-Lippe and Rhineland associations of local authorities in North Rhine – Westphalia or the state welfare organizations (*Landeswohlfahrtsverbände*) in Baden – Württemberg.

5 The main reason for this variance is the creation of joint authorities for several smaller municipalities in some *Länder*.

6 If the European Union is taken into account as another level, municipalities and counties represent the fourth administrative tier.

7 A prominent example for this is the demand that the Federation should not be authorized to legislate that individual citizens may claim a place for their child or children in a kindergarten (Isensee 1995).

8 Art. I/5 (1), EU constitutional treaty: "The union shall respect the equality of Member States before the constitution as well as their national identities, inherent in their fundamental structures, political and constitutional, inclusive of regional and local self-government."

9 The performance of tasks within the municipalities' own field of activity is subject to legal supervision which, however, does not relate to the suitability of municipal decisions. The performance of tasks in the field of transferred activities are subject to expert supervision, which relates not only to the legality, but also to the aptness of municipal decisions. See section 3, below.

10 West Berlin was not considered to be a *Land*. Its citizens were not authorized to vote in federal elections but were indirectly represented in the Federal Parliament by twenty deputies (without voting rights) chosen by the West Berlin House of Representatives. Correspondingly, representatives sent by the West Berlin Senate (that is, the government) to the Federal Council had no voting rights.

11 In a political system, several tasks must be fulfilled: maintenance of internal and external security, (re)distributive policies, stabilization policies, maintenance of sustainability, and the allocation of public goods and services. The distribution of these responsibilities and functions amongst the different levels of a political system should follow the fundamental principle that services provided by the state shall correspond with the needs of the citizens and their preferences. In this context, the normative principle of subsidiarity applies, according to which public tasks should be performed at the lowest level possible; the *Land* should take action only if municipalities are not capable of doing so properly.

12 For example, 120 out of approx. 300 EU directives concerning the Internal Market had to be implemented by the municipalities. In general, these EU directives have to be transformed in federal and *Länder* laws (Thränhardt 1998, 365).

13 An example of a special purpose association is the Lake Constance Water Supply (*Bodensee-Wasserversorgung*), which was set up by 126 municipalities and 31 smaller *Zweckverbände* to provide nearly half of the *Land* Baden-Württemberg with drinking water.

14 The jurisdiction over taxes encompasses three elements of fiscal sovereignty: the claim to tax revenue; the authority to introduce, alter, and repeal taxes, including the right to change tax rates and the assessment basis, thereby increasing or decreasing the revenue; and the responsibility for the imposition, enforcement, and control of taxes. In a system of separate taxes (*Trennsystem*), specific tax revenue exclusively accrues to one

territorial authority. The alternative option is the distribution of specific tax revenue amongst several levels of government. In a system of joint taxes (*Verbundsystem*), tax revenue is distributed amongst the territorial authorities via quotas. The lower levels of government receive a share of tax revenue which is imposed by a higher level. In these systems, the fiscal autonomy of each level of government remains relatively high. The level of autonomy is considerably lower in an allocative system (*Zuweisungssystem*), where allocations of funds are transferred to the recipients by other levels of government (top-down as well as bottom-up) (Scherf and Hofmann 2003, 313 – 316).

15 Often, there is a *Hebesatz* differential between cities and municipalities. Larger cities especially are forced to set their *Hebesatz* at a higher percentage than smaller municipalities in their vicinity (Karrenberg and Münstermann 1998, 445).

16 This applies to Berlin and Hamburg. The situation in Bremen is different, because it consists of two municipalities (see section 2).

17 This source of revenue has become more salient in recent years. A growing number of tasks has been delegated from the municipalities to the counties without adequate financial compensation by the *Land*. Thus, many counties can only secure their budget by increasing this form of allocation from their municipalities.

18 The expression commonly used by municipal representatives, including the central associations, is "He who orders, has to pay" (in German: *Wer bestellt, bezahlt;*) See DStGB 2005a).

19 There are examples of conflicts between the federal government and German municipalities. In 1986, Munich's city council decided to help out Nicaraguan municipalities. At the same time, the federal Ministry for Economic Cooperation and Development decided to discontinue all assistance (Nuscheler 1996, 385). Another case in point relates to the current situation in Iran. After the Iranian nuclear program was relaunched, members of the conservative Christian Democratic Party heavily criticized the mayor of Freiburg, a member of the Green Party, for the continuation of the town-twinning activities between Freiburg and the Iranian city of Isfahan.

20 Only the federal chancellor (Helmut Kohl) intervened when the *Länder* reluctantly agreed that municipalities would be represented in the Committee of the Regions (3 out of 24 seats). With the exception of Germany (with strong *Länder*) and Belgium (with very strong regions and communities as entities of the federal state at the subnational level), all other EU member states have incorporated the municipalities more strongly (Thränhardt 1998, 368).

21 Prominent examples are Chancellor Willy Brandt (former governing mayor of Berlin), Chancellor Helmut Schmidt (former senator of the interior in Hamburg), Chancellor Helmut Kohl (former prime minister in Rhineland-Palatinate), and Chancellor Gerhard Schröder (former prime minister of Lower Saxony).

22 In the medium and long term, however, most of these organizations are faced with recruitment problems.

23 Accordingly, disasters are threats to the life and health of the population, to the environment, or to tangible assets. In quantitative terms, a disaster is marked by the need to coordinate a variety of actors, by a longer time frame, and by the necessity to foster the coordination and networking of several authorities. A state of disaster can be declared

following natural disasters, such as floods and storms, and also in reaction to large traffic crashes, accidents in chemical or nuclear power plants, and terrorist attacks.

24 Note that the German term *Bevölkerungsschutz* (protection of the population) illustrates the new, comprehensive approach. The traditional term *Zivilschutz* (civil protection), which was associated with the state of defence, is no longer used in this context.

25 These were the lowest numbers since 1991. They include foreign students, German citizens, and EUcitizens, as well as seasonal workers, recent repatriates, asylum seekers, and Jewish immigrants.

26 There are two different terms for immigration in the German language: *Einwanderung* and *Zuwanderung*. The first refers to the lawful entry and residence of foreigners who intend to settle permanently in Germany from the outset (i.e., legal immigration). *Zuwanderung* has become the accepted term to describe all forms of long- and short-term migration across national borders (BMI 2005).

27 With 31.8 percent, the city of Offenbach (in the metropolitan area of Frankfurt) has the highest percentage of inhabitants of immigrant origin. Other cities with more than 20 percent include Frankfurt, Stuttgart, and Munich.

28 In accordance with the Law Governing the Application Procedure for Asylum (*Asylverfahrensgesetz*), asylum seekers whose applications are still being processed are subject to the *Residenzpflicht*: they are not allowed to leave the district in which the foreigners' authority at which they are registered is located. A federal distribution arrangement apportions the refugees among the *Länder* who then assign asylum-seekers to their counties.

REFERENCES

Andersen, Uwe. 1995. "Gemeinden/Communale Selbstverwaltung." In Handwörterbuch des politischen Systems der Bundesrepublik Deutschland, ed. Uwe Andersen and Wichard Woyke, 78–87. Liske & Budrich

Articus, Stephan. 2002. "Zukunft der Stadt? Stadt der Zukunft! Anmerkungen zur Situation und Zukunft der kommunalen Selbstverwaltung in Deutschland." *Deutsche Zeitschrift für Kommunalwissenschaften* 41 (1): 3–23

Baden-Württemberg (BW). 2005. www.baden-wuerttemberg.de/en/Municipal_regional_federal/86230.html (accessed 25 August 2005)

Beauftragte der Bundesregierung für Migration und Flüchtlinge (BAMF). 2004. *Migrationsgeschen. Daten, Fakten, Trends.* www.integrationsbeauftragte.de (accessed 25 August 2005)

Bogumil, Jörg, and Lars Holtkamp. 2002. "Liberalisierung und Privatisierung kommunaler Aufgaben: Auswirkungen auf das kommunale Entscheidungssystem." In *Liberalisierung und Privatisierung öffentlicher Aufgabenerfüllung: Soziale und umweltpolitische Perspektiven im Zeichen des Wettbewerbs*, ed. Jens Libbe, Stephan Tomerius, and Jan Hendrik Trapp, 71–87. Berlin: Difu

Bönker, Frank, and Helmut Wollmann. 2004. "L'évolution du role des collectivités locales dans l'État providence allemande." *Revue française des Affaires sociales* 58 (4): 245–66

Bundesministerium des Innern (BMI). 2005. *Zuwanderungsrecht in Deutschland.* www.zuwanderung.de/index.html (accessed 25 August 2005)

Bundesregierung 2005. *Koalitionsvertrag zwischen CDU, CSU und SPD 11.11.2005: Gemeinsam für Deutschland – mit Mut und Mitmenschlichkeit.* www.bundesregierung.de/ Anlage920135/Koalitionsvertrag.pdf (accessed 25 November 2005)

Committee of the Regions of the European Union (COR) 2004. *Strengthening Regional and Local Democracy in the European Union.* Vol. 1 of *CoR Studies*, E-1/2004. Luxembourg: Office for Official Publications of the European Communities

Deutscher Landkreistag (DLT) 2005. www.kreise.de/landkreistag/ (accessed 25 August 2005)

Deutscher Städte- und Gemeindebund (DStGB). 2005a. *Neustart in der Arbeitsmarktpolitik fortsetzen: Investitionskraft stärken – Arbeitsplätze schaffen.* www.dstgb.de/index_inhalt/ homepage/index.phtml (accessed 19 August 2005)

– 2005b. *Datenreport Kommunalfinanzen 2005: Fakten, Trends, Einschätzungen.* DStGB-Dokumentation, no. 48. www.dstgb.de/index_inhalt/homepage/index.phtml (accessed 25 August 2005)

Dieckmann, Jochen. 1998. "Die Städte im Bundesstaat." In *Kommunalpolitik*, ed. Helmut Wollmann and Roland Roth, 292–305. Opladen: Leske&Budrich

– 2001. "Die Städte im Bundesstaat." In *Empirische Policy- und Verwaltungsforschung: lokale, nationale und internationale Perspektiven*, ed. E. Schröter 15–25. Opladen: Leske&Budrich

Gburreck, Tim, and Ralf Kleinfeld. 2005. "Die kommunalen Spitzenverbände in der Kommission von Bundestag und Bundesrat zur Modernisierung der bundesstaatlichen Ordnung." In *Die unvollendete Föderalismus-Reform: Eine Zwischenbilanz nach dem Scheitern der Kommission zur Modernisierung der bundesstaatlichen Ordnung im Dezember 2004*, ed. Rudolf Hrbek and Annegret Eppler, 119–37. Occasional Paper No. 31. Tübingen: Europäisches Zentrum für Föderalismus-Forschung

Geiger, Christian. 2004. "Konnexitätsprinzip und Konsultationsgremien – aktuelle Entwicklungen im Bundesvergleich" www.staedtetag-nrw.de (accessed 31 August 2005)

Goldsmith, Mike. 2003. "Variable Geometry, Multi-level Governance: European Integration and Sub-national Government in the New Millennium." In *The Politics of Europeanization*, ed. Kevin Featherstone and Claudio Radaelli, 112–33. Oxford: Oxford University Press

Heinz, Werner, Nicole Langel, and Walter Leitermann. 2004. "Kooperationsbeziehungen zwischen deutschen Städten und Kommunen in Entwicklungs*Ländern*." *Aus Politik und Zeitgeschichte* 15–16, 21–7

Holtmann, Everhard. 1998. "Parteien in der lokalen Politik." In *Kommunalpolitik*, ed. Helmut Wollmann and Roland Roth, 208–26. Opladen: Leske&Budrich

Hrbek, Rudolf. 1986. "Doppelte Politikverflechtung: Deutscher Föderalismus und europäische Integration. Die deutschen Länder im EG-Entscheidungsprozess." In *Die deutschen Länder und die Europäische Gemeinschaft*, ed. Rudolf Hrbek and Uwe Thaysen, 17–36. Baden-Baden: Nomos

– 2001. "Die föderale Ordnung – Anspruch und Wirklichkeit." In *Bilanz: 50 Jahre Bundesrepublik Deutschland*, ed. Marie-Louise Recker, Burkhard Jellonek and Bernd Rauls, 33–68. St. Ingbert: Röhrig

Hrbek, Rudolf, and Annegret Eppler, ed. 2004. *Deutschland vor der Föderalismus-Reform: Eine Dokumentation.* Occasional Paper No. 28. Tübingen: Europäisches Zentrum für Föderalismus-Forschung

Isensee, Josef. 1995. "Der Rechtsanspruch auf einen Kindergartenplatz: Ein Verfassungsproblem des Bundesstaates und der kommunalen Selbstverwaltung." *Deutsches Verwaltungsblatt* 1:1–9

Jarass, Hans D., and Bodo Pieroth. 2004. *Grundgesetz für die Bundesrepublik Deutschland. Kommentar.* 7th edn. München: Beck

Karrenberg Hanns, and Engelbert Münstermann. 1998. "Kommunale Finanzen." In *Kommunalpolitik*, ed. Hellmut Wollmann and Roland Roth, 437–60. Opladen: Leske&Budrich

Keller, Stephan. 2006. "Die Kommunen im Verhältnis zu Bund und Ländern." In *Der deutsche Föderalismus im Reformprozess*, ed. Michael Borchard and Udo Margedant, 101–17. St. Augustin: Konrad-Adenauer-Stiftung

Kipke, Rüdiger. 2000. "Gemeinden in der politischen Ordnung der Bundesrepublik Deutschland." In *Einführung in die Kommunalpolitik*, ed. Jürgen Bellers, Rainer Frey and Claudius Rosenthal, 75–88. München: Oldenbourg

Knodt, Michèle, and Martin Große Hüttmann. 2005. "Der Multi-Level-Governance-Ansatz." In *Theorien europäischer Integration*, ed. Hans-Jürgen Bieling and Marika Lerch, 227–51. Wiesbaden: VS Verlag für Sozialwissenschaften

Kost, Andreas, and Hans-Georg Wehling, ed. 2003. *Kommunalpolitik in den deutschen Ländern*, 7–19. Wiesbaden: Westdeutscher Verlag

Kuban, Monika. 2004. "Die Anliegen der Kommunen in der Kommission zur Modernisierung der bundesstaatlichen Ordnung." *Zeitschrift für Kommunalfinanzen* (5): 113–16

Marks, Gary, et al., eds. 1996. "Competencies, Cracks, and Conflicts: Regional Mobilization in the European Union" In *Governance in the European Union*, ed. Marks et al. London: Sage

Nierhaus, Michael. 2003. "Art. 28 GG." In *Grundgesetz*, ed. Michael Sachs. München: Beck, Rdnr. 31

Norton, Alan, ed. 1994. *International Handbook of Local and Regional Government: A Comparative Analysis of Advanced Democracies.* Aldershot: Elgar

Nuscheler, Franz. 1996. "Lern- und Arbeitsbuch Entwicklungspolitik." Bundeszentracle für Politische Bilding, Bonn

Ott, Yvonne. 1994. *Der Parlamentscharakter der Gemeindevertretung: Eine rechtsvergleichende Untersuchung der Qualität staatlicher und gemeindlicher Vertretungskörperschaften.* Baden-Baden: Nomos

Papier, Hans-Jürgen. 2003. "Steuerungs- und Reformfähigkeit des Staates." Vortrag bei der Stiftung für Ordnungspolitik held on 10 April in Freiburg. www.sfop.de/sfop/Papier.pdf (accessed 29 August 2005)

Püttner, Günter. 2004. *Kommunalrecht in Baden-Württemberg.* 3rd edn. Stuttgart: Boorberg

Reichwein, Alfred, and Stephanie Vogel 2004. *Integrationsarbeit – effektiv organisiert: Ein Handbuch für Kommunen.* Kommunale Gemeinschaftsstelle für Verwaltungsvereinfachung (KGST)

Rosamond, Ben. 2000. *Theories of European Integration.* New York: St Martin's Press

Sachsen. 2002. *Bericht der Unabhängigen Kommission der Sächsischen Staatsregierung.* Flutkatastrophe 2002

Scharpf, F. 1985. "Die Politikverflechtungs-Falle. Europäische Integration und deutscher Föderalismus im Vergleich." In *Politische Vierteljahresschrift*, 26 (4): 323–56

Scheffler, Thomas. 1998. "Aus*Länder*politik in der Kommune." In *Kommunalpolitik*, ed. Hellmut Wollmann and Roland Roth, 764–79. Opladen: Leske&Budrich

Scherf, Wolfgang, and Kai Hofmann. 2003. "Die kommunale Finanzverfassung in Deutschland." In *Kommunalpolitik in den deutschen Ländern*, ed. Andreas Kost and Hans-Georg Wehling, 313–34. Wiesbaden: Westdeutscher Verlag

Schmidt-Eichstaedt, Gerd. 1998. "Autonomie und Regelung von oben." In *Kommunalpolitik*, ed. Hellmut Wollmann and Roland Roth, 323–37. Opladen: Leske&Budrich

Schrader, Christian. 2004. *Die kommunalen Spitzenverbände und der Schutz der kommunalen Selbstverwaltungsgarantie durch Verfahren und Verfahrensgestaltung.* Baden-Baden: Nomos

Schulze, Claus J. 1997. *Die deutschen Kommunen in der Europäischen Union: Europabetroffenheit und Interessenwahrnehmung.* Baden-Baden: Nomos

Sellers, Jeffrey M. 2002a. "The Nation-State and Urban Governance: Toward Multilevel Analysis." *Urban Affairs Review* 37:611–41

– 2002b. *Governing from Below: Urban Regions and the Global Economy.* Cambridge: Cambridge University Press

Statistisches Bundesamt (DESTATIS). 1994–2004. www.destatis.de/basis/d/fist/fist01.php (accessed 29 August 2005)

Thränhardt, Dietrich. 1998. "Die Kommunen und die Europäische Union." In *Kommunalpolitik*, ed. Hellmut Wollmann and Roland Roth, 361–77. Opladen: Leske&Budrich

Witte, Gertrud. 2004. *Die kommunale Sicht zu Migration, Integration und Prävention*, www.staedtetag-nrw.de (accessed 31 August 2005)

Wollmann, Hellmut. 1998. "Kommunalvertretungen: Verwaltungsorgane oder Parlamente?" In *Kommunalpolitik*, ed. Hellmut Wollmann and Ronald Roth. 50–66. Opladen: Leske&Budrich

– 2002. "Die traditionelle deutsche kommunale Selbstverwaltung – ein 'Auslaufmodell'?" *Deutsche Zeitschrift für Kommunalwissenschaften* 41 (1): 24–51

– 2004a. "The Two Waves of Territorial Reform of Local Government in Germany." In *Redrawing Local Government Boundaries: An International Study of Politics, Procedures, and Decisions*, ed. John Meligrana, 106–29. Vancouver: University of British Columbia Press

– 2004b. "Wird der deutsche Typus kommunaler Selbstverwaltung den Druck von EU-Liberalisierung, New Public Management und Finanzkrise überleben?" In *Die europäische Stadt*, ed. Walter Siebel, 359–70. Frankfurt/M: Suhrkamp

THE INTERACTION OF MUNICIPAL AND FEDERAL GOVERNMENTS IN MEXICO: TRENDS, ISSUES, AND PROBLEMS

Allison Rowland

1 INTRODUCTION

The gradual fall of the one-party political system in Mexico, beginning in the 1970s and culminating in 2000 with the election of the first non-PRI president in seven decades,[1] has transformed nearly all aspects of governance in the country, including intergovernmental relations and the activities of the local unit of government, the *municipio* (municipality). Everything from constitutional provisions to fiscal arrangements to interactions of federal and state line agencies with municipal government has been altered in recent decades, either as part of an attempt by the former ruling party to maintain its hold on power or in reaction to these attempts. As a result, the system of more than 2,400 local governments, 31 states, and one Federal District continues to be characterized by uneven change and increasing regional variation in practices and activities.

The present paper attempts to identify and explain the most significant trends and patterns in municipal-federal relationships in Mexico, as well as to suggest some directions in which things are likely to evolve in coming years. Throughout, it argues that the context for effective and appropriate local and urban policy has improved in Mexico as the result of decentralization in many aspects of government. The text also identifies several areas in which modifications in federal and state legal structures could improve this framework. Nevertheless, it stresses that noticeable gains in governance will take time, since dramatic change in political and legal spheres has taken place in an environment characterized by inexperienced and technically deficient local governments, whose current practices are a result of nearly a century of weakness relative to other levels of government (Merino 1998). Even the most advanced municipalities are immersed in an intense process of "learning by doing" as they try to respond to mixed and sometimes confused messages both from higher levels of government and from their own electorates.

Thus, the panorama of intergovernmental relations in Mexico is varied and rapidly evolving. The general direction appears promising, but many obstacles to improved policymaking remain to be overcome. Two examples of this pattern are explored in more detail in section 11. Here, the discussion of federal-municipal interactions in the use of federal property and the examination of strategies of image definition and promotion for certain places bring to light the specific challenges facing municipalities, as well as the uneven process of change across the country.

2 CONSTITUTIONAL DIMENSION

Municipalities predate the establishment of modern Mexico by more than three hundred years. Their relatively disadvantaged legal and political status today reflects the reduction in their importance as part of the long process of consolidation of power at the central level, especially during the early part of the twentieth century (Merino 1998). Nevertheless, the Constitution of 1917, which remains in effect in amended form, defines municipalities in Article 115 as a republican, representative, popular, and "free" unit of government; most of the muncipalities' faculties, responsibilities, and revenue sources are specifically enumerated in this article. The structure of local government is laid out in the same article: a local council (*ayuntamiento*) to be led by the mayor (*presidente municipal*) and composed of a group of councillors (*regidores*) and comptrollers (*síndicos*), whose number varies according to municipal population and state law. These officials are elected for three-year nonrenewable terms on the basis of municipality-wide party slates, with Mexico's version of proportional representation laws providing for a minimal presence of opposition parties in municipal governance.

In practice, this is a "strong-mayor" system, not only because the municipal president is guaranteed a party majority in council sessions, but also because the role of other council members is not clearly stated in law (Rowland 2004). This helps explain why the latters' activities vary widely, both from place to place and within a single jurisdiction over time. The mayor names department directors for such areas as public works, police and transit, and treasury. Their number and profile depend on population and budget sizes as well as on other characteristics of the local jurisdiction. These directors are responsible for most government operations and report directly to the mayor. Since there is no career civil service in Mexican local government, the majority of these authorities remain in their positions only briefly, which often implies a limited amount of expertise.

The extent to which activities in a particular municipality truly conform to the list laid out in the Constitution varies substantially for several reasons. First, the precise wording of the constitutional text has left room for diverse interpretations over the decades. For example, one prominent legal scholar insists that "free" refers to the form of electing local officials and not to any characteristic of their policymaking (Tena 1997). Historically, this interpretation provided legal support to federal and state governments that wished to control municipal affairs for political purposes or, more recently, that sought to maintain control of local revenue sources for their own purposes.

In fact, until the 1980s, common extraconstitutional practices essentially obviated the provisions of Article 115. In particular, the ruling party subsumed the formal constitutional arrangements of government into its own practices, making the election of local officials, for example, an exercise of simply reaffirming the candidate chosen by the party hierarchy through its internal processes.

Recent trends towards increased attention to the formal rule of law in all areas of Mexican government, not to mention the rise of parties to compete with the PRI, have led to some new developments. Constitutional reform in 1999 defined municipalities as formal units of government rather than mere administrative sub-divisions of the states, as they had been before. This paved the way for a growing number of "constitutional controversies" through which municipalities (and, in some cases, states) ask the Supreme Court to mediate in intergovernmental disputes. Municipalities rarely win these cases, since their scope of action is relatively restricted in legal terms, and all powers not reserved for them explicitly in law are considered state or federal domains. However, the growing importance of the law in determining municipal faculties and responsibilities, combined with more competitive and "cleaner" elections, has encouraged the expansion of the range of policies chosen at the local level, has improved local service provision, and has led to the development of new administrative and technical capacities.[2]

These trends have also favoured the reassertion of state power in intergovernmental relations after decades of federal government domination. Local governments face the threat of dissolution of the *ayuntamiento* by state congresses, although this is infrequent. Another, less direct, source of state control is the requirement that the state congress approve each municipality's annual revenue plan. However, regional practices are increasingly varied. One reason is that although state constitutions play a growing role in the practice of municipal government, in many cases these have either not been reformed to reflect changes at the national level or have been reformed in such a way as to reaffirm political and fiscal control by the states, rather than reducing it.

Regardless of the role of the states, Article 115 essentially treats all municipalities as identical, in the face of notable differences in population, economic structure and dynamism, levels of poverty, political practices, and ethnic composition (the appendix presents a variety of data to illustrate this point). Government programs purportedly designed to compensate for imbalances among municipalities are rarely effective (Rowland 2001). The national Constitution does allow for states to step in to assist local governments in tasks they declare themselves to be unable to handle on their own. However, given the legacy of intrusive and unhelpful state meddling in their affairs, many municipalities are reluctant to ask for such help.

The major exception to this rule of equal legal status for very unequal politico-administrative units is the Federal District (*Distrito Federal*, DF). The seat of national political power is neither a state nor a municipality, and the form of local administration is notably problematic. The level of complexity is heightened by the fact that the DF is home to nearly half the population of one of the largest cities in the world, Mexico City, but the urban area spills across jurisdictions to include other states and municipalities with whom coordination is difficult. The large amount of national investment dedicated to the DF during the twentieth century resulted in an area well endowed with physical infrastructure compared with the rest of the country, and the contrast with adjoining politico-administrative units is notable. In addition, long-running attempts to reform the structures of government of the DF have led to a confused and contradictory local administration. Finally, few options for representation of local citizens exist in the government of the DF, and there are perhaps even fewer opportunities for them to influence local policy choices.

In other jurisdictions, it is not common to encounter local bodies of government besides the municipality. One exception to this rule appears in indigenous villages, which typically are organized through councils of elders or community councils that distribute responsibility for public service provision among residents (usually only adult males). In addition, in the State of Oaxaca, many municipalities in which indigenous villages are located select local officials through a process known as "uses and customs" (usos y costumbres) rather than conducting local political-party-based elections. These types of system supplement but do not completely replace the formation of municipal governments according to constitutional provisions.

Another type of local government structure, parallel but not integrated into the municipality and common throughout rural and semi-rural areas, is based on arrangements for shared landholding known as ejidos or tierras comunales. These structures, which date from the first half of the twentieth century, enjoy significant governmental powers thanks to their direct links to the federal Ministry of Agrarian Reform. Because of this autonomy, they work at times in coordination and at times in conflict with the ayuntamientos.

Finally, national (and, less often, state) government programs sporadically include the establishment of agencies or committees with substantial power relative to local government; the PRONASOL program of the 1980s is a well-known example (Cornelius, Craig, and Fox 1994; Dresser 1991). These groups, whose constitutionality is often questionable, tend to be controlled closely by the higher level of government and interact minimally with the municipalities. Still, their impact on local issues has at times surpassed the importance of local governments themselves.

3 THE RANGE OF MUNICIPALITIES' RESPONSIBILITIES AND FUNCTIONS

The Mexican Constitution charges municipalities with a range of local public responsibilities and functions that could be considered typical and appropriate according to international literature (Bahl and Linn 1992; Shah 1994). Formally, as listed in Article 115, these include local water and sewerage systems; garbage collection and public sanitation; local streets; public lighting; police and local transit; civil protection; parks and open spaces; environment; zoning, land use, and urban planning; and civic and cultural activities.

This list may seem straightforward, but on closer examination not only is it rather vague in terms of the nature and extent of certain responsibilities ("environment," to name just one) but it glosses over the evidently intergovernmental character of several others. For example, local water systems in mostly arid Mexico are rarely autonomous; they depend on the linkages of each community to the broader national or regional network of water collection and distribution. "Public security" is interpreted to include local "preventive" policing, but these police officers must deliver suspects they capture to state officials, since municipalities do not have their own criminal courts.

The lack of precision in law about the ways that responsibilities should in practice be distributed among different levels of government may not be unusual in federal systems, but in Mexico this has resulted in some problems. On the one hand, as mentioned previously, it has facilitated the usurping of municipal spheres by state government. Some dramatic examples include state control of local police forces in the metropolitan area made up of the municipalities Port of Veracruz and Boca del Rio in the State of Veracruz; and state control of local mass transit in the immense municipality of Nezahuacóyotl, State of Mexico. In strictly constitutional terms, these practices are illegal, and many other examples elsewhere could be cited.

So why do these practices persist? Often, states justify their action on the grounds that most municipalities do not have sufficient administrative capacity to take charge of the responsibilities and obligations granted by the Constitution (Cabrero 1996). This is in part because of persisting and dramatic imbalances in the size of local government relative to other levels. For example, in 2002 the combined expenditures by all municipalities amounted to little more that 25 percent of spending by states and about 10 percent of national government expenditures (table 1).

Table 1
Expenditures by Level of Government, 2002 (millions of pesos)

	Total amount	Share
Federal expenditure	1,459,951	68%
State expenditure (including DF)	562,738	26%
Municipal expenditure (does not include *delegaciones* of the DF)	122,343	6%
TOTAL PUBLIC EXPENDITURE	2,145,032	100%

Source: Derived by author from INEGI 2005; INEGI, SIMBAD 2005

On the other hand, only in a few of the large cities can this broader expenditure imbalance be construed as a reason for state intervention. In fact, as discussed in more detail later, urban municipalities tend to be more dynamic in terms of administration and governance than most rural ones. State control of local service provision instead appears to be either a financial manoeuvre or an attempt to maintain control over some critical aspect of politics in the region.

In addition to the tasks delineated in Article 115 as exclusive jurisdiction of municipalities, other sections of the Constitution envision shared responsibility for certain government functions, including basic education and public security.

However, if state governments are prone to ignore or usurp the areas in which municipalities have exclusive jurisdiction, they are, not surprisingly, even more likely to do so where responsibilities are nominally shared among levels of government. In other words, truly shared responsibility is more common on paper than in practice.

On the other hand, and perhaps more commonly, some basic public functions routinely go unmet by any level of government. Shared responsibility can often mean that residents have difficulty in deciphering just whom they should hold responsible for failures in government performance. Again, in part because of budget constraints, this kind of administrative limitation is more common in rural than urban areas. Thus, although the Constitution does not distinguish between different types of municipalities, in practice those in rural areas tend to handle fewer and less complex tasks. Still, they often are involved in aspects of rural life (such as agriculture and natural resource management) that urban local governments do not handle.

Indeed, as alluded to previously, urban and rural municipalities are substantially different in their practice of government, in spite of their equivalent constitutional status. And while 67 percent of the total national population was concentrated in 364 cities[3] in 2000 (the latest census), the vast majority of Mexican municipalities are rural rather than urban in character. So it is a relatively small group of local governments that plays a large role for an important part of the total population, as well as in total local expenditures.

Some indication of the limited overall impact of municipal activities in Mexico is evident in a comparison of per capita local expenditure among different kinds of municipalities. In 1997 the expenditure of municipalities with populations of more than 50,000 residents amounted to about US$51 per capita, while smaller municipalities spent only US$30 (Rowland 2001). The national average for all municipalities was US$44 per capita. Direct comparison of amounts spent by federal and state governments in each municipality on a per capita basis is nearly impossible, since these budgets are not broken down by region. However, simply as a general reference, total federal spending in 2002 surpassed US$1,000 per capita, while average state spending neared US$500 per capita.[4]

Within the group of urban municipalities, two different types of situation should be distinguished: those in which the urban area is fully encompassed by a single local government, and those in which more than one jurisdiction is involved. In the first group, the importance of the municipality in any urban agenda is fundamental, since it is the only organ of government with jurisdiction in most relevant issues. In certain cases, especially where the city is the seat of state government powers, the state may play some role in local government, but in general the municipality has sole responsibility for defining and promoting the urban agenda. For this, it depends on internal resources, local interest groups, and the occasional support or intervention of higher authorities. A recent example of this kind of support is the Hábitat program, directed by the national Social Development Ministry (SEDESOL), which aims to promote attention to urban issues and programs aimed at resolving them.

The definition and promotion of an urban agenda for the second type of cities – those that overlap municipal (and state) jurisdictions – is much more complex and problematic. Legally, the function of urban planning in such cases is assigned to the state and federal governments, but they rarely are active or successful in carrying out this role. In part, the problem is that the political benefits of doing so are not clear: few states appear willing to take over officially and manage such thankless and expensive tasks as urban waste disposal, water provision, or public security, even where economies of scale and greater efficacy clearly would be achieved. The increasingly plural political affiliation of Mexican municipalities has complicated this situation further, since many municipal presidents and governors see little reason to cooperate with politicians of other parties, even when improved urban governance is at stake.

These problems are especially dramatic in the Mexico City Metropolitan Area, where nearly twenty million residents, spread over two states, forty-one municipalities, and the Federal District (itself composed of sixteen precincts or *delegaciones*, the local unit of government in the DF) live in close physical proximity but under dramatically different governing structures. In forty other cities around the country, coordination among multiple municipal jurisdictions is also problematic.

4 THE FISCAL POSITION OF MUNICIPALITIES

An analysis of the fiscal position of Mexican municipalities must start with two general observations. First, the total amount of public revenue of all three levels of government amounted to slightly over 15 percent of GDP in 2000 (Rowland 2005). This is considered a low level of collection by international standards and may indicate other problematic aspects in the system. Second, the central government receives by far the largest share of this public revenue – even after taking intergovernmental grants into consideration – which is also notable in international terms.

Indeed, vertical imbalance has been a feature of Mexican public finance since at least the 1930s, when growth in the share of central government revenue began to surpass that of state and local governments. However, the problem was little noticed during much of the twentieth century, because local governments were in fact expected to fulfill few tasks (Fagen and Tuohy 1972; Graham 1968). Meanwhile, state governments typically received massive ad hoc subsidies from the central government, provided that their leaders cooperated with their federal counterparts.

The trend towards the increasing vertical concentration of public revenue began to reverse itself in the 1980s (Díaz Cayeros 1995), but the general pattern persists to this day, in spite of the vastly expanded role of municipalities in public service provision since then. In 2000, federal government collections amounted to 75 percent of total public revenue, states contributed 18 percent and municipalities 7 percent (IMF 2002).[5]

These national-level figures mask wide variation among particular jurisdictions. Still, part of the reason for the municipalities' small overall share in revenue raising is related to the assignment of revenue bases. According to Article 115 of the Constitution, municipalities are entitled to exclusive access to the following revenue sources: property taxes, fees and charges for local services, and certain fines. Not surprisingly, the most important of these revenue sources in urban areas are the taxes on property ownership and sales (table 2). However, municipalities do not have independent taxing authority, so neither do they set their own tax rates (a state function) nor can they invent new taxes to cover expenditures. In fact, most municipalities depend much more on federal conditional grants and revenue sharing than on local tax revenues. These transfers have amounted to two-thirds of combined local budgets in recent years, as will shortly be discussed in more detail.

Table 2
Revenue Sources for Mexican Municipalities, 2002

	Percent[1]
Federal revenue sharing	34.4
Federal conditional grants	33.7
Local taxes	10.0
Fees for local services	5.2
Loans and credits	4.4
Fines	3.8
Cash on hand	3.7
Other	4.9
TOTAL	100.0

[1]Figures rounded to one decimal point
Source: Derived by author from INEGI, SIMBAD 2005

In spite of this general pattern, the total amount of revenue collected by local governments has expanded dramatically in recent years, both in terms of amounts collected (a result of the arduous process of updating property values) and the number of potential tax bases actually tapped (figure 1). However, gains tend to be concentrated in urban areas; rural municipalities have very low local tax bases because of the high prevalence of poverty and low economic dynamism in these jurisdictions (Rowland 2001).

Local sources of revenue are particularly important to municipal policymaking because of the lack of predictability in the yearly amounts of intergovernmental transfers and the lack of fiscal flexibility at this level. Property tax revenues, in particular, have tended to be more stable over time and, from the local standpoint, have the advantage of having no strings attached in terms of how they may be spent.

Figure 1
Evolution of Major Sources of Municipal Revenue, 1989–2002

Millions of constant pesos

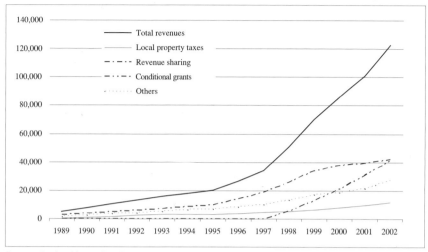

Source: Derived by author from INEGI, SIMBAD 2005

Municipal governments in Mexico must balance their budgets on an annual basis. Loans can be contracted only from domestic sources, including the national development bank (Banco nacional de obras y servicios públicos, BANOBRAS), commercial banks, private organizations, and decentralized bodies of federal public administration, such as the Federal Electricity Company (Compañía federal de electricidad, CFE) or the National Water Commission (Comisión nacional de agua, CNA). Any loan to municipal government must be approved by the state legislature.

The principal way to address issues of vertical imbalance is through intergovernmental transfers. These are classified in Mexico as either federal conditional grants (*transferencias*, also known as Ramo 33) or federal revenue sharing (*participaciones*). The total amount dedicated to both types has grown rapidly in recent years. In 2000, 25 percent of total federal revenue was transferred to states and 3 percent to local governments (derived by author from IMF 2002).

Since 1994, the amount of federal conditional grants (*transferencias*) has increased especially dramatically, reaching 14 percent of total federal expenditure in 2000 (SHCP 2000). This reflects, in part, the fact that as decentralization efforts intensified during the 1990s, both municipal and state governments began to assume new responsibilities. Federal government responded in some measure to their claims to need more money with new programs to support specific types of activity (PND 1995).

The revenue-sharing (*participaciones*) program is designed, in part, to address horizontal fiscal imbalances, which as mentioned earlier are especially glaring between urban and rural municipalities. In 2000, federal revenue sharing to the municipalities nearly equalled the amount spent on conditional grants (SHCP 2000). However, unlike federal grants, revenue-sharing monies are distributed to municipalities via the states, according to their own criteria. The states are obligated to distribute 20 percent of the total revenue-sharing funds they receive among municipalities within their jurisdictions, but their internal rules do not always reflect concern for issues of horizontal imbalance among local governments. Instead, political criteria often appear to dominate these decisions.

In fact, Mexico has been remarkably ineffective – or uninterested – in addressing equalization among municipalities. Rowland (2001) argues that state and especially federal governments prefer to spend directly in rural areas rather than allowing municipal governments in these areas to exercise larger budgets. Again, the reason is that this direct spending by higher levels presumably offers the possibility of converting public monies into electoral advantage.

5 HOW MUNICIPALITIES ORGANIZE AMONG THEMSELVES TO DEAL WITH THE FEDERAL LEVEL

The federal structure of Mexico, along with its evolving political traditions, militate against direct, one-on-one relationships between central and municipal governments. Even under the one-party system, the state government or its party machine was normally consulted when the federal government planned any substantial activity in a municipality. Today, states jealously attempt to maintain their role as intermediaries in the federal-municipal relationship. It is not clear, at any rate, that the federal level has the administrative capacity to develop relationships of any depth or importance with many of the 2,400-odd municipalities. For example, the federal conditional grant program mentioned above is often criticized both as an illegitimate intrusion into state affairs and for its perceived ineffectiveness in ensuring that municipalities use these ostensibly conditional grants in the way they are intended to be used.

Nor is there any official body to represent the interests of municipal officials at the national or state levels. The official organs, such as INAFED (Instituto nacional para el federalismo y el desarrollo municipal) and its state counterparts, are oriented towards information-gathering and training programs rather than representing local interests. However, in recent years, at least three major non-governmental organizations have arisen in response to the needs and interests of local public officials. In spite of the fact that each of these groups – AALMAC (Asociación de autoridades locales de México), AMMAC (Asociación de municipios de México), and FENAMM (Federación nacional de municipios de México – is loosely affiliated with an important national political party, they do appear to have served the purpose of uniting local officials to promote common agendas for negotiation with other levels of government. Recently, these groups have agreed to pool their resources under the rubric of the National Conference of Mexican Municipalities (Conferencia nacional de municipios de México).

Still, while these non-governmental organizations have become important in terms of the definition of the agenda for improvements in municipal government (as shown by their work in the constitutional reforms to Article 115 in 1999), they are far from exerting a notable influence on other issues of government. A clear example of this is that although representatives of these groups were allowed to attend the first national convention of public finance in 2004 (Primera convención nacional hacendaria), their ability to influence decision making in that event was virtually non-existent. Not only are federal and state officials generally dubious of the potential of these organizations – and of their members – to contribute to the affairs of national and state government, but the extent to which municipal officials can agree on lobbying agendas is limited by the great differences among the interests of different types of municipality. The very profile of local government authorities in terms of administrative experience and educational background can also mean that political issues take a back seat to capacity-building efforts.

6 THE SCOPE OF MUNICIPAL-FEDERAL INTERACTION

Given the role of the states as intermediaries between municipal and federal governments, as discussed in previous sections, the scope of the direct relationship between the latter two is relatively circumscribed. In general, federal programs and financial support – even those with an explicit focus on municipalities – tend to be channelled via the states. Depending on the political importance and practices of each state, this level exerts different degrees of influence over the shape of programs within its jurisdiction. The major exception, as noted earlier, is the federal grant program known as Ramo 33, which has been controversial precisely because it aims to avoid state intervention.

The federal government does attempt – at least nominally – to include municipalities in some of its most important programs, including three that are defined in the constitution: the National System of Democratic Planning (SNPD), the National System of Public Security (SNSP), and, as of 2004, the National System of Social Development (SNDS). However, it is unclear whether municipalities play more than a symbolic role in any of these systems, which tend to be dominated by federal and state agendas. In addition, education, health, communications, and transport, as well as other line ministries, have some direct dealings with local governments, but these generally take place within a framework (*convenio*) negotiated with and approved by each state government on an annual basis.

Unfortunately, it is almost impossible to devise quantitative measures of the amount that local governments spend on programs or policies linked to federal initiatives. Not only is there enormous variation both among municipalities and from year to year but, in addition, the methods of reporting such data are inadequate for this kind of calculation. For example, the federal Social Development Ministry (SEDESOL) carries out some actions directly related to urban areas, including the growing Hábitat program. But the states maintain wide discretion and bargaining power in the precise definition of these programs, and the results of their negotiations are rarely made available to the public.

Exceptions to this general pattern of limited direct federal-municipal interaction include international border zones, areas of domestic armed conflict, and regions in which federal property is particularly important in fiscal terms, such as the sites of petroleum extraction and processing, electricity generation, and federally developed tourist resorts. In these areas, the actions of the federal government are generally carried out in a flexible and ad hoc manner by particular line agencies (the Secretary of Defence or of Tourism) or semi-autonomous units (PEMEX, the state-owned oil company, or CFE, the Federal Electricity Commission).

7 THE NATURE OF THE MUNICIPAL-FEDERAL INTERACTION

As explained in the previous section, the extent of independence of Mexican municipal governments from the federal level depends in part on the issue at hand. It also depends on other variables, such as population and political and economic importance. For example, if the central government intends to undertake extensive new activities in large and prosperous municipalities like León or Tijuana, which are important both in terms of their role in the national economy and the number of voters who live in these jurisdictions, it must engage in a certain amount of negotiation with local authorities. In smaller and poorer jurisdictions, both federal and state governments have more leeway to ignore or try to manipulate local affairs.

Still, the formal constitutional definition of areas of exclusive municipal responsibility, combined with trends towards greater adherence to the law and growing dynamism in local government, mean that at the local level there is an increasing number of issues that the federal government tends to leave to its local counterparts. It is still possible, and even common, for federal government infrastructure or social welfare programs – which may have a substantial direct and indirect local impact – to be undertaken with little or no consultation with local authorities. Indeed, municipal, state, and federal governments at times appear to pursue parallel but unrelated agendas, with none adhering to plans or taking a more comprehensive view of a region or locality. Paradoxically, this does not imply much competition among levels of government: rarely is more than one actor involved in providing the same type of service, nor are voters normally given a choice among distinct service "packages."

It should be noted, however, that the very existence of local policy agendas is relatively new in the Mexican context. Until at least the late 1980s, local elections tended to revolve around national issues, including both the management of the national economy and the desirability (or not) of unseating the PRI (Rowland 1997). This is no longer the case. While municipal authorities still routinely complain of the imposition of federal and state programs and priorities, the need to win competitive local elections (since the 1980s, in most municipalities) has increasingly ensured a greater margin of independence in policy decisions. Thus, although local governments are far from equal in their interaction with the central government, they do enjoy wider spheres of autonomous action than they did at the beginning of the 1980s.

8 MEDIATION OF MUNICIPAL-FEDERAL RELATIONS BY STATE GOVERNMENTS

State governments have long been important intermediaries in municipal-federal relations in Mexico. This is both a cause and a consequence of the traditional constitutional definition of local governments as mere "territorial divisions for the political and administrative organization" of the states. Indeed, it was only as the result of the constitutional reforms of 1999 that municipalities achieved the status of full-fledged governments, with rights that include bringing constitutional controversies against the states and the federation. In spite of this legal change, as explained previously, states continue to see themselves as legitimate actors in essentially all aspects of local affairs, often to the point of intruding on clearly defined municipal responsibilities and prerogatives.

The establishment of intermediate authorities between municipalities and states is explicitly prohibited in the national constitution. However, in recent years, a number of states have established their own ministries of municipal affairs, ostensibly to support local governments, especially in the area of capacity building. The true motivation of these actions varies from state to state. It appears that in some cases these efforts have been provoked precisely by the states' reasonable and legitimate interest in fostering improved local government. However, in other cases, partisan and even financial interests appear to be at play, and some municipalities complain that these agencies are used inappropriately by state governments either to promote particular candidates for political office or to wrest control over certain tax bases from the local level.

All the states have a full range of administrative line departments, but with varying degrees of interest and capacity to involve themselves in local affairs. Of particular importance throughout the country are the state ministries of social development, education, and health. The specialization of these executive agencies in issues that are easily and often incorporated into clientelistic relationships means that, typically, they are closely aligned with the governor's own political agenda. Depending, then, on the interaction of the governor with his or her national-level counterparts, the state line departments may take a more or less active role in mobilizing popular support for federal and state actions. This involves different degrees and types of intervention in different municipalities.

In other words, as the potential alternatives for party affiliation have widened at all levels of government in recent years, municipalities are increasingly likely to get caught up in partisan intergovernmental wrangling. Whether or not this implies more supportive or more conflictual relationships between states and municipalities depends on the interaction of specific and constantly changing regional variables. It should be stressed, however, that in general terms, state (and federal) line agencies are motivated as much by partisan political strategies as by any internal norms of professionalism or organizational goals.

9 MUNICIPAL FORAYS INTO INTERNATIONAL RELATIONS

There is a relatively narrow legal scope for formal international relations on the part of municipalities in Mexico. The federal government is the only level authorized by the Constitution to undertake dealings with foreign entities; and in contrast to many other developing countries, even international aid agencies are prohibited from working directly with local governments without the approval of the national level. This also means that local and state governments are prohibited from contracting loans with international agencies; this type of assistance must be channelled through the national development bank (BANOBRAS).

Nevertheless, hundreds of municipalities participate in international organizations dedicated to more modest (and less controversial) goals. Many have established "sister city" relationships in other parts of the world, both to promote trade and to promote the exchange of information about local governance. In addition, organizations such as ICMA (International City Management Association) have established offices in Mexico and are promoting international linkages for local government, as well as a domestic political agenda aimed at improving municipal government. Along the northern border, and in spite of constitutional provisions to the contrary, dozens of municipalities have long-established relationships with their neighbours on the U.S. side, ranging from cooperation among police forces to cultural exchanges.

Several factors suggest that international contacts and concerns will continue to play an increasing role for Mexican residents and their local governments. First, the nationwide shift from a closed economy to a relatively open one since the mid-1980s has radically altered the comparative economic advantage of certain regions of the country (Rowland and Gordon 1996). While entrance into the OECD and NAFTA during this period merely formalized broader pre-existing trends towards the internationalization of Mexico's economy, the changes allowed some northern and urban municipalities to become more closely integrated into the U.S. economy. The impact on municipal-federal relations for those localities that have benefited directly from economic liberalization is essentially the establishment of new and different incentives for local government behaviour. For example, greater percentages of municipal spending may be directed to investment in physical infrastructure (pavement, water supplies, etc.) to support export activities. This, in turn, means that relatively less expenditure is available to pursue the goals or preferences – often merely electoral – of the national government; in addition, those municipalities that enjoy newfound economic importance tend to be less dependent on their relationships with the federal government for their own fiscal health.

Still, it should be recalled that the majority of municipalities, especially in the central and southern regions of the country, have reaped little if any direct benefit from economic liberalization. However, these regions tend to be responsible for much of the migration to the United States in recent years, and this factor may exert a different kind of impact on local government behaviour. Approximately 21 million people born in Mexico or with family in Mexico live and work in the United States (CONAPO 2001), permanently or temporarily. Many of these migrants appear to adopt new expectations for their municipalities of origin. This is reflected in the large number of "hometown" associations in the United States (and elsewhere) that have organized themselves to finance and otherwise support community development programs at the local level back in Mexico.

Finally, international organizations such as the World Bank and the IMF have pressed the Mexican government in recent years to allow direct dealing with states and, in some cases, with municipalities. These efforts are a way to open up options for financing new projects; they also, implicitly, seek to avoid the partisan political manipulation of projects by national authorities.

As in other parts of the world, it is increasingly difficult for the federal government to intervene in the changes in local governments brought about by globalization and in the incentive system surrounding them. Nor is it clear to what extent the current federal administration is interested in doing so. Indeed, a highly publicized program of the national Social Development Ministry, known as Three for One for Migrants (*3 por 1 para Migrantes*), attempts to leverage the millions of dollars in remittances, sent by Mexicans working outside the country, with funds matched by local, state, and federal governments. Thus, barring a radical retrenchment at the national level, the internationalization of municipal government in Mexico is likely to continue to expand, regardless of constitutional strictures.

10 THE POLITICAL DIMENSION OF THE MUNICIPAL-FEDERAL RELATIONSHIP

As has been alluded to throughout this text, the current situation of local governments in Mexico is inseparable from the three decades of rapid political change that has been occurring throughout the country. Greater municipal autonomy and dynamism is both a cause and a consequence of "cleaner" and more intense electoral competition at all levels. At the same time, greater attention to legal norms in government proceedings has allowed some municipalities to establish a more balanced relationship with other levels. This process may represent a virtuous cycle, in the sense that it appears increasingly unlikely that even a return to more authoritarian government at the national level would suffice for recentralization in the short run. New political and economic interests in defending local prerogatives have been created, and these would resist efforts to remove the new powers and privileges from the municipal sphere.

Nevertheless, uncertainty over short-run national electoral and political outcomes persists. The paucity of tangible gains as a result of the political and economic changes in recent years – at least in certain regions of the country and for certain sectors of the population – has spawned support for national- and state-level candidates who call for a return to earlier nondemocratic practices of government. The success of such candidates might imply a return to previous patterns of intergovernmental relations, as well as greater government intervention in the economy.

Part of the threat of these candidates is their power within what is still highly centralized, albeit plural, political-party system. The privileged place of political parties in Mexico includes their monopoly on elected offices at all three levels of government: nonaffiliated candidates are not permitted. At the same time, the internal organization of parties remains highly centralized and hierarchical, so "success" for many local politicians continues to be defined as their recruitment for national posts in their party or in the government in Mexico City. New civil service laws at the federal level may begin to change this practice of partisan-controlled bureaucracy, but it is too soon to be sure.

National laws regarding the formation of new parties are so restrictive that their creation is virtually impossible, particularly at the regional level. Local (and all other) aspiring candidates must join existing political parties, if they are not already members. Inevitably, these hopefuls must adjust their own political positions in large or small ways in order to triumph in internal struggles for the right to compete as candidates for their parties. Certainly, since electoral competition began to be tolerated at the municipal level during the 1980s, the number of "citizen-politicians" in local government has increased. They tend to be successful local business people or professionals, who agree to serve as local public officials (elected or appointed) for one term but who have no intention of making a career in politics. Still, for ambitious career politicians and many public servants, adjustment to the priorities of the national party remains unavoidable.

Another way in which issues at the national level affect local government is in debates over the assignment of tasks among levels of government. It may be significant that calls for increased central government control are being heard regarding some topics of particular concern to public officials and voters, especially crime control and environmental protection. The pendulum swing of the 1980s and 1990s towards increased decentralization may have peaked.

Finally, the persistence of extreme poverty and isolation in hundreds of municipalities throughout the country appears to facilitate continued clientelist practices by politicians and public officials at all levels of government. Economic desperation for families,[6] combined with difficulties in oversight both by public entities (such as electoral institutes) and by the media, undermine the gains that elsewhere in the country have been achieved from improved electoral competition and respect for the rule of law. The poorest and most isolated regions of the country tend to be those where democratic practices and electoral competition are least established. Certain aspects of globalization, particularly the constant and massive migration of residents from rural areas to other states and other countries, may help overcome some of these persistent problems, but the personal cost and risk for individuals and families who opt to migrate remain high.

The growing internationalization of Mexican society may be more readily felt in urban municipalities, where migration is accompanied by the increasing presence of international firms and products, as well as by television and Internet access. The long-term impact of these changes is, of course, unknown, but they at least offer new sources of information to residents and may encourage them to demand more responsive and effective government. If this is the case, such demands may be most evident at the local level, where many of the services that affect residents most are provided. One illustration of the tendency to demand more from government is evident in the proliferation in recent years of non-governmental and non-partisan organizations, a novelty in this country after many decades of PRI cooptation or repression of independent social movements.

Other profound shifts in economic and demographic patterns may support social changes that favour the trend towards greater municipal autonomy and dynamism. As mentioned previously, the liberalization of the Mexican economy since the mid-1980s has resulted in a massive reallocation of comparative advantage in the northern regions of the country. Both domestic and international firms have increasingly settled outside the traditional consumer market of Mexico City to take advantage of new export opportunities to the United States. Residents have followed in search of employment opportunities, transforming what were until recently small cities into large metropolitan areas, as occurred with Tijuana and Ciudad Juárez. This has resulted in a shift of traditional migrant streams all over the country. The north has replaced the central valley of Mexico City as the primary destination both for rural-urban and urban-urban migrants. Thus, the twin patterns of diversification and privatization of the economy, on the one hand, and urbanization and the distancing of the population from the political centre, on the other, make old-style clientelism more difficult to sustain. Again, the growing need to compete for votes changes the bases of municipal-federal interactions.

11 RECENT TRENDS

The changing relationship between municipal and federal governments in Mexico is inextricably tied to broader changes in the basic political and economic practices in the country. This results in a highly complex and uneven panorama across local governments, one that is constantly and rapidly transforming itself and is subject to permanent or temporary reverses. To the extent that broad trends are discernable, they can be summarized as follows:

- Greater pluralism and respect for divergent electoral outcomes over the past two decades means increasing intergovernmental conflict, much of which is played out in public. Local officials are no longer always willing to subsume their activities to the preferences of state and national authorities. Increasingly, local politicians try to defend their autonomy with recourse to legal norms, when these exist.

- Change in the country's basic economic model has served to undermine municipal dependence on higher levels of government in many regions. New market opportunities, cutbacks in state-owned enterprises, and reductions in federal subsidies for diverse activities have served to reorient the incentives for local government action, as well as those for citizens and firms.
- States, reacting to the same changes in context as local governments, are also reasserting their role in intergovernmental relations. In some cases, this may lead to support for improved local government; but in others, state governments appear to try to replicate the previous centralized, authoritarian system within their jurisdictions.
- The possibilities of fruitful interaction with federal and state governments are increasingly divergent for large (urban) and small municipalities. Urban municipalities have been much more successful in raising local revenues, which makes them less dependent on higher-level largesse. The rise of non-governmental municipal associations may help alleviate some of the problems for small localities, to the extent that these associations are not also dominated by the interests of their large counterparts.
- Remaining spheres of federal prerogatives in municipalities (such as *ejido* landholdings and tourist enterprises, as explained below) are the subject of increasing tension and demands by local governments for clearer rules.
- Frustration with some especially difficult social problems – such as crime and environmental protection – has led to calls for the recentralization of government as a general panacea. The fact that recentralization is commonly proposed, in lieu of reflection on how to improve the framework of intergovernmental actions, suggests that gains in municipal autonomy in recent decades remain fragile.

12 POLICY CASE STUDIES

12.1 FEDERAL PROPERTY AND ITS USE IN MEXICO

As a result of the Constitution of 1917, which attempted to establish a strong role for the central government in the redistribution of wealth, as part of the "gains of the Revolution" that preceded it, a relatively large proportion of Mexican national territory is still controlled by federal authorities. The extent and nature of this control varies from direct ownership for "strategic activities" (such as military bases, seaports and airports, and some small offshore islands) to sites expropriated from local communities for the extraction and processing of petroleum or the generation of electricity, to rural lands administered (and technically owned) under the systems of *ejidos* and *tierras comunales*. These two forms of federal property are the result of the land redistribution efforts of the 1930s and 1940s, which aimed to (re)establish communal landholding as a way of fighting rural poverty and making good on the promises of the Revolution.

The potential intergovernmental tensions derived from this pattern of federal government property within municipal jurisdictions were suppressed during most of the twentieth century, because of the hierarchical (top-down) nature of the political system. Specific problems or crises were resolved by the federal government, often via intervention by the corresponding state, on an ad hoc basis. However, as municipalities have gained a measure of power and autonomy since the 1980s, a variety of intergovernmental conflicts related to federal property have begun to emerge. This increase in conflicts is also partly a result of rapid population increases in cities and towns of all sizes, which has put pressure on members of surrounding *ejido* and *comunal* lands to sell (legally or not) their holdings for much more highly priced urban uses.

The precise nature of the interaction between the federal and municipal governments regarding federal property depends on two basic factors. First is the degree of activity and capacity of the local government to request (or demand) changes in the status quo. The second factor is the type of use of the federal property in question. Some examples can help illustrate these basic patterns, given the lack of hard data on specific cases.

Military bases in municipalities that have not improved their capacity for property tax collection (as is the case for most rural municipalities) are typically not viewed as net losses by local governments, whereas their urban counterparts often bemoan the forgone property taxes on these and other types of federal property. Other potential conflicts related to military land use, including water provision and the activities of off-duty soldiers, are typically negotiated on a case-by-case basis. They occasionally erupt into public protests, especially in zones such as Chiapas and Guerrero, where civil conflict is endemic or drug trafficking is entrenched, but these are exceptions at the national level.

Airports and some federal highways and bridges have been sources of conflict, especially in urban areas where enterprising local politicians have attempted to apply property taxes or to recover some fraction of the fees charged to users. This issue has become especially controversial in cases where federal authorities have included concessions to private firms in the construction or operation of these installations. For many local authorities, it is not clear why these concessionaires should enjoy the same tax-exemption privileges as the federal government or, in some cases, why the federal government is involved at all in the management of these facilities. In recent years, federal authorities have occasionally begun to grant affected municipalities a proportion of the user fees for these services.

Petroleum extraction and processing, as well as electricity generation, have long provoked conflict with local settlements, even in rural and poorly administered municipalities. One recurring complaint concerns the substantial negative consequences of these activities on the local environment, but there is also considerable discontent that the "riches" produced in these regions appear to offer little benefit to local residents. Again, the traditional method of quelling these disagreements was to cede certain benefits, for example, by constructing schools or health clinics in nearby communities. It is commonly alleged that large quantities of cash often changed hands between the federal petroleum and electricity enterprises and the local or state politicians involved in mediating these conflicts.

Partly to help control this problem, some of these exchanges were gradually formalized into special programs for intergovernmental transfers targeted to municipal governments in affected regions. One case in point is the "additional fee on petroleum extraction" (*Derecho adicional sobre extracción de petróleo*), which ostensibly compensates municipal governments for the activities of PEMEX (the government-owned petroleum monopoly) within their jurisdictions. However, in spite of a general increase in transparency in public finances, it is difficult to gather firm data on the actual amounts of these transfers. While formal rules specify that payments should reflect the current price of petroleum as well as the precise quantities extracted in each locale, compliance with this rule is almost impossible to monitor, and many municipalities and states complain of arbitrariness and manipulation of these funds by the federal finance ministry (SHCP) for electoral purposes.

These examples pale in comparison to municipalities' problems related to the use of *ejido* and *comunal* lands. Estimates suggest that just over 50 percent of national territory is governed under this system and that at least 20 percent of the nearly 31,000 *ejidos* and *tierras comunales* have been illegally subdivided and sold. Since 1992, legal mechanisms have existed to transform this type of property into private holdings, but members of these communities appear unwilling to confront this complex process and prefer to sell illegally, since buyers are willing and such sales are rarely prosecuted by federal authorities (Caire 2001).

The issue is much more than a legal technicality, however, in terms of urban management by municipalities. Until former *ejido* lands are "regularized" by federal and state authorities, local governments cannot charge property tax on housing and other urban land uses, and they are typically resistant to extending urban services to these areas since it is not clear that they are legally empowered to so. Nevertheless, they face pressure from new residents to cover the considerable costs of expanding urban infrastructure such as water and sewage facilities and public lighting.

In earlier decades, the problem of service provision to new informal settlements on federal property was effectively resolved by exceptional federal, state, or municipal spending, usually timed to coincide with elections. Essentially, residents would be promised "regularization" of their land titles or the extension of urban services in exchange for voting in favour of particular candidates or parties. While such practices persist in many parts of the country, increasing transparency and autonomy of local governments have brought to light some of the worst abuses and highlighted the difficulty for municipalities of adopting alternatives. The common complaint from the local level is that the federal ministry charged with "regularization" of *ejido* lands, the Ministry of Agrarian Reform, is needlessly slow in acting on local requests for action.

Thus, there continues to be a substantial range in the character of interactions between municipal and federal governments in Mexico regarding federal property. That such issues are becoming more common and more openly discussed in this country represents a notable advance towards the possibility of improved local government. However, as this discussion has suggested, there is still room for much improvement in clarifying the rules and procedures that guide these processes, as well as in reaching consensus among different levels of government over the best way to confront these tensions.

12.2 IMAGE BUILDING VIA TOURISM IN MEXICO

Tourism, particularly international resort-oriented tourism, was identified by the Mexican national government as a promising source of foreign exchange in the 1970s (Jiménez 1998). Not surprisingly for this era, the strategy selected to promote this line of economic growth was the creation of a new federal agency, FONATUR, which was charged with identifying promising sites and investing massive quantities[7] of public monies in the construction of roads, water supplies, and other infrastructure. The emblematic Cancún is the first and best known of these sites and can be credited with shifting the attention of international tourists from the 1950s and 1960s jet-set destinations of Acapulco and Puerta Vallarta to other regions of the country, including Ixtapa, Los Cabos, and Huatulco.

In large part because of FONATUR, tourism has come to represent the third-largest source of foreign revenue for the country, trailing in importance only petroleum and remittances by Mexicans living abroad. The efforts of FONATUR to promote Mexico in general, and certain beach resorts in particular, in the United States and Canada have centred on a combination of the natural attractions of these places and a sort of homogenized version of Mexican culture and cuisine. This point is especially obvious in Cancún, whose true regional traditions derive from the dominant Mayan cultures and centuries of interaction with non-indigenous *hacienda* owners. In the original resort developments of Cancún, these local patterns are typically glossed over in a frenzy of mariachis and tequila, neither of which form any part of traditional Yucatecan culture. Rather, this is the image of "Mexico" which central government functionaries chose to sell to international tourists during the 1970s and 1980s.

Over the years, problems have developed in the FONATUR strategy, partly because central government revenues were dramatically reduced as a result of macroeconomic crises and general cutbacks in government expenditure. At the same time, local residents, and at times local governments, began to reassert their cultural identities. One of the early signs of trouble appeared in the 1980s in Huatulco, in the State of Oaxaca, when local peasants resisted the attempts of FONATUR to expropriate their communal landholdings and to construct tourist facilities on sacred sites that date from prehispanic eras. A mix of negotiation and brute force by state and federal authorities eventually allowed the resort project to proceed, but resentment and tension lingered among the local population and helped to fuel small-scale guerrilla movements in the region.

This type of problem was new for FONATUR at the time, since its biggest successes, Cancún and Ixtapa, were constructed on essentially unoccupied territory (the ancient town of Zihuatanejo is about ten kilometres from Ixtapa and has only gradually and partially become incorporated into the tourist zone). However, both the process of construction and the potential for employment later on, in what are regions of exceptional poverty, made these projects the site of spectacular rates of immigration. The population of the Municipality of Benito Juárez, for example, where Cancún is located, grew from 37,000 in 1980 to more than 177,000 in 1990 and to nearly 420,000 in 2000. The growth rate of the entire State of Quintana Roo from 1970 to 1990, at 8.9 percent per year, was more than double that of its closest follower (CONAPO 1994; INEGI, SIMBAD 2005). Perhaps predictably, central planners had not taken into account the massive influx of new and impoverished residents and their need for housing and urban services. The result is a stark contrast between fully equipped luxury tourist services – airports, hotels, restaurants, shopping centres, discotheques, etc. – along the beachfront and extensive slums of self-built housing for workers, which typically lack even such basic urban services as access roads and public transportation for the inhabitants' journeys to work. More damning yet to the legacy of FONATUR is the absence of adequate wastewater treatment facilities for these new cities. Ironically, the pristine beaches that are used to draw tourists are being increasingly polluted by untreated wastewater discharged directly into the sea.

Given this context, the gradual and partial decentralization of Mexican political and administrative practices, discussed throughout this paper, has given rise to some interesting effects in these areas of international tourism. In cases like Cancún and other FONATUR sites, municipal governments – and municipal politics more broadly – have been highly problematic. The contrasting demands of impoverished local voters and high-end international hotel and restaurant chains have complicated the formation of coherent local policy agendas. In addition, coincidentally or not, the states that are home to these sites are among the least innovative, dynamic, and democratic in the country in terms of their own governments. This pattern has clearly constrained the development of new types and practices of municipal government in these tourist zones.

The contrast between these struggling local governments and those in many other parts of the country points up some dramatic differences in the character of federal-municipal interaction. At one extreme are municipalities like León, Tijuana, Monterrey, and Aguascalientes, home of large modern cities which have adopted image-building strategies based on business-related activities, combined with some elements of their own local heritage and identity. Other cities, where business is less dominant and colonial urban infrastructure is plentiful, such as Guanajuato, Morelia, and Xalapa, occupy a sort of middle ground, promoting tourism through the preservation and restoration of their architectural treasures with support from international organizations (particularly UNESCO's program of World Heritage Sites), as well as some branches of the Mexican national government, especially INAH, the prestigious National Institute of Archaeology and History. A much smaller number of municipalities have embarked on similar identity-building strategies based on their proximity to prehispanic archaeological sites. Finally, a handful of municipalities – Puerto Escondido, Ensenada, Las Tuxtlas, and others with smaller-scale natural, archaeological, or historic tourist attractions – also appear to be more successful in balancing this development strategy with the needs of local residents, especially when ownership and management of tourist facilities are in local or non-corporate hands. Clearly, changing tastes in international tourism support this trend towards smaller-scale facilities and different kinds of experience.

Thus, while the period of the massive, ground-up creation of new tourist destinations by the federal government appears to be over, the profile of today's image-building efforts is more complex to characterize. In some areas, especially those previously dominated by federal tourism investment, municipal governments still struggle merely to operate. While these are not the only local governments in Mexico that face severe obstacles to their functioning, it is important to note that federal intervention in their jurisdictions has generally only exacerbated their plight. In others areas, the support of international agencies and state tourism boards have stimulated municipal efforts to define and preserve a unique cultural heritage. In still other parts of the country, municipal government has come to play the key role in defining and promoting a local image chosen by local residents and businesses. This mix is consistent with the overall growth in complexity and variation of federal municipal interactions in Mexico during the past quarter-century.

13 IS THE SYSTEM OF MULTILEVEL GOVERNANCE ADEQUATE IN RELATION TO MUNICIPAL AND URBAN POLICY?

It is difficult to assess the adequacy of an intergovernmental system that is immersed in a context of profound political, economic, and administrative change, as Mexico's has been during the past two decades. Any judgment is influenced by explicit or implicit expectations about the ultimate outcome of these broader changes – for example, democratic consolidation versus a return to authoritarianism. Put another way, the degree of institutionalization of the new types of intergovernmental practice discussed in this text is insufficient to guarantee their continued existence, even in the short run.

On the one hand, the persistence of loopholes and vagueness in the legal framework of intergovernmental affairs makes a return to highly centralized government possible, especially if authoritarian forces retake national power. Even in a less extreme scenario, municipalities could see an erosion in their current space for action, as part of the common pattern in federal systems of shifts in levels of centralization over time (Wright 1990).

On the other hand, it may be significant that the three major political parties in Mexico eventually came to embrace decentralization efforts during the 1980s and 1990s. Local politicians of each party have come to balance, in varying degrees, the parties' inherent centripetal tendencies. In general, the consensus endures among the country's political classes that greater municipal dynamism and autonomy is a key to improved public policy and government effectiveness. Still, in certain circumstances – including compelling social problems, partisan political objectives, and entrenched corruption in all levels of government – these lofty ideals tend to be abandoned, especially by national actors.

In part, the challenge for maintaining the new style of decentralized multilevel governance in Mexico lies in convincing citizens that what is portrayed publicly as greater levels and frequencies of intergovernmental conflict is not necessarily an indicator of government ineffectiveness. However, the persistent reality of government failure – at all levels – in such key issues as poverty reduction, crime control, and environmental protection, has begun to undermine the optimism and goodwill generated by the peaceful transition to multiparty electoral competition. After decades of struggle to democratize and decentralize Mexico (two goals tightly linked in rhetoric and practice), it is becoming more common to hear calls for a return to centralized rule and a "firm hand" on the part of national authorities. The open question is whether the proliferation of local experiences and local interest groups will be sufficient to resist these proposals.

In sum, the current system of multilevel governance in Mexico is inadequate, but this is a reflection of many other related problems in the rapidly evolving political and governmental system. Not all of the problems in the intergovernmental system can be addressed in the absence of continued progress on other fronts. Perhaps the most pressing challenge for municipalities at present is to take advantage of the current relatively wide space for local initiative to press for the establishment of certain ground rules that would hinder future attempts at recentralization. Such reforms should begin with efforts to sort out some of the tensions that are evident in the system (for example, between large and small municipalities), as well as to formalize those procedures and practices that would help preserve hard-won spaces for local government autonomy.

APPENDIX
Basic Data on Mexican Municipalities (number of cases in each category)

Note that the creation of new municipalities makes the following data subject to constant change. All the tables except A1 and A5 include the *delegaciones* of the Federal District in addition to the 2,442 municipalities.

Table A1
Size of Territory, 1994

Size (km²)	No.
0–99	666
100–499	992
500–999	317
1,000–4,999	358
5,000–9,999	49
10,000 +	21

Table A2
Population Ranges, 2000

Residents	No.
1–4,999	796
5,000–14,999	714
15,000–99,000	782
100,000–499,000	121
500,000–999,999	22
1 million +	7

Table A3
Occupied Residences With Dirt
Floors in Municipality, 2000

Percent	No.
90.0 or more	42
50.0–89.9	550
10.0–49.9	1,374
1.5–9.9	477
Nationwide share	15.5%

Table A4
Nonagricultural Municipal Value
Added, 1999

Million pesos	No.
Less than 10	1,260
10–99	679
100–999	335
1,000–9,999	132
10,000–19,999	23
20,000–61,000	14
Nationwide average (million pesos)	565

Table A5
Governmental Practices, 1994

Practice	No.
Popular election	2,023
"Uses and customs"	419

Table A6
Municipal Residents Who Speak an
Indigenous Language, 2000

Percent	No.
90.0 or more	224
50.0–89.9	241
10.0–49.9	347
1.0–9.9	630
0.0–0.9	1000
Nationwide share	7.1%

Sources: Derived by author from Rowland 2000b; INEGI, SIMBAD 2005

NOTES

1 The PRI is the common designation for the Institutional Revolutionary Party (Partido revolucionario institutional); for English-language introductions to the party and its impact on the Mexican political system, see Camp 1996 and Cornelius 1996.

2 The variety and intensity of municipal innovation is evident in the cases documented in the annual editions of *Premio de gobierno y gestión local* ("Prize for Local Government and Management"), www.premiomunicipal.org.mx/Premio2004

3 Defined by Mexican authorities as the home of 15,000 or more residents each. Together, this group represented nearly 65 million people in 2000.

4 Figures derived by author from the national statistical institute INEGI, www.inegi.gob.mx (accessed 9 March 2005). Federal government figures refer only to the programmable budget.

5 Data on expenditures are presented in section 3.
6 A recent estimate suggests that more than 18 million Mexicans, 17.3 percent of the national population, have incomes below that necessary to afford the "basket" of basic food items (Comité técnico 2005).
7 The precise amount and beneficiaries of these programs have not been made available to the public.

REFERENCES

Bahl, R.W., and J.F. Linn. 1992. *Urban Public Finance in Developing Countries*. New York: Oxford University Press

Cabrero Mendoza, E., ed. 1996. *Los dilemas de la modernización municipal: estudios sobre la gestión hacendaria en municipios urbanos de Mexico*. Mexico City: CIDE–Miguel Ángel Porrúa

– 1998. *Las políticas descentralizadoras en Mexico (1983–1993): logros y desencantos*. Mexico City: Miguel Ángel Porrúa

Caire, G. 2001. "La gestión urbana municipal en el proceso de incorporación de la tierra ejidal al suelo urbano ante el nuevo orden institucional." *Revista federalismo y desarrollo* 72:38–85

Camp, R.A. 1996. *Politics in Mexico*. 2nd edn. New York: Oxford University Press

Carmangani, M., ed. 1993. *Federalismos latinoamericanos: México / Brasil / Argentina*. Mexico City: Colegio de México and Fondo de cultura económica

Carpizo, J. 1978. *El presidencialismo mexicano*. Mexico City: Siglo XXI

Comité técnico. 2005. "Medición de la pobreza, 2002–2004." Comité técnico para la medición de la pobreza en México (photocopied paper dated 14 June)

CONAPO. 1994. *La población de los municipios de México, 1950–1990*. Mexico City: Consejo nacional de población

– 2001. La migración de mexicanos a los Estados Unidos. *Población de México en el nuevo siglo*. www.conapo.gob.mx/publicaciones/Lapoblacion/05.pdf (accessed 6 June 2005)

Cornelius, W.A. 1996. *Mexican Politics in Transition: The Breakdown of a One-Party-Dominant Regime*. La Jolla: Center for U.S.–Mexican Studies, University of California, San Diego

Cornelius, W.A., A.L. Craig, and J. Fox, eds. 1994. *Transforming State-Society Relations in Mexico: The National Solidarity Strategy*. La Jolla: Center for U.S.–Mexican Studies, University of California, San Diego

Díaz Cayeros, A. 1995. *Desarrollo económico e inequidad regional: hacia un nuevo pacto federal en México*. Mexico City: Fundación Friedrich Naumann, CIDAC, and Miguel Ángel Porrúa

Dresser, D. 1991. *Neopopulist Solutions to Neoliberal Problems: Mexico's National Solidarity Program*. La Jolla: Center for U.S.-Mexican Studies, University of California, San Diego

Fagen, R.R., and W.S. Tuohy. 1972. *Politics and Privilege in a Mexican City*. Stanford: Stanford University Press

Graham, L.S. 1968. *Politics in a Mexican Community*. Gainesville: University of Florida Press

Guillén López, T. 1996. *Gobiernos municipales en México: entre la modernización y la tradición política*. Mexico City: Miguel Ángel Porrúa and Colegio de la frontera norte

– 2000. *El federalismo en México: una historia en construcción*. Tijuana: Colegio de la frontera norte (photocopy)

Hansen, R.D. 1971. *The Politics of Mexican Development*. Baltimore: Johns Hopkins University Press

Hernández Chávez, A. 1993. "Federalismo y gobernabilidad en México." In *Federalismos latinoamericanos: México / Brasil / Argentina*, ed. M. Carmangani, 263-99. Mexico City: Colegio de México and Fondo de cultura económica

International Monetary Fund (IMF). 2002. *Government Finance Statistics Yearbook 2002*. Washington, DC: International Monetary Fund Publication Services

Instituto nacional de estadística, geografía, e informática (INEGI). 2005. www.inegi.gob.mx

– *Sistema municipal de base de datos* (SIMBAD). 2005. jweb.inegi.gob.mx/simbad/index.jsp?c=125

Jiménez, A. 1998. *Desarrollo turístico y sustentabilidad: el caso de México*. Mexico City: Miguel Ángel Porrúa

Marván Laborde, I. 1997. *Y después del presidencialismo? Reflexiones para la formación de un nuevo régimen*. Mexico City: Océano

Merino, M. 1998. *Gobierno local, poder nacional: la contienda por la formación del Estado mexicano*. Mexico City: Colegio de México

Plan nacional de desarrollo (PND). 1995. *Plan nacional de desarrollo, 1995–2000*. Mexico City: Presidencia de la República

Rodríguez, V. 1997. *Decentralization in México: From Reforma Municipal to Solidaridad to Nuevo Federalismo*. Boulder, Colo: Westview

Rowland, A. 1997. "Decentralization and the Challenge of Local Governance: The Case of Mexico." Doctoral dissertation, School of Policy, Planning, and Development, University of Southern California

– 2000a. "Los municipios y la coordinación intergubernamental." *Cuadernos de debate: agenda de la reforma municipal en Mexico*. Mexico City: CIDE

– 2000b. *La organización territorial de la administración y las políticas públicas*. DT-AP, no. 83. Mexico City: CIDE

– 2001. "Population as a Determinant of Local Outcomes under Decentralization: Illustrations from Small Municipalities in Bolivia and Mexico." *World Development* 29 (8): 1373–89

– 2004. *A Comparison of Decentralization and Subnational Government in Mexico and the United States*. DT-AP, no. 151. Mexico City: CIDE

– 2005. *A Comparison of Federalism and Fiscal Federalism in Mexico and the United States*. DT-AP, no. 164. Mexico City: CIDE

Rowland, A., and P. Gordon. 1996. "Mexico City: No Longer a Leviathan?" In *The Mega-City in Latin America*, ed. Alan Gilbert, 173–202. Tokyo: United Nations University Press

Rowland, A., and L.S. Graham. 2002. *An Historical Perspective on Federalism and Decentralization in Mexico, Brazil, and the United States*. DT-AP, no. 112, Mexico City: CIDE

Secretaría de hacienda y crédito público (SHCP). 2000. www.shcp.gob.mx

Sempere, J., and H. Sobarzo. 1996. *Federalismo fiscal en México*. Mexico City: Colegio de México, CEE-DT 96/IV

Shah, A. 1994. *The Reform of Intergovernmental Fiscal Relations in Developing and Emerging Market Economies*. Policy and Research Series 23. Washington, DC: World Bank

Tena Ramírez, F. 1995. *Leyes fundamentales de México, 1808–1995*. Mexico City: Editorial Porrúa

– 1997. *Derecho constitucional mexicano*. Mexico City: Editorial Porrúa

Wright, D.S. 1990. "Federalism, Intergovernmental Relations, and Intergovernmental Management: Historical Reflections and Conceptual Comparisons." *Public Administration Review* 50 (March/April): 168–78

NATIONAL, PROVINCIAL, AND LOCAL RELATIONS: AN UNCOMFORTABLE *MÉNAGE À TROIS*

Professor Nico Steytler

1 INTRODUCTION

In South Africa's recently engineered system of multilevel government, where local government plays a significant role in the governance of the country, a direct and extensive relationship between municipalities and national government has been forged. This relationship parallels, competes with, and ultimately overshadows the relationship between provinces and local government. This is nowhere more visible than in the financial transactions between local and national government. However, provincial governments, falling outside the financing loop, remain in the wings; they have retained an important monitoring and support function. While the two sets of relationships function on parallel tracks, they are often not aligned, and this results in an uncomfortable *ménage à trois*.

The direct relationship between the national government and municipalities flows from the constitutional dispensation that found its final imprint in 1996, signifying a radical departure not only from the pre-1994 apartheid state but also from the constitutional settlement of 1993.

2 CONSTITUTIONAL DIMENSION

2.1 CONSTITUTIONAL DEVELOPMENTS

Given the race-based and authoritarian nature of the apartheid state, the relationship between the centre and local government was dictated by race and central control (see Cloete 1988, ch 8). From the formation of the Union in 1910, white local authorities fell under the jurisdiction of the four provincial governments (which had limited powers of legislation). With the abolition of the provincial legislatures in 1983 and the institution of the tricameral parliamentary system, comprising whites, coloureds, and Indians, local government became the responsibility of the three race-based national departments responsible for local government. In white areas, the four provincial administrations (continuing without legislatures) remained the primary institutions managing local government. The national government directly governed the black townships that fell outside the "independent" homelands and self-governing territories. Despite the race-based "federation," the South African state was highly centralized, and the dominant relationship was between the central government and local authorities.

The advent of democratic rule in South Africa in April 1994 saw not only the formal abolition of race-based politics but also the decentralization of the state, with the formation of nine provinces of limited but protected legislative and executive competences. Provincial autonomy was one of the most contested elements of the new dispensation, and the ambivalence about provinces from the governing party, the African National Congress (ANC), still affects the national government's relationship with local government directly. The ANC favoured a strong central government, arguing that this was essential for the great transformative project of the new nonracial society. The then white minority government, joined by some of the black homeland leaders, argued for the limitation of powers at the centre and the accommodation of regional differences. The eventual compromise produced provinces with a list of functional areas, one of which was local government (Steytler 2005a, 316).

The negotiated interim Constitution of 1993 was to be replaced within two years after the first democratic election by a "final" constitution drafted by the new parliament. An innovative feature of the "final" Constitution of 1996 was the status of local government. Elevating local government to a "sphere" of government signified a real and symbolic change from its previous status as a subservient "tier" of government (Murray 2001, 77). Moreover, the Constitution removed local government from the direct tutelage of the provinces and constructed a set of direct relationships between the national government and municipalities.

2.2 THIRD SPHERE OF GOVERNMENT

The Constitution of 1996 provides that the South African state be composed of three spheres of government – national, provincial, and local – which are "distinctive, interdependent and interrelated" (s. 40(1)). The three concepts capture the basic elements of the South African system of decentralization. The distinctiveness of each sphere reflects the measure to which each sphere is the final decision maker over matters falling in its domain; autonomy is of a limited nature for both the provinces and the municipalities. "Interdependence" refers to the constitutional object of cooperative government and "interrelatedness" to the hierarchical relationship of supervision that exists between the three spheres. In terms of the Constitution, there is an explicit relationship between the national government and local government with regard to both cooperative government and the supervision of the latter. This relationship exists alongside the provincial-local relationship.

Autonomy

Local government's powers are closely tied to those of the provinces. Schedules 4 and 5 of the Constitution list the concurrent and exclusive powers of provincial government, respectively. The two schedules are divided into parts A and B, the latter parts containing municipal functional areas. However both the national and provincial governments have regulatory powers over how municipalities exercise their listed competencies (s. 155(7)). Regulation refers to setting frameworks within which local autonomy can be exercised responsibly. It has thus been argued that this does not include control that refers to the prescription of outcomes (De Visser 2005). Regulation, therefore, does not extend to the "core" of Schedules 4B or 5B matters; rather, it provides a framework within which, for example, local government can make bylaws.

There is a hierarchy of powers; the basic rule of paramountcy is that a municipal bylaw in conflict with national or provincial legislation is invalid (s. 156(3)). However, in some instances, a bylaw may trump a provincial or even a national law if the latter "compromises or impedes a municipality's ability or right to exercise its powers or perform its functions" (s. 151(4)). This may be interpreted to mean that the national and provincial governments may not use their legislative powers in an unduly intrusive or prescriptive manner (De Visser 2005, 125). As far as internal matters are concerned, the appointment and dismissal of staff fall squarely within the competence of municipalities.

In sum, it could be said that municipalities enjoy a measure of autonomy against both the national and the provincial governments. This autonomy must, however, be exercised within the framework of cooperative government and under the supervision of both "superior" spheres of government.

Cooperative Government

Like the provinces, local government is drawn into the national legislative process by being part of the second house of Parliament, the National Council of Provinces (NCOP). Along with ten-member delegations of each of the nine provinces, organized local government also is entitled to a ten-member delegation, which may participate "when necessary" but may not vote (s. 67).

Although the NCOP has limited veto powers over legislation affecting provinces and local government, it has significant supervisory powers over provincial governments when they intervene in municipalities. It may set aside a provincial executive's decision to intervene in a municipality by assuming any of its executive functions or dissolving a municipal council (s. 139).

Apart from the institutional architecture, hearing the voice of local government is also regarded as vital for the proper exercise of the national legislative function. Whenever the national (or provincial) government drafts legislation that affects the status, institutions, powers, or functions of local government, it must allow organized local government and municipalities to make representations (s. 154(2)).

Supervision

The national government plays an extensive supervisory role over local government. First, the basic institutional architecture of local government must be provided for in national legislation, including the establishment of municipalities, their demarcation, their structures and procedures, and their, financial management. Second, as noted above, the national government may play a regulatory role over how municipalities exercise their autonomy (s. 155(7)). Third, along with the provinces, the national government must support local government (s.154(1)). Fourth, while a general monitoring power is implicit, the national government must monitor local government's financial affairs. Fifth, the national government may indirectly intervene in a municipality in cases of maladministration. It may stop the transfer of funds for a limited period of time where a municipality is guilty of a persistent breach of good financial management. Although it is primarily the provinces' responsibility to intervene when a municipality fails to comply with its executive obligations or to adopt a budget or impose revenue-raising measures, the national government may step into the provinces' shoes when they fail to perform this function (s. 139(9)).

The Constitution has thus made it explicit that there is, alongside the provincial-local relationship, a clear national-local relationship. This relationship has been fleshed out in a number of laws. The practice of supervision has, however, been influenced by the constitutional recognition of different categories of municipalities.

Categories of Municipalities and Demarcation

The Constitution entrenches three categories of municipalities: A, B, and C. While category A is a self-standing, metropolitan municipality, "shared" local authority for B and C category municipalities is established for the areas falling outside the metropolitan areas. The basic units are the B category municipalities, termed local municipalities, a number of which combined to form a C category municipality, termed a "district municipality" (see Steytler 2003a).

The first round of demarcation in the democratic era saw the more than 2,000 race-based local authorities being reduced to 842 nonracial municipalities (including three metropolitan municipalities: Johannesburg, Cape Town, and Durban). The demarcation was done by nine provincial demarcation boards that made recommendations to the provincial governments.

In terms of the 1996 Constitution, the nine provincial demarcation boards were replaced by a single national Municipal Demarcation Board (MDB), on the argument that there was a need for a uniform application of policy, allowing also for the better use of the limited demarcation expertise (Cameron 2005). The MDB, whose independence was ensured, makes final binding determinations, without any direct provincial involvement. The task of the MDB was to demarcate the entire country into "wall-to-wall" municipalities. The outcome was a dramatic reduction in municipalities to 284, comprising 6 metropolitan, 46 district, and 232 local municipalities.

Although the three existing metropolitan areas remained the same, the new dispensation saw a radical change in their (and the three additional metros') governing structure. Whereas before there was a two-tier structure (a weak metropolitan council and strong substructures), the new system, much influenced by the Toronto model, created a single unified governing body. The size, land area, and provincial localities of the six metropolitan municipalities are set out in table 1.

Table 1
Metropolitan Cities: Population Size, Land Area, and Provincial Location

City	Population in millions (1996)	Territory in km²	Province
eThekwini (Durban)	2.7	2,291	KwaZulu-Natal
Johannesburg	2.6	1,664	Gauteng
Cape Town	2.5	2,498	Western Cape
Ekurhuleni	2.0	1,923	Gauteng
Tshwane (Pretoria)	1.6	2,198	Gauteng
Nelson Mandela (Port Elizabeth)	1.0	2,100	Eastern Cape

In the central province of Gauteng – the business and industrial heartland of South Africa – three contiguous metropolitan municipalities were established, containing most of the provincial population. Individually, their resources are more than those of some provinces and collectively are equal to that of the Gauteng provincial government. The metropolitan City of Cape Town contains 70 precent of the Western Cape's population. With lower urbanization in KwaZulu-Natal and the Eastern Cape, the metropolitan municipalities in the Durban and Port Elizabeth conurbations have one-third and one-sixth of the provincial population, respectively. As will be shown, the creation of the new unified metropolitan governments fundamentally changed their relationship with the provinces. In many instances they have competed with provinces, they are often beyond the supervisory capacity of provinces, and theynforge their primary relationship with the national government.

Below the metropolitan municipalities are a number of local municipalities that have aspirations for metropolitan status. These secondary cities are, however, significantly smaller and have less resources than the top five (see table 1) municipalities (MDB 2005a). In contrast to the large metros, the smallest local municipality in population size has 6,000 residents. Most local municipalities have populations in excess of 50,000. The amalgamation has meant that local municipalities do not consist of a single town or city but represent a collective of towns and rural areas. This has brought its own dynamics of intertown rivalry and conflict.

3 THE RANGE OF MUNICIPALITIES' RESPONSIBILITIES AND FUNCTIONS

Local government is posited as the developmental arm of government. The objects of this sphere of government thus include the provision of services to communities in a sustainable manner and to promote social and economic development (*Constitution*, s. 152). Local government must also participate in national and provincial development programs (*Constitution*, s. 153). To fulfill this developmental function, the Constitution entrenches in Schedules 4B and 5B thirty-eight functional areas to municipalities. The national and provincial governments may, in addition, assign any of their legislative or executive competencies to municipalities.

The principal areas of competence are:

- planning and building regulation
- household services (electricity, gas, water and sanitation, waste removal)
- social services (childcare facilities, health care, cemeteries)
- protective services (firefighting)
- economic activities (tourism, trading regulations, billboards, liquor sales, food sales, street trading, markets, abattoirs)
- transport (airports, public transport, ferries, traffic and parking)
- infrastructure (stormwater management, public works, roads)
- environment (air pollution)
- public spaces (public places, cleansing, public nuisance, fences, amenities, street lighting, noise pollution)
- recreation (beaches and amusement facilities, sport facilities, parks)
- animals (care, pounds, impounding, licensing of dogs).

The match between the developmental mandate of local government and the allocated competences is, however, questioned (see HSRC et al. 2003). The discrepancy between the functional areas listed in the schedules and the holistic vision of developmental local government contained in the *White Paper on Local Government* and the *Municipal Systems Act* of 2000 has been pointed out. It was argued that the schedules were ad hoc lists of functions, with little focus on development and little conception of integration among functions. A review of the schedules would suggest that many of the provincial functions in part A of the schedules that are related to developmental local government should be allocated to municipalities. In practice this is already occurring and the activities of municipalities frequently transcend their constitutionally demarcated areas. While "economic development" is not a listed functional area, municipalities routinely engaged in a variety of "local economic development" programs (FFC 2005, 23). Moreover, there is a progressive delegation of functions to local government by the national government in particular.

The influence of the national government is also felt in another way. Although local constitutional competences fall, theoretically at least, within the discretionary authority of municipalities, national legislation increasingly imposes duties on municipalities to perform basic services by setting norms and standards for the delivery of municipal services. The *Municipal Systems Act* of 2000 empowers the national minister to establish essential national standards and minimum levels for any municipal service (s. 108). This has now been done in relation to free basic services in the areas of water, electricity, and sanitation.

4 THE FISCAL POSITION OF MUNICIPALITIES

Unlike the provincial government, which may exercise its constitutionally en-shrined revenue-raising powers only within a nationally set regulatory framework, local government has exclusive access to property rates and user charges. The exercise of such powers may, however, be regulated by national legislation. The immediate consequence is that provincial finances show the worst case of vertical fiscal imbalance (provinces raising only 3 percent of their income), while local governments are largely self-sufficient (raising overall 87 percent of their income).

Although local governments can rely directly on the Constitution to levy prop-erty rates, most aspects of local finances are now done within a framework set in national legislation, as permitted or required by the Constitution. In this regard, provincial governments play no regulatory role but, as will be discussed below, emerge from the wings with the task of overseeing the implementation of the national regulatory framework.

Local governments' operating income budgets for 2003–4 of R72.9 billion[1] (comprising 82.4 percent of the total budgets) were based on the following revenue sources:

user charges (mainly electricity and water)	42.5%
property rates	19.6%
other (tariffs, fines, subsidies, etc.)	19.6%
intergovernmental grants	11.1%
business payroll and turnover levies	7.1%

With the abolition of the business payroll and turnover levies by the National Treasury in 2006, the lost income will in the short term be compensated by addi-tional national transfers.

For the capital expenditure budgets of R16.7 billion, 45.9 percent of the rev-enue came from national and provincial transfers. Municipal borrowing has remained at low levels, the bulk (93 percent) being done by the metros.

4.1 REVENUE-RAISING POWERS

The Constitution entitles a municipality to impose rates on property and surcharges on fees for services – and, if authorized by national legislation – other taxes, levies, and duties "appropriate to local government," but not income tax, value-added tax, general sales tax, or customs duty (s. 229(1)). The power to levy property rates and user surcharges is subject to the general limitation that it may not be exercised "in a way that materially and unreasonably prejudices national eco-nomic policies, economic activities across municipal boundaries, or the national mobility of goods, services, capital or labour" and may be regulated by national legislation (s. 229(2)).

The regulation is now done via the *Municipal Systems Act* of 2000 (insofar as user charges are concerned) and the *Municipal Property Rates Act* of 2004. Not only have these Acts provided an extensive regulatory framework, but they make provision for direct intervention by the National Treasury in municipal finances. A few examples will suffice. First, if a rate imposed by a municipality is materially and unreasonably prejudicing any of the matters listed in section 229(2) of the Constitution (listed above), the national minister responsible for local government must set an appropriate rate (*Municipal Property Rates Act*, 2004, s. 16). Second, the national minister of finance may set the upper limit on the percentage by which rates (or rates on a specific category of property) may be increased annually (s. 20). Third, while the Act lists a number of properties that are excluded from property rates (for example, the first R15,000.00 of the market value of any property), a municipality may apply to the national minister of finance to be exempted from any of the limitations if they compromise or impede the municipality's ability to exercise its powers (s. 18).

In a major policy initiative from the national Department of Mineral and Energy Affairs, municipalities are set to lose direct control over the surcharges on electricity. In an effort to rationalize the electricity distribution for the entire country, the national government intends to establish six regional electricity distributors (REDs) that would take over the electricity function from municipalities. Although municipalities will be shareholders in the REDs, they will not be able, individually, to set the rate of the surcharge and thus determine the revenue to be raised for cross-subsidizing other services. Indeed, the scheme is built on the premise that each of the six metropolitan municipalities would anchor one RED in an attempt to effect cross-subsidization of rural municipalities.[2] To implement this scheme may well require a constitutional amendment deleting "electricity reticulation" as a Schedule 4B municipal competence.

4.2 TRANSFERS

Along with provinces, local government is entitled to an "equitable share of the revenue raised nationally to enable it to provide basic services and perform the functions allocated to it" (*Constitution*, s. 227(1)). The equitable share is largely based on recommendations by the independent Financial and Fiscal Commission and serves as a horizontal equalization device. Municipalities may also receive conditional grants from the national government (s. 227(1)(b)). Table 2 sets out the distribution of revenue raised nationally between the three spheres of government in terms of the Medium Term Expenditure Framework (Wheelan 2004).

Relative to the provinces, local government's share of income raised nationally remains small (4.4 percent compared with the provincial stake of 57 percent). Transfers play a limited role in the budget of the larger municipalities, including all the metros, which collect between 94 and 97 percent of their own revenue. Poorer rural municipalities are much more reliant on transfers, which, in the worst case, amount to 92.1 percent of their revenue.

Transfers to local government have increased rapidly over the past four years, doubling to R8.8 billion in 2002–3 and rising to R12.3 billion in 2003–4. This trend is projected to continue over the next four years. With conditional grants

Table 2
**Distribution of Revenue Raised Nationally between National, Provincial, and
Local Government**

	2003–4	*2004–5*	*2005–6*	*2006–7*
NATIONAL GOVT.	110.5 (38.9%)	120.6 (38.2%)	131.0 (37.8%)	139.6 (37.4%)
PROVINCIAL GOVT.	161.4 (56.8%)	181.9 (57.3%)	199.7 (57.6%)	216.3 (58.0%)
Equitable share	(50.9%)	(50.6%)	(50.1%)	(50.1%)
Conditional grants	(5.9%)	(6.7%)	(7.5%)	(8.0%)
LOCAL GOVT.	12.3 (4.4%)	14.2 (4.5%)	15.9 (4.6%)	17.0 (4.6%)
Equitable share	(2.2%)	(2.4%)	(2.5%)	(2.5%)
Conditional grants	(2.1%)	(2.1%)	(2.1%)	(2.1%)
TOTAL	R284.3 bn	R315.9 bn	R373.1 bn	R373.1 bn

currently constituting slightly less than half of the transfers, there is a slow
movement over a four-year period towards increasing the equitable share and
thus local discretion.

Although the primary responsibility for supervising local government lies with
the provinces, the primary source of conditional grants is the national government, rendering the role of provinces peripheral in this area. With transfers
constituting the bulk of provincial income, and much of their expenditure predetermined by national norms on the payment of pensions, social grants, and salaries,
there is precious little provincial largesse left transfer to struggling municipalities. Moreover, the administration of conditional grants for municipal infrastructure
that was previously done by provinces has now been centralized at the Department of Provincial and Local Government (DPLG) (see section 11.2 below).
Funding for housing is an exception. Housing is a provincial function, but all
housing developments are undertaken by municipalities in terms of subsidies provided by provinces. Thus, the bulk of the funds that provinces receive from national
transfers for housing is passed on by the provinces to "accredited" municipalities.

4.3 BUDGET

Like revenue raising, municipalities' expenditure is largely governed by national
legislation. According to the Constitution, the national government must prescribe
measures to ensure both transparency and expenditure control in each sphere of
government. With regard to local government this is being done by the *Municipal
Finance Management Act* of 2003, which sets an expansive and demanding framework for budget formation and expenditure control. Municipalities must approve

of an annual budget, but there is no direct bar against deficit budgeting. The Act prescribes the process, form, and content of the budget. The specific format of the budget may be further detailed in regulations issued by the National Treasury.

In the preparation of actual budgets, the parallel supervisory roles of national and provincial governments emerge. In drafting the budget, a mayor must consult with the provincial treasury and, when required by the National Treasury, with it as well. When the budget is tabled, the council must consider not only the views of the local community but also those of the National Treasury and the provincial treasury. The approved budget is then forwarded to both the national and provincial treasuries.

4.4 SUPERVISION

This dual relationship that municipalities have with the national and provincial governments is also strong when it comes to monitoring and interventions. The supervision of municipal finances was for long a contentious issue between the national government and the provinces. Within the broader constitutional scheme, the national government supervises compliance by provinces with their executive obligations (*Constitution*, s.100), while provinces do the same with regard to municipalities in their jurisdiction (*Constitution*, s. 139). Provinces have also the constitutional duty of monitoring municipalities (*Constitution*, s. 155(6)), a power that is implicit only in the case of the national government.

In designing the *Municipal Finance Management Act* (and the constitutional amendments to authorize its provisions), the various drafts vacillated between giving the National Treasury or the provinces the upper hand, with no conclusive resolution of the matter in the end. The final text of the constitutional amendments and the Act are thus an uncomfortable, and at times confusing, dualistic system of supervision.

On the monitoring front, the provincial treasuries, the provincial departments of local government, and the National Treasury perform a variety of often overlapping functions. When it comes to intervening in the case of financial difficulties, a similar parallel approach is followed.

Where a municipal council does not or cannot fulfill the specific obligation to approve a budget or any revenue-raising measure to give effect to the budget, the province is in charge, but the National Treasury keeps a watching brief. A provincial executive must intervene by taking "appropriate steps" to ensure that these financial obligations are fulfilled. The steps include dissolving the council and appointing an administrator and approving a temporary budget or revenue-raising measure to provide for the continuing functioning of the municipality. Failure of a province to interevene, or its failure to do so adequately, allows the national government to act in its stead.

In the case of "a financial emergency" (where a municipality, as a result of a crisis in its financial affairs, is in serious or persistent material breach of its obligations to provide basic services or to meet its financial commitments), the National Treasury plays an even stronger role. The provincial executive must intervene by imposing a financial recovery plan on the municipality. This plan must, however, be prepared by the Municipal Financial Recovery Service, a unit of the National Treasury. The effect of this requirement is that provinces become the implementers of nationally prescribed measures. Moreover, the national government may also intervene instead of the province if the latter fails to discharge its duty or does so inadequately.

While the province has the primary responsibility to monitor and enforce prudent financial management, the National Treasury hovers in the background, performing selected monitoring functions, devising recovery plans, and keeping a close watch on the way provinces execute their supervisory duties.

5 ORGANIZED LOCAL GOVERNMENT

In a rather unusual feature, the Constitution requires the formation of organized local government (Steytler 2005b). This flows from the integral part that local government plays in the overall governance of the country and the needs of the system of intergovernmental relations to hear the national voice of municipalities. The Constitution requires an Act of Parliament for the recognition of national and provincial organizations representing municipalities (s. 163). In terms of the *Organised Local Government Act* of 1997, it is the national minister responsible for local government who recognizes, first, the bodies representing the majority of municipalities in the provinces, and then the body representing the majority of provincial bodies. The South African Local Government Association (Salga) has received this recognition both at the provincial and the national level.

At first Salga was the collective of provincial associations. However, to find a more national voice, the organization's constitution of 2004 provides that membership consists of both individual municipalities and provincial local government associations. The aim is to get a direct mandate from municipalities, and consequently membership dues and fees are payable by municipalities directly to Salga at its head office. It is important to note that Salga is not entirely self-funded – it receives a grant from the national government to cover some of its expenses.

While Salga's constitution does not deal with the relative weight of the large metros compared with that of small rural local municipalities, the dominance of the metros is apparent. The leadership is drawn from the ranks of metropolitan mayors and other large district municipalities. In such a large organization, unity of interest is not always at hand, since large cities move on a different trajectory from that of their poor rural cousins. Already the metros and the four largest local municipalities have joined forces in the Cities Network (referred to as a "learning network").

The performance of Salga has thus far not matched the constitutional recognition it enjoys. It has been unable to participate in the National Council of Provinces in any meaningful way. While its engagement with sectoral intergovernmental forums (the so-called MinMECs) has been more successful, its response to numerous consultation processes has been uneven at best. To improve its functioning, Salga has opted for the policy position of elected full-time office bearers, who would be able to devote their full attention and time to Salga business (Salga

2003). In terms of its 2004 constitution, the Salga national executive has the power to stipulate which of the elected office bearers should serve Salga full-time. As this policy is yet to be implemented, the achievement of its objectives cannot yet be judged.

The formidable task of organized local government to be a true partner in government is apparent from the scope of municipal-national interaction, a significant part of which has been structured and formalized in law.

6 SCOPE OF MUNICIPAL-NATIONAL INTERACTION

The scope of municipal-national interaction is broad and multisectoral. Apart from the structured regulatory and supervisory relationships, the interaction occurs in formal intergovernmental forums, in terms of a consultation obligation, and in national sectoral programs. While Salga deals extensively with national departments, the bulk of the day-to-day interactions occur directly between line departments and municipalities.

6.1 FORMAL INTERGOVERNMENTAL FORUMS

A striking feature of the South African set-up is the extent to which relations between the three spheres have been formalized in intergovernmental relations (IGR) structures. The inclusion of organized local government in most of the national IGR forums brings local government directly into contact with the national government.

Salga participates at a national level in both legislative and executive institutions. As noted above, it has a right to participate in the National Council of Provinces. Organized local government has also a guaranteed seat on the Finance and Fiscal Commission, the body that advises government concerning the division between spheres of government of the revenue raised nationally.

In terms of national legislation, Salga is a member of the Budget Forum, a statutory intergovernmental forum where the minister of finance consults with his or her counterparts in the provinces and with Salga on, among other things, the annual Division of Revenue Bill. Salga also has membership in a number of administrative bodies, including the Committee for Environmental Coordination (*National Environmental Management Act,* 1998) and the Road Traffic Management Corporation's shareholders committee (*Road Traffic Management Corporation Act,* 1999).

Before 2005, Salga interacted with the national government (and its line departments) through a number of informal IGR structures, the most prominent being the President's Coordinating Council (PCC) and a number of sectoral forums between line ministers, their provincial counterparts, and organized local government (the MinMECs). These informal structures have now been given statutory form by the *Intergovernmental Relations Framework Act* of 2005 in terms of which local government has a prominent seat at the table of government. In reflecting practice, the chairperson of Salga is a member of the PCC, the body at the apex of the IGR system, consisting of the president, the deputy president, four designated cabinet members, and the nine premiers. The PCC is styled "a consultative forum for the President" to discuss matters of national interest with provincial governments and organized local government and to hear their views. It is also a forum of consultation on the implementation of national policy and legislation in provinces and local government, and on the coordination and alignment of priorities.

A similar approach is followed in the various sectoral MinMECs; their composition includes a representative of organized local government where it is appropriate for the functional area (for example, in housing, transport, and health).

6.2 CONSULTATION OBLIGATION

The inclusion of local government in IGR forums flows from the more general constitutional principle that organized local government must be provided with the opportunity to make representations on behalf of its members on national and provincial legislation affecting their interests (s. 154(2) *Constitution*). In addition a number of legislative instruments oblige the national government, before initiating legislation, to consult Salga. For example, section 229(5) of the Constitution requires that national legislation, that regulates the powers of municipalities to impose revenue-raising measures, may be enacted only after organized local government has been consulted.

6.3 NATIONAL PROGRAMS

Through the Department of Provincial and Local Government (which, despite its name, is devoted mainly to local government), the national government has launched, in conjunction with the provinces, several programs aimed at the well-being of municipalities. Its flagship programs have been the Urban Renewal Programme (URP) and the Integrated Sustainable Rural Development Programme (ISRDP). Their main aim has been to provide strategic leadership and coordination across the three spheres of government to ensure development initiatives and sustainable service delivery. The DPLG identified municipal nodes across the country that are in need of support and thus sought to mobilize resources to these nodes (see South Africa, DPLG 2004d).

Given widespread perceptions that local government is failing in its mandate, the national government, with the DPLG as the lead department, launched Project Consolidate in 2004, a project aimed at assisting municipalities to perform their basic functions. This project, driven by the presidency, identified 136 municipalities that face serious difficulties and are in immediate need of assistance. Working through the provincial governments, a number of remedial strategies have been put in place (South Africa, DPLG 2004e).

The DPLG also seeks to encourage municipalities to better performance through the annual Municipal Performance Excellence (Vuma) awards. This program was launched in 2003 as a partnership between the department and Salga. After provincial rounds of awards administered by the provinces, the national awards are made (South Africa, DPLG 2004a; Mutobvu 2004).

7 THE NATURE OF THE MUNICIPAL-NATIONAL INTERACTION

The Constitution establishes a clear hierarchy between the three spheres of government, which is clearly reflected in the relationship between the national government and municipalities. The national government determines the broad framework of local government, exercises some financial supervision, and transfers limited but significant funds to the municipalities. Outside these hierarchical relationships, there is arguably scope for a more equal relationship when the two spheres meet in intergovernmental forums. However, both the emerging legal framework and the practice of intergovernmental relations suggest a hierarchical bias towards the centre.

The *Intergovernmental Relations Framework Act* of 2005, in a subtle yet significant way, portrays the relationship between the spheres as a hierarchy. As noted above, the PCC is seen as "a consultative forum *for the President*" to discuss matters of national interest with provincial governments and organized local government and to hear their views (s. 8). It is also a forum of consultation on "the implementation of national policy and legislation" in provinces and local government (s. 9). A similar approach is adopted for MinMECs – they are the consultative forums "for the [national] ministers." In contrast, the Premier's Intergovernmental Forum (where a premier meets with district and metropolitan mayors and one representative of organized local government) is described as a forum for the premier *and* local government. The national bias reflects past practices; MinMECs were experienced as discussion forums dominated by the centre, with provinces as passive recipients of national guidance and information.

The same approach is evident in the formulation of municipal policy. The most significant national intervention in municipal policy has been the provision of free basic services. It came to the fore in the ANC's local government election campaign of 2000 (Wheelan 2004, 6) and soon became national policy. Because of the massive costs involved in implementing free basic services in the area of water, electricity, and sanitation, municipalities had to be assisted. Although the National Treasury increased local government's equitable share substantially to cover the cost, it did so only partially; municipalities still have to subsidize part of the costs from their own resources, and this places considerable strain on the financial viability of some. Despite their constitutionally protected status, the most significant factor in defining the relationship between the centre and municipalities is probably the overall political climate, in which government in all spheres is dominated by one party, a theme to which we will return later.

In spite of the implicit hierarchy underpinning the relationship, municipalities and Salga are not entirely docile and subservient, and they have sought to protect their limited constitutional space and interests. In the National Assembly Portfolio

Committee on local government, Salga has been very active over the years in commenting on key pieces of legislation on local government (Salga 2003). The push is towards a more equal relationship, as the following interchange between Salga and the minister for local government illustrates.

The minister has the power to make regulations or guidelines on the assignment of functions to local government but may do so only after consultation with Salga (*Municipal Systems Act*, 2000, s. 120(1)). The Minister thus forwarded a set of draft guidelines to Salga for comment within fourteen days (letter from Minister F.S. Mufamadi to the chairperson of Salga, 30 March 2005). The chairperson of Salga (and mayor of the Johannesburg Metropolitan Council) responded as follows: "It is submitted that being given the opportunity to comment unilaterally on a product does not constitute consultation. Consultation by definition requires a level of bilateral engagement and implies an attempt by the consulting parties to reach *consensus (although such consensus is of course not a necessary outcome)*" (letter dated 15 April 2005, emphasis in original). Salga thus proposed that a technical team be composed of Salga and DPLG representatives to commence the "consultation" process. The importance of this exchange is that consultation is seen as a joint decision-making process, a view to which national departments have not been subscribing.

8 THE ROLE OF PROVINCIAL GOVERNMENTS IN MEDIATING MUNICIPAL-NATIONAL RELATIONS

Local government's relationship with the national government runs parallel to its relationship with the provinces. Formally, in terms of the Constitution, provinces have the power to regulate the municipalities' exercise of their competences (s. 155(7)). In this they parallel the national government, although the provincial powers of regulation with regard to Schedule 5B matters (exclusive provincial matters) are relatively wider than those of the national government. Provinces are under the constitutional obligation to monitor and support municipalities, a duty they share with the national government. Their only exclusive function is the power of intervention in terms of section 139. As noted above, the primary monitoring role of the provinces has been affirmed in the *Municipal Finance Management Act* of 2003. Accordingly provinces have established departments of local government answerable to a member of the Executive Council (MEC). While these departments are primarily concerned with the institutional arrangements and functioning of municipalities, most other provincial line departments also interact to varying degrees with municipalities.

The two-track relationships do not always mesh; often they exhibit a measure of duplication and sometimes competition and conflict. The provincial treasuries are acutely aware that much of their monitoring efforts are duplicating those of the National Treasury, leaving the impression that they are simply a mailbox for municipal financial reports. Moreover, these parallel relationships are coloured by the fact that the funds lie at the centre, not in the provinces. Provincial departments of local government were much stymied when the municipal infrastructural grants were removed from their jurisdiction and located centrally in the DPLG (see section 11.2 below).

Because of the parallel relationships, the mediation by provincial government of local concerns to the national government is not a major issue although there are some indications that the province can play a communication role. In terms of the *Intergovernmental Relations Framework Act* of 2005, the Premier's Intergovernmental Forum, consisting of the premier and the mayors of metropolitan and district municipalities, may forward matters of national importance to the PCC. These formal institutional arrangements do not, however, constrain municipalities from dealing directly with national departments. More specifically, metropolitan municipalities are more likely to do business with the national government than with their provincial governments.

Metropolitan councils control budgets that compete with those of their provinces. Not that size necessarily matters, but the disposable income in the hands of the metropolitan councils makes the difference – they have raised over 95 percent of their own revenue. Moreover, they have the same if not better skills than a number of provincial departments. This inevitably has led to the perception that the metropolitan councils do not need provinces for their health and well-being. This is also evident in the difficulties provincial departments experience in performing their usual monitoring and support functions. Not only do some departments lack the capacity to monitor the functioning of metros, but they also lack the resources to provide meaningful support. When in 1999 Johannesburg Metropolitan Council required a R500 million grant to effect institutional reform, it did not approach the province of Gauteng (which in any event would not have been able to afford a grant of such magnitude); rather it secured the grant from the National Treasury. The result of this power discrepancy is that provincial departments of local government are seen to be concerned mostly if not exclusively with the non-metropolitan municipalities.

9 MUNICIPAL INTERNATIONAL RELATIONS

The Constitution grants neither provinces nor municipalities the power to conclude international agreements; it reserves this competency for the national government (see Steytler 2003b). Nevertheless, provinces and municipalities have been active in engaging with other subnational entities across the national borders. Such international relations have taken a variety of forms – from friendly visits and trade missions to formalized written twinning agreements.

Salga has also been an active member of a number of international local government organizations. Most notable is the recent establishment of United Cities and Local Governments of Africa (UCLGA), a continent-wide organization with the objective of supporting the process of decentralization, consolidating the African municipal movement, and strengthening the capacity of local governments to deliver services (Baatjies 2005).

The focus of most foreign links has been Europe, North America, and China. The aim has been mainly the pursuit of trade links and cultural exchanges. However, some municipalities along the border region of South Africa are establishing links with their neighbours, and cooperation agreements are emerging (Steytler et al. 2004).

The flourishing of local government's international forays did not escape the attention of the national government. Already in July 1999 the Ministry for Provincial and Local Government had issued an official policy document, *Municipal International Relations (MIR): A Policy Framework for South Africa*, providing nonbinding guidelines. Although municipal international relations are encouraged as an important developmental and strategic instrument for local government, the policy framework cautioned that international relations and networking do not become "activities in and for themselves" (para. 4.1.2). Rather, international relations should add value to municipal development programs. The policy framework also sought to give political direction to the focus of cooperation. Noting that most international linkages are with the northern hemisphere, it urged local government to develop stronger relationships with developing countries of the South; in particular, links with African countries should be emphasized in support of an African Renaissance. Although there is recognition that it would be inappropriate for national and provincial governments to regulate municipal international relations tightly (or "to approve all international involvement before it can proceed" (para. 5.1), the policy framework asserted that "organized local government in conjunction with national and provincial government needs to set a direction for municipal international relation." (para. 5.2.1). With municipalities giving little credence to the policy framework, the DPLG is currently considering legislation to regulate more closely municipalities' uncoordinated and mostly unprofitable foreign forays.

10 THE POLITICAL DIMENSION OF THE MUNICIPAL-NATIONAL RELATIONSHIP

Local politics are profoundly party-political and in most cases are dominated by national politics. This flows in part from the electoral system. The Constitution provides for a system of ward representation combined with proportional representation. Thus, in all metros and local municipalities with more than seven councillors, the German system of a mixed proportional representation system has been adopted. Fifty percent of councillors are elected in wards, while the other half are elected from compensatory party lists.[3] Given that the final result must be proportional to the votes for political parties, parties are an integral part of the system. Moreover, with an imperative mandate, political parties exercise strict control over their members, because loss of party membership also means loss of elected positions. However, constitutional amendments in 2001 allow floor crossing in two window periods during a council's five-year term.

The major political parties dominate local politics. Although localized parties have been formed during election time, few have succeeded in getting elected. Likewise, although independent candidates are permitted, only in exceptional cases have they been elected. Because the major political parties dominate local politics, municipal governance has been drawn into the national arena. Moreover, the major parties have also made local issues a key aspect of their national policies. The result is that local politics are, to a large extent, dictated by national political imperatives. Two illustrations will suffice.

The ANC, with a national support base of over 70 percent of the popular vote, functions in a very centralized manner. Having adopted a policy of "democratic centralism," party leadership at both provincial and local government is decided at the national level (Steytler 2004). Along with the ANC candidates for the premiers of the provinces, the mayors of the metropolitan cities also are nominated by the ANC's central committee (and not by the local party structures). For the 2006 local election, the ANC leadership even refused to disclose the candidates for the mayorships prior to election day.

The main opposition party, the Democratic Alliance (DA), approaches local politics no differently from the ANC. Indeed, good governance at local government level is used by the party as a national campaign strategy, seeking to show that it can run a clean and effective municipal government in contrast to the ineptitude of the ANC-led governments. At the 2000 local election, the DA captured the metropolitan City of Cape Town. When its mayor, Peter Marais, was accused of dishonest conduct, the DA's national executive committee instructed him to vacate his position as mayor. Although Marais succeeded in his legal challenge against his dismissal as mayor, the DA eventually expelled him from the party, effecting the loss of his seat (Smith 2002). With good governance as a main plank in its attack on the ANC, the provincial structures of the DA in the Western Cape have removed mayors in two rural municipalities following charges of corruption.

The "national" nature of local politics comes to the fore most vividly at election time. A single election date is set for all the municipalities by the national minister responsible for local government. The major political parties develop a uniform local government policy platform and the national leaders hit the campaign trail. For the election of 1 March 2006 the national parliament went into recess for the fortnight preceding the polling date, enabling MPs to canvass alongside the local candidates.

The national interest in local politics is not surprising given the important repercussions that the election results have on intergovernmental relations. Within a highly party-politicized local government, party differences have played a major role in shaping the functioning of relationships between some municipalities, provinces, and the national government. Until June 2004 the Inkatha Freedom Party led the government in the Province of KwaZulu-Natal, while the Ethekwini Metropolitan Council was in the hands of the ANC. The council's relationship with the province was strained (although at the officials level some cooperation was evident), in contrast to the expansion of direct relations with the national government. The same occurred in the Western Cape. When the City of Cape Town Metropolitan Council was in the hands of the ANC and the province was controlled by the New National Party / Democratic Alliance coalition, the relationship was conflictual. Since the ANC gained political power in both institutions, the provincial-local relationships have been more harmonious and conflicts are resolved within party structures.

11 POLICY CASE STUDIES

In the two policy areas selected – emergency planning and infrastructure development – a strong municipal-national relationship is clearly evident.

11.1 EMERGENCY PLANNING

In the area of emergency planning – referred to in South Africa as "disaster management" – the national government has taken the lead in developing a comprehensive policy that seeks to integrate and align the efforts of all three spheres of government when meeting the challenge of natural disasters. Because South Africa has a semi-arid to arid climate, the main natural disasters are droughts, floods, and veld and forest fires (Buys 2005).

Given the distribution of competencies between the three spheres of government, all three have some role to play in disaster management. In terms of Schedules 4B and 5B, local government is responsible for firefighting services. Ambulances services are an exclusive by provincial competence, while disaster management is a functional area of concurrent national and provincial competence. Given this diffusion of responsibilities, the national *Disaster Management Act* of 2002 seeks to establish an integrated and coordinated disaster management policy across the three spheres. Significantly, the administration of the Act was given to the Department of Provincial and Local Government.

The Act established the Intergovernmental Committee on Disaster Management, consisting of relevant national ministers, provincial members of the Executive Council responsible for disaster management, and members of municipal councils selected by Salga. The object of the committee is to give effect to the principles of cooperative government relating to disaster management. Contradicting the general principles of cooperative government, the committee "is accountable and must report to [the national] Cabinet on the coordination of disaster management among the spheres of government" and "must advise on the establishment of a national framework for disaster management aimed at ensuring an integrated and uniform approach to disaster management" (s. 4(2)). This political committee is shadowed by the technical National Disaster Management Advisory Forum, which draws its members from all the spheres of government as well as from role players in the private sector and civil society concerned with disaster management.

The system establishes a hierarchy of functionaries. Each district municipality must establish a disaster management centre, which is linked to a provincial disaster management centre, while at the apex is the National Disaster Management Center (NDMC), which must promote an integrated and coordinated system with the provincial and municipal disaster centres. The NDMC also performs a monitoring function and must review the disaster management plans of provinces and municipalities. It also classifies disasters as a local, provincial, or national disaster. Until classified otherwise, all disasters are local. The classification of a disaster designates primary responsibility to a sphere of government.

A provincial disaster management centre must monitor the disaster management plans and strategies of municipalities. In each province the responsible members of the Executive Council must also convene a provincial disaster management advisory forum composed of provincial officials, the heads of each municipal disaster management centre, representatives of organized local government in the province, and role players in the private sector and civil society. Their function is to provide the link between national objectives and provincial and municipal disaster risk management activities and priorities. When a disaster occurs, the advisory forum must provide support and guidance to the provincial disaster management centre (*National Disaster Management Framework*, 2005, para. 1.2.4).

As noted the *Disaster Management Act* prescribes the formation of a disaster management center in each metropolitan and district municipality. An extensive regulatory framework is provided relating to the functions of the centres, the development of disaster management plans, the management of the centres, and their relationship with the national and provincial centres. The municipal centres must, for instance, assist the provinces when so requested. The Act also creates parallel relationships between the municipal centre and the national and provincial centres. In general, a municipal centre "must liaise and coordinate its activities with the National Centre and the relevant provincial disaster management centre" (s. 44(4)). For example, when a "disastrous event" occurs, the municipal centre must inform both the national and the provincial centres. The parallel relationship may also work the other way; both the national and provincial disaster management frameworks may designate municipal entities (entities controlled by municipalities, such as utility companies) that must prepare disaster management plans.

There are also instances where the only relationship is that between the municipality and the NDMC. Where a municipality establishes a unit of volunteers to participate in disaster management, it must submit the names of the volunteers to the NDMC. The volunteer unit also functions in terms of a framework established nationally.

The overall structure of disaster management reflects a complex set of relationships. First, there is a set of relationships that follows the overall constitutional hierarchy, the primary relationship of a municipality being with its province. Second, there is the parallel set of relationship where municipalities relate to both national and provincial governments on the same matters at the same time. Finally, there is the direct relationship between municipalities and the NDMC to the exclusion of the provinces. The hierarchical nature of this system is further enforced by the fact that disaster relief funds are doled out by the national government.

11.2 INFRASTRUCTURE

One of apartheid's legacies was the huge infrastructural backlog at the municipal level for the provision of basic services. With the formation of nonracial municipalities it was clear that municipalities would not be able to cover infrastructural development from own-source revenue. With provinces hardly raising any revenue, funding had to be forthcoming from the national government. At first, funds were channelled through provinces to municipalities in terms of the Consolidated

Municipal Infrastructure Programme (CMIP). In addition, national departments such as Water and Forestry, Transport, and Mineral and Energy had specific conditional grants for water, sanitation, roads, and electricity.

In a significant policy shift in 2004, all national infrastructural grants were centralized in the Department of Provincial and Local Government (South Africa, DPLG 2004b). Infrastructural grants are to be administered by the national government, and all existing national infrastructural grants[4] are to be combined in one consolidated grant, termed the Municipal Infrastructure Grant (MIG) and administered by the DPLG. The consolidation of the grants was said to flow from the uncoordinated and fragmented approach by different departments, often leaving municipalities out of control of infrastructural projects (South Africa, DPLG 2004c).

With the purse strings firmly in hand, the DPLG laid down policy. The MIG program is aimed at providing all South Africans with at least basic levels of services by 2013 through the provision of grant finance to cover the capital costs of basic infrastructure for the poor (ibid.). The DPLG thus describes the MIG as "a mechanism for the coordinated pursuit of national policy priorities with regard to basic municipal infrastructure while avoiding duplication and inefficiency associated with sectorally fragmented grants" (ibid., 12). The MIG may be used for infrastructure for basic household services (water, electricity, sanitation, roads, street lighting), public municipal facilities (transport, fire stations, cemeteries), and other nonmunicipal facilities (schools, clinics).

While the DPLG prescribes the pro-poor focus, the responsibility for prioritization, planning, and implementation lies with the municipalities. The objective of the MIG is to fully subsidize the capital costs of providing basic services to poor households. The MIG thus complements the unconditional "equitable share" allocation to municipalities that should be used to supplement municipal revenue to deliver free basic services of water, electricity, and sanitation to the poor. The third leg of grant support is the Municipal System Improvement Grant, aimed at building in-house capacity.

The allocation of MIG funds between municipalities is determined by the National Treasury. Using a formula, the funds are divided first among the different sectors (water, roads, etc.) and then among all municipalities based on their infrastructural backlogs. Each municipality's allocation is according to a schedule attached to the annual *Division of Revenue Act*. The conditionalities of the grant come with regard to the purposes for which its may be used (prioritizing residential infrastructure), implementation methods (labour-intensive construction methods), and other procedural requirements (inclusion in an integrated development plan (IDP)). There may also be sectoral conditions in, for example, water and sanitation infrastructure. While there is an automatic transfer of funds annually, the enforcement mechanism is the decrease in size of the grant the following year.

In addition to the basic MIG, there is a Special Municipal Infrastructure Fund to which municipalities may apply for grants for special innovative or regional investment projects. Apart from the MIG Management Unit administering the MIG program, the DPLG established in 1998 the Municipal Infrastructure

Investment Unit (MIIU) – a stand-alone company with the task of assisting municipalities with advice on the financing and management of essential municipal services such as water supply, sanitation, waste, energy, and transport.

Infrastructure policy and funding has thus become an entirely nationally driven enterprise. After losing the function to administer the Consolidated Municipal Infrastructure Programme (CMIP), provinces play only a peripheral role in municipal infrastructural development. Their role, described by the DPLG, is confined to their general constitutional role of monitoring and support, ensuring that IDPs are properly prepared, and providing technical advice on infrastructure for which they have responsibility, such as roads. The complaint of provinces is that on losing control over the distribution of funds through the CMIP, they have lost an important regulatory device. Without the sanction of manipulating money flows, provincial monitoring has lost much of its clout.

12 RECENT TRENDS

The recent trends in local-national relations, alluded to in the above text, can be summarized as follows. First, the national government is increasingly setting urban and rural policy. This has been most evident in the case of the policy on free basic services. Second, the national policy setting has resulted in a dramatic increase in the national transfers of funds to municipalities for the provision of free basic services through the "equitable share" allocation and conditional grants for infrastructure. The national restructuring of the electricity distribution through the creation of the regional electricity distributors (REDs) will impact significantly on municipal revenue, which, again, will result in national influence through increased transfers to municipalities.

Third, the increased policy intervention by the national government is followed by much closer national and provincial supervision of local government, aimed at ensuring the delivery of basic services. Project Consolidate is the most recent example of such a nationally driven but provincially implemented initiative. A further example is the nationally appointed and paid-for community development workers (CDWs). Paid by the national government and trained by the provinces, the CDWs have from 2006 been placed in selected municipalities to unblock linkages between municipalities and communities. This has resulted in an uncomfortable situation, where CDWs are working in municipalities and communities but are not finally answerable to the municipal councils concerned.

Fourth, the ever-shrinking realm of local autonomy is not arrested by the conduct of municipalities; they have not shown themselves uniformly to be prudent and successful custodians of local self-rule. Given local government's constitutionally protected unfettered employment powers, the extravagant salaries paid to municipal managers have been the obvious argument for constitutional reform. In the worst case, the municipal manager of an impoverished district council in Mpumalanga earned more than the president of the country. His salary of R1.2million for 2003–4 exceeded the presidential pay of R1.05million for 2004–5. Yet 73 percent of households in the district had no basic refuse removal,

60 percent lived in poverty, and 36 percent had no electricity (Le Roux 2005, 22). High salaries, coupled with appointments of underqualified persons (often as political patronage), have prompted the DPLG to promise legislative intervention, and a unified civil service for all three spheres of government is also in the cards. National legislation will structure the grades and salaries of municipal employees, leaving only the hiring and firing to municipalities.

A frequently articulated complaint is that some municipalities have become inwardly focused – the vehicle for a self-serving elite – rather than being community-centred. Popular perceptions are shaped by the use of municipal funds to support a high life of conferencing and overseas travel for the top management, and the dominance of party political appointments for both high and low municipal positions. The ultimate form of a self-serving municipality is corruption in its various forms. Numerous examples abound. The most dramatic recently was the arrest in August 2005 of the mayor and municipal manager of Mangaung (Bloemfontein) on multimillion-rand corruption charges.

Fifth, despite the negative perceptions of local government's ability to deliver development, its role as a key partner in the governance of the country was affirmed in the *Intergovernmental Relations Framework Act* of 2005. The Act institutionalizes the place of organized local government at the heart of the intergovernmental relations system, the President's Coordinating Council. Through the channels of communication created by the various provincial and district intergovernmental forums, local concerns are set to permeate decision making throughout the entire system of government.

13 THE ADEQUACY OF THE SYSTEM OF MULTILEVEL GOVERNANCE IN RELATION TO MUNICIPAL AND URBAN POLICY

Within the context of the parallel relationship that both the national and the provincial governments have with local government, it is clear that the national relationship dominates. This reality also reflects the uncertainty around the shape and role of the provinces in the future. Are they going to increase in significance with more functions and own-revenue-raising powers, or is there a slow demise in their governance role? Although it is sometimes argued that the growth in status of local government is not a zero-sum game vis-à-vis the provinces, the strengthening of local government's relations with the national government in South Africa has taken place at the expense of the provinces.

The critical point where provinces must still play the leading role is with regard to monitoring and support. Even this relationship is being undercut, because the primary financial relationship is between national and local government. Without independent revenue at their disposal, provinces do not have much of a stick or a carrot for municipalities. In the case of metropolitan municipalities, it is virtually non-existent.

In the municipal-national relationship, the dominance of the national government is clearly evident. Assessing the adequacy of the system of multilevel governance relating to good public policy affecting municipal and urban policy has, therefore, become an evaluation of the adequacy of national policy. Any assessment is inevitably a comment on the functionality and value of a decentralized system of government in South Africa, seen against the background of the often inept and frequently self-serving performance of local government.

The first critique of the national-municipal policy is that local government is overregulated. Law has been thrown at every conceivable problem. While the Constitution holds out the promise of local democracy, the statutory framework created for municipalities is extremely complex and burdensome. Where the requirements are so onerous and costly, nonobservance becomes the inevitable reality, resulting in a state of lawlessness. Where a municipality has the skill to comply, there is a high compliance cost. Legislation is experienced as a hindrance, an obstacle rather than an empowering tool. Overregulation has led to under-compliance – the exact opposite of the intended outcome. Part to the problem has been the assumption of equal capacity.

The legal framework is premised on a notion of uniform municipalities; the law applies in equal measure to all municipalities, irrespective of their size, skills, or resources. While compliance is not an insurmountable problem for large municipalities, it is for small rural municipalities in impoverished rural areas. For the first time, this reality was recognized in the phrasing in of the *Municipal Finance Management Act*. Three categories of municipalities were created – high capacity, medium capacity, and low capacity – but this recognition holds only for three years. After that, the smallest rural local municipality with six thousand residents in the heart of the Kalahari Desert must have the same skills base as the largest metro to comply with the rigours of the Act. The inadequacy of national legislation dealing with local government is, then, the failure to deal with the huge disparities between institutions that on the surface are the same but in reality are very different. Conversely, despite the possibility of the asymmetrical devolution of powers to well-performing municipalities, the best are kept to the level of the weakest. Capable municipalities have not been assigned additional powers or functions.

The third critique is the lack of coherence and alignment between sectoral departments; the left hand of the national government does not know what the right hand is doing – let alone both doing so in unison. National legislation is often contradictory and confusing. Legislation from the national Health Department on the definition of "municipal health service" (*National Health Act,* 2003) is at odds with the DPLG's division of functions between district and local municipalities (MDB 2005b). The procurement provisions of the *Municipal Systems Act* (sponsored by the DPLG) and the *Municipal Finance Management Act* (sponsored by the National Treasury) are not aligned. While the DPLG has managed to coordinate all the sectoral infrastructural grants to municipalities, this has not happened at a legislative or policy level.

The lack of a coordinated national approach to local government is exacerbated by inconsistencies between national and provincial approaches to the same subject. There is a large number of national statutes that impose roles and responsibilities relating to local government on provincial departments or on the provincial government as a whole. Often the roles are not clearly defined, and sometimes they overlap with national responsibilities. The enactment of the *Municipal Finance Management Act* is an example of the creation of such overlapping responsibilities. The lack of clarity on roles, overlaps in jurisdiction, and uncertainties over responsibilities results in municipalities often receiving poor service.

On the one hand, without a proper integrated approach to local government, the result is uncoordinated policies, inconsistent practices, and duplication of services or the development of service gaps. The loser in all cases is local government. On the other hand, effective coordination of departmental activities would lead to complementarity of effort, the concentration of resources, and the synergy of activities. The need for a coordinated approach to local government has finally been emphasized in the nationally driven Project Consolidate. The aim is to ensure unified state-led action and support for local government in critical areas of service delivery and transformation.

Fourth, where the national government prescribes the contours of development (goals as well as performance targets), the very purpose of a democratic local government is undercut. The danger exists that the municipalities will become mere appendages of the national government. Not only does this often result in unfunded mandates, but it creates a democratic deficit – development is no longer shaped by communities. While the impoverished residents applauded the free basic services policy, municipalities are being held accountable for policies imposed elsewhere. Not since the violent protest in the black townships in the 1980s have South Africans witnessed protests of such magnitude in the streets of a number of municipalities. They started in 2004 in the eastern Free State, where residents violently expressed their anger about a lack of service delivery. Soon similar protests emerged in the Western Cape and Eastern Cape.

However, municipal performance should be assessed against what local government can realistically deliver. Nationally imposed policies and expectations that demand too much set local government up for failure. It is simply unrealistic to expect that many municipalities (particularly in rural areas) can effect local economic development while the growth in the national economy is slow and urban-based. A review of IDPs indicates that the expectations of citizens often fall beyond the scope of local government's competences – the urgent need is jobs and houses. Municipalities can only seek to promote the former, while hey can provide housing only on an agency basis.

14 CONCLUSION

The South African case study provides an example of how multilevel government has produced a complex set of relationships between three spheres of government. Without a clear hierarchy between the three spheres, a strong direct relationship has been forged between the national government and municipalities. Provinces still play an important monitoring and support role, but they do not perform an essential mediating role between local and national government. Given the very centralized nature of South Africa's decentralized form of government, the national government's dominance of local government matters is not surprising. However, overregulation and overly prescriptive policies may emaciate local democracy, resulting in poor municipal and urban policy.

NOTES

1 Exchange rate: R5 equals Can$1 (date February 2006).
2 At the time of writing (February 2006), the establishment of the six REDs is being reconsidered by the national cabinet as a result of concerns raised by the metros regarding the prospective loss of income.
3 The councils of district municipalities are composed of 40 percent directly elected members on closed party lists and 60 percent indirectly elected councillors from the local municipalities in the district.
4 The grants were CMIP, Water Services Projects, Community-based Public Works Programme, Local Economic Development Fund, Urban Transport Fund, Building for Sport and Recreation Programme, and National Electrification Programme.

REFERENCES

Baatjies, Reuben. 2005. "United Cities and Local Governments of Africa: Crystallisation of Local Government in Africa." *Local Government Bulletin* 7 (3): 15–16

Buys, L.J. 2005. "Status of Disaster Management in South Africa." Unpublished paper. Pretoria: Directorate, Disaster Management, Department of Provincial and Local Government

Cameron, Robert. 2005. "Local Government Boundary Reorganization." Unpublished paper, Department of Political Science, University of Cape Town

Cloete, J.J.N. 1988. *Central, Regional, and Local Government in South Africa*. Pretoria: J.L. van Schaik

De Visser, Jaap. 2005. *Developmental Local Government: A Case Study of South Africa*. Antwerp and Oxford: Intersentia

Financial and Fiscal Commission (FFC). 2005. *Annual Submission for the Division of Revenue 2006/7*. Pretoria: FFC

Human Sciences Research Council (HSRC) et al. 2003. "Review of Schedules 4 and 5." Unpublished research report submitted to DPLG, 21 March

Le Roux, Mariette. 2005. "Municipal Managers' Pay Absurd." *Business Report*, 14 September, 22

Mastenbroek, Rudolf, and Nico Steytler. 1997. "Local Government and Development: The New Constitutional Enterprise." *Law, Democracy and Development* 1: 233–50

Municipal Demarcation Board (MDB). 2005a. "Cities Report." Unpublished report. Pretoria: MDB

– 2005b. "Capacity Assessment Report 2004/5." Unpublished report. Pretoria: MDB

Murray, Christina. 2001. "The Constitutional Context of Intergovernmental Relations in South Africa." In *Intergovernmental Relations in South Africa: The Challenges of Co-operative Government*, ed. Norman Levy and Chris Tapscott, 66–83. Cape Town: School of Government, University of the Western Cape; and Political Information and Monitoring Service, IDASA

Mutobvu, Takalani. 2004. "Vuna Awards Gets Off the Ground in Spectacular Way." *dplgNews* 1 (1): 6

National Disaster Management Framework. 2005. Issued by the Minister for Provincial and Local Government, *Government Gazette* 27534, 29 April

Smith, Geraldine. 2002. "Firing the Mayor with a 'Double Barreled' Motion." *Local Government Bulletin* 4 (2): 15

South Africa. Department of Provincial and Local Government (DPLG). 2004a. *Annual Report 2003/2004*. Pretoria: DPLG

– 2004b. *Policy Framework for the Introduction of the Municipal Infrastructure Grant (MIG)*. Pretoria: DPLG, 5 February

– 2004c. *The Municipal Infrastructure Grant (MIG) 2004–2007*. Pretoria: DPLG

– 2004d. *Urban News: Newsletter of Department of Provincial and Local Government on Urban Renewal Programme* 1 (1)

– 2004e. *Project Consolidate: A Hands-on Local Government Support and Engagement Programme*. Pretoria: DPLG

– National Treasury. 2004. *Modernising Financial Governance: Implementing the Municipal Finance Management Act, 2003*. Pretoria: National Treasury

South African Local Government Association (Salga). 2003. "Enhancing the Role of Salga in Intergovernmental Relations: A Position Paper on the Role and Functioning of the Political Office Bearers of South African Local Government Association." Unpublished report. Pretoria: Salga

Steytler, Nico. 2003a. "District Municipalities: Giving Effect to Shared Authority in Local Government." *Law, Democracy, and Development* 7 (2): 227–42

– 2003b. "Cross-Border External Relations of South African Provinces." In *External Relations of Regions in Europe and the World*, ed.Rudolf Hrbek, 247–64. Baden-Baden: Nomos Verlagsesellschaft

– 2004. "One Party Dominance and the Functioning of South Africa's Decentralised System of Government." In *Political Parties and Federalism*, ed. Rudolf Hrbek, 159–68. Baden-Baden: Nomos Verlagsesellschaft

– 2005a. "Republic of South Africa." In *Constitutional Origins, Structure, and Change in Federal Countries*, ed. John Kincaid and Alan Tarr, 211–346. Montreal & Kingston: McGill-Queen's University Press

– 2005b. "The Role of Organized Local Government in Intergovernmental Relations in South Africa." In *Decentralisation and Local Governance: Essays for George Matthew*, ed. L.C. Jain, 495–520. New Delhi: Orient Longman

Steytler, Nico, et al. 2004. "Transfrontier Cooperation: Towards a Provincial Strategy." Unpublished discussion document prepared for the Premier's Office, KwaZulu-Natal Provincial Government

Wheelan, Paul. 2004. *Local Government and Budget 2004*. Occasional Papers, IDASA–Budget Information Service, May

MULTILEVEL GOVERNANCE IN THE UNITED STATES

Ronald K. Vogel

1 INTRODUCTION

I don't want to see anybody do anymore goddamn press conferences. Put a moratorium on press conferences ... Don't tell me 40,000 people are coming here. They're not here. It's too doggone late. Now get off your asses and do something, and let's fix the biggest goddamn crisis in the history of this country.

Ray Nagin, mayor of New Orleans, 2 September 2005

Today, the complicated nature of local, state, and federal relations in the United States belies simple characterization. Political scientists commonly refer to multilevel governance as reflective of the "new forms of governance and dispersion of decision making away from central states" (Hooghe and Marks 2003, 233). Liesbet Hooghe and Gary Marks point to the benefits that flow from centralization. "Large (i.e., territorially extensive) jurisdictions have the virtue of exploiting economies of scale in the provision of public goods, internalizing policy externalities, allowing for more efficient taxation, facilitating more efficient redistribution, and enlarging the territorial scope of security and market exchange" (ibid., 235). However, the benefits of centralization are offset by the disadvantages: "Large jurisdictions are bad when they impose a single policy on diverse ecological systems or territorially heterogeneous populations. One criticism of centralized government is that it is insensitive to varying scale efficiencies from policy to policy. Economies of scale are more likely to characterize the production of capital-intensive public goods than of labor-intensive services because economies accrue from spreading costs over larger outputs (Oakerson 1999)" (ibid., 235–6).

Conceptualizing federalism as multilevel governance "allows decision makers to adjust the scale of governance to reflect heterogeneity" (Hooghe and Marks 2003), a hallmark of large modern states such as the United States. In this paper, I explore the nature of the multilevel governance system in the United States at two levels. First, I outline the basic features of the system. Second, using the case of New Orleans, I assess whether the multilevel governance arrangements in the United States produce good public policy.

2 CONSTITUTIONAL DESIGN

The U.S. Constitution has no provisions concerning the place of cities in the federal order. American federalism is predicated on a constitutional division of power between the national government and state governments. At the nation's onset, the national government was weak and the states were strong. Indeed, the national government under the Articles of Confederation lacked its own authority to raise revenue or armies without the approval of the states. The Constitution adopted in 1789 was designed to overcome these limitations by creating a strong national government with a single chief executive charged with specific responsibilities for conducting foreign policy, ensuring national defence, and promoting commerce – albeit subject to checks and balances – while leaving the states largely responsible for domestic policy.

Although the United States is characterized as a federal system, this characterization refers to the national and state governments. The states are not organized as federal systems internally. Rather, they are unitary entities, and their authority over municipalities is limited only by their own constitutions and laws. This authority is embraced in a judicial doctrine known as Dillon's Rule, which is followed by the courts in the United States. The rule emerged out of an 1865 court case of Judge John F. Dillon, chief justice of the Iowa Supreme Court. Dillon, an expert on municipal law, later wrote a legal treatise, *Commentaries on the Law of Municipal Corporations*, expounding his views, which were widely accepted by state and federal courts (Richardson, Gough, and Puentes 2003). Dillon's Rule, which has been in effect for more than a century, states:

> It is a general and undisputed proposition of law that a municipal corporation possesses and can exercise the following powers and no others: First, those granted in express words; second, those necessarily or fairly implied in or incident to the powers expressly granted; third, those essential to the declared objects and purposes of the corporation, not simply convenient, but indispensable. Any fair, reasonable doubt concerning the existence of the power is resolved by the courts against the corporation, and the power is denied.

Dillon's Rule supplanted the prior "inherent right of local self-government" view that led state legislatures to interfere freely in municipal affairs (Lang 1991). Of course, it was not until the mid-to-late 1800s that cities began rapid expansion in public services and infrastructure, often under the direction of political machines (DiGaetano 1991). Dillon's Rule was partially an effort to reduce political corruption and provide greater oversight of municipal administration (Richardson, Gough, and Puentes 2003). Dillon's Rule did not so much lead to good governance as replace local corruption with state corruption.

In the twentieth century, the Home Rule movement sought to reduce state intrusion and reassert local authority to address growing urban problems (Krane, Rigos, and Hill 2001). Home Rule was intended to restore the inherent right of local self-governance. State legislatures passed state statutes or constitutional amendments providing for municipalities to have greater control over local affairs and to avoid undue state interference. In some instances, states may have been trying to provide municipalities with sovereignty akin to that of federal systems. In other instances, the states may have been seeking to provide a greater delegation of authority. However, in practice, Home Rule has had limited impact, for Dillon's Rule still tends to prevail in court cases, and municipal legal offices tend to take a conservative position with regard to local powers; and state legislatures continue to control municipalities. Even where clear Home Rule grants are made, when local laws or actions clash with state laws or where state law explicitly or implicitly "pre-empts," local laws are struck down by the courts (Richardson, Gough, and Puentes 2003).[1]

To what, then, do municipalities owe their reputation for a great deal of local autonomy? It is not the formal authority in which they are vested by their state governments. Rather, the answer lies in the high regard for localism in the American political system and culture. Officials in state and national government have a healthy respect for local preferences and values. Americans look to their local authorities to solve their problems. Most elected officials in the state and federal governments got their start in local offices. The local orientation is reinforced by a weak party system and the local system of representation. The national Democratic and Republican parties are actually aggregations of the 50 state parties and 3,000 county party systems. The localist political culture limits state intervention by restraining state and national governments from being very interventionist in local affairs. Moreover, members of the state House of Representatives and the state Senates meet together as a delegation from the local community to set local priorities.

American political culture also emphasizes individualism and pragmatism. Local public officials do not hesitate to "just do it," as the Nike sneaker commercial says. This is the credo of an American mayor. Local political leaders find creative ways around the barriers that confront them. Whether the barriers are legal or political, American mayors are very innovative and imaginative in trying to address their problems, and they often get involved in issues over which their city governments have limited legal authority.

Still, citizens do have high expectations of state and federal governments. Since the Great Depression, Americans have looked to the national government to provide income security and a social safety net. In the 1960s, the national role expanded to ensure protection for civil rights, to promote equal opportunity in employment and education, and to address the urban decline in the nation's largest cities. The election of Ronald Reagan in 1980 reversed the extension of federal involvement in urban affairs. While direct federal aid to cities and a commitment to urban revitalization declined dramatically, federal expenditures in the form of entitlement programs to individuals and support for education and health policy continued to grow.

3 THE RANGE OF MUNICIPALITIES' RESPONSIBILITIES AND FUNCTIONS

Municipalities in the United States are generally responsible for the provision of urban services, including land use planning and zoning, solid waste collection and disposal, waste water and storm water drainage, public works such as roads and highways, street cleaning, and public safety. The exact services supplied by municipalities are determined by the states, as provided for in their state constitutions and legislation. Thus, there is wide variation in the specific responsibilities assigned to municipalities and the degree of discretion in carrying out those assignments.

Historically, education was provided as a municipal service in many large cities in the Northeast and Midwest. In the reform era, education services were often insulated from municipal authorities, including from the mayor. However, education continued to be included in municipal budgets. In the 1990s, concern about the declining quality of large school systems led to efforts to bolster the mayor's authority over education. In the South, public education is usually provided by a separate school district whose boundaries often match county boundaries.

The Census of Governments gives an indication of the kind of responsibilities that cities have and the relative weight of those functions within the local agenda.[2] Basic public services provided by the largest U.S. cities are police protection, fire protection, highways, parks and recreation, sewerage, solid waste, housing and community development, and health and hospitals.[3] Other public services provided by less than half of the largest cities are corrections, education, and public welfare.

Although municipalities have the primary responsibility to provide these basic public services, state and federal governments do provide aid to pay for infrastructure and operating costs in varying amounts. In addition, state and federal government regulations and grant conditions have a significant effect on urban service provision. For this reason, we usually emphasize the intergovernmental dimension in public services in the United States. Virtually all municipal services involve the cooperation of a multitude of local (municipalities, counties, special districts, regional agencies), state, and federal governments. Table 1 illustrates the range of federal involvement in programs that are primarily reserved to the states under the Constitution. However, a large share of federal aid goes to benefit individuals rather than places; as much as two-thirds of federal aid is for "payments for individuals, such as Medicaid and welfare" (Kincaid 1997, 376).

The scale and importance of local government vis-à-vis the federal and state governments is readily apparent by comparing employment in each level of government (see figure 1). State and local government employment accounted for 87 percent of total government employment in 2002, up from 78 percent in 1970. The major growth in local government employment has been in special districts (162 percent), counties (122 percent), and school districts (92 percent) (see figure 2). The growth in county employment probably represents the increasing importance of urban counties as municipal service providers in the unincorporated areas. In addition, counties generally are responsible for health and corrections, both services with sharply rising costs.

Table 1
Federal Aid to State and Local Governments, 2003

Program for 2003	$ millions
Grant-in-aid shared revenue[1]	387,281
National defense	(NA)[6]
Energy	589
Natural resources and environment	5,593
Environmental Protection Agency[2]	3,917
Agriculture	800
Commerce and Housing Credit	3
Transportation	41,029
Grants for airports[2]	2,681
Federal-aid highways[3]	29,960
Urban mass transportation[2]	7,448
Community and regional development	15,082
Homeland Security(FEMA)	7,861
Appalachian regional development programs	74
Community development fund	5,569
Education, training, employment, and social services	51,543
Compensatory education for the disadvantaged[4]	11,204
School improvement programs[4]	5,964
Impact aid	1,103
Vocational and adult education	1,908
Social services block grant	1,740
Children and family services programs	8,161
Training and employment services	4,291
Office of museum and library services	239
Health	173,814
Substance abuse and mental health services[4]	2,171
Grants to states for Medicaid[4]	160,805
Income security	86,476
Food stamp program	4,162
Child nutrition programs[4]	10,664
Veterans benefits and services[4]	403
Administration of justice	4,498
General government[5]	7,449

[1]Includes items not shown separately

[2]Grants include trust funds

[3]Trust funds

[4]Includes grants for payments to individuals

[5]Includes general-purpose fiscal assistance

[6]Not available

Source: U.S. Census Bureau, *Statistical Abstract of the United States, 2004*, table 424

Figure 1
Local, State, and Federal Government Employment, 1970–2002

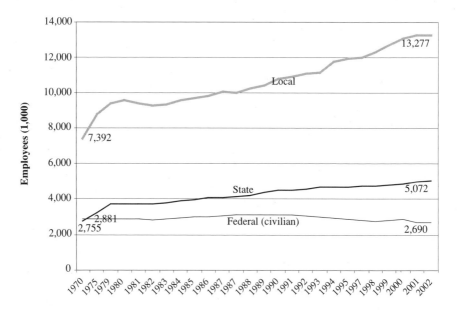

Figure 2
Local Government Employment, 1970, 1980, 1990, 2002

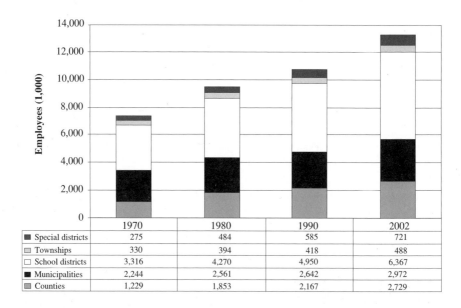

	1970	1980	1990	2002
■ Special districts	275	484	585	721
▨ Townships	330	394	418	488
☐ School districts	3,316	4,270	4,950	6,367
■ Municipalities	2,244	2,561	2,642	2,972
▨ Counties	1,229	1,853	2,167	2,729

4 THE FISCAL POSITION OF MUNICIPALITIES

U.S. municipalities generate a significant share of their revenue – well over 65 percent of their budgets – from their own sources. This is a major reason why American municipalities are usually viewed as highly autonomous when compared with cities in some other countries. Although the cities generate the greater share of their revenues, they are still dependent on aid from the states and the federal government. The long-term trend has been for federal aid to decline from a high of over 15 percent in 1979 to about 5 percent from 1990 onwards. State aid to municipalities has continued to stay above 20 percent in the same timeframe (U.S. Bureau of Census, Government Finances, 1979–2000).

The primary source of revenue for most municipalities remains the property tax, which accounts for just under 27 percent of own-source revenues.[4] However, since the property tax revolt movements, which began with Proposition 13 in California and spread across the country in the 1980s, the property tax has declined in importance. Few U.S. local governments, including cities, have access to income taxes (Pagano 1999, 255). The remainder of city-generated revenues comes from sales taxes and user fees, which the cities and counties are increasingly relying on for new revenue growth. User fees now account for about 40 percent of city and county revenues (ibid., 255). Cities may also derive revenue from municipal enterprises such as water companies.

Figure 3
Large Cities Revenue, 2002–03

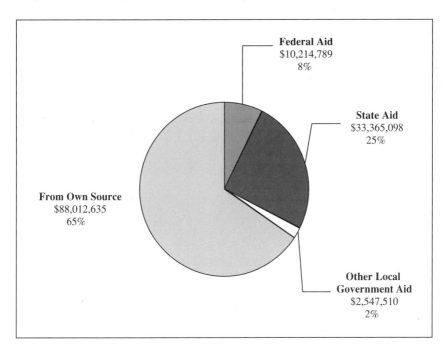

Federal Aid
$10,214,789
8%

State Aid
$33,365,098
25%

From Own Source
$88,012,635
65%

Other Local
Government Aid
$2,547,510
2%

The National League of Cities issues an annual report, *The State of American Cities*, based on a survey of municipalities. In 2005, about one-third of municipal officials reported "that if city tax rates and fees are not increased, city service levels next year will be decreased" (NLC 2005, 3). When only cities with more than 100,000 persons are included, the figure is 43 percent. Thus, although American cities may have greater revenue-generating capacity than cities in other countries, they are still dependent on aid from higher-level governments. Moreover, their revenue is strongly related to economic conditions.

Municipalities may not run deficits for their operating budgets, though they do incur long-term debt to finance large-scale physical infrastructure such as sewerage systems, roads and highways, landfills, and the like. In the past, General Obligation Bonds were the main mechanism to finance infrastructure. These require referendums, which are frequently voted down. More recently, cities have been inclined to finance facilities such as stadiums and arenas with revenue bonds that do not require referendums. Other tools have been developed to extend revenues, such as tax increment financing. Where possible, public officials will often seek to create public authorities or special districts to offload the debt and service responsibilities to the new entity, allowing them to reallocate the money previously budgeted to these functions.

5 THE CITIES AND WASHINGTON

The main associations concerned with national policies affecting localities are the U.S. Conference of Mayors, the National League of Cities (NLC), the National Association of Counties (NACO), and the International City/County Managers Association (ICMA). In addition, a multitude of organizations represent specific units of local government, categories of local public servants (e.g., National Association of Chiefs of Police), professionals (e.g., National Association of Social Workers, American Public Works Association), and agencies or bodies (e.g., National Association of Clean Water Agencies, National Association of Regional Councils). There are also several local government unions including the National Education Association (NEA) and the American Federation of State, County, and Municipal Employees (AFSCME). The Council of State Governments (CSG) and the Association of Governors represent state interests in national policymaking that bears on state or local issues.

More and more, local governments are operating as interest groups seeking to influence federal policy and secure infrastructure investment in their communities. Most medium and large cities employ lobbyists in Washington, DC, specifically to promote local interests and ensure a share of the congressional pork barrel, and indeed an ever-increasing flow of federal money is going to local governments from this source. According to the Congressional Research Service, about $53 billion was spent on earmarks in 2004, up from $29 billion in 1994 – a 45 percent increase over ten years (*Washington Post* 2006). There is not an authoritative definition of earmarks, but they are usually thought of as funds provided to specific "projects, locations, or institutions" inserted into appropriation bills,

Table 2
Local Government Associations

Group	Year created	Represents	Mission	Policy agenda
United States Conference of Mayors	1932	Mayors in cities of over 30,000 (1,183 members)	Development of effective national urban/suburban policy Strengthen federal-city relationships Ensure that federal policy meets urban needs Provide mayors with leadership and management tools Create a forum in which mayors can share ideas and information	Metro agenda: "Keeping America Strong," acknowledging prime role of city-regions as "engines that drive this nation's economy." Jobs Infrastructure Transportation investment Public safety Brownfields redevelopment
National League of Cities	1924	Municipal governments (18,000 cities, villages, towns; 1,600 paid members)	Advocates for cities and towns in Washington, DC Promotes cities and towns in media Trains local leaders Keeps leaders informed Provides opportunities for involvement and networking	Enact a transportation bill Support municipal economic development (CDBG and Section 8 housing vouchers) Homeland Security funding (money for training) Protect local tax authority and revenue in tax reform (deduction of state and local income and property taxes, tax-exempt bond financing) Preserve local government's authority to regulate and tax communications services

...continued

Table 2
(Continued)

Group	Year created	Represents	Mission	Policy agenda
National Association of Counties	1935	Counties (3,066; 2,000 members)	Advocacy in Washington Membership Communications to present good image for counties Products, resources, and services for members	Assuring necessary federal funding for critical county programs, the protection of county authorities, and opposition to unfunded mandates Support health-care financing Support remote sales tax collection legislation Support surface transportation reauthorization Support social services and workforce programs reauthorization Support an extension of deadlines for Help America Vote Act Support reauthorization of Forest Counties Safety Net Oppose preemption of local authorities and unfunded mandates
International City/County Management Association	1914	City and county managers	Create excellence in local governance by developing and fostering professional local government management worldwide. [Activities engaged in include advocacy, professional development, and research.]	

Excerpted from the following sources:

United States Conference of Mayors, *Keeping America Strong: Mayors '04 Metro Agenda for America's Cities*, www.usmayors.org/uscm/news/press_releases/documents/chicagoagenda_081004.pdf

National League of Cities, "NLC Leaders Set 2005 Advocacy Agenda," *Nation's Cities Weekly*, 17 January 2005. Online at www.nlc.org/Newsroom/nation_s_cities_weekly/weekly_ncw/2005_01_17/1746.cfm

National Association of Counties, "2004 Legislative Priorities," *County News Online*, 22 December 2003. Online at www.naco.org/CountyNewsTemplate.cfm?template=/ContentManagement/ContentDisplay.cfm&ContentID=10715

International City/county Management Association, *ICMA's Strategic Plan 2000*, www.icma.org/main/bc.asp?ssid1=17&ssid2=2752&ssid3=2752&from=search&hsid=1&bcid=32

bypassing normal grant and bureaucratic review processes (Streeter 2004, 1). Not all of this money goes to local governments. However, local governments find earmarks sufficiently lucrative that they are increasingly employing lobbyists to get their share of benefits. The number of cities with lobbyists in 2006 was 511, compared with 234 in 1998. For counties, the number rose from 85 to 186 and for public schools from 19 to 59 (Rudoren and Pilhofer 2006).

The U.S. Conference of Mayors continually complains about federal mandates and declining federal support for cities. Federal mandates include environmental regulations for waste water treatment, clean water, brownfield clean-up standards, and special education requirements in schools. These federal programs alone may add $50 to 100 billion to local spending, without money being transferred to pay for them. Many unfunded mandates are uncounted because they are "conditions-of-aid" rather than an "enforceable duty" (Nivola 2003, 3). Pietro Nivola refers to the "shift and shaft" game which national officials are likely to play, since they can claim to address problems without paying for them. A good example is the *No Child Left Behind Act* which requires public schools to document children's progress annually with standardized tests. If public schools want to qualify for federal funding, they must comply with the federal policies. However, the federal government lacks the authority to order public schools to test annually. Although Congress passed the *No Child Left Behind Act* with these requirements, it did not adequately fund the programs. Thus, the national government can claim it has addressed educational problems, though without actually providing much support – and in effect causing state and local governments to increase their own spending drastically.

The National League of Cities' agenda mirrors that of the U.S. Conference of Mayors. The NLC complains that federal mandates add to responsibilities without providing sufficient fiscal resources or local flexibility in administering the regulations; it also complains of federal intrusion into local governmental responsibilities, such as zoning, and intrusion into local development codes (NLC 2005, 1). The NLC favours an intergovernmental partnership with the federal government. Focusing specifically on the grant system, it calls for a simpler grant process, with more aid distributed through block grants, and it wants the federal government to absorb the indirect costs of administering grants.

Historically, the Advisory Commission on Intergovernmental Relations (ACIR) played an important role in studying and recommending changes in the federal system. The ACIR's members were appointed to reflect all parts of the federal system, including the cities, the states, and the federal government. It thus provided a mechanism with which to balance competing views on how the federal system should operate and to negotiate changes in the intergovernmental system. The ACIR was disbanded in 1996 as part of the Republican revolution. There is no longer an institutional platform in the United States that regularly monitors and assesses the workings of the intergovernmental system. However, the continued existence of the ACIR would not have halted the declining priority of cities in the national agenda. Indeed, the Clinton administration contemplated the elimination of the Department of Housing and Urban Development (HUD) as part of its efforts to reduce the national budget deficit.

6 THE SCOPE AND NATURE OF MUNICIPAL-FEDERAL INTERACTION

The defeat of the Southern states in the Civil War clearly established that central authority did not derive from the states. However, even after the Civil War, the federal government continued to play a limited role. Following the dual-sovereignty theory of federalism (also referred to as the layer-cake model of federalism), the central government and the states have specifically enumerated functions in the Constitution. Each is sovereign when acting within its appropriate sphere. The functions and authority granted each level are considered independent, with the Supreme Court arbitrating in cases of dispute. The Constitution delegates to the federal government the conduct of foreign affairs and the promotion of commerce. The Constitution leaves to the states the regulation of public safety and domestic affairs. The states are not subordinate to the national government. Beyond conservative ideology about the proper role of the federal government, there were practical limitations on federal expansion, such as limited financial resources and administrative capacity.

The theory of federalism in the United States underwent significant revision following the Great Depression. Although, under the Constitution, the federal government lacked specific enumerated authority to act in domestic affairs, the Congress clearly had the right to "appropriate" money for legitimate public purposes. In addition, the federal "commerce" clause of the Constitution clearly held the national government pre-eminent in regulating interstate commerce. Thus, there was room for extensive growth of federal involvement in state and local affairs. The national government had earlier enacted a national income tax, which greatly enhanced the national revenue-raising capacity. The collapse of the economy in the Great Depression and the accompanying national crisis, as well as the expansion of national defence and war industries during the Second World War, certainly provided a rationale for greater federal involvement (Vogel and Harrigan 2007). With the conclusion of the war, both the Congress and the president sought to meet citizens' rising expectations with a dramatic increase in federal activity in domestic affairs.

The theory of federalism needed to catch up to the changed reality regarding the way the intergovernmental system actually functioned and normative concern with promoting social equity (Kincaid 1996). The new perspective, cooperative federalism (often referred to as the marble-cake model), replaced the layer-cake version of federalism. Cooperative federalism acknowledged and promoted the expanded federal role, adopting the dynamic language of intergovernmental relations rather than the more static and legalistic language of federalism. Under cooperative federalism, both the federal government and the states have joint responsibility for addressing domestic policy, and their actions are virtually inseparable. The grants-in-aid system is the mechanism that binds the federal and state governments together. The federal government sets the policy priorities and provides financial aid and the states and local governments implement the policies (Kleinberg 1995). Initially, grants were targeted towards the states, which determined how to allocate money and to administer the programs. Of course, states and local governments often sought federal aid for their own purposes lead-ing federal officials to complain of poor implementation, while state and local officials complain of overly rigid rules and little discretion.

Changes in the grants-in-aid system and federalism are related to the political interests of presidents and their re-election fortunes. The extension of the cat-egorical grant programs under Lyndon Johnson's presidency rewarded Democratic mayors in the big cities of the Northeast and Midwest, the base of the Democratic Party. The federal government was able to ensure that money went directly to the mayors and groups in the cities rather than being redirected by state governments, which are less responsive to city interests. Two signs of the new place of cities on the national agenda were the creation of the Office of Economic Opportunity (OEO), directly in the Executive Office of the President, and the newly created Department of Housing and Urban Development (Vogel and Harrigan 2007).

The place of cities on the national agenda was short-lived however Republican Presidents Nixon, Ford, Reagan, Bush I, and Bush II had little regard for the mayors and were uninterested in or hostile to the interests of large cities. The cities are not central to the Republican strategy to gain and hold the White House. Republicans have secured the presidency by appealing to the growing suburbs, especially in the South and West. Moreover, the Republican presidents have fa-voured a more limited federal role in domestic affairs.

Under Richard Nixon (1968–74), there was concern that the federal govern-ment was growing too large and eclipsing state and local initiative with the growth of federal grants. Under New Federalism I, also known as fiscal federalism, the federal government provided revenue sharing to states and local governments with no strings attached. Categorical grants, which were primarily aimed at large cities, were targeted for consolidation into block grants. This marked a shift away from the grant policies that bolstered big-city mayors in the Northeast and Mid-west, the Democratic strongholds. The *New York Daily Post*'s headline, "Ford to New York, Drop Dead," during the New York City bankruptcy crisis of 1975, highlighted the declining position of cities on the national agenda.

Under Ronald Reagan (1980–88), New Federalism II took a sharp turn to the right. Citizen attitudes had changed, with few people still believing in an active and positive national government (Self 2000). It was markets, not governments, that were seen as contributing to an improved standard of living. This called for privatization, deregulation, and tax cutting, leading to a federal withdrawal from the concerns of cities. The national policy agenda emphasized deficit reduction, budgetary policy, and eliminating bureaucracy. This meshed well with the subur-ban electorate and the growing population shift to the south and west, benefiting Republicans.

Bill Clinton represented the new breed of Democrats who were anxious to balance traditional liberal-democratic ideals and concern for the plight of cities with fiscal conservatism in order to appeal to suburban voters. However, contin-ued emphasis on reducing the national deficit left little room for expanding national urban policies. The federal government encouraged large cities to address con-centrated poverty by developing local strategic plans to revitalize poor neighbourhoods and by forming public-private partnerships. The federal government brought a small amount of money to the table, about $3.5 billion, and hoped to leverage this with other federal, state, and non-governmental support. The thrust was to fuse liberal intervention policies that focused on places with more neoconservative policies that emphasized reliance on markets. Thus, HUD helped finance the destruction of large-scale public-housing complexes alongside local efforts to build more mixed-income neighbourhoods. The federal government helped initiate local community development banks that would help jumpstart more entrepreneurialism in inner city minority communities to create jobs and stabilize neighborhoods. At the same time, the federal government would help finance the hiring of 100,000 new police in the cities (and suburbs) to fight the rising rates of violent crime.

In 2000 George W. Bush ran on a platform of "compassionate conservatism" but whether this was a coherent policy approach or rhetoric was never clear. The terrorist attacks on 9/11 and later the Iraq War moved urban policies and the cities entirely off the national agenda. The costs of the Iraq War, estimated at $1.2 trillion (Bilmes and Stiglitz 2006), together with the large tax cuts adopted in 2001, estimated at $1.35 trillion (Gale and Potter 2002), mean that even if liberal Democrats were to return to power, there would be no money available for urban policy initiatives.

There has been "*de facto* devolution" occurring in the United States over the last four decades (Kincaid 1999). Devolution was not a deliberate policy to bolster local autonomy. Rather, the federal government abandoned cities and their problems (Caraley 1992), changing the nature of urban politics (Eisinger 1998). Cities must now be more fiscally and administratively self-reliant. Local public management takes on increasing importance, leading urban managers to focus less on issues of social justice and racial equality and more on economic development and central city revitalization. Mayors in such cities as New York, Los Angeles, and Chicago have embraced the new public management policies to reduce costs, keep taxes low, and create a good business climate, and are now being hailed as saviours of the cities (Savitch and Vogel 2005).

The mayors were helped by the booming U.S. economy and a new wave of immigration in the 1990s, which benefited even older central cities. In this climate, it is easy to see how mayors were managing devolution successfully. Although they were less inclined to pursue redistributive policies, the stronger economy produced jobs and income for all levels of the workforce. The economic recession in the first few years of the twenty-first century has again raised questions about the cities' social, fiscal, and economic health. The National League of Cities reports: "A federal and state fiscal crisis that is the largest the nation has experience in decades is trickling down to city governments, making it increasingly difficult for city officials to balance their own budgets" (Hoene and Pagano 2003). The report points out that nearly half the states cut revenue for cities in 2003 and 2004, resulting in a 9.2 percent drop in state aid to cities. The NLC polled city finance officials to gauge their response to the reduced federal and state aid. According to the poll, the city officials planned to raise user fees and cut services, including laying off employees. In addition, they planned to defer infrastructure projects (ibid).

Although there has been a *de facto* devolution in American cities with mixed effects, the national government continues to play a strong role in domestic policy. The entitlement programs that aid people instead of places account for a large share of the national budget. This includes programs such as social security and Medicare. Overall, the evidence indicates that in spite of the language of devolution and decentralization, the national government has actually centralized policy, even in areas which the Constitution traditionally reserves to the states (Bowman and Krause 2003).

Increasingly, national policymaking is made without reference to the problems of cities and with little direct input from city officials. Local officials lament that the federal government no longer accepts responsibility for urban problems. According to the National League of Cities, "the intergovernmental partnership ... is slowly deteriorating." The NLC points to the increasing deficits as a factor in "the smaller federal role in assisting municipal governments with domestic priorities." Local governments are left shouldering the costs of infrastructure and services without federal assistance. Further, the federal government adds insult to injury by increasing unfunded federal mandates and pre-empting local authority (NLC 2005, 5). Close observers of the federal system decry the current state of intergovernmental relations in the United States. William Barnes (2005), the research director of the NLC, bluntly states, "The era of federal urban policy is, like, way over" (ibid., 575). John Kincaid, former executive director of the Advisory Commission on Intergovernmental Relations refers to the current state of federalism as "coercive federalism" (1996, 29). Others call it "fend-for-yourself-federalism" (Hoene and Pagano 2003).

Robert Waste (1998, 21) attributes the "political invisibility of American cities" to the U.S. Constitution's provision for there to be two Senators for each state resulting in a "structural bias" against cities and towards rural areas. In the 1990s a coalition of the twenty-six smallest states with 16.5 percent of the population could block urban policy in the Senate (Waste 1998, 23). This bias against cities is reinforced by the Electoral College system used for presidential elections since a state's electoral vote is tied to the number of seats held in the U.S. House of Representatives and Senate. Hence, the anomaly of George W. Bush's failure to capture the popular vote in 2000 while gaining a majority of the Electoral College.

7 THE STATES AND THE CITIES

George W. Bush and the Republican Congress through 2006 preferred to work through state governments rather than directly with municipal officials. There are few ties between big-city mayors and the national government today. Most federal aid to local government now flows through the state governments. This has led to significant problems for mayors, who have difficulty being heard. Although cities, especially the larger cities, are more likely to be targets of terrorism (Savitch 2003), most aid to municipalities to protect against terrorism flows through state governments (Eisinger 2004). The states have been reluctant to give the largest cities their share of the resources. Even in an area such as Homeland Security, which is central to Bush's policy agenda, cities have been given the short end of the stick.

Large cities often fare poorly in their dealings with state governments. State and federal governments still tend to overrepresent rural interests in policymaking. Increasing suburbanization and a declining central city population have reduced city representation in state and national legislative bodies (Weir, Wolman, and Swanstrom 2005). In the past, city representatives were able to forge coalitions in the Democratic Party caucuses, which they often dominated, with rural legislators representing poor and distressed small towns. With these coalitions, they could address common concerns over poverty, education, and economic development (ibid., 737). But declining political parties, the election of Republican mayors, and greater division among city representatives have left cities with greatly reduced political influence in their state capitals. The challenge for cities is to build statewide coalitions with often hostile suburbs and rural communities when they lack the aid of strong political party institutions through which to build coalitions and forge common bonds.

Large cities have been unsuccessful at building alliances among themselves within a state or with other medium or smaller cities through a state league of cities. Historically, large cities in a state competed with one another for commerce, while small and medium-sized cities were jealous of their resources and suspicious of their agendas. Although some suggest that central cities can build coalitions with inner-ring suburbs (e.g., Orfield 1997), there is little evidence that these types of interest-based coalitions have actually occurred.

Rather, state governors are now crucial to the fortunes of cities. Weir, Wolman, and Swanstrom (2005, 743) point to the increasing importance of governors in "building cross-party legislative coalitions to support urban priorities," most often for infrastructure investment. Governors often see the cities as essential for the state economy, even if the cities were not central to their election. The governors may be responding to urban corporate interests, which make significant financial contributions to the governors' campaigns. Although the governor-brokered coalitions have been important to cities, Weir, Wolman, and Swanstrom point out that they come at a price:

> Yet, in all cases, reliance on governor-brokered coalitions contains significant drawbacks for cities. The final terms of the legislative bargains that governors strike may be far from ideal from the city's perspective ... Moreover, the growing independence of state legislative leaders limits the governors' ability to cement such coalitions so that this strategy is far from reliable. (ibid., 746)

From the 1960s through 1980, cities were often able to bypass the state government. Since 1980, direct federal aid to cities has declined, and the national government has favoured block grants passed through state governments rather than direct ties with cities. This has reinforced the power of the state governors and state legislatures in the distribution of federal aid to cities. Mayors of large cities are still more likely to be Democrats, while Republicans have greater influence in the suburbs and in rural parts of the state. The complaints of mayors and city officials are reflected in the national agendas of their primary associations, especially the National League of Cities and the U.S. Conference of Mayors. What cities really want from state government is more autonomy, especially to raise revenues and to be free from state mandates that raise costs. Cities also seek greater aid and investment from the state (ibid., 747–8).

At the substate level, regional governments are almost non-existent, with the exception of the Metropolitan Planning Organizations (MPOs) and voluntary associations such as a Council of Governments (COGs). In the 1990s there appeared to be some promise of greater regionalism in U.S. metropolitan areas (Savitch and Vogel 1996). Two factors were promoting greater regionalism. First, the federal government, through its transportation policies, required an MPO to be established for every metropolitan area in order to develop short and long-term transportation plans. Further, significant transportation projects required MPOs to undertake major investment studies to consider costs and benefits and to ensure that transportation projects were consistent with regional transportation and land-use plans. No federal highway trust fund money can be spent without MPO review and support. Second, research pointed to the interdependence of cities and suburbs and to the cities as engines of the national economy (Savitch et al. 1993; Barnes and Ledebur 1993; Peirce 1993; Rusk 1995; Savitch and Vogel 1996; Orfield 1997).

Unfortunately, the promise of regionalism at the metropolitan level did not match performance (Frisken and Norris 2001). The MPOs did not lead to integrated regional planning (Vogel and Nezelkewicz 2002). Today, there is little concrete evidence that cities and suburbs can forge effective regional coalitions or that the federal government will return to the field. This has not dampened the optimism of some scholars and policy advocates and big cities continue to call for the federal government to resume its previous level of commitment to cities and city-regions (Dreier, Mollenkopf, and Swanstrom 2001).

8 CITIES ON THE WORLD STAGE

Globalization and concern with enhancing the city's competitiveness in a world economy have led U.S. cities increasingly to cast their gaze beyond the national borders. The economies of a number of American metropolitan areas dwarf that of many nations, as highlighted in a U.S. Conference of Mayors' report:

> The flow of goods and services among metro areas is comparable to trade flows between nations. Consider how these engines of growth compare in a broader international context. Indeed, when comparing the output of the nation's metro economies with those of international economies, the importance of metros to the U.S. is clearly revealed. Out of the 100 largest international economies in the world, 42 are U.S. metro areas, with New York in the top 10, and Los Angeles and Chicago in the top 20. (Global Insight 2006, 7)

Local and state officials seek to enhance their cities' competitive position in the world economy in response to globalization (Scott 2001). Mayors and governors frequently make overseas jaunts in an effort to recruit business and increase trade. In addition, American cities are the recipients of international migration, with significant economic consequences. On the one hand, municipalities face added costs to such services as bilingual education, housing assistance, and job training. On the other hand, immigration leads to increased cultural diversity, neighbourhood revitalization, and improved economic development. Richard Florida (2005), for example, trumpets the benefits of attracting the creative class, which enjoys the more cosmopolitan and culturally rich environment that is frequently found in cities with large immigrant communities.[5]

Is the increasingly global world leading municipal officials to engage more actively in international relations and even develop municipal foreign policies? There is little systematic study of municipal foreign policy and the place of cities in international relations, but Heidi Hobbs (1994) provides a baseline. Hobbs points to four significant areas where municipalities "challenged federal supremacy in foreign policy." These are "the comprehensive test ban movement, nuclear free zone declarations, divestment of local funds from South Africa, and provisions of sanctuary for Central America refugees" (ibid., 3). According to Hobbs, 900 cities called for a nuclear freeze, 157 cities and 32 counties set up nuclear-free zones, 101 cities and 25 counties adopted sanctions against South Africa, and 28 cities and 2 states called for sanctuary for Guatemalans (ibid., 4). Hobbs attributes increased municipal activism in international relations to the grassroots activism that arose in response to the more conservative foreign policy of the Reagan era in the 1980s. In addition, cities needed to promote international trade and foreign investment in light of deindustrialization and New Federalism policies at the national level, which reduced federal aid and called for state and local governments to take charge of local economic development.

States are particularly concerned that international trade agreements may undermine state tax and trade policies. For example, Enid Beaumont points to the "Beer II case, in which the World Trade Organization (WTO) determined in a dispute resolution that a Minnesota law that gave tax preference to microbreweries was a violation of free trade, because it discriminated against larger breweries" (Beaumont 1996, 376). The U.S. trade representative, a federal official, plays an important role in defending state taxes and policies that may violate WTO agreements. State and local governments want guarantees for state sovereignty, greater input into national government decisions in dispute resolutions, and the right to act directly in disputes rather than through the national government (ibid., 377). States also worry about treaty obligations that require standard treatment when the states' policies vary so widely. Beaumont reports that the U.S. trade representative has set up a formal communication link in each state to improve consultation on issues of concern (ibid). It is also unclear whether state incentives to recruit business violate trade agreements.

Mildred Warner and Jennifer Gerbasi find that "NAFTA is eroding subnational government authority in legislative and judicial arenas" (Werner and Gerbasi 2004, 858). The North American Free Trade Agreement (NAFTA) and World Trade Agreement (WTA) treaties limit cities' ability to favour local industries. The U.S. Constitution provides that national treaties negotiated by the president and approved by the U.S. Senate are supreme and "trump subnational domestic policies" (ibid., 861). Under NAFTA, municipal policies promoting local industries are regarded as trade barriers. The effect of this kind of agreement is to centralize greater authority in the federal executive branch over domestic policies that are otherwise under the authority of state and local officials.

In practice, NAFTA has led to greater federal centralization in the executive branch. Warner and Gerbasi highlight that NAFTA has redefined property rights that otherwise are determined by the fifty states following state laws and constitutions. NAFTA provides for "foreign investors to bring nations into international arbitration to defend government measures that affect their private investments (property) negatively, and redefining property to include future profits, market access and market share" (ibid., 862). State and local governments no longer set the boundaries for balancing the public good with property rights. The U.S. Government will represent state and local interests in arbitration. "In effect, this system replaces domestic processes with international courts and law, shifting disputes regarding domestic state matters to an international venue" (ibid., 863). The US government is likely to trade off state and local government interests and prerogatives on behalf of broader national goals. Of course, the same holds true for Canada and Mexico, which also are parties to NAFTA.

Warner and Gerbasi examine the case of Methanex in California to explore the consequences of NAFTA for subnational governments. In 1999 the California legislature imposed a ban on the chemical methyl tributyl ethanol (MTBE), a chemical gas additive, after evidence was found that public drinking water was contaminated. A study for the California State Senate reported that $160 million to $300 million was required for remediation and that residents had suffered property value loss due to contaminated wells. Some California cities had also been awarded about $40 million from U.S. courts after suing refineries for groundwater pollution. The Canadian company Methanex challenged "the United States over the California ban in a NAFTA arbitration and is claiming US$970 million in damages including good will, reputation and future profits" (ibid., 864). Methanex produces methane, which is an ingredient of MTBE. Among the claims made by Methanex is that the additive ethanol, manufactured by U.S. companies, is used, thus favouring U.S. companies over Canadian ones. According to Warner and Gerbasi,

These claims would not be successful within the US legal system. First, the damage claim would not survive. Methanex is asking for a partial takings ruling based on the loss of 6% of their production. In the US system, property must lose nearly all of its value to require compensation for damages due to regulations. Second, most legislation bears the burden of being rationally related to a legitimate government objective. The US courts give great deference to the states' legislative intent, and allow states to have laws more stringent than the federal system. The NAFTA arbitration tribunals apply strict scrutiny that requires regulations affecting trade be narrowly tailored. Thus, the trade analysis has a singular focus on supporting free trade rather than considering common criteria (e.g. pubic health) used by subnational governments to balance competing objectives. Finally, in the US system the focus would be on the harm caused by the product, not the incidental positive impact on substitutes. (ibid., 864)

Although the Methanex claim was rejected by the NAFTA tribunal in 2005 (Corsi 2006), many believe that it is just a matter of time before some actions of state or local government are deemed to have violated NAFTA provisions. Warner and Gerbasi point out that once this occurs, "the federal preference for free trade is substituted for democratic legislative and judicial action at the subnational (state and local) levels" (2004, 864).

Clearly, cities are engaged in the international arena. Yet there remains little systematic study of the scope and scale of their involvement. This is an area ripe for further investigation. Certainly, the Seattle WTO riots reveal increased awareness by cities and citizens of the possible effects of international trade agreements on urban life. Many states and cities maintain permanent overseas trade offices. Many cities have created international offices to coordinate "sister cities" programs. Cities appear to be taking a strategic approach to this kind of partnership focusing on building ties that offer new markets or opportunities for local firms and industries.

9 THE PLACE OF CITIES IN U.S. POLITICS[6]

As suburbs grew and absorbed migrants from the central cities, some analysts believed that these suburbs would be influenced by liberal (often-Democratic) values (Scammon and Wattenberg 1971). They reasoned that areas outside the city core were not inherently conservative but were a product of the people who composed them. Democrat optimism dissolved as the suburban experience worked in the opposite direction. Home ownership, private clubs, seemingly limitless space, a flood of inexpensive automobiles, and class homogeneity contributed to increasingly conservative attitudes in what had become predominantly white suburbs.

The political transformation of America's suburbs can be traced back to the 1960s during the halcyon days of Democratic liberalism. While followers of Lyndon Johnson and Robert Kennedy were celebrating the War on Poverty, Republicans were building a conservative foundation in white suburbs and in the South. Lisa McGirr (2001) analyses the roots of this movement and explains its ideological appeal. For McGirr, the Republican right arose in the natural American soil of respect for limited government, the value of free enterprise, the sanctity of private property, and a deep-seated patriotism. The ideology of the "new right" was coupled with a reverence for traditionalism that emphasized religious observance and archetypal ideals of the nuclear family.

While the new right was still an emerging idea, more centrist Republicans, such as Richard Nixon, diligently created political coalitions between the suburban North and West as well as with a conservative South (Phillips, 1969). Nixon's fall following the Watergate scandal was followed by years of Democratic rule, but in 1980 Ronald Reagan hoisted the new right's banner over the White House. While the Reagan legacy was followed by the Democratic centrism of Bill Clinton, Republicans had established that Democrats could no longer cling to a left-wing constituency. Furthermore, the Republican right remained strong. It had carried congressional races, and it maintained a substantial hold over important state governorships. Both would later furnish George W. Bush with a powerful base.

National elections in 2000 (Bush v Gore) and 2004 (Bush v Kerry) were the crucible over whether the new right or centrist Democrats would prevail. After a controversial defeat in 2000, hopeful Democrats pointed out that while Bush had captured the Electoral College, Gore held the real American mandate by having won the popular vote. By 2004, the nation had a clear answer. Relying on the suburban-southern coalition, Bush and his strongly conservative allies were swept into office. Clearly, the political outcome rested on a sharply divided geographic landscape whose contours would shape domestic policy for years to come.

Figure 4 shows the extent of this political split. It uses twelve central cities and their surrounding suburbs to illustrate the sharply different voting patterns between Democrat John Kerry and Republican George Bush in the presidential election of 2004.

Figure 4 depicts a bifurcation of political behaviour. Cities are moving decisively towards the left and suburbs are moving just as decisively towards the right. Kerry won almost all the core cities, while Bush carried almost all the suburbs. These differences were not only very clear but also overwhelming. Kerry won upwards of 70 percent in eight out of twelve cities. Although Bush's victory in the suburbs was less substantial, he carried the suburban electorate by a comfortable margin. Moreover, cities that voted most heavily for Kerry were more densely populated, contained greater mixed uses, or held larger minority populations (Baltimore, New Orleans, New York, San Francisco, St Louis and Washington, DC) than those where Kerry's margins were slimmer (Indianapolis, Louisville, Nashville). In sum the more "urbane" the city, the more heavily it voted Democrat, while sprawled metropolitan areas outside the central city voted Republican in greater numbers. These observations are confirmed by exit polls and other studies that found a distinct relationship between the size of a jurisdiction and its political disposition. Cities, especially large cities, vote for candidates on the left (or in the American context, that are more "liberal") while smaller, less dense jurisdictions elect more "conservative" candidates on the right (Sauerzopf and Swanstrom 1999; Wolman and Marckini 2000).

Clear and polar social attitudes underlined these differences in voting behaviour. Core cities voted for the "liberal" candidate who favoured a greater degree of income redistribution, social welfare programs, and a separation between religion and state. By contrast, suburbs opted for the "conservative" candidate who favoured fewer restrictions on private enterprise, a less progressive tax system, fewer social programs, and a closer relationship with religion. By the year 2000, the highly polarized politics that once characterized the body politic of core cities was transferred into sharp distinction between jurisdictions.

Exactly why centrist Democrats, first under Gore and later under Kerry, could not prevail can be explained by structural (or underlying) factors as well as by apparent (or circumstantial) factors. From a structural point of view, American elections are decided in "winner-take-all" single-member districts. Proportional representation is virtually unknown, and there are no "run-offs" (second rounds)

Figure 4
Selected Central Cities and Suburbs 2004: Votes for President

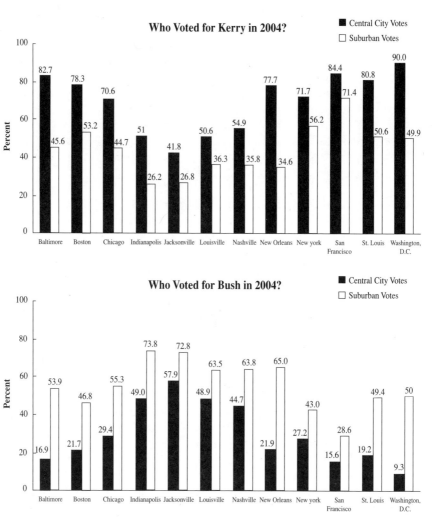

Source: H.V. Savitch, and R.K. Vogel, "L'hyperpluralisme des Villes aux Etats-Unis," 2006

in national elections. This encourages "forced majorities" that are channelled into one or two major parties, and this reduces the chances of minority candidates winning office. Constricted political choices often depress voting turnout among the least affluent sectors of the population. It is no coincidence that on average less than 60 percent of the population votes in national elections and about 30 percent of citizens vote in local elections.[7] Moreover, core cities hold only 30 percent of America's population, and opportunities for establishing coalitions outside these areas are limited.

Clinton was unable to pass the mantle in 2000 in a contested election, weakened by impeachment. Clinton's success was due in large measure to his own charismatic personality, his southern roots, and his ability to blend liberal ideology with market-based policies. Democratic coalitions cannot win in the cities alone. Few Democrats can garner votes in the suburbs and the South while retaining the central cities and minorities in the Midwest and Northeast. Even Clinton was unable to translate this into policies that were greatly beneficial to large cities. The locus of American national politics has shifted to the more conservative and Republican suburbs and exurbs.

10 MULTILEVEL GOVERNANCE AND THE FLOODING OF NEW ORLEANS

The 2005 disaster in New Orleans raises questions about the way the multilevel governance system actually operates and the effectiveness of current arrangements. Political scientist Brian Jones (1980) reminds us: "Delivering services is the primary function of municipal government. It occupies the vast bulk of the time and effort of most city employees, is the source of most contacts that citizens have with local government, occasionally becomes the subject of heated controversy, and is often surrounded by myth and misinformation. Yet, service delivery remains the "hidden function" of local government" (quoted from Melosi 2000, 1). In the modern era, delivering services may be a primary function of municipal governments, but the state and federal governments are certainly integral partners in financing and delivering those services, beginning with the basic physical infrastructure found in the city. In this section I review the basic contours of infrastructure support in the cities, provide background on emergency planning, and then examine the circumstances leading to the New Orleans flooding and the response, in order to explore the effectiveness of the system of multilevel governance in the United States.

10.1 INFRASTRUCTURE

Critical urban infrastructure includes water supply, sewerage, solid waste disposal, and transportation. Without sound physical infrastructure, a city cannot grow and prosper. Yet urban policymakers often neglect infrastructure placement, maintenance, and operations in favour of economic development policies, including glamour projects such as stadiums, arenas, and museums. Martin Melosi (2000, 10) highlights path dependence in understanding how choices in urban infrastructure today are linked to past choices and history.

The intergovernmental system in the United States is bound together by the grants-in-aid system established in the 1930s during Franklin D. Roosevelt's New Deal (Kleinberg 1995). Essentially, the national government agrees to appropriate federal dollars to serve national purposes. Initially, this was in the form of the categorical grants, with the federal government identifying national goals and establishing programs to further these goals. The state and local governments were to implement these programs. This partially explains the small size of federal employment when compared with that of state and local governments (see figure 1). Under categorical grants, the federal government typically picks up 80 percent of the costs of a program, and the state and local share is 20 percent. The initiative for applying for the grant remains with the local government as well as responsibility for administering the grant.

In the latter half of the twentieth century, metropolitan growth and sprawl led to concern over a crisis in city infrastructure. Older cities had deteriorating infrastructure while newer suburbs and the Sunbelt lacked infrastructure. In the past, urban infrastructure was a city problem. Now the city no longer contained the bulk of the urban population, yet county government, small cities, and unincorporated areas lacked the capacity or resources to plan, finance, build, or operate costly urban infrastructure. This coincided with a fiscal crisis in the larger cities of the Northeast and Midwest, which faced declining populations and revenue, related to deindustrialization. The cities looked to Washington for help. In the 1960s, Lyndon Johnson was eager to meet the need with a growing flow of federal aid that went directly to the cities, especially large cities in the Northeast and Midwest.

The revenue-sharing programs of the Nixon and Ford administrations also provided needed dollars but began to shift resources to the suburbs and the Sunbelt. Categorical grants for urban renewal, model cities, housing-code enforcement, water supply, and sewers were combined into the Housing and Community Development Block Grant. Revenue sharing was extended to eighty urban county governments in 1974. While central cities often had to use their revenue sharing to keep services afloat, suburbs were able to keep taxes low while building new infrastructure (Melosi 2000, 359).

In the 1980s, when the federal government under Reagan drastically reduced federal aid to cities while they were in the midst of severe economic and fiscal crisis, cities frequently stopped maintaining urban infrastructure. Melosi refers to this as a period of federal "disinvestment," with reports such as *America in Ruins: the Decaying Infrastructure* appearing (Melosi 2000, 359). The newly created Council on National Public Works Improvement, stemming from the *Public Works Improvement Act of 1984*, released a report, *Fragile Foundations*, that rated public works. The highest grade was a B for water, while a D was given to hazardous-waste cleanup. The reported investment in public works capital of $34 billion spent each year by state and local government and $25 billion by the federal government (1984 dollars) was deemed insufficient (ibid., 362).

A 1987 council study said the infrastructure crisis with regard to water supply was overblown and less federal subsidy was needed; rather, the greater need was said to be in the area of transportation. The amount needed was $2 trillion compared with $125 billion for water supply and $100 billion for waste water. Indeed, federal support for water and sewerage in the 1980s paled in comparison with state and local government support – $900 million versus $11.6 billion (Melosi 2000, 373, 378). The U.S. Conference of Mayors complains that there is still an infrastructure crisis. The mayors call for $295 billion over six years for transportation (TEA-21) (Thaniel and Rosenberg 2005). The mayors pointed to the

American Society of Civil Engineers' 2005 infrastructure report card, which found transit infrastructure went from a C– to D–, and road infrastructure improved slightly from a D- to a D. The five-year cost was pegged at $1.6 trillion.

Certainly, the federal government plays a significant role in financing and promoting urban infrastructure. This brief review has not even addressed federal support for airports and ports.

10.2 EMERGENCY PLANNING

The basic framework for emergency planning in the United States is premised on local, state, and national officials (1) preparing emergency plans for responding to disasters, (2) managing the response to the disaster, (3) ensuring recovery from the disaster, and (4) mitigating disasters or reducing their severity. Local officials are charged with basic planning and are the first responders to natural disasters. In response to local requests (or in the governor's own judgment), the governor requests the president to declare a disaster under national law whenever they are faced with a catastrophic disaster. "A catastrophic disaster is one that affects an entire nation and requires extraordinary resources and skills for recovery" (Hoetmer 1991, xviii). The federal government mandates state and local governments to undertake emergency planning, and it provides significant resources through grants to underwrite the emergency-planning offices in state and local governments. Once the president declares a national disaster, the Federal Emergency Planning Agency (FEMA) is expected to coordinate the federal response to the disaster, drawing upon the full resources of the national government. The state and local governments are expected to plan effectively, respond to local disasters, and request what assistance they may need from the federal government. The state governor has available the National Guard "to preserve peace, order, and public safety" (Durham and Suiter 1991, 110).

FEMA was created in 1978 under Jimmy Carter. The rationale for FEMA was to ensure that a single official was charged with overseeing emergency preparedness and response, with direct responsibility to the president (Durham and Suiter 1991, 112):

> As envisioned by the coalition of groups at the state and local levels that supported the reorganization, FEMA would become the lead agency – the central point of contact for emergency managers, volunteer agencies, business and industry, the fire service community, the law enforcement community, and other groups with responsibility for public safety and protection of property in the event of disaster. From a federal perspective, the reorganization would centralize planning and coordination for natural, technological, and civil hazards within one independent, lead federal agency. (ibid., 113)

10.3 HURRICANE KATRINA AND THE NEW ORLEANS FLOODING

On 29 August 2005, Hurricane Katrina came ashore with devastating effects on the Gulf Coast region, including Florida, Mississippi, Louisiana, and Alabama.

The course of the hurricane seemed to spare New Orleans from the worst of the storm. However, initial relief turned to horror as officials realized that dam levees were failing, leading to the flooding of 80 percent of the city (Federal Response to Hurricane Katrina: Lessons Learned 2005). Although most citizens evacuated, some 100,000 people were left behind, most of them poor and black. The city was ill prepared to evacuate so many people, and insufficient shelters or provisions were in place. About 25,000 people were trapped in the Superdome without enough water or food and with poor sanitary conditions. Another 20,000 people went to the Convention Center, which was never intended as a shelter (Comfort 2006, 501, 506).

Americans watched images on their televisions of survivors having to fend for themselves with no sign of local, state, or federal officials coming to the rescue. Many tried to leave on foot, crossing the Crescent City Convention Bridge, only to be turned back at gunpoint by sheriffs of Gretana, Louisiana, who apparently feared invasion by mobs of black looters (Comfort 2006, 506). Viewers had trouble believing that this was a disaster in a modern American city rather than in a Third World country. The hurricane was a natural disaster, but it appears that the flooding was the result of human disaster – an incomplete, poorly designed, poorly constructed and poorly maintained levee and flood-control system (ibid., 503). The costs of the disaster are estimated at between $100 billion and $150 billion, with 1,293 dead in New Orleans and southern Louisiana, and 306 dead in southern Mississippi (University of California, Berkeley 2006, 15–1).

A number of national commissions and studies have been undertaken to try to account for the disaster (see table 3). The Hurricane Pam exercise in the summer of 2004 warned that a category 3 hurricane would lead to the flooding of New Orleans with some 300,000 people "trapped" in the city (van Heerden 2004). The report highlighted the vulnerability of the city sitting below sea level. The exercise pointed to the need to develop "a long-term coastal restoration plan to ensure New Orleans' survival." Unfortunately, the city, state and federal government failed to act to address the issues that the Hurricane Pam exercise foreshadowed.

Following 9/11, the framework for emergency planning had been changed. The Office of Homeland Security was created, and FEMA and other agencies were brought under the new cabinet department's auspices. The emphasis of Homeland Security was on planning and responding to terrorism. Although FEMA has a role to play in this, as evidenced in the response to the destruction of the Twin Towers, FEMA lost its direct access to the president and Congress, since it was no longer an independent agency. As initial assessments are made regarding the disaster in New Orleans, the national reorganization certainly appears to have significance (Stehr 2006, 21). The testimony of Michael Brown, former FEMA head, before a congressional committee pointed out that FEMA was down one-fourth of its workforce and that Secretary Michael Chernoff of Homeland Security did not support FEMA budget requests for equipment and personnel. The testimony also highlighted the Republican view of the president and Congress that the federal government take a secondary role in emergency planning and response. Of course, this explanation does not match the expectations of citizens and emergency-planning laws that the federal government respond when the scale of the disaster overwhelms state and local capacity or resources.

Table 3
Studies Analysing the New Orleans Flood

	Findings
U.S. Army Corps of Engineers	Most of the flooding should not have occurred and was due to "breaches in floodwalls and levees." Flood protections system "did not perform as a system." No redundancy in the system; pumps not operating. "Incompleteness of the system." "Inconsistent levels of protection" and problems with materials, design, and construction.
U.C. Berkeley-led Independent Levee Investigation Team (NSF Study)	"The resulting catastrophe had its roots in three main causes: (1) a major natural disaster (the Hurricane itself), (2) the poor performance of the flood protection system due to localized engineering failures, questionable judgments, errors, etc. involved in the detailed design, construction, operation, and maintenance of the system, and (3) more global 'organizational' and institutional problems associated with the governmental and local organizations responsible for the design, construction, operation, maintenance and funding of the overall flood protection system." Among the failures related to governance were (1) "failures of foresight" to prepare for hurricanes, (2) "failures of organization" which "lacked centralized and focused responsibility and authority for providing adequate flood protection," (3) "failures of resource allocation" with state and federal governments failing to fund many Army Corps of Engineers projects and pursuing less expensive solutions, (4) "failures of diligence" in completing the flood protection system set up following Hurricane Betsy in 1965, "failures of decision making" emphasizing "efficiency" over "effectiveness" to save costs, (5) "failures of management" with the Corps reducing its focus on flood control and "engineering quality" as it responded to other agendas pushed on it, (6) "failures of synthesis" in failing to recognized that the parts did not equal a whole, and (7) "failures of risk assessment and management" in underestimating the "risks (likelihoods and consequences) associated with hurricane surge and wave induced flooding."
Senate Homeland Security and Governmental Affairs Committee	The report pointed to "the failure of government at all levels to plan, prepare for and respond aggressively to the storm ... Among the many factors that contributed to these failures were four overarching ones: (1) long-term warnings went unheeded and government officials neglected their duties to prepare for a forewarned catastrophe; (2) government officials took insufficient actions or made poor decisions in the days immediately before and after landfall; (3) systems on which officials relied on to support their response effort failed; and (4) government officials at all levels failed to provide effective leadership. These individual failures, moreover, occurred against a backdrop of failure, over time, to develop the capacity for a coordinated, national response to a truly catastrophic event, whether caused by nature or man-made."

Sources:
U.S. Army Corps of Engineers, *Performance Evaluation of the New Orleans and Southeast Louisiana Hurricane Protection System, Draft Final Report of the Interagency Performance Evaluation Task Force, Volume I—Executive Summary and Overview,* 1 June 2006
University of California, Berkeley, *Investigation of the Performance of the New Orleans Flood Protection Systems in Hurricane Katrina on August 29, 2005 (Draft Final Report Version 1.2 June 1, 2006) Volume I: Main Text and Executive Summary*
Committee on Homeland Security and Governmental Affairs, United States Senate, "Hurricane Katrina: A Nation Still Unprepared," May 2006

In the case of New Orleans, the flood destroyed the local communication and transportation infrastructure. This raises certain questions: Why did some first responders abandon their posts? Why did others lack the resources or ability to assess the situation and intervene? The state also was ill-prepared to deal with the storm. Some amount of blame for the disaster rests with local officials. Researchers Peter Burns and Matthew Thomas (2006) consider that the failure to evacuate the city and deal with the immediate crisis facing the citizens can be traced to a poorly developed local governing coalition or regime. The mayor had few networks or established patterns of relations to draw upon to help evacuate the city, to relate to state and federal officials, or to call in the aid and resources of private and non-governmental agencies that could assist him. The lack of trust and bonds was an obstacle. Mayor Ray Nagin waited until Sunday morning, 28 August 2005, to order a mandatory evacuation of New Orleans. He wanted to consult the city's attorneys, fearful that the city could be held liable for business losses resulting from evacuation (Brinkley 2006, 22–23). The city had no plan for evacuating poor and elderly residents of the city, in spite of the Hurricane Pam exercise the previous year. The mayor had no emergency communications and did not even stay at the city's emergency operations command post at City Hall. Apparently, the city had no satellite telephones available, even though it had received a "$7 million grant to connect all first responders like ambulance drivers, police, and firemen" (ibid., 216). The city had a mobile command centre in an eighteen-wheeler, but it was not prepositioned out of the city in advance (ibid., 108).

There is also concern that the state had insufficient National Guard and equipment available because of the Iraq War. However, an additional problem was that the National Guard was based at Jackson Barracks in the city and was itself flooded and unable to respond effectively (Brinkley 2006). Additional obstacles to the state being the lynchpin to make the intergovernmental system work were that Governor Blanco (Democrat) had poor relations with the mayor (Democrat), who had endorsed the Republican opponent in the governor's election and that the governor also distrusted the president and resisted the calls to federalize the National Guard.

Others, such as urbanist Peter Dreier, point a finger more directly at the federal government and the ideology of conservatives such as President Bush who favour market solutions over government action, thus eroding the capacity of governments at all levels to act positively, provide effective services, and address urban problems. He says:

> Katrina was a human-made disaster more than a natural disaster. The conditions that led to the disaster, and the response by government officials, were the result of policy choices. Government incompetence was an outgrowth of a more serious indifference to the plight of cities and the poor. As a result, the opportunity to reconstruct New Orleans as part of a bold regional renewal plan was lost. Whatever positive things happen in Katrina's aftermath will be due, in large measure, to the long-term work of grassroots community and union-organizing groups who mobilized quickly to provide a voice for the have-nots and who found allies among professionals to

help formulate alternative plans to those developed by business and political elites. (Dreier 2006, 528)

Dreier denounces the Bush administration for its "crony capitalism" and its reliance on "disaster profiteers" to rebuild the Gulf area (ibid., 533). He cites the fact that many no-bid contracts worth billions of dollars went to companies such as Kellogg Brown & Root, which is a subsidiary of Haliburton with little effort being made to steer rebuilding jobs and resources to New Orleaners. He also points out that the president suspended the Davis-Bacon law to allow companies to avoid paying prevailing wages (union level), thus lowering wages. For Dreier, the real tragedy is that the rebuilding effort in New Orleans could have set the stage for really dealing with urban problems in America. With more than $100 billion in federal money going towards the rebuilding of housing, schools, transportation, parks, and commercial redevelopment, there was an opportunity to cooperate, and in a democratic fashion, set a vision for rebuilding the city and the region. Moreover, the disaster could have led to a more ambitious urban agenda that would provide a model for cities throughout the nation with the return of a federal partner for cities.

In the aftermath of the storm, Governor Blanco created the Louisiana Recovery Authority to lead the effort to restore the economy, rebuild housing, and assist in the recovery of New Orleans and Louisiana. Mayor Ray Nagin has created the Bring New Orleans Back Commission to develop a master plan to direct federal and state aid in order to ensure New Orleans' recovery. Burns and Thomas (2006) are hopeful that these may lead to a stronger regime that will govern New Orleans more effectively. However, they acknowledge a lack of consensus about the rebuilding agenda. Serious concern remains about whom the city will serve and whether the African American majority will return. The mayor was widely criticized for his speech calling for the return of a *"chocolate"* city. However, many blacks fear that there is an agenda to prevent New Orleans from being an African American city by depriving the poorer black residents the location or means to return. The federal government, the state, and the city still appear to have divergent agendas, and coordination remains weak.

11 ASSESSING MULTILEVEL GOVERNANCE IN THE UNITED STATES

Hurricane Katrina and the flooding of New Orleans in August 2005 revealed significant weaknesses in the intergovernmental system to deal with emergency planning. First, the current federal budget process that supports emergency response emphasizes response and recovery over mitigation and preparedness (Donahue and Joyce 2001, 728). The failure of the levee system and the difficulty of evacuating New Orleans and the Gulf of Mexico region were anticipated in a simulation exercise in 2004. Moreover, the levee system was built to protect New Orleans from a category 3 hurricane, not a category 5. Little effort had been made to plan or mitigate for likely flooding in New Orleans. Observers had warned of the consequences of the decline in the coastal wetlands as a brake on a hurricane, as well as the migration of the population to coastal regions. Local, state, and national officials were unprepared to deal with the disaster. While the specific failures of various officials, agencies, and systems is likely to be studied in detail over the next several years, the intergovernmental system and lack of coordination are undoubtedly a major part of the story.

Local, state, and federal officials have been hard pressed to develop effective multilevel governance. State and local officials have had fiscal difficulties related to declining federal support and a sluggish economy. Citizens are reluctant to raise taxes although they desire increased public services. The challenge for modern government is to improve coordination across (horizontal) and between (vertical) levels of government. The federal government has not developed a coherent urban policy for municipalities. Agencies of the federal government and the operation of Congress lead to a fragmented approach to policymaking. State and local governments respond to the myriad of regulations and grants provided by the federal government rather than forming their own policies. The United States is ambivalent about cities and the people who live in them. The U.S. system of government does not encourage policymakers to develop coherent and long-term policy for cities.

The U.S. system of local government is fragmented and varied across the fifty states. The American political system places a high regard on localism. The orientation of citizens and decision makers is that decisions should be made at the level closest to the people (the principle of subsidiarity). The political structure reinforces this normative orientation. With the exception of the president and governor, all elected officials in the U.S. represent local districts. This leads to parochialism and difficulty in forging clear national, state, or local agendas or priorities. As Charles Lindblom pointed out, the American system values incrementalism over rational-comprehensive decision making. As problems become more complex and as organizations do too, coordination becomes more difficult. While hierarchy once presented the means to develop coordination, increasing centralization leads to less information and often to greater challenges for coordination.

Increasingly, political scientists refer to "governance" rather than "government". This shift is indicative of the need to find ways to coordinate agencies and actors in the intergovernmental system as well as coordination between the public and private sectors. In U.S. policymaking, this can be seen in the advent of Metropolitan Planning Organizations (MPOs) that tie together numerous actors in local, state, national, and private and non-profit sectors concerned with transportation planning (Vogel and Nezelkewicz 2002). While MPOs have stimulated greater dialogue among diverse interests in transportation planning, they have not necessarily led to improved governance. Transportation planning is still disjointed, and much financing for transportation policies flows to communities outside the formal transportation funding process. For example, the Big Dig in Boston is best viewed as a pork barrel project and not a rational transportation policy emerging from a coordinated intergovernmental system (Altshuler and Luberoff 2003, chs. 4 and 9).

The system of multilevel governance is not producing good public policy at the municipal or urban level. Municipal officials say the federal government provides too few resources and continues to scale back its commitment. The municipal officials view state officials – the beneficiaries of national New Federalism policies – as obstacles to improved urban governance. State officials often divert money, which the federal officials had intended to benefit cities (e.g., Homeland Security), and mayors often have strained relations with governors. Federal and state officials tend to view local and municipal officials as corrupt and incompetent, and in need of close monitoring.

Municipal officials have generally adjusted to the unlikelihood of national or state support. Most cities have strong-mayor systems in place. American mayors can and do the "impossible" with limited resources. In many cities, the mayor takes the lead role in organizing a local regime to mobilize the resources of large local businesses and foundations to support community development that is beyond the resources of the city treasury (Stone 1989). Mayors recruit business, redevelop their cities, and attempt to ensure that their cities thrive in the world economy. Of course, there are trade-offs, and many fear that local democracy suffers as public-private partnerships become the norm. Although these partnerships have led to revitalized central business districts, the poor have not benefited significantly from these policies (Squires 1989; Cummings 1988; Kantor 1988).

The New Orleans flood had the potential to propel dramatic changes in the American federal system and politics. In the past, large-scale national disasters have sometimes led to significant political change. For example, the destruction of Galveston, Texas in the early 1900s greatly accelerated the local government reform movement. The debate ensuing from the New Orleans disaster is likely to raise questions about whether New Federalism policies, including declining federal support for cities and urban problems, have gone too far. The slow federal response and the severe poverty and racial disparities were laid bare by the disaster. However, the structural and demographic conditions that undermine political support for more socially centred urban policy are unchanged. The more conservative suburbs remain. Further, the national government once again faces large structural deficits because of tax cuts, the Iraq War, and higher costs for health care. Even if Democrats were to be returned to office, they would face similar problems to those that Clinton experienced in the absence of resources and a strong mandate.

Mayors may be able to develop intergovernmental regimes if they find willing partners at the state and national levels. In recent years, the mayors have not found these governments willing to support their efforts to a significant degree. The national government denies responsibility for the problems of large cities, suggesting that these are a function of failed liberal policies, profligate mayors, and a culture of poverty. Compassionate conservatism has proved to be more rhetorical than real. Indeed, the failure of FEMA to respond effectively to the

New Orleans flooding partly reflects a shift in national policy orientation – that Washington plays a supporting rather than leading role in national-disaster relief.

Nonetheless, mayors will likely accept the challenge to try. It is instructive to American politics to notice that the mayor of New Orleans is not reticent to lecture the president or the governor. Moreover, in 2005 the mayor defied reluctant federal and state officials to bring the citizens of New Orleans back even before the levees and the infrastructure or housing are rebuilt. The mayor knew that he had the media's attention and that the window for action was short. A mayor without a people is quickly relegated to irrelevancy. The mayor is keeping pressure on the national government to follow through on its commitment to rebuild New Orleans. This is a lesson that American mayors may teach to municipal officials in other countries. Political authority may derive less from formal grants than from political entrepreneurship and politics. In this regard, American mayors excel. The national government may or may not keep its commitment to fund the rebuilding. On the one hand, the Republican dominated 109th Congress (2005–2006) wanted to fulfill the president's promise. On the other hand, it said that tax cuts must not be undone and that funds for rebuilding New Orleans will have to come at the expense of Medicare and Medicaid.

12 CONCLUSION

Multilevel governance has been proposed as a new framework for understanding intergovernmental relations in nations and the place of cities in the federal order. However, this analytical perspective implies a cooperative system of intergovernmental relations. In the United States, from the 1930s to about the 1970s, there was a liberal Democratic consensus about the shared responsibilities of the federal, state, and local governments in domestic policies and cities. The consensus eroded in the 1970s and 1980s as congressional and presidential elections were decided in suburbs, small towns, and rural communities. A new Republican and conservative consensus has emerged that endorses more limited government. Although the federal government continues to play a strong role in domestic policy, the federal partnership with cities has completely evaporated. In place of cooperative federalism, we now have "coercive" or "fend-for-yourself" federalism, which are apparent in the response to the disaster in New Orleans.

Under New Federalism, the central government looks to markets and a strong economy to drive all other domestic policies. State and local governments must follow suit. In good economic times, such as the mid to late 1990s, state and local governments were flush with resources. In periods of recession, such as the opening years of the twenty-first century, state and local governments were forced to cut services and defer infrastructure and maintenance. The case of New Orleans dramatically illustrated the continuing urban crisis of concentrated poverty and the racial inequality in American cities. No level of government is seriously addressing these problems in the cities, and for this reason the current multilevel governance system must be judged poorly. Since the problems are linked to structural features of American politics, multilevel governance is unlikely to improve.

Although disasters may precipitate change, the incipient problems of cities have been exposed before – in the Miami Riot of 1980 and the Los Angeles Riot of 1992. In these instances, the federal, state, and local (county and cities) governments vowed in the short term to tackle severe inner-city problems but failed to take concrete action. Few expect New Orleans to change this.

Finally, although the focus of this paper is on multilevel governance and obstacles to good public policy in the cities, the disaster in New Orleans reveals that incompetent political leaders and politicization of the bureaucracy at all three levels of government may be equally important in understanding the failure to prepare for and respond to the hurricane and flooding. The president, the governor, and the mayor failed to demonstrate strong or effective leadership. Heads of critical federal, state, and local agencies had little professional qualifications or experience, and the bureaucracy of all three were highly politicized, thus undermining the coordination necessary to make a federal system work (Koven and Brennan, forthcoming).

NOTES

1 Dillon's Rule is followed in thirty-nine of the fifty states, with thirty-one always applying Dillon's Rule and eight applying it to some municipalities (Richardson, Gough, and Puentes, 2003, 17–18). The states that do not follow Dillon's Rule are Alaska, Iowa, Massachusetts, New Jersey, New Mexico, Ohio, Oregon, South Carolina, and Utah (ibid., appendix A).

2 By examining city budgets, we can get a rough indication of the responsibilities of cities in the United States. However, analysing U.S. city budgets is not an exact science. The Census of Governments collects data on city finances annually by surveying cities, but the quality of the data is uneven. City officials have little incentive to ensure that the data provided to the Census of Governments is accurate, and there is no way of knowing who actually reported the data for each city; it may be an intern or it may be the budget director. In addition, each city uses its own budget categories and must translate these into the general classifications of the Census of Governments. This requires assigning budget items to categories and involves a great deal of discretion and, probably, guesswork. The ideal data source of city budgeting would be each city's individual annual budget. However, an analyst would need to make judgments with little direct knowledge of their accuracy.

3 Twenty-four of the twenty-five largest cities provided parks and recreation and housing and community development; twenty-one of the twenty-five provided health and hospitals, and all twenty-five provided the rest of the listed services.

4 Calculated from U.S. Census Bureau, *Statistical Abstract of the United States: 2004–2005*, table 449, "City Governments: Revenue for Largest Cities: 2001."

5 Globalization is frequently cited as a factor in the rescaling of the state (Newman and Thornley 2005; Brenner 2004). City-regions – not cities – are the territory around which local economic development strategy is oriented. This leads federal, state, and local officials to think about reorganizing territorial boundaries (e.g., annexation, city-county consolidation) to enhance economic opportunity. However, formal boundary adjustment

or the creation of metropolitan governments is unlikely in the United States (Savitch and Vogel 2006a).

6 This section is drawn from Savitch and Vogel (2006b).

7 Voting turnout in the 2004 election was relatively high, reaching 60.7 percent (McDonald, 2005).

REFERENCES

Altshuler, Alan, and David Luberoff. 2003. *Mega-Projects: The Changing Politics of Urban Public Investment*. Washington, DC: Brookings Institution

Barnes, William R. 2005. "Beyond Federal Urban Policy." *Urban Affairs Review* 5:575–89

Barnes, William R., and Larry C. Ledebur. 1993. *The New Regional Economies: The U.S. Common Market and the Global Economy*. Thousand Oaks, Calif.: Sage

Beaumont, Enid F. 1996. "Domestic Consequences of Internationalization." In *Globalization and Decentralization,* ed. Jong S. Jun and Deil S. Wright, 374–87. Washington, DC: Georgetown University Press

Bilmes, Linda, and Joseph Stiglitz. 2006. "The Economic Costs of the Iraq War: An Appraisal Three Years after the Beginning of the Conflict." Cambridge, Mass.: John F. Kennedy School of Government. Online at www.ksgnotes1.harvard.edu/Research/wpaper.nsf/rwp/RWP06-002

Bowman, Ann M., and George A. Krause. 2003. "Power Shift Measuring Policy Centralization in U.S. Intergovernmental Relations, 1947–1998." *American Politics Research* 31:301–25

Brenner, Neil. 2004. *New State Spaces: Urban Governance and the Rescaling of Statehood*. Oxford: Oxford University Press

Brinkley, Douglas. 2006. *The Great Deluge: Hurricane Katrina, New Orleans, and the Mississippi Gulf Coast*. New York: William Morrow

Burns, Peter, and Matthew Thomas. 2006. "The Failure of the Nonregime: How Katrina Exposed New Orleans as a Regimeless City." *Urban Affairs Review* 41 (4): 517–27

Caraley, Demetrios. 1992. "Washington Abandons the Cities." *Political Science Quarterly* 10:1–30

Comfort, Louise. 2006. "Cities at Risk: Hurricane Katrina and the Drowning of New Orleans." *Urban Affairs Review* 41 (4): 510–16

Corsi, Jerome. 2006. "North American Union Would Trump U.S. Supreme Court." www.vivelecanada.ca/article.php/20060620071235810

Cummings, Scott, ed. 1988. *Business Elites and Urban Development*. Albany: State University of New York Press

DiGaetano, Alan. 1991. "Urban Political Reform: Did It Kill the Machine?" *Journal of Urban History* 18:37–67.

Donahue, Amy K., and Philip G. Joyce. 2001. "A Framework for Analyzing Emergency Management with an Application to Federal Budgeting," *Public Administration Review* 6:728–40.

Dreier, Peter, John Mollenkopf, and Todd Swanstrom. 2001. *Place Matters: Metropolitics for the Twenty-first Century*, 2nd edn. Lawrence, Kans.: University of Kansas Press

Durham, Tom, and Lacy E. Suiter. 1991. "Perspectives and Roles of the State and Federal Governments." In *Emergency Management: Principles and Practice for Local Government*, ed. Thomas E. Drabek and Gerard J. Hoetmer, 101–27. Washington, DC: International City Management Association

Eisinger, Peter. 1998. "City Politics in an Era of Federal Devolution." *Urban Affairs Review* 33 (3): 308–25

– 2004. "The American City in the Age of Terror: A Preliminary Assessment of the Effects of September 11." *Urban Affairs Review* 40:115–30.

Florida, Richard. 2005. *Cities and the Creative Class*. New York, NY: Routledge

Frisken, Frances, and Donald F. Norris. 2001. "Regionalism Reconsidered." *Journal of Urban Affairs* 23 (5): 467–78

Gale, William, and Samara R. Potter. 2002. "The Bush Tax Cut: One Year Later." Policy Brief no. 101. Washington, DC: Brookings Institution

Global Insight. 2006. *The Role of Metro Areas in the U.S. Economy*. Lexington, Mass.: Global Insight

Hobbs, Heidi. 1994. *City Hall Goes Abroad: The Foreign Policy of Local Politics*. Thousand Oaks, Calif.: Sage

Hoene, Christopher, and Michael Pagano. 2003. "Fend-for-Yourself Federalism: The Impact of State and Federal Deficits on America's Cities." *Government Finance Review*, 37–42

Hoetmer, Gerard J. 1991. "Introduction." In *Emergency Management: Principles and Practice for Local Government*, ed. Thomas E. Drabek and Gerard J. Hoetmer. Washington, DC: International City Management Association

Hooghe, Liesbet, and Gary Marks. 2003. "Unraveling the Central State, but How? Types of Multi-level Governance." *American Political Science Review* 97:233–43

Kantor, Paul. 1988. *The Dependent City: The Changing Political Economy of Urban America*. Glenview, Ill. Scott Foresman

Kincaid, John. 1996. "From Dual to Coercive Federalism in American Intergovernmental Relations." In *Globalization and Decentralization: Institutional Contexts, Policy Issues, and Intergovernmental Relations in Japan and the United States*, ed. Jong S. Jun and Deil S. Wright 29–47. Washington, DC: Georgetown University Press

– 1997. "Global Interdependence and Local Independence in American Federalism." In *Future Challenges of Local Autonomy in Japan, Korea, and the United States*, ed. Fukashi Horie and Masaru Nishio, 371–88. Tokyo: National Institute for Research Advancement

– 1999. "De Facto Devolution and Urban Defunding: The Priority of Persons Over Places." *Journal of Urban Affairs* 21:135–67

Kleinberg, Benjamin. 1995. *Urban America in Transformation: Perspectives on Urban Policy and Development*. Thousand Oaks, Calif.: Sage

Koven, Steven G., and Michael Brennan. Forthcoming 2007. "Hurricane Katrina: Preparedness, Response and the Politics Administration Dichotomy." In *Handbook of Crisis and Emergency Management*, ed. Ali Farazmand. New York: Marcel Dekker, Inc.

Krane, Dale, Planton N. Rigos, and Melvin Hill. 2001. *Home Rule in America: A Fifty-State Handbook*. Washington, DC: Congressional Quarterly

Lang, Diane. 1991. "Dillon's Rule ... and the Birth of Home Rule." *Municipal Reporter*. www.nmml.org/Dillon.pdf

McDonald, Michael. 2005. *United States Elections Project: Voter Turnout*. George Mason University. www.elections.gmu.edu/Voter_Turnout_2004.html

McGirr, Lisa. 2001. *Suburban Warriors: The Origins of the New American Right*. Princeton, NJ: Princeton University Press

Melosi, Martin V. 2000. *The Sanitary City*. Baltimore: Johns Hopkins University Press

National League of Cities. 2005. *The State of America's Cities 2005*. Washington, DC

Newman, Peter, and Andrew Thornley. 2005. *Planning World Cities: Globalization and Urban Politics*. New York City, NY: Palgrave Macmillan

Nivola, Pietro S. 2003. "Fiscal Millstones on the Cities: Revisiting the Problem of Federal Mandates." Policy Brief no. 122. Washington, DC: The Brookings Institution

Orfield, Myron. 1997. *Metropolitics*. Washington, DC: Brookings Institution

Pagano, Michael. 1999. "Metropolitan Limits: Intrametropolitan Disparities and Governance in U.S. Laboratories of Democracy. In *Governance and Opportunity in Metropolitan America*, ed. Alan Altshuler et al., 253–9. Washington, DC: National Academy Press

Peirce, Neal R., Curtis W. Johnson, and Stuart Hall. 1993. *Citistates: How Urban America Can Prosper in a Competitive World*. Washington, DC: Seven Locks Press

Richardson Jr, Jesse J., Meghan Z. Gough, and Robert Puentes. 2003. *Is Home Rule the Answer? Clarifying the Influence of Dillon's Rule on Growth Management*. Washington, DC: Brookings Institute

Rudoren, Jodi, and Aron Pilhofer. 2006. "Hiring Federal Lobbyists, Towns Learn, Money Talks." New York Times, 2 July. Online at www.nytimes.com/2006/07/02/washington/02earmarks.html?ex=1309492800&en=c4371dd2dab7497c&ei=5088&partner=rssnyt&emc=rss

Rusk, David. 1995. *Cities without Suburbs*, 2nd edn. Washington, DC: Woodrow Wilson Center Press

Sauerzopf, Richard, and Todd Swanstrom. 1999. "The Urban Electorate in Presidential Elections." *Urban Affairs Review* 35:72–91

Savitch, Hank V. 2003. "Does 9-11 Portend a New Paradigm for Cities?" *Urban Affairs Review* 39 (1): 103–27

Savitch, H.V., and Ronald K. Vogel. 2005. "The United States: Executive-Centred Politics." In *Comparing Local Governance, ed. Bas Denters and Lawrence Rose*, 211–27. Basingstoke, Hampshire: Palgrave Macmillan

Savitch, Hank V. and Ronald K. Vogel. 2006a. "Local and Regional Governance: Rescaling the City." In *Metropolitan Governing: Canadian Cases, Comparative Lessons*, ed. Eran Razin and Patrick J. Smith, 214–45. Jerusalem: Hebrew University Magnus Press

– 2006b. L'hyperpluralisme revisité: la poursuite de la fragmentation des villes aux Etats-Unis." In *Les métropoles au défi de la diversité culturelle*, ed. Bernard Jouve and Alain-G. Gagnon, 193–222. Grenoble: Presses Universitaires de Grenoble

– 1996. *Regional Politics: America in a Post-City Age* (Urban Affairs Annual Reviews no. 45). Thousand Oaks, Calif.: Sage

Savitch, H.V., David Collins, Daniel Sanders, and John P. Markham. 1993. "Ties that Bind: Central Cities, Suburbs, and the New Metropolitan Region." *Economic Development Quarterly* 7 (4): 341–57

Scammon, Richard, and Ben J. Wattenberg. 1971. *The Real Majority*. New York: Coward, McCann and Geoghegan

Scott, Allen J., ed. 2001. *Global City-Regions: Trends, Theory, Policy*. Oxford: Oxford University Press

Self, Peter. 2000. *Rolling Back the Market: Economic Dogma and Political Choice*. Basingstoke, Hampshire: Macmillan

Squires, Gregory. 1989. "Public Private Partnerships: Who Gets What and Why." In *Unequal Partnerships: The Political Economy of Urban Redevelopment in Postwar America*, ed. Gregory Squires, 1–11. New Brunswick: Rutgers University Press

Stehr, Steven D. 2006. "The Political Economy of Disaster." *Urban Affairs Review* 41:492–500

Stone, Clarence N. 1989. *Regime Politics: Governing Atlanta 1946–1988*. Lawrence, Kans.: University of Kansas Press

Streeter, Sandy. 2004. *Earmarks and Limitations in Appropriations Bills*. CRS Report for Congress, order code 98–518 GOV, Congressional Research Service

Thaniel, Ron, and Brett Rosenberg. 2005. "Mayors Nickels, Palmer, Wallace Call in Urgent Federal Investment in City Transportation, Water Infrastructure." The United States Conference of Mayors, 27 June. www.usmayors.org/uscm/us_mayor_newspaper/documents/06_27_05/water_survey.asp

University of California, Berkeley. 2006. *Investigation of the Performance of the New Orleans Flood Protection Systems in Hurricane Katrina on August 29, 2005*. www.ce.berkeley.edu/~new_orleans

Van Heerden, Ivor L. 2004. "Coastal Land Loss: Hurricanes and New Orleans." Baton Rouge, La.: Center for the Study of Public Health Impacts of Hurricanes, LSU Hurricane Center, Louisiana State University

Vogel, Ronald K. 2000. "Globalization and the American Metropolis." *Comprehensive Urban Studies* 71:257–64

Vogel, Ronald K., and John J. Harrigan. 2007. *Political Change in the Metropolis*, 8th edn. New York: Longman

Vogel, Ronald K., and Norman Nezelkewicz. 2002. "Metropolitan Planning Organizations and the New Regionalism: The Case of Louisville." *Publius* 32:107–29

Warner, Mildred, and Jennifer Gerbasi. 2004. "Rescaling and Reforming the State under NAFTA: Implications for Subnational Authority." *International Journal of Urban and Regional Research* 28:858–73

Washington Post. 2006. "Up to Their Earmarks." 27 January. Online at www.washingtonpost.com/wpdyn/content/graphic/2006/01/27/GR2006012700168.html

Waste, Robert J. 1998. *Independent Cities: Rethinking U.S. Urban Policy*. New York: Oxford University Press

Weir, Margaret, Harold Wolman, and Todd Swanstrom. 2005. "The Calculus of Coalitions: Cities, Suburbs, and the Metropolitan Agenda." *Urban Affairs Review* 40:730–60

White House. 2005. *Federal Response to Hurricane Katrina: Lessons Learned*. Washington DC: The White House. Online at www.whitehouse.gov/reports/katrina-lessons-learned.pdf

Wolman, Harold, and Lisa Marckini. 2000. "The Effect of Place on Legislative Roll Voting: The Case of Central City Representatives in the U.S. House." *Social Science Quarterly* 81:764–81

Queen's Policy Studies
Recent Publications

The Queen's Policy Studies Series is dedicated to the exploration of major public policy issues that confront governments and society in Canada and other nations.

Our books are available from good bookstores everywhere, including the Queen's University bookstore (http://www.campusbookstore.com/). McGill-Queen's University Press is the exclusive world representative and distributor of books in the series. A full catalogue and ordering information may be found on their web site (http://mqup.mcgill.ca/).

School of Policy Studies

Fulfilling Potential, Creating Success: Perspectives on Human Capital Development, Garnett Picot, Ron Saunders and Arthur Sweetman (eds.), 2007
Paper ISBN 1-55339-127-6   Cloth ISBN 1-55339-128-4

Reinventing Canadian Defence Procurement: A View from the Inside, Alan S. Williams, 2006
Paper ISBN 0-9781693-0-1 (Published in association with Breakout Educational Network)

SARS in Context: Memory, History, Policy, Jacalyn Duffin and Arthur Sweetman (eds.), 2006
Paper ISBN 0-7735-3194-7 Cloth ISBN 0-7735-3193-9

Dreamland: How Canada's Pretend Foreign Policy has Undermined Sovereignty, Roy Rempel, 2006
Paper ISBN 1-55339-118-7 Cloth ISBN 1-55339-119-5 (Published in association with Breakout Educational Network)

Canadian and Mexican Security in the New North America: Challenges and Prospects, Jordi Díez (ed.), 2006   Paper ISBN 1-55339-123-3 Cloth ISBN 1-55339-122-7

Global Networks and Local Linkages: The Paradox of Cluster Development in an Open Economy, David A. Wolfe and Matthew Lucas (eds.), 2005
Paper ISBN 1-55339-047-4 Cloth ISBN 1-55339-048-2

Choice of Force: Special Operations for Canada, David Last and Bernd Horn (eds.), 2005
Paper ISBN 1-55339-044-X Cloth ISBN 1-55339-045-8

Force of Choice: Perspectives on Special Operations, Bernd Horn, J. Paul de B. Taillon, and David Last (eds.), 2004   Paper ISBN 1-55339-042-3 Cloth 1-55339-043-1

New Missions, Old Problems, Douglas L. Bland, David Last, Franklin Pinch, and Alan Okros (eds.), 2004   Paper ISBN 1-55339-034-2 Cloth 1-55339-035-0

The North American Democratic Peace: Absence of War and Security Institution-Building in Canada-US Relations, 1867-1958, Stéphane Roussel, 2004
Paper ISBN 0-88911-937-6 Cloth 0-88911-932-2

Implementing Primary Care Reform: Barriers and Facilitators, Ruth Wilson, S.E.D. Shortt and John Dorland (eds.), 2004   Paper ISBN 1-55339-040-7 Cloth 1-55339-041-5

Social and Cultural Change, David Last, Franklin Pinch, Douglas L. Bland, and Alan Okros (eds.), 2004   Paper ISBN 1-55339-032-6 Cloth 1-55339-033-4

Clusters in a Cold Climate: Innovation Dynamics in a Diverse Economy, David A. Wolfe and Matthew Lucas (eds.), 2004   Paper ISBN 1-55339-038-5 Cloth 1-55339-039-3

John Deutsch Institute for the Study of Economic Policy

Health Services Restructuring in Canada: New Evidence and New Directions, Charles M. Beach, Richard P. Chaykowksi, Sam Shortt, France St-Hilaire and Arthur Sweetman (eds.), 2006
Paper ISBN 1-55339-076-8 Cloth ISBN 1-55339-075-X

A Challenge for Higher Education in Ontario, Charles M. Beach (ed.), 2005
Paper ISBN 1-55339-074-1 Cloth ISBN 1-55339-073-3

Current Directions in Financial Regulation, Frank Milne and Edwin H. Neave (eds.), Policy Forum Series no. 40, 2005   Paper ISBN 1-55339-072-5 Cloth ISBN 1-55339-071-7

Higher Education in Canada, Charles M. Beach, Robin W. Boadway and R. Marvin McInnis (eds.), 2005   Paper ISBN 1-55339-070-9 Cloth ISBN 1-55339-069-5

Financial Services and Public Policy, Christopher Waddell (ed.), 2004
Paper ISBN 1-55339-068-7 Cloth ISBN 1-55339-067-9

The 2003 Federal Budget: Conflicting Tensions, Charles M. Beach and Thomas A. Wilson (eds.), Policy Forum Series no. 39, 2004
Paper ISBN 0-88911-958-9 Cloth ISBN 0-88911-956-2

Our publications may be purchased at leading bookstores, including the Queen's University Bookstore (http://www.campusbookstore.com/), or can be ordered directly from: McGill-Queen's University Press, c/o Georgetown Terminal Warehouses, 34 Armstrong Avenue, Georgetown, Ontario L7G 4R9; Tel: (877) 864-8477; Fax: (877) 864-4272; E-mail: orders@gtwcanada.com

For more information about new and backlist titles from Queen's Policy Studies, visit the McGill-Queen's University Press web site at: **http://mqup.mcgill.ca/** OR to place an order, go to: **http://mqup.mcgill.ca/ordering.php**

Institute of Intergovernmental Relations
Recent Publications

Available from McGill-Queen's University Press:

Canada: The State of the Federation 2004, vol. 18, *Municipal-Federal-Provincial Relations in Canada*, Robert Young and Christian Leuprecht (eds.), 2006
Paper ISBN 1-55339-015-6 Cloth ISBN 1-55339-016-4

Canadian Fiscal Federalism: What Works, What Might Work Better, Harvey Lazar (ed.), 2005
Paper ISBN 1-55339-012-1 Cloth ISBN 1-55339-013-X

Canada: The State of the Federation 2003, vol. 17, *Reconfiguring Aboriginal-State Relations*, Michael Murphy (ed.), 2005 Paper ISBN 1-55339-010-5 Cloth ISBN 1-55339-011-3

Money, Politics and Health Care: Reconstructing the Federal-Provincial Partnership, Harvey Lazar and France St-Hilaire (eds.), 2004
Paper ISBN 0-88645-200-7 Cloth ISBN 0-88645-208-2

Canada: The State of the Federation 2002, vol. 16, *Reconsidering the Institutions of Canadian Federalism*, J. Peter Meekison, Hamish Telford and Harvey Lazar (eds.), 2004
Paper ISBN 1-55339-009-1 Cloth ISBN 1-55339-008-3

Federalism and Labour Market Policy: Comparing Different Governance and Employment Strategies, Alain Noël (ed.), 2004 Paper ISBN 1-55339-006-7 Cloth ISBN 1-55339-007-5

The Impact of Global and Regional Integration on Federal Systems: A Comparative Analysis, Harvey Lazar, Hamish Telford and Ronald L. Watts (eds.), 2003
Paper ISBN 1-55339-002-4 Cloth ISBN 1-55339-003-2

Canada: The State of the Federation 2001, vol. 15, *Canadian Political Culture(s) in Transition*, Hamish Telford and Harvey Lazar (eds.), 2002
Paper ISBN 0-88911-863-9 Cloth ISBN 0-88911-851-5

Federalism, Democracy and Disability Policy in Canada, Alan Puttee (ed.), 2002
Paper ISBN 0-88911-855-8 Cloth ISBN 1-55339-001-6, ISBN 0-88911-845-0 (set)

Comparaison des régimes fédéraux, 2ᵉ éd., Ronald L. Watts, 2002 ISBN 1-55339-005-9

Health Policy and Federalism: A Comparative Perspective on Multi-Level Governance, Keith G. Banting and Stan Corbett (eds.), 2002
Paper ISBN 0-88911-859-0 Cloth ISBN 1-55339-000-8

Comparing Federal Systems, 2nd ed., Ronald L. Watts, 1999 ISBN 0-88911-835-3

The following publications are available from the Institute of Intergovernmental Relations, Queen's University, Kingston, Ontario K7L 3N6
Tel: (613) 533-2080 / Fax: (613) 533-6868; E-mail: iigr@qsilver.queensu.ca

Open Federalism, Interpretations Significance, collection of essays by Keith G. Banting, Roger Gibbins, Peter M. Leslie, Alain Noël, Richard Simeon and Robert Young, 2006
ISBN 978-1-55339-187-6

First Nations and the Canadian State: In Search of Coexistence, Alan C. Cairns, 2002 Kenneth R. MacGregor Lecturer, 2005 ISBN 1-55339-014-8

Political Science and Federalism: Seven Decades of Scholarly Engagement, Richard Simeon, 2000 Kenneth R. MacGregor Lecturer, 2002 ISBN 1-55339-004-0

The Institute's working paper series can be downloaded from our website www.iigr.ca